Neuropsychology

Handbook of Perception and Cognition
2nd Edition

Series Editors
Edward C. Carterette
and Morton P. Friedman

Neuropsychology

Edited by
Dahlia W. Zaidel
Department of Psychology
University of California, Los Angeles
Los Angeles, California

Academic Press
San Diego New York Boston
London Sydney Tokyo Toronto

This book is printed on acid-free paper. ∞

Academic Press, Inc.
A Division of Harcourt Brace & Company
525 B Street, Suite 1900, San Diego, California 92101-4495

United Kingdom Edition published by
Academic Press Limited
24-28 Oval Road, London NW1 7DX

Library of Congress Cataloging-in-Publication Data

Neuropsychology / edited by Dahlia W. Zaidel.
        p.   cm. -- (handbook of perception and cognition)
    Includes index.
    ISBN 0-12-775290-0
    1. Neuropsychology.   I. Zaidel, Dahlia W.   II. Series.
QP360.N4939   1994
612.8--dc20

PRINTED IN THE UNITED STATES OF AMERICA
94   95   96   97   98   99   BC   9   8   7   6   5   4   3   2   1

Contents

3 Evolution of the Brain
Harry J. Jerison

4 *Neuropsychology of Perceptual Functions*
Michael C. Corballis

5 *Neuropsychology of Attention*
Marcel Kinsbourne

9 Neuropsychology of Movement Sequencing Disorders and Apraxia

Eric A. Roy and Paula A. Square

10 Developmental Aspects of Neuropsychology: Childhood
Maureen Dennis and Marcia Barnes

11 Neuropsychology of Aging and Dementia
Elisabeth Koss

12 Cognitive and Emotional Organization of the Brain: Influences on the Creation and Perception of Art

Wendy Heller

13 Sex Differences in the Brain

Nicole Yvette Weekes

14 *Neuropsychological Rehabilitation*
Robert Hanlon

Contributors

Numbers in parentheses indicate the pages on which the authors' contributions begin.

Marcia Barnes (219)
Department of Psychology
The Hospital for Sick Children
Toronto, Ontario
Canada M5G 1X8

Jeffrey M. Clarke (29)
Department of Psychology
University of North Texas
Denton, Texas 76203

Michael C. Corballis (83)
Department of Psychology
University of Auckland
Auckland, New Zealand

Maureen Dennis (219)
Department of Psychology
The Hospital for Sick Children
Toronto, Ontario
Canada M5G 1X8

Stanley Finger (1)
Department of Psychology
Washington University
St. Louis, Missouri 63130

Jordan Grafman (159)
Cognitive Neurosciences Section
Medical Neurology Branch
National Institutes of Health
Bethesda, Maryland 20892

Robert Hanlon (317)
Neuropsychology Department
Baylor Institute of Rehabilitation
Dallas, Texas 75246

Kenneth M. Heilman (139)
Department of Neurology
University of Florida College of
  Medicine
and Veterans Affairs Medical Center
Gainesville, Florida 32610

Wendy Heller (271)
Department of Psychology
University of Illinois
Champaign, Illinois 61820

Harry J. Jerison (53)
Department of Psychiatry
University of California, Los Angeles
Los Angeles, California 90024

Helen J. Kahn (125)
Department of Communication
Sciences and Disorders
University of Vermont
Burlington, Vermont 05405

Marcel Kinsbourne (105)
Center for Cognitive Studies
Tufts University
Medford, Massachusetts 02155

Elisabeth Koss (247)
Alzheimer Center
University Hospitals of Cleveland
Case Western Reserve University
and University Hospitals of Cleveland
Cleveland, Ohio 44106

Eric A. Roy (183)
Department of Kinesiology
University of Waterloo
Waterloo, Ontario
Canada N2L 3G1

Paula A. Square (183)
Graduate Department of Speech
Pathology
University of Toronto,
Toronto, Ontario
Canada M5S 1A8

Nicole Yvette Weekes (293)
Department of Psychology
University of California, Los Angeles
Los Angeles, California 90024

Harry A. Whitaker (125)
Laboratoire de Neuroscience de La
Cognition
Université du Québec à Montréal
Montreal, Quebec
Canada H3C 3P8

Foreword

The problem of perception and cognition is in understanding how the organism transforms, organizes, stores, and uses information arising from the world in sense data or memory. With this definition of perception and cognition in mind, this Handbook is designed to bring together the essential aspects of this very large, diverse, and scattered literature and to give a précis of the state of knowledge in every area of perception and cognition. The work is aimed at the psychologist and the cognitive scientist in particular, and at the natural scientist in general. Topics are covered in comprehensive surveys in which fundamental facts and concepts are presented, and important leads to journals and monographs of the specialized literature are provided. Perception and cognition are considered in the widest sense. Therefore, the work will treat a wide range of experimental and theoretical work.

The *Handbook of Perception and Cognition* should serve as a basic source and reference work for all in the arts or sciences, indeed for all who are interested in human perception, action, and cognition.

Edward C. Carterette and Morton P. Friedman

Preface

Psychological research for the most part ignores the mind–body position. For example, in my department of psychology about ten years ago during a guest talk on a classic psychology topic, I heard an amazing statement from an established psychologist in the audience. It was a response to the conclusion made by the speaker, himself a psychologist, namely that the ultimate answer to his study would have to come from investigations of patients with unilateral focal brain damage. The statement from the psychologist in the audience was, "Why look for answers in other fields? Psychologists should seek answers within psychology!" He seemed to be promoting the notion that the mind operates within a black box rather than within a brain, a "box" that can be studied and understood. To me, a neuropsychologist, this did not make sense. How can we know what the mind or mental phenomenon is made of in real terms? How can we agree upon the units that make up behavior, who decides, and on what basis? Philosophical answers are clearly insufficient. The chapters in this volume indicate that the brain is *not* a black box.

The metaphor for neuropsychology: Imagine the Brain as a magnificent great house, established long ago through the millennia with the help of Mother Nature and evolution. The building blocks were carefully chosen and all the rooms, corridors, and staircases have been designed to function efficiently in the service of the chief resident, the Mind. The two are interwoven, the house and its chief resident, so that the one, the Mind, is a reflection of the conditions which exist in the house. The mind would not be what it is if it were not for the unique architecture of the brain. This metaphor illustrates the mind–body position. It is the approach adopted in all chapters of this book.

The view adopted throughout this book is that studies of normal subjects provide only a partial window to the mind, that the components of behavior are obscured by the very unity of behavior. On the other hand, brain damage causes the fractionation of behavior and disentangles the complexities of perception, cognition, personality, memory, and language so that they can be studied in detail.

The classical approach of neuropsychologists to the study of behavior has been through investigations of patients with unilateral focal brain damage. What is amiss in their behavior tells us the composition of the mind. This is important not only for understanding normal behavior, but also for improving the often anguished lives of brain-damaged patients. There is a logic to the juxtaposition of behavioral functions in specific anatomical structures. Neuropsychology attempts to map this juxtaposition to understand the nature of the organization of the mind in the brain.

Whereas in traditional neuropsychology the specific localization of damage in the brain is crucial for obtaining clues, in cognitive neuropsychology individual cases with any type of brain damage are investigated if they show signs of breakdown in normal behavior. The focus is on proving or disproving the reality of psychological theories through "brain preparations" rather than on charting the way the mind is organized in the brain.

Hemispheric specialization is at the heart of neuropsychology, and every topic discussed in this volume assumes its presence in the brain. The concept of hemispheric specialization is a major organizing principle in the brain and it represents the notion that the left and right hemisphere are specialized for different yet complementary cognitive functions. The idea that the cerebral hemispheres of humans represent two complementary spheres of consciousness gained scientific popularity in the early 1960s in Roger Sperry's psychobiology laboratory, at Caltech in Pasadena, California. Commissurotomy (split-brain) patients, operated on for the relief of drug-resistant, intractable epilepsy by neurosurgeons P. J. Vogel and J. E. Bogen, were tested in that laboratory. These patients had the major fiber tracts between the left and right hemispheres sectioned surgically (corpus callosum, anterior commissure, and the hippocampal commissure) in order to alleviate severe, intractable epilepsy. This type of surgery is called complete commissurotomy. The results of the laboratory studies which were conducted by many investigators were dramatic; they showed two separate hemispheres, each with its own range of cognition, memory, emotion, and consciousness. Such a conception of the human brain has never been presented before with such clear evidence. Indeed, in 1981 Roger Sperry received the Nobel Prize for his work with the commissurotomy cases. Our current understanding of the way the mind is organized in the brain has been shaped and enriched by the concept of hemispheric specialization.

Neuropsychology saw its modern beginning with the localization of language to the left posterior frontal lobe by the French neurologist Paul Broca. In Chapter 1, Stanley Finger traces the historical background and development of neuropsychology, and in Chapter 6, Harry Whitaker and Helen Kahn discuss current issues in brain and language. Since Broca, more details became known about patterns of language lateralization through the use of new medical techniques. Brenda Milner has collected the most widely accepted statistics on language lateralization in the brain: In 96% of right handers, language is lateralized to left hemisphere, while in 4% language is lateralized to the right hemisphere. In 70% of the left handers, language is lateralized to the left hemisphere, in 15% to the right hemisphere, and in 15% it is bilaterally represented. After language, functional localization of other abilities followed.

The new techniques and the findings that stemmed from using them are described in Chapter 2, by Jeffrey Clarke. Chapter 3, by Harry Jerrison, traces the evolution of the human brain. In Chapter 4, by Michael Corballis, critical current issues on perception and the brain are discussed with extensive important description of the visual system. Chapter 5, by Marcel Kinsbourne, describes brain processes for attentional mechanisms, including the much-debated topics of hemi-neglect and consciousness. Chapter 7, by Kenneth Heilman, discusses the current views on how emotions are processed in the brain. Chapter 8, by Jordan Grafman, focuses on the perceptual and cognitive functions in the prefrontal cortex, a part of the brain that for many years has puzzled neuropsychologists. In Chapter 9, by Eric Roy and Paula Square, cerebral control of motor output as well as the condition of apraxia are described. Chapter 10, by Maureen Dennis and Marcia Barnes, and Chapter 11 by Elisabeth Koss, describe and trace developmental issues in neuropsychology, from childhood to aging. Chapter 12, by Wendy Heller, is unusual for a neuropsychology book; it discusses the topic of art and the brain and shows the important lessons in art about the brain and vice versa. In Chapter 13, Nicole Weekes puts constraints on the topics discussed in previous chapters by describing and discussing sex differences in various cognitive functions, and in Chapter 14, Robert Hanlon shows how the scientific findings by neuropsychologists can be profitably tapped in the rehabilitation of brain-damaged patients.

The chapters in this volume represent some of the critical areas in human neuropsychology. They review and discuss both the traditional approach to neuropsychology and current views in this field. The authors are from the fields of medicine, experimental psychology, cognitive psychology, and clinical psychology, and have all made important scientific contributions to the study of mind–brain relations.

Dahlia W. Zaidel

CHAPTER 1

History of Neuropsychology

Stanley Finger

I. ROOTS OF THE WORD *NEUROPSYCHOLOGY*

In the post-Renaissance era, the words *neurology* and *psychology,* from which the term *neuropsychology* is derived, were introduced. In his *Cerebri anatome* of 1664, Thomas Willis (1621–1675), the most outstanding anatomist of the time, presented the word neurology in Greek. Willis based the prefix of his new word on the Greek word for *sinew* or *tendon,* and applied the term to the peripheral and autonomic nerves, but not to the brain or spinal cord. In his 1681 translation of Willis's works, Samuel Pordage (1633–1691?) translated the Greek word for neurology into *neurologie* and defined the term as the doctrine of the nerves.

The word *psychologia,* in contrast, was used prior to the time of Willis. It may have been coined by Rudolf Goclenius (Goclenio; 1547–1628) in the 1590s. Goclenius employed the Latin word in the title of his moralistic book, *Psychologia: hoc est, De hominis perfectione,* which can be translated as *Psychology: Or on the Improvement of Man* (1594).

In *De anima brutorum,* Willis's Latin text of 1672, the Greek word for psychologia was used with some frequency. In 1683, Samuel Pordage translated this volume into *Two Discourses Concerning the Soul of Brutes,* presented the Old English word *psycheology,* and defined this word as the doctrine of the soul. This was probably the first time that the word that would become shortened to *psychology* appeared in print in the English language (Cranefield, 1961; Spillane, 1981).

With the passage of time, the terms neurology and psychology, Willis's doctrines of the nerves and the soul, respectively, became a part of the common vocabulary. But as the years passed, these words also took on new meanings. At present, neurology usually refers to the branch of medicine that deals with the nervous system and its disorders, whereas psychology has been defined as the study of behavior or the mind, rather than the soul.

Many terms have been derived from the words *neurology* and *psychology.* One, the subject of this chapter, is *neuropsychology,* a word sometimes attributed to the famous American experimentalist, Karl Lashley (1890–1958; see Cobb, Hisaw, Stevens, & Boring, 1959). Lashley used neuropsychology in the context of brain damage and behavior in a 1936 presentation before the Boston Society of Psychiatry and Neurology. His Boston address appeared in print in 1937.

Lashley was not, however, the first to use this compound word (Bruce, 1985). It had been used in 1913 by William Osler (1849–1919) in a published speech dealing with training at the Phipps Psychiatric Clinic of the Johns Hopkins Hospital. Osler mentioned "neuro-psychology" in the context of students being able to take specialized courses dealing with so-called mental disorders. Nevertheless, he did not take the time to define his new word, and presented it only in passing.

Another person who used the word neuropsychology before Karl Lashley was Kurt Goldstein (1878–1965), the German-born neuropsychiatrist who emigrated to the United States (Frommer & Smith, 1988). Goldstein employed it in his 1934 classic, *Der Aufbau des Organismus,* a work that would become well known to many people under its English title, *The Organism* (1939). The latter bore the suitable subtitle, *A Holistic Approach to Biology Derived from Pathological Data in Man.* In his insightful book, Goldstein (p. 365) presented the term "neuro-psychological" when introducing the topic of aberrant thought processes in patients suffering from brain damage.

Lashley cited Goldstein's 1934 book in 1936/1937, in the same sentence in which he first spoke about neuropsychology. Nevertheless, Lashley did not credit Goldstein or anyone else with the word. But the fact that Lashley did not use the word before 1936, and now used it when citing Goldstein's thought, makes it very likely that he took the word from Goldstein, rather than from Osler, even though he had been in residence at Johns Hopkins when Osler gave his 1913 address.

Because Osler viewed mental disorders as brain diseases, he, Goldstein, and Lashley all looked up neuropsychology as the study of higher functions following brain injuries or diseases. At the present time, neuropsychology still deals largely with the study of higher functions and their disturbances after brain insult, although some definitions of neuropsychology may encompass more than just aberrant behaviors. Furthermore, although most individuals who call themselves neuropsychologists are professionals involved with assessing and treating human patients (i.e., clinical neuropsychology), there has also been a growing branch of neuropsychology concerned with hard-core experimentation, including the use of laboratory animal models (i.e., experimental neuropsychology).

II. NEUROPSYCHOLOGY AND THE EARLY HISTORY OF LOCALIZATION THEORY

Whether neuropsychology is defined narrowly or broadly, its history can be linked to changing concepts of localization of function (Benton, 1988). This is the idea that different parts of the brain are specialized to contribute to behavior in different ways. Given that people have attempted to localize higher functions and to treat intellectual and related disturbances during the Greco-Roman period, one can say that neuropsychology, or at least its theoretical backbone, has well over a 2000-yr-old history.

In ancient Greece, opinions about the function of the brain were far from uniform. Aristotle (384–322 B.C.), the greatest of the Greek naturalist–philosophers, believed the heart controlled sensory, cognitive, and related higher functions, and that the cool brain simply tempered "the heat and seething" of the heart. In contrast, Democritus (ca. 460–370 B.C.) and Plato (ca. 429–348 B.C.), both of whom achieved great stature before the time of Aristotle, were more modern in believing that intellectual or rational functions belonged not in the heart, but in the head.

Aristotle's tremendous influence notwithstanding, by the time of the Roman Empire, most behavioral functions were associated with the brain. The major exceptions were the passions and desires, still tied by most individuals to the liver and the heart.

The most important medical figure during this era was Galen (A.D. 130–200). Born in Pergamon, educated in Alexandria, and physician to emperors in Rome, Galen suggested that the front of the brain received sensory impressions, whereas the cerebellar area was responsible for motor functions. His reasoning rested largely on attempts to trace the nerves and the premise that the anterior region was softer than the posterior region, thus being better able to receive and record sensory impressions. In *De usu partium* he wrote:

> In substance the encephalon is very like the nerves, of which it was meant to be the source, except that it is softer, and this was proper for a part that was to receive all sensations, form all images, and apprehend all ideas. For a substance easily altered is most suitable for such actions and affections, and a softer substance is always more easily altered than one that is harder. This is the

reason why the encephalon is softer than the nerves, but since there must be two kinds of nerves, as I have said before, the encephalon itself was also given a two fold nature, that is, the anterior part (the cerebrum) is softer than the remaining hard part (the cerebellum), which is called *encranium* and *parencephalis* by anatomists. Now . . . the posterior part had to be harder, being the source of the hard nerves distributed to the whole body.

(Galen, 1968, p. 398)

Galen tied intellect and thought to the divine (rational) soul and associated intellect with the substance of the brain itself. In his *Commentaries on Hippocrates and Plato*, Galen listed imagination, reason, and memory as the basic components of intellect, and added that they could be affected independently by brain damage. Yet in his surviving works, he stopped short of actually localizing imagination, cognition, and memory in separate parts of the brain.

Galen was intrigued by the hollow ventricles of the brain. Around 300 B.C., Herophilus of Alexandria (ca. 335–280 B.C.) placed the soul in the fourth ventricle. In contrast, Galen believed the ventricles only "prepared the instruments of the soul" by making and storing the ethereal animal spirits (*psychic pneuma*) that penetrated the brain and traveled through the nerves to and from the various body parts. He maintained that injuries to the ventricles can be paralyzing. Still, he noted, they do not destroy life and mind, two basic properties of the brain itself.

Galen's known works do not provide evidence for functional localization within the ventricular system. Nevertheless, perhaps having access to lost manuscripts, or for theological reasons alone (a cavity being a more suitable dwelling place for a noncorporeal soul than a mass of tissue), the Church Fathers of the fourth and fifth centuries clearly took the three basic functions of the rational soul (imagination, reason, and memory) and localized them in the different ventricles of the brain (Clarke & Dewhurst, 1972; Pagel, 1958).

One of the earliest advocates of ventricular localization was Nemesius (fl, A.D. 390), Bishop of Emesia, who had studied the writings of Galen. He localized sensory reception (*sensus communis*) and image formation (*imaginativa, fantasia*) in the two lateral ventricles (treated as a single, anterior functional cavity), reason or knowing (*ratio, cognitativa, æstimativa*) in the middle ventricle, and memory (*memorativa*) in the most posterior ventricle.

This early attempt to localize higher functions was embraced by Nemesius's contemporary, St. Augustine (354–430), who suggested shifting memory to the middle ventricle. Loosely rooted in metaphysics and theology, but presented as physiology, ventricular localization in one form or another was accepted without serious challenge for well over 1000 years.

During the Renaissance, when scientists eventually returned to the tasks of dissection and experimentation, demonstration and observation began to

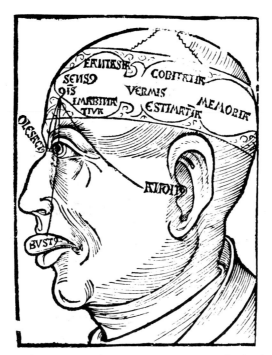

FIGURE 1   More than 1000 yr after its emergence, ventricular localization ("cell doctrine") was still a guiding doctrine. This plate, from the 1525 edition of Hieronymous Brunschwig's (ca. 1450–1533) 1497 text shows sensation, fantasy, and imagination in the first ventricle, cognition and estimation in the second ventricle, and memory in the posterior ventricle.

replace philosophy and conjecture. In Italy, Leonard da Vinci (1472–1519) made molds of the ventricles of oxen to reveal their true shapes. Soon afterward, Andreas Vesalius (1514–1564), who was invited to Padua to teach anatomy by conducting public dissections, noted that the ventricles did not vary much across species.

The anatomical studies of Vesalius and da Vinci drew new attention to the substance of the brain itself. Slowly, ventricular theory started to wane and the forebrain began its formative rise to prominence as the source of things intellectual.

The willingness to look at the brain in new ways during the Renaissance set the stage for Thomas Willis to write his celebrated *Cerebri anatome*. Published in 1664, Willis proposed that the corpus striatum was a meeting place for both sensory and motor spirits. He added that the cerebellum (which included the colliculi and pons as its appendages) regulated vital and involuntary motor systems (e.g., heartbeat, breathing). As for the cere-

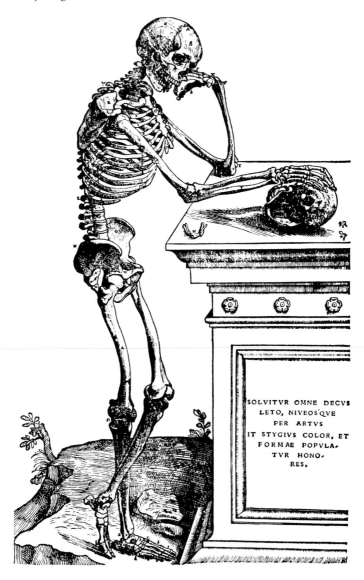

SOLVITVR OMNE DECVS
LETO, NIVEOS'QVE
PER ARTVS
IT STYGIVS COLOR, ET
FORMAE POPVLA-
TVR HONO-
RES,

FIGURE 2   Figure of a skeleton contemplating a human skull. The pensive skeleton appeared in Andreas Vesalius's *Fabrica* and in his *Epitome*, a shorter version of the *Fabrica* also published in 1543. Only the Latin captions differed in plates from the two books, this plate from the *Epitome* presenting a funereal verse from *Punica* by Silius Italicus (ca. 25–101).

brum, Willis postulated it controlled the will (initiating ideas and movements) and played a role in memory. He associated the weak intellects of wild animals and mental deficiency in humans with less convoluted brains and with small hemispheres, respectively. He also saw a close association between memory and imagination, assigning the latter to the corpus callosum, which he broadly defined as all cerebral white matter.

To quote Willis on the distinction between the functions of the cerebellum and the cerebral hemispheres:

> The Cerebel is a peculiar Fountain of animal Spirits designed for some works, wholly distinct from the Brain. Within the Brain, Imagination, Memory, Discourse, and other more superior Acts of the animal function are performed; besides, the animal spirits flow also from it into the nervous stock, by which all the spontaneous motions, to wit, of which we are knowing and will, are performed. But the office of the Cerebel seems to be for the animal Spirits to supply some Nerves; by which involuntary actions . . . are performed. As often as we go about voluntary motion we seem as it were to perceive within us the Spirits residing in the fore-part of the Head to be stirred up to action, or an influx. But the Spirits inhabiting the Cerebel perform unperceivedly and silently their works of Nature without our knowledge or care.
>
> *(1664, p. 111)*

And, to quote Willis again, this time with regard to the forebrain and the higher functions of imagination and memory:

> If that this (sensory) impression, being carried farther, passes through the *callous Body,* Imagination follows the Sense: Then if the same fluctuation of Spirits is struck against the *Cortex* of the Brain, as its utmost banks, it impresses on it the image of character of the sensible Object, which, when it is afterwards reflected or bent back raises up the Memory of the same thing.
>
> *(1664, p. 96)*

Willis's division of the brain into functional parts, based on comparative anatomy, clinical material, existing theories, and even some quirky correlations (e.g., "we rub the Temples and the forepart of the Head" to remember), markedly changed existing thinking about the physiology of the brain. It also stimulated genuine experimentation as scientists set forth to test Willis's many new ideas.

III. THE BIRTH OF CORTICAL LOCALIZATION THEORY

The opening decades of the 1800s proved to be an especially important time in the history of the brain sciences. First, Julien Jean César Legallois (1770–1840) provided an accepted example of localization within a brain structure. In 1812, on the basis of lesion experiments performed primarily on rabbits, Legallois associated respiration with a small region of the medulla.

FIGURE 3   Thomas Willis (1621–1675), whose *Cerebri anatome* of 1664 provided a new way of looking at brain anatomy and physiology, and stimulated considerable research.

Second, Sir Charles Bell (1774–1842) and François Magendie (1783–1855), both of whom experimented on dogs, showed that the spinal roots could be split into sensory (dorsal) and motor (ventral) divisions (Bell [1811]; Magendie [1822]; also see Brazier [1959] and Finger [1994] for some of the controversies behind this discovery). In his 1811 pamphlet, *Idea of a New Anatomy of the Brain* (1811/1936) Bell even hypothesized that sensory and motor distinctions might also apply to the organization of the brain.

During this same period, new attention was drawn to the cerebrum by Franz Joseph Gall (1757–1828). Gall's theory of phrenology held that different areas of the cerebrum subserved different higher mental faculties. He further proposed that cranial features reflected the development of discrete underlying organs of mind. Gall and his followers were convinced that our highest functions, including speech, belonged in the front of the cerebral

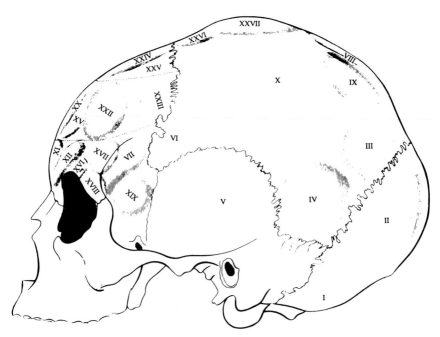

FIGURE 4   One of Franz Gall's phrenological diagrams of the skull showing the location of some of the faculties of mind.

cortex, whereas those functions shared more equally with the brutes could be localized more caudally (e.g., Gall & Spurzheim, 1810–1819).

To say the least, Gall's theory was revolutionary. Indeed, only Emanuel Swedenborg (1688–1772) seemed to have developed a theory of cortical localization before him. Swedenborg said nothing about cranial features when he divided the cerebral cortex in smaller functional areas (or units). Instead, he seemed to base his ideas of discrete areas for vision, hearing, and the like on what he had learned by studying pathology and anatomy, as well as his deep-seated belief that separate controlling areas were essential to prevent physiological chaos. Remarkably, Swedenborg even seemed to have inferred the intellectual functions of the frontal lobes, as can be noted in the following passage:

> These fibres of the cerebrum proceed from its anterior province, which is divided into lobes—a highest, a middle, and a lowest. . . . These lobes are marked out and encompassed by the carotid artery. . . . If this portion of the cerebrum therefore is wounded, then the internal senses—imagination, memory, thought—suffer; the very will is weakened, and the power of its determination blunted. . . . This is not the case if the injury is in the back part of the cerebrum.
>
> *(1938, p. 73)*

FIGURE 5   Emanuel Swedenborg (1688–1772) proposed a theory of cortical localization in the eighteenth century, but his work was not recognized before the late nineteenth century.

Unfortunately, Swedenborg's (1740–1741, 1887, 1938, 1940) functional neurology was not made public in his lifetime. He turned to theology in the second half of his life, and his ideas about localization in the cerebrum only became known toward the end of the nineteenth century (Schwedenberg, 1960). By this time, cortical localization of function had already been "proven" to the satisfaction of most scientists and physicians, leading some scholars to call Swedenborg's cortical theory simply a remarkable premonition (Akert & Hammond, 1962).

With Swedenborg effectively absent from the picture, the revolutionary ideas of the phrenologists, which were based largely on individuals who either exhibited extreme behaviors or very unusual crania, attracted by far the most attention. Some scientists thought phrenological theory had merit and rushed to embrace it, while others, including the conservative French

FIGURE 6   Marie Jean Pierre Flourens (1794–1867), the French experimentalist, led the movement against the phrenologists and vigorously opposed cortical localization.

establishment, which was led by Marie Jean Pierre Flourens (1794–1867), thought phrenology was utterly absurd. Relative to these two opposing forces, there was a small group of scientists who believed cortical localization made sense, but that Gall's cranioscopic procedures and small samples were not the way to make the point.

The latter position was championed by Jean-Baptiste Bouillaud (1796–1881), a man who had been trained in phrenology. By 1825, Bouillaud was presenting actual cases of brain damage, as opposed to individuals with bulging eyes or large foreheads, to argue for the localization of speech in the frontal lobes. In fact, after examining a fairly large number of cases, Bouillaud postulated the existence of two frontal speech areas in each hemisphere. According to Bouillaud, one was responsible for the creation of ideas, whereas the other governed the movements necessary for smooth articulation.

It is evident that the movements of the organs of speech must have a special centre in the brain, because speech can be completely lost in individuals who present no other signs of paralysis, whilst on the contrary other patients have the free use of speech coincident with paralysis of the limbs. . . . From the observations I have collected, and from the large number I have read in the literature, I believe I am justified in advancing the view that the principle lawgiver of speech is to be found in the anterior lobes of the brain.

(Bouillaud, 1825, p. 158; translated in Head, 1926, p. 15)

With each passing year, Bouillaud became more convinced that the conclusions he drew from his autopsy cases were fundamentally sound. Nevertheless, he found himself fighting a very strong and determined opposition. One reason for this was that he was still associated with the phrenological movement by some scientists. Another was that his critics found many instances of severe injuries to the frontal lobes that did not produce lasting aphasias.

It never occurred to Bouillaud, or to the opposition, that the variability across patients might be associated with the specific hemisphere damaged. In fact, had Bouillaud compared the effects of right- and left-hemispheric lesions, he might have recognized that the left hemisphere played a special role in language decades before Paul Broca (1824–1880) made this important association (Benton, 1984). Indeed, in his *Traité Clinique et Physiologique*

FIGURE 7   Jean-Baptiste Bouillaud (1796–1881) turned from phrenology to pathological material to argue for localization of speech in the anterior lobes. Bouillaud presented a number of cases to make his point in 1825 and continued to add to his sample.

FIGURE 8   Paul Broca's (1824–1880) 1861 presentation of the case of "Tan" ignited the localizationist revolution.

de l'Encéphalité of 1825, Bouillaud described 25 patients with unilateral lesions and 4 with bilateral lesions. Among the 11 individuals with left hemispheric damage, 8 (73%) showed aphasia. In contrast, just 4 (29%) of the 14 cases with right-hemispheric damage were aphasic.

With Bouillaud and Simon Alexandre Ernest Aubertin (1825–1865) spearheading the attack, the debates in the French academies over cortical localization grew in intensity (Schiller, 1979). It was in this charged atmosphere that, in 1861, Paul Broca, who previously had not taken sides, presented his celebrated case of M. Leborgne. Nicknamed "Tan" by the other patients because this was one of the few sounds he made, this 51-yr-old man had lost his capacity for voluntary language 21 yr earlier, and had not been able to use his right arm for 10 yr.

Tan died soon after Broca saw him and his autopsy revealed a lesion centered in the third frontal convolution of the left hemisphere. On the basis of this case, Broca became absolutely convinced that Bouillaud and Aubertin were in fact correct about cortical localization. Broca's new-found willingness to take sides and his detailed localization of a frontal center for articulate language were like the fall of the Bastille or the first shots of the American Revolution to many scientists who had been sitting on the sidelines during the debates.

In 1865, Broca published another landmark paper. He now told his audience that his case studies revealed that the left hemisphere was special for speech. Interestingly, Broca was not the first to recognize this. It was something Marc Dax (1770–1837) had found in 1836. Unfortunately, like Swedenborg before him, Dax failed to make his findings public before he died. In fact, Dax's report on more than 40 cases only appeared in print in 1865, the year in which Broca's own major paper on the subject was published, and two years after Broca began talking about the unexpected correlation between aphasia and damage to the left hemisphere (Joynt & Benton, 1964; Schiller, 1979).

IV. THE DISCOVERY OF ADDITIONAL CORTICAL CENTERS

In 1870, Gustav Fritsch (1838–1927) and Eduard Hitzig (1838–1907) identified the motor cortex in the dog using electrical stimulation, and then confirmed their findings with ablation. The discovery of the motor cortex in the precentral gyrus of the frontal lobe was especially important because it meant that cortical localization was not restricted to speech. In addition, Fritsch and Hitzig showed that at least some cortically dependent functions could be studied under controlled conditions in laboratory animals.

In the wake of the Fritsch and Hitzig paper, many lesion studies were conducted to confirm and extend this work, as well as to localize sensory functions, such as vision and hearing. One of the leading figures in the new localization movement was David Ferrier (1843–1928), a British experimentalist. Ferrier was a close friend and admirer of John Hughlings Jackson (1835–1911), the remarkable British neurologist who, after studying patients with seizures or hemiplegias, postulated the existence of a somatotopically organized motor cortex well before Fritsch and Hitzig firmly localized this structure in dogs (see Jackson, 1863).

Ferrier (1873, 1875) first extended the motor cortex experiments of Fritsch and Hitzig to monkeys, adding more details. He described behaviors as intricate as the twitch of an eyelid, the flick of an ear, and the movement of one digit. This resulted in maps of the motor cortex that appealed not just to the experimentalists, but to those clinicians who were convinced that only primates could serve as a suitable model for human patients.

In 1881, Ferrier even took a monkey with a unilateral lesion of the left

FIGURE 9   Eduard Hitzig (1838–1907) was the codiscoverer of the motor cortex with Gustav Fritsch (1838–1927) in 1870.

motor cortex to the Seventh International Medical Congress in London. Over 120,000 people were invited to this huge Victorian spectacle, including all the crowned heads of Europe. When Ferrier's hemiplegic monkey limped into the demonstration room, Jean Martin Charcot (1825–1893), the leading French neurologist of the era declared, "It is a patient!"

During the 1870s and 1880s, Ferrier also explored the superior temporal gyrus. He found that monkeys perked up the opposite ear and turned to the opposite side when this region was stimulated. This suggested a role for this area in audition. An ablation experiment confirming this hypothesis soon followed. This work, however, led to a prolonged and bitter debate between Ferrier and Edward Albert Schäfer (1850–1935) about the boundaries of the auditory cortex and whether bilateral lesions of the temporal lobe auditory region leave primates stone deaf or less severely impaired (see Finger, 1994).

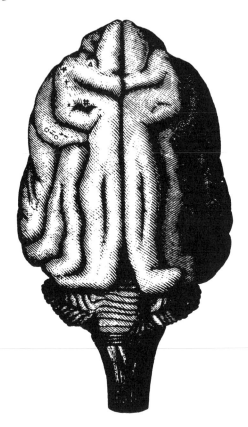

FIGURE 10   Diagram of a dog brain from Fritsch and Hitzig's 1870 paper. This figure shows the areas (triangle, cross, hash marks) from which movements of the opposite side of the body were evoked with electrical stimulation.

Ferrier was clearly on the mark when he placed audition and olfaction in the superior and inferior parts of the temporal lobe, respectively. Unfortunately, his conclusion that one could also localize gustation and somesthesis in the temporal lobes was wrong (Finger, 1994). In addition, Ferrier was very slow to recognize the real importance of the occipital lobe for vision. At first he thought the angular gyrus of the parietal lobe housed the center for sight, and then that the occipital lobes were involved in vision, but only in a subordinate way (see Ferrier, 1876, 1878, 1881, 1886, 1888).

The credit for the more accurate localization of the visual cortex is typically given to Hermann Munk (1839–1912), who associated vision with the occipital cortex in 1878, and then replicated his findings on dogs and monkeys in 1881 (Munk, 1881; see von Bonin, 1960, pp. 97–117). Credit has also been given to Bartolomeo Panizza (1785–1867), an often overlooked

FIGURE 11   Edward Albert Schäfer (1850–1935). Although he believed firmly in cortical
localization of function, Schäfer disagreed with David Ferrier about the boundaries of some of
the functional areas (e.g., the auditory cortex) and the nature of the deficit that followed
damage to these areas.

Italian investigator, who studied vision in both dogs and humans with brain
damage in the 1850s, before the modern era of cortical localization had
begun (Panizza 1855, 1856; also see Finger, 1994).

Many of Ferrier's findings and conclusions were presented in his book,
The Functions of the Brain, published in 1876. Ferrier not only summarized
his own data in this landmark publication, but went on to show how his
preparations with animals related to clinical cases. This book, with its many
figures, had an immense impact. In addition to advancing basic science, it
played an important role in opening the "modern" era of neurosurgery.
Surgeons, beginning with William Macewen (1848–1924) in 1879, turned
to Ferrier's functional maps for guidance in localizing brain tumors (Finger,

FIGURE 12   The German experimentalist Hermann Munk (1839–1912) associated vision with the occipital cortex in 1878. Although Munk favored localization of sensory and motor processes, he believed that intellect itself could not be localized in any one part of the cortex.

1994; Jefferson, 1960; Trotter, 1934). The successful surgical cases, in turn, offered further confirmation of the growing theory of localization.

V. HIGHER FUNCTIONS AND THE ASSOCIATION AREAS

The search for additional structure–function relationships was not restricted to sensory-perceptual and motor functions. It was recognized that not all cortical areas were electrically excitable, and that damage to some parts of the cortex led to more complex phenomena than the loss of the voluntary usage of a limb or one part of the field of vision.

In particular, attention was drawn to the frontal cortex anterior to the precentral gyrus, a favorite target of neuropsychologists today. This part of the cerebrum was seen as evolving most rapidly, and many nineteenth-century investigators believed it was the part of the brain that most distinguished civilized humans from their more apish ancestors (see Finger, 1994). It was also one of the last parts of the brain to develop, thus correlating well with the slow emergence of intellectual functions. In the 1740s, Emanuel Swedenborg felt compelled to call this region "the highest court of the cerebrum" and, as noted, even Gall and the phrenologists chose to house the highest faculties of mind here.

But was this structure–function relationship consistent with findings based on injury or pathology? The answer seemed to be yes. In fact, even in the first half of the nineteenth century there were brain damage cases that could have been used to support the association between the frontal lobes and intellect. The best known involved Phineas Gage (1823–1860), a railroad foreman for the Rutland and Burlington Railroad who suffered a severe brain injury in 1848 when he turned and accidently dropped his tamping iron on a rock, igniting some blasting powder. The explosion caused the huge iron to shoot point-first through the left side of his jaw and up through the front of his cranium.

Gage's recovery over the next few months, although unsteady, was far better than anyone expected. Nevertheless, it was clear that Gage's intellect and personality had been altered. He now exhibited poor judgment, impulsivity, and lack of restraint. Because "the equilibrium or balance . . . between his intellectual faculties and animal propensities, seems to have been destroyed" (Harlow, 1868, p. 13), he was unable to win back his job, although he previously had been a very capable foreman. In fact, Gage had become so "childish" that friends and acquaintances said he was no longer the same man, no longer Gage.

In addition to the acute damage suffered by Gage, several revealing frontal tumor cases were presented in the prelocalization era. One came from Jean Cruveilhier (1791–1874) and involved a 45-yr-old school teacher who was found to have a huge meningioma pressing upon her right frontal lobe (1829–1842). In addition to her tumor-induced headaches, loss of balance, and weakness of one leg, she became unusually apathetic and lost all interest in what was going on around her. Cruveilhier also mentioned a girl of 15, mentally defective from the time of birth. The distinguishing feature of the latter case was that the anterior two-thirds of her front lobes were missing.

The scientist most responsible for initiating lesion experiments on the frontal association cortex in laboratory animals was Eduard Hitzig. Even Leonardo Bianchi (1848–1927), the Italian who devoted a lifetime to studying the frontal lobes, stated that Hitzig should be given full credit for first bringing frontal lobe research into the laboratory, where various ideas gleaned from comparative anatomy could be tested (Bianchi, 1920, 1922).

Hitzig's work on the frontal association cortex began in 1870 when he and Gustav Fritsch discovered it was not electrically excitable and that damaging it did not cause paralyses (see Finger, 1994). By 1874, the idea that these areas must be contributing to higher mental functions seemed irrefutable to Hitzig (1874a, 1874b). Ten years later, at a meeting for German neurologists and psychiatrists, Hitzig (1884) summarized his studies on the anterior frontal areas. He stated that dogs trained to find food before surgery seemed unable to do so after bilateral frontal cortex lesions. Although healthy and hungry, they even appeared to forget about pieces of food they had just been shown. Hitzig added that this unusual deterioration in intellect was not observed after other cortical lesions. Nevertheless, he did not propose that intellect was limited to just one part of the brain. Instead, he argued that the frontal lobes were special for just one specific aspect of intellect—abstract thought (see also Goldstein, 1934, 1939).

A somewhat different opinion came from the experimentalist camp in Britain. David Ferrier (1876) studied three monkeys with near complete ablations of the anterior frontal areas and wrote:

> Notwithstanding this apparent absence of physiological symptoms, I could perceive a very decided alteration in the animal's character and behaviour, though it is difficult to state in precise terms the nature of the change. The animals operated on were selected on account of their intelligent character. . . . Instead of, as before, being actively interested in their surroundings, and curiously prying into all that came within the field of their observation, they remained apathetic, or dull, and dozed off to sleep, responding only to the sensations or impressions of the moment, or varying their listlessness with restless and purposeless wanderings to and fro. While not actually deprived of intelligence, they had lost, to all appearance, the faculty of attentive and intelligent observation.
>
> *(1876, pp. 231–232)*

Ferrier observed the same behavior in dogs, but unlike Hitzig, he concluded that the fundamental function of the "silent" region of the frontal lobes was to govern attention. To Ferrier, it was because of severe attentional deficits, and not a loss of abstraction, that monkeys and dogs with anterior frontal lobe lesions show a pathological absence of curiosity, apathetic behaviors, restlessness, and impulsivity.

Leonardo Bianchi, who gave lavish credit to Hitzig for his pioneering experiments on the frontal lobes, began his own work on the prefrontal areas of monkeys and dogs in 1888. Over the years, Bianchi (1894, 1895, 1920, 1922) emphasized that bilateral damage to the prefrontal areas markedly changed the social characteristics, emotional makeup, and personalities of his animals. He wrote the following about one of his monkeys:

> Her behaviour is altered, her physiognomy stupid, less mobile; the expression of the eyes is as if uncertain and cruel, devoid of any flashes of intelligence, curiosity, or sociability. Shows terror, even by shrieks and gnashing of teeth,

when threatened or hurt, but never reacts aggressively. She is in a state of unrest; when placed in a large closed room, it walks aimlessly around it, always in the same direction, without stopping near any object or person. Any action done with apparent purpose remains incomplete, unfinished; if she runs towards a door she stops near it, goes back, runs to the door again, and so on several times. . . . She is unsociable with the other monkeys, does not play; cannot overcome the least difficulties in her way by new adaptations, nor learn anything new, nor recover what she has forgotten.

(1895, p. 517)

Bianchi concluded that the "psychical tone" of his animals had been affected by the bilateral prefrontal cortical lesions. He argued that the "dissolution of the psychical personality" can manifest itself in many ways, including the loss of careful planning and assessment, intellectual blunting, and restlessness.

In the final quarter of the nineteenth century, there were many clinical reports on the effects of anterior frontal lobe tumors and injuries (see Finger, 1994). In some, there was an absence of intellectual deterioration. But in others, the situation was quite different. Although hardly constant from patient to patient, among the symptoms most frequently described were loss of attention, apathetic behaviors, poor social skills, and intellectual deterioration or "mental dullness." These were in fact the most important changes described by Hitzig, Ferrier, and Bianchi in their early lesion experiments on dogs and monkeys.

VI. NEUROPSYCHOLOGY'S DEBT TO ANATOMY AND PHYSIOLOGY

The advancement of localization theory and the birth of neuropsychology as a field of specialization within psychology, were not based solely on pathological material. They also received support from other sources. In 1875, for example, Richard Caton (1842–1926) reported that regional cortical electrical activity changed when his animals were chewing, looking at flashing lights, or engaged in other activities. Caton noted that the changes were very much in line Ferrier's functional maps of the cortex.

Growing evidence favoring neuron doctrine (i.e., the idea that neurons are actually independent entities that are not fused together to form massive nets) also enhanced acceptance of the idea that different parts of the brain could be specialized to do different things. Neuron doctrine was greatly stimulated by Camillo Golgi's discovery of *la reazione nera* (the black reaction) in 1873 (see Santini, 1975), although it was Santiago Ramón y Cajál (1852–1934), and not Golgi, who became the standard bearer for the theory of independent neurons as opposed to fused nets (see Ramón y Cajál, 1906/1967; Shepherd, 1991).

FIGURE 13   Richard Caton (1842–1926) was the scientist who first recorded regional changes in cortical activity in animals, using light, sound, and other stimuli.

In the field of developmental anatomy, Paul Flechsig (1847–1929) was able to show that different cortical areas became myelinated at different times. From the start, Flechsig (1895, 1896, 1898, 1900) correlated the slow myelination of the association areas with the development of intellect, and the destruction of these areas with loss of intellect.

Several anatomists, including Oscar Vogt (1870–1950) and his wife Cécile Vogt (1875–1962), Grafton Elliot Smith (1871–1937), and Alfred Walter Campbell (1868–1937) studied the cellular anatomy of the cerebral cortex at about the same time. Although their maps did not overlap perfectly, all reported many regional differences in cellular features. As for what cyto-architectonic differences meant, Korbinian Brodmann (1868–1918), who recognized 52 discrete cortical areas, might have expressed it best when he wrote the following:

The specific histological differentiation of the cortical areas proves irrefutably their specific functional differentiation—for it rests as we have seen on the

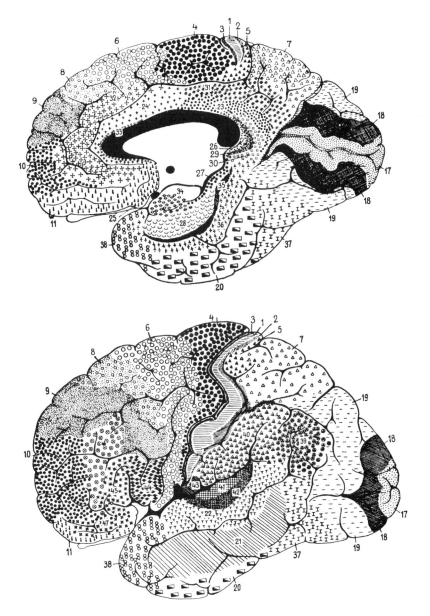

FIGURE 14 Korbinian Brodmann's (1868–1918) map of the cortex. Published in 1909, this map delineated 52 discrete cortical areas. Brodmann expressed the belief that each had a unique function.

division of labor—the large number of specially built structural regions points to a spatial separation of many functions and from the sharp delineation of some fields there follows finally the sharply delimited localization of the physiological processes which correspond to it.

(1909; see von Bonin, 1960, p. 217)

VII. FACTS, THEORIES, AND THE FUTURE OF NEUROPSYCHOLOGY

The dominant trend in the brain sciences since the days of Broca, Hitzig, and Ferrier has been to try to divide all parts of the brain into smaller functional units. Nevertheless, some scientists, beginning with John Hughlings Jackson, have urged caution, recognizing that boundaries between areas may be considerably more "fuzzy" than they often are made out to be, and arguing that it is very important to remember that no part of the brain really functions independently of all others.

In particular, there has been growing recognition that previous generations of scientists might have been too quick to equate anatomical markers and "localization of symptoms" with localization of specific functions (Finger & Stein, 1982; Kosslyn & Van Kleeck, 1990). At the present time, no one would dispute the idea that the central nervous system is made up of many specialized parts. Yet it is also clear that the "functions" of some of these parts can only be *inferred* from human case studies and lesion experiments on animals.

Although it may seem trivial to emphasize that lesion data can only show what the brain can do in the absence of one or more of its parts, and not how the part may be functioning under normal conditions, the failure to distinguish adequately between fact and theory has continued into the present era. Indeed, even when anatomical and physiological measures are added to the equation, one still can only theorize how the individual parts may be contributing to higher behavioral (psychological) functions such as speech, memory, and abstract thought. Indeed, it is primarily because neuropsychologists can only theorize about structure–function relationships that there is still so much debate about the functions of specific brain parts and how certain functional systems should be defined.

In his 1910 Presidential Address before the American Neurological Association, Morton Prince (1854–1929), spoke about three distinct types of localization: (1) anatomical localization, based on where the nerve tracts terminated, (2) localization of symptoms, based on behavior after brain lesions, and (3) localization of function, an inference derived from the response to brain damage and, in some cases, anatomy and physiology. Prince was convinced that his colleagues were too quick to equate symptoms with functions without really thinking the issues through. He wrote:

The present doctrine of cerebral localization regarded as a mapping of the brain into areas within which lesions give rise to particular groups of symptoms is one of the triumphs of neurology which cannot be valued too highly. Regarded as a localization of the psychophysiological functions represented by these symptoms within narrowly circumscribed areas it is in large part naive to a degree with will excite the smiles of future neurologists.

(1910, p. 340)

Because an inference is involved, and because structure–function relationships may change with development and after injury, neuroscientists, including neuropsychologists, are likely to continue to debate the precise functions of particular parts of the brain for years to come. This will probably be true even as orientations shift from sharply defined independent "centers" that only process serially (the models of Hitzig and Ferrier) to more diffuse, overlapping, and interrelated neural networks, which can also process in parallel (Benton, 1991; Damasio & Damasio, 1989).

Although predicting the future is never easy, three other trends are likely to continue in the field of neuropsychology: (1) behavioral approaches for treating brain-damaged patients will increase along with a proliferation of drug therapies; (2) more sensitive behavioral tests will emerge for detecting and tracking some neurological diseases; and (3) there will be more emphasis on preventing diseases of the nervous system, especially as causal factors are identified.

In conclusion, it seems fairly safe to say that how we will view and treat the brain in health and disease will change over the coming decades. The ways in which perception, cognition, and memory may be mediated are likely to command the most attention, being the most intriguing and least understood functions at this time. Once housed deep in the ventricles, these three components of the rational soul of antiquity promise to be especially fertile territory for those neuropsychologists willing to labor to understand the diverse effects of brain damage and to provide new insights into the functional organization of the brain.

References

Akert, K., & Hammond, M. P. (1962). Emanuel Swedenborg (1688–1772) and his contribution to neurology. *Medical History, 6,* 255–266.

Bell, C. (1936). *Medical Classics, 1,* 105–120. Reprinted from *Idea of a new anatomy of the brain submitted for the observations of his friends.* London: Strahan & Preston, 1811.

Benton, A. (1984). Hemispheric dominance before Broca. *Neuropsychologia, 22,* 807–811.

Benton, A. (1988). Neuropsychology: Past, present and future. In F. Boller, J. Graffman, G. Rizzolatti, & H. Goodglass (Eds.), *Handbook of neuropsychology* (Vol. 1, pp. 3–27). Amsterdam: Elsevier.

Benton, A. (1991). The Hécaen-Zangwill legacy: Hemispheric dominance examined. *Neuropsychology Review, 2,* 267–280.

Bianchi, L. (1894). Ueber die Function der Stirnlappen. *Berliner Klinische Wochenschrift, 31,* 309–310.

Bianchi, L. (1895). The functions of the frontal lobes. *Brain, 18,* 497–530. (Translated by A. de Watteville)

Bianchi, L. (1920). *La meccanica del cervello e la funzione dei lobi frontali.* Torino: Bocca.

Bianchi, L. (1922). *The mechanism of the brain* (J. H. MacDonald, Trans.). Edinburgh: Livingstone.

Bouillaud, J. (1825). *Traité clinique et physiologique de l'encéphalite ou inflammation du cerveau.* Paris: Baillière.

Brazier, M. (1959). The historical development of neurophysiology. In *Handbook of physiology: Vol. 1. Neurophysiology* (pp. 1–58). Baltimore MD: Waverly Press.

Broca, P. (1861). Remarques sur le siège de la faculté du langage articulé; suivies d'une observation d'aphémie (perte de la parole). *Bulletins de la Société Anatomique, 6,* 330–357, 398–407.

Broca, P. (1865). Sur la siège de la faculté du langage articulé. *Bulletins de la Société d'Anthropologie (Paris), 6,* 337–393.

Brodmann, K. (1909). *Vergleichende Lokalisationslehre der Grosshirnrinde in ihren Prinzipien dargestellt auf Grund des Zellenbaues.* Leipzig: Barth.

Bruce, D. (1985). On the origin of the term "neuropsychology." *Neuropsychologia, 23,* 813–814.

Brunschwig, H. (1525). *The noble experyence of the vertuous handy warke of surgeri . . .* London: P. Treveris.

Caton, R. (1875). The electric currents of the brain. *British Medical Journal, 2,* 278.

Clark, E., & Dewhurst, K. (1972). *An illustrated history of brain function.* Berkeley: University of California Press.

Cobb, S., Hisaw, F. L., Stevens, S. S., & Boring, E. (1959, February). Karl Spencer Lashley. *Harvard University Gazette,* pp. 115–116.

Cranefield, P. F. (1961). A seventeenth century view of mental deficiency and schizophrenia: Thomas Willis on "stupidity or foolishness." *Bulletin of the History of Medicine, 35,* 291–316.

Cruveilhier, J. (1829–1842). *L'anatomie pathologique du corps humain* (2 vols.) Paris: Baillière.

Damasio, H., & Damasio, A. R. (1989). *Lesion analysis in neuropsychology.* New York: Oxford University Press.

Dax, M. (1865). Lésions de la moitié gauche de l'encéphale coincidant avec l'oubli des signes de la pensée. *Gazette Hebdomadaire de Médecine et de Chirurgie, 2,* 259–262.

Ferrier, D. (1873). Experimental researches in cerebral physiology and pathology. *West Riding Lunatic Asylum Medical Report, 3,* 30–96.

Ferrier, D. (1875). Experiments on the brain of monkeys. *Philsophical Transactions of the Royal Society of London, 165,* 433–488.

Ferrier, D. (1876). *The functions of the brain.* London: Smith, Elder.

Ferrier, D. (1878). *Localisation of cerebral disease.* London: Smith Elder.

Ferrier, D. (1881). Cerebral ambylopia and hemiopia. *Brain, 3,* 456–477.

Ferrier, D. (1886). *The functions of the brain* (2nd ed.). New York: Putnam's.

Ferrier, D. (1888). Schäfer on the temporal and occipital lobes. *Brain, 11,* 7–30.

Finger, S. (1994). *Origins of neuroscience.* New York: Oxford University Press.

Finger, S., & Stein, D. G. (1982). *Brain damage and recovery: Research and clinical perspectives.* New York: Academic Press.

Flechsig, P. E. (1895). Weitere Mittheilungen über die Sinnes- und Associationscentren des menschlichen Gehirns. *Neurologisches Centralblatt, 14,* 1118–1124, 1177–1179.

Flechsig, P. E. (1896). *Gehirn und Steele.* Leipzig: Veit.

Flechsig, P. E. (1898). Neue Untersuchungen über die Markbildung in den menschlichen Grosshirnlappen. *Neurologisches Centralblatt, 17,* 977–996.

Flechsig, P. E. (1900). Les centres de projection et d'association du cerveau humain. *13th Congrès International de Médecine, Paris, Section de Neurologie*, pp. 115–121.

Fritsch, G., & Hitzig, E. (1870). Uber die elektrische Erregbarkeit des Grosshirns. *Archiv für Anatomie und Physiologie*, 300–332.

Frommer, G. P., & Smith, A. (1988). Kurt Goldstein and recovery of function. In S. Finger, T. E. LeVere, C. R. Almli, & D. G. Stein (Eds.), *Brain injury and recovery: Theoretical and controversial issues* (pp. 71–88). New York: Plenum.

Galen, (1968). *De usu partium*. M. T. May (Trans.), *On the usefulness of the parts of the body*. Ithaca, NY: Cornell University Press.

Gall, F. J., & Spurzheim, J. (1810–1819). *Anatomie et physiologie du système nerveux en général, et du cerveau en particulier*. Paris: F. Schoell. (Gall was the sole author of the first two volumes of the four in this series)

Goclenius, R. (1594). *Psychologia: hoc est, De hominis perfectione, amino, et in primus ortu hujus, commentationes ac disputationes quorundam theologorum & philosophorum nostrae ætatis*. Ex officina typographica Pauli Egenolphi.

Goldstein, K. (1934). *Der Aufbau des Organismus*. The Hague: Martinus Nijhoff.

Goldstein, K. (1939). *The organism*. New York: American Book Co.

Golgi, C. (1873). Sulla struttura della grigia del cervello. *Gazetta Medica Italiani Lombardi, 6*, 244–246.

Harlow, J. M. (1868). Recovery from the passage of an iron bar through the head. *Bulletin of the Massachusetts Medical Society, 2*, 3–20.

Head, H. (1926). *Aphasia and kindred disorders of speech*. New York: Macmillan.

Hitzig, E. (1874a). Ueber Localisation psychischer Centren in de Hirnrind. *Zeitschrift für Ethnologie, 6*, 42–47.

Hitzig. E. (1874b). *Untersuchungen über das Gehirn*. Berlin: Hirschwald.

Hitzig, E. (1884). Zur Physiologie des Grosshirns. *Archiv für Psychiatrie und Nervenkrankheiten, 15*, 270–275.

Jackson, J. H. (1863). Convulsive spasms of the right hand and arm preceding epileptic seizures. *Medical Times and Gazette, 1*, 110–111.

Jefferson, G. (1960). Sir William Macewen's contributions to neurosurgery and its sequels. In *Selected papers of Sir Geoffrey Jefferson* (pp. 132–149). Springfield, IL: Charles C. Thomas.

Joynt, R. J., & Benton, A. L. (1964). The memoir of Marc Dax on aphasia. *Neurology, 14*, 851–854.

Kosslyn, S. M., & Van Kleeck, M. (1990). Broken brains and normal minds: Why Humpty-Dumpty needs a skeleton. In E. L. Schwartz (Ed.), *Computational neuroscience* (pp. 190–402). Cambridge, MA: MIT Press.

Lashley, K. S. (1937). Functional determinants of cerebral localization. *Archives of Neurology and Psychology, 38*, 371–387.

Legallois, J. J. C. (1812). *Expériences sue le principe de la vie, notamment sur celui des movemens du coeur, et sur le siége de ce principe*. Paris: Hautel.

Macewen, W. (1879). Tumour of the dura mater removed during life in a person affected with epilepsy. *Glasgow Medical Journal, 12*, 210–213.

Magendie, F. (1822). Expériences sur les fonctions des racines des nerfs rachidiens. *Journal de Physiologie Experimentale et Pathologie, 2*, 276–279.

Munk, H. (1878). Weitere Mittheilungen zur Physiologie der Grosshirnrinde. *Verhandlungen der Physiologischen Gesellschaft zu Berlin*, pp. 162–178.

Munk, H. (1881). *Uber die Funktionen der Grosshirnrinde (3rd Mitt*, pp. 28–53). Berlin: Hirschwald.

Osler, W. (1913). Specialism in the general hospital. *Johns Hopkins Hospital Bulletin, 24*, 167–233.

Pagel, W. (1958). Medieval and Renaissance contributions to knowledge of the brain and its functions. In M. W. Perrin (Chair), *The brain and its functions* (pp. 95–114). Oxford: Blackwell/Wellcome Foundation.

Panizza, B. (1855). Osservazioni sul nervo ottico. *Instituto Lombardo di Scienze e Lettere, Milan. Giornale di Scienze e Lettere, 7,* 237–252.

Panizza, B. (1856). Osservazioni sul nervo ottico. *Memoria, Istituto Lombardo di Scienze, Lettere e Arte, 5,* 375–390.

Prince, M. (1910). Cerebral localization from the point of view of function and symptoms. *Journal of Nervous and Mental Disease, 37,* 337–354.

Ramón y Cajál, S. (1967). The structure and connexions of neurons. In *Nobel Lectures Physiology or Medicine 1901–1921* (pp. 220–253). New York: Elsevier. (Original work published 1906)

Santini, M. (1975). On the structure of the gray matter of the brain. In M. Santini (Ed.), *Golgi Centennial Symposium, Proceedings* (pp. 647–650). New York: Raven Press.

Schiller, F. (1979). *Paul Broca: Founder of French anthropology, explorer of the brain.* Berkeley: University of California Press.

Schwedenberg, T. H. (1960). The Swedenborg manuscripts. *Archives of Neurology (Chicago), 2,* 407–409.

Shepherd, G. (1991). *Foundations of the neuron doctrine.* New York: Oxford University Press.

Spillane, J. D. (1981). *The doctrine of the nerves.* Oxford: Oxford University Press.

Swedenborg, E. (1740–1741). *Oeconomia regni animalis.* Amsterdam: Changuion.

Swedenborg, E. (1887). *The brain, considered anatomically, physiologically, and philosophically* (2 vols., R. L. Tafel, Ed. and Trans.). London: Speirs.

Swedenborg, E. (1938). *Three transactions on the cerebrum: A posthumous work of Emanuel Swedenborg* (Vol. 1; A. Acton, Ed. and Trans.). Philadelphia: Swedenborg Scientific Association.

Swedenborg, E. (1940). *Three transactions on the cerebrum: A posthumous work of Emanuel Swedenborg* (Vol. 2). Philadelphia: Swedenborg Scientific Association.

Trotter, W. (1934). A landmark in modern neurology. *Lancet, 2,* 1207–1210.

von Bonin, G. (1960). Some papers on the cerebral cortex. In G. von Bonin (Ed.), *On the comparative localization of the cortex* (pp. 201–230). Springfield, IL: Thomas.

Willis, T. (1664). *Cerebri anatome: cui accessit nervorum descriptio et usus.* London: J. Martyn and J. Allestry.

Willis, T. (1672). *De anima brutorum.* Oxonii: R. Davis.

Willis, T. (1681). The remaining medical works of . . . Dr. Willis. Translated from the Latin by S. Pordage. London: Dring, Harper, Leigh & Martyn.

Willis, T. (1683). *Two discourses concerning the soul of Brutes* . . . (Translated from the Latin by S. Pordage). London: Dring, Harper & Leigh.

CHAPTER 2

Neuroanatomy
Brain Structure and Function

Jeffrey M. Clarke

I. INTRODUCTION

This chapter will serve as an introduction to a number of issues concerning the relationship between brain anatomy and brain function. First, I will show how an understanding of anatomical–behavioral relationships begins at the microscopic level. One may wonder how we can ever comprehend the underlying functioning of the human brain given that some 50 billion brain cells, known as neurons, are involved in information processing, and that each of these neurons can receive up to 15,000 connections from other neurons (Kolb & Whishaw, 1990). Yet, anatomical studies have shown that functionally distinct brain regions often exhibit striking differences in the physical characteristics of the neurons present (e.g., specific type, size, and shape) as well as the pattern of connections between them. I will then turn to the issue of localizing functionally distinct regions of the brain. The subdivisions or lobes of the brain will be presented along with an overview of the primary functions ascribed to each region. As will be the case throughout this chapter, the focus will be on the neocortex (also referred to as the cortex), which comprises about 80% of the human brain and consists of the two cerebral hemispheres, the left and the right. In the subsequent section, I will describe the technological tools that are providing researchers with powerful means for studying the anatomy and the physiology of the

Neuropsychology

living human brain. As a final topic I will focus on structure–function relationships associated with brain size and two brain structures, the planum temporale and the corpus callosum. Do normal variations in the size of particular brain regions have measurable behavioral–functional significance? Indeed, such relationships do appear to exist for measures of the planum temporale and the corpus callosum.

II. CYTOARCHITECTURE: FUNCTIONAL CORRELATES AT THE CELLULAR LEVEL

A. Anatomical Maps of the Brain

If different regions of the neocortex carry out different functions, then one might expect to see regional differences in the underlying neuronal structure. Brodmann (1909) examined the cellular architecture of the cortex, and systematically partitioned it into 52 different regions based on the particular size, type, shape, and distribution of cells. An example of one of Brodmann's maps is shown in Figure 1 (see also chapter 1, p. 23). Today, the Brodmann cytoarchitectonic maps are classic, and the subdivisions, although sometimes

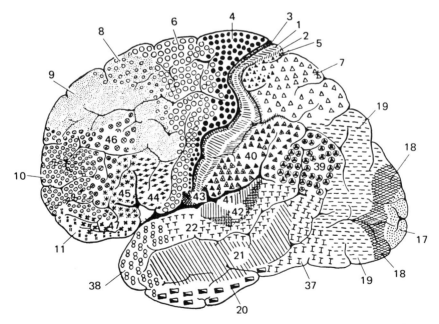

FIGURE 1   One of Brodmann's cytoarchitectonic maps of the human brain, in this case an external view of the left cerebral hemisphere. The distinct regions differ in terms of their microscopic-anatomical features. (After Brodmann, 1909.)

revised, are frequently used as a neuroanatomical reference. Many of the Brodmann areas have turned out to have fairly circumscribed functions, particularly those related to the initial stages of sensory processing (i.e., visual, auditory, and the somatosensory or body senses) and motor processing (i.e., control of movement). Higher order cognitive processing seems to be less constrained to particular cytoarchitectonic areas. For instance, evidence from functional electrical brain stimulation in epileptic patients undergoing neurosurgery suggests that essential language areas can vary in location among individuals, and these language areas do not correspond to any particular cytoarchitectonic area (Ojemann, Ojemann, Lettich, & Berger, 1989).

B. Cortical Layers and Columns

Most areas of the cortex have six distinct layers of cells (identified as I through VI). Certain layers are primarily dedicated to receiving information, whereas other layers emphasize conveying information to other cortical or noncortical regions. Furthermore, the thickness or elaboration of particular layers can vary for functionally distinct cortical regions. For example, cortical regions concerned with the control of body movement (e.g., Brodmann area 4 in Figure 1) have a thick layer V, for *outputting* commands to move the body, and a relatively thin layer IV. The reverse is found in primary sensory areas, such as for visual functions (e.g., Brodmann area 17 in Figure 1), where there is a greater reliance on the *input* of sensory information from the eyes rather than on the output of information, and consequently layer IV is thick and layer V is relatively thin.

A number of cortical regions have been found to be organized in cortical columns, in addition to being organized into different layers. Columnar organization has been demonstrated by measuring the electrical responses of individual brain cells in animals during different kinds of sensory stimulation (e.g., Hubel & Wiesel, 1962; Kaas, Nelson, Sur, Lin, & Merzenich, 1979; Mountcastle, 1957). The striking feature of a cortical column is that all of the cells in the column share a functional characteristic that is distinct from neighboring columns. For instance, cells within a 1-mm-wide column in the somatosensory cortex may respond selectively to the light touch of the little finger. The neighboring column may respond preferentially to the movement of hairs of the little finger, or to the movement of a corresponding joint. Nearby there will be columns dedicated to such senses for other parts of the hand, and so on. The columnar organization has also been systematically investigated in the visual cortex, and it is likely that columnar organization is a pervasive feature of the cortex. These findings suggest that cortical columns are the simplest functional unit of cortex, acting like minicircuits. Specific neuronal information is received by a column, the information is processed in some manner, and then the transformed neuronal information is exported out of the column.

C. Cellular Changes Associated with Experience

A remarkable characteristic of cortical cytoarchitecture is its apparent dynamic property. That is, the brain may undergo constant cellular changes that are related to experiential and environmental factors. Diamond and colleagues (see Diamond, 1990) have shown that rats trained to run mazes of increasing difficulty have thicker cerebral cortices than do rats that did not receive such training. Moreover, rats raised in enriched environments, consisting of such objects as ladders, wheels, and mazes, have thicker cortices than do rats that were not given such objects to interact with. Interestingly, the "toys" in the enriched environment had to be replaced with new toys at least twice a week in order to observe the increase in cortical thickness. The increased cortical thickness was not because of a change in the number of neurons. Instead, there were qualitative changes in the neurons, such as an increase in the length of the neuron's branch-like dendrites, and an augmentation in the number of dendritic protrusions or spines. These types of changes enhance a neuron's potential for interacting with a greater number of other neurons, possibly allowing for more complex types of neural processing. Neurons are one of two classes of cells in the brain, the other being glial cells. Glial cells did increase in number in the rats with thicker cortices. In contrast to the communicatory role of neurons, glial cells serve a support role for the neurons, such as metabolic functions and the production of the myelin sheath that is found on some neurons and acts to facilitate neuronal transmission.

These findings raise questions as to whether similar cellular changes occur in the human brain. Although this remains to be systematically explored, an anecdotal report by the neuroanatomist Arnold Scheibel (1990) suggests that there may be parallel findings in humans. In examining the brains of two gifted individuals, he noticed that a distinguished violinist had an enhanced thickness of layer IV of the primary auditory cortical region, being twice as thick as that of normal individuals. The other brain was from a prominent artist who apparently had a remarkable capacity for intense eidetic imagery. In this latter case, layer IV was atypically thick in the primary visual cortex.

D. Hemispheric Differences in Cytoarchitecture

It is well established that the two sides or cerebral hemispheres of the brain exhibit functional differences. Most notable of these is the greater linguistic competence possessed by the left cerebral hemisphere. Scheibel and colleagues (see Scheibel, 1990) investigated whether there are cellular differences between a language region in the left hemisphere, known as Broca's area, and the corresponding region in the right hemisphere. They compared neurons from the two hemispheres in terms of the "branchiness" of the neuron's branch-like dendritic processes. The left hemisphere had neurons with a greater degree of branching than was the case for the right hemisphere, and this was particularly true for the later developed branches. This apparent neuronal embellishment in the left hemisphere may well be important for supporting language-related processing. Interestingly, the growth of these higher order branches in the left hemisphere are particularly marked starting at about 2 yr of age, a time of tremendous language acquisition.

Differences in neuronal architecture between the left and right cerebral hemispheres have also been demonstrated in the auditory cortex. Neurons in the left auditory cortex have dendrites that extend further tangentially within a cortical layer than do those in the right side (Seldon, 1985). Furthermore, there is greater separation between cortical columns in the left than in the right auditory cortex. Seldon suggests that this greater segregation between columns on the left side may be related to the left hemisphere's superiority in distinguishing certain auditory stimuli based on specific features. For instance, the left hemisphere is superior at identifying very short auditory signals, such as certain consonants (e.g., distinguishing /BA/ from /DA/). In contrast, the greater overlap between columns in the right auditory cortex may be advantageous in circumstances that require a more integrated or holistic, rather than a feature-specific, type of processing (Seldon, 1985).

III. FUNCTIONAL LOCALIZATION: THE CORTICAL LOBES AND THEIR FUNCTIONS

A. Approaches for Localizing Brain Functions

1. Lesion Studies

Our current understanding of the localization of different brain functions is a product of converging evidence from a variety of neuroanatomical and neuropsychological approaches. Foremost of these are lesion studies that examine behavioral changes that follow localized brain alterations that are either of a natural origin (e.g., stroke) or that are realized by accident (e.g., head injury; gunshot wounds to the head) or as a consequence of neurosurgery (e.g., removal of brain tumors; epilepsy surgery). Here, the typical logic is that if a particular brain region participates in a particular function, then that function should be impaired if the corresponding brain region is removed or damaged. Although this logic is often valid, other interpretations can sometimes apply. For instance, brain lesions can lead to reorganization of brain functions, or to the release of previously inhibited functions (see Kolb & Whishaw, 1990, for further discussion).

2. Electrical Brain Stimulation

Cortical localization of brain functions has also been investigated using electrical brain stimulation. In humans, this technique was pioneered by Penfield and Roberts (1959) as a protocol in the neurosurgical treatment of epilepsy. Here, weak electrical currents are briefly applied to points on the brain of conscious patients, during which time ensuing sensorial, motor, or behavioral experiences are noted. Importantly, this technique can be used to reveal critical language areas, since stimulation of such areas will disrupt speech. The neurosurgeon can then avoid such areas during neurosurgery. More recent brain stimulation studies have been carried out by Ojemann and colleagues, and they have found that critical language areas involve smaller cortical areas with greater between-subject variability in cortical localization than had been suspected from classical lesion studies (Ojemann et al., 1989). Brain stimulation has also been informative for mapping out the homunculus, that is, the sensory and motor cortical representations of the different parts of the body (Penfield & Jasper, 1954).

3. Recording Electrical Activity and Imaging Studies

In addition to stimulating the brain, it is also possible to record the electrical activity of brain cells. As was noted above, the recording of individual brain cells in animals has revealed such neural circuitry as the organization of cortical columns. In humans, the electrical activity of a large number of neurons can be measured using electroencephalography (EEG). This will be discussed further in the subsequent section, along with other imaging techniques that are being used to reveal localized brain functions in patients and, importantly, in neurologically normal individuals as well.

B. Functions of the Cerebral Lobes

The two cerebral hemispheres are approximately symmetrical in shape, and by convention, each cerebral hemisphere can be subdivided into four different lobes as depicted in Figure 2. With the exception of the occipital lobes, which are dedicated to visual processing, each right and left pair of cerebral lobes participates in a variety of disparate functions, as will be described. The following descriptions of the cerebral lobes are intended to provide an overall picture of the cortical localization of different sensory, motor, and cognitive functions as we understand this to date. This will serve as a general overview, as other chapters of this volume will concentrate on specific brain functions. Finally, it is important not to come away with the impression that the brain is partitioned into a large number of autonomous functional areas. There are vast neural connections between different areas within a cortical lobe, between the different lobes, between the cerebral

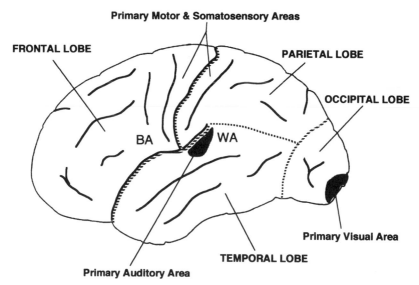

FIGURE 2   The division of the cerebral cortex into the four cortical lobes as depicted in the left hemisphere. Also indicated are the cortical locations of the primary sensory and motor areas, as well as the approximate locations of Broca's area (BA) and Wernicke's area (WA), which are considered to be critical language areas.

hemispheres, and between cortical and subcortical areas. Therefore, when one considers a cognitive function such as memory, several brain regions are involved, each contributing a qualitatively different type of processing (e.g., such as processing related to memory storage, memory retrieval, short-term vs. long-term vs. procedural vs. implicit memories, temporal information, modality-specific information, etc.).

1. The Occipital Lobes

Cortical processing of visual sensory information begins in the primary visual area of the occipital lobes. Animal studies have led to great advances in our understanding of the functional neural circuitry of the visual system. Visual processing involves both serial and parallel connections between multiple cortical visual areas that differ in their responsiveness to such visual attributes as color, shape, motion, orientation, and depth (e.g., DeYoe & Van Essen, 1988). The later stages of visual processing extend beyond the occipital lobe, forming two primary pathways that have been described as the "what" and "where" pathways (Ungerleider & Mishkin, 1982). These pathways are related to object perception, involving primarily the temporal lobe regions (i.e., identifying *what* an object is), and to spatial perception, involving primarily the parietal lobes (i.e., locating *where* an object is).

Lesions of the occipital lobes can produce blindness for parts of the visual field. More complex visual disorders result when brain damage includes either the temporal lobe, the parietal lobe, or both regions, resulting in deficits that commonly correspond to the "what" and "where" distinction. Lesions to occipitotemporal regions can produce visual agnosias, such as a selective deficit in recognizing objects, colors, or faces, despite otherwise normal vision. Meanwhile, occipitoparietal lesions can cause deficits related to visuospatial functioning. (see McCarthy & Warrington, 1990, for further discussion).

2. The Temporal Lobes

In addition to the temporal lobes' role in higher order visual functions, the temporal lobes are concerned with hearing and also participate in functions related to language, memory, and emotion. Damage to the temporal lobes' primary auditory area can impair hearing or even cause deafness. Damage to areas neighboring the primary auditory area can lead to more selective hearing deficits. In particular, lesions of the temporal lobe in the left hemisphere are often associated with disorders of speech perception, whereas right temporal lobe damage can produce deficits in music perception (e.g., Milner, 1962; Zatorre, 1984). Patients who can hear but have problems comprehending and repeating verbal information that they have heard are considered to have a language disorder (i.e., type of aphasia) known as Wernicke's aphasia. These patients can speak, but often their sentences make little or no sense. Wernicke's aphasia is commonly, but not always, associated with damage to a left temporal lobe region known as Wernicke's area (Figure 2). The right hemisphere is known to participate in prosodic processing of language, such as discerning the particular intonation of someone's speech (e.g., E. Zaidel, 1985). Such prosodic processing likely occurs within the temporal lobe of the right hemisphere. Another key function of the temporal lobes is integrating sensory information from the auditory, visual, and somatic (e.g., tactile) modalities.

Within the temporal lobes are structures that are part of the limbic system, which is considered to be distinct from, and phylogenetically older than, the neocortex. The limbic system is known to play a role in emotion, affect, and sexual behavior. It also has critical memory functions. In Alzheimer's disease, in which patients have marked memory deficits, the limbic system undergoes severe degeneration (Brun, 1983). A limbic structure known as the hippocampus has been shown to be essential for forming long-term memories. If both hippocampi of the left and right hemisphere are damaged, this can have profound effects on the formation of new memories, while sparing memories that were present before the damage took place (Milner, 1966). Findings from epileptic patients, who have had surgical removal of part of their left or right temporal lobe for the treatment of epilepsy, suggest that both the temporal neocortex and the hippocampus participate in memory functions. Left temporal lobe removal tends to produce memory deficits for verbal material (e.g., numbers, words, and stories), whereas right lobe removal impairs memory for nonverbal material (e.g., line drawings, faces, and melodies) (e.g., Kimura, 1963; Milner, 1967; Shankweiler, 1966; Warrington & James, 1967).

3. The Parietal Lobes

Memory functions are also an attribute of the parietal lobes, which is not surprising given the substantial neural connections between the parietal lobes and the hippocampus. In particular, the parietal lobes are associated with short-term memory functions, also known as working memory. For example, the ability to repeat a series of numbers that was just heard is often impaired in patients with left-hemisphere lesions involving both the temporal and parietal lobes. Here too, one finds hemispheric asymmetries for verbal and nonverbal material, in this case for working memory (see McCarthy & Warrington, 1990).

The parietal lobes are responsible for processing somatosensory information from the body; this includes touch, pain, temperature, and the sense of limb position. Like the temporal lobes, the parietal lobes are also involved in integrating information from different modalities. This is particularly the case for the convergence of visual information and both sensory and motor information concerning the body. Consequently, the parietal lobes are important for visuomotor guidance.

Language deficits often accompany damage to the left parietal lobe. Acquired reading and writing deficits have been associated with left parietal lobe lesions, and arithmetic abilities can be similarly impaired (e.g., Hécaen, 1969; Hécaen & Albert, 1978). Thus, left parietal lobe regions appear to be especially adept at processing stimuli of a symbolic nature.

As already mentioned, the parietal lobes have important visuospatial functions, especially the right parietal lobe. Although a distinction was made between the temporal lobe "what" visual system and the parietal lobe "where" system, this is more of a relative description than an absolute one. For instance, patients with parietal lobe damage can have difficulty identifying objects from unusual views (e.g., a bucket that is photographed from directly above; Warrington & Taylor, 1973). This situation suggests a role of the parietal lobes in the interplay between visuospatial processing and object recognition.

Right and left parietal lobes also appear to differ in the manner that sensory information is attended to in each hemisphere. Right parietal lobe lesions can cause a remarkable deficit called unilateral neglect, in which the patient neglects visual, auditory, and somatosensory information on the left side (e.g., McFie & Zangwill, 1960). Unilateral neglect is considerably less common following left parietal lobe damage.

4. The Frontal Lobes

The frontal lobes are characterized by regions devoted to (1) controlling the body's movements, (2) participating in language functions, and (3) serving general executive functions. The control of body movement is carried out by motor cortical regions, situated adjacent to the somatosensory cortex of the parietal lobe. Damage to the primary motor area of a particular cerebral hemisphere can cause paralysis on the opposite side of the body.

Language functions have been ascribed to the frontal lobe region in the left hemisphere known as Broca's area (Figure 2). The functions of the corresponding frontal lobe region in the right hemisphere are not well understood. Broca's area is situated in front of the motor cortical area that controls movements of the face, mouth, and tongue. Lesions to Broca's area frequently produce a language disorder known as Broca's aphasia, which is somewhat the converse of Wernicke's aphasia. Broca's aphasics have a problem with speech output, which is disproportionately greater than any problems they may have with speech comprehension. The classification of Broca's area as a language area has met with controversy because some researchers have proposed that Broca's area may be related more to general motor functions required for speech, than to language functions per se (e.g., Petersen, Fox, Posner, Mintun, & Raichle, 1988; Zangwill, 1975).

A large portion of the frontal cortex seems to be involved in a diverse repertoire of functions that contribute to or enhance cognitive processing. For instance, the frontal lobes seem to be important for problem solving and the ability to shift strategies. Other functions ascribed to the frontal lobes include associative learning, temporal memory, and cognitive functions related to purposeful and planned behavior.

IV. IMAGING THE LIVING BRAIN

One avenue in which neuropsychological research has been undergoing rapid and exciting changes concerns technologies for imaging the living brain. These techniques tend to be characterized by their ability to reveal either brain structure or brain function, although even this distinction is narrowing for some instruments (e.g., functional magnetic resonance imaging [MRI]). Furthermore, it is likely that through computerized image processing it will become relatively common to combine images from different techniques to provide a final image that reveals functional changes in brain activity mapped onto views of the brain that possess exquisite anatomical detail.

A. Techniques That Reveal Brain Anatomy

1. Computerized Tomography

Computerized tomography (CT) is known for being the first widely used imagery technique to reveal brain anatomy. By combining X-ray techniques with computerized data acquisition and image reconstruction, CT provides horizontal-sliced images of the brain. With CT, tissues are distinguished by their different absorptions of X rays. Although CT does not show the details of the brain to the extent that is now possible with MRI, the advent of CT was a great medical advancement because of its ability to detect tumors, lesions caused by stroke, and other brain abnormalities. Since cognitive deficits often accompany brain damage, CT has been a useful research instrument in enabling researchers to infer the cognitive functions subserved by different brain regions or pathways. The technology incorporated in CT has helped pave the road for the development of still more sophisticated imaging techniques such as positron emission tomography (PET) and single photon emission computed tomography (SPECT).

2. Magnetic Resonance Imaging

MRI provides views of the brain in amazing lifelike detail. Furthermore, whereas CT requires the use of X rays, MRI acquires images noninvasively through the use of a strong magnetic field and radio waves. A key feature of MRI is its sensitivity to properties of hydrogen atoms, one of the two elements found in water. This is fortunate because all brain tissues contain water in varying degrees. Although the physics of MRI is complicated, in brief, hydrogen nuclei align with the magnetic field, much like a compass needle behaves within the earth's magnetic field. A brief pulse of radio waves is then introduced, which dislodges the spinning hydrogen nuclei. Following the pulse, the nuclei return to alignment with the magnetic field, and emit radio waves themselves in the process, which are detected by antennae-like receivers situated around the head. Since these emitted radio waves will vary for different tissues, this provides the means by which MRI can construct images of the anatomy of the brain.

Like CT, MRI affords the possibility of studying relationships between localized brain injuries or abnormalities and the type of cognitive deficits that ensue. Unlike CT, MRI has a great facility to obtain images of the brain at different angles or planes of view, as well as the possibility of constructing three-dimensional representations of regions of interest. Subsequently, MRI is a useful research tool for carrying out morphometric studies, that is, the ability to measure the size and shape of different brain regions in living individuals. Since MRI can be performed on healthy individuals who can then also participate in behavioral testing, this permits investigations of whether individual differences in specific cognitive abilities or patterns of hemispheric specialization can have measurable anatomical correlates.

Recent advances in MRI technology have resulted in functional or high-speed MRI, which can reveal brain activity in addition to brain structure. This will be discussed further (Section IV.B.5).

B. Techniques That Reveal Brain Function

1. Positron Emission Tomography

Although MRI has become the technique of choice for revealing brain anatomy, PET is renown for its sensitivity in revealing functional activity of the brain. PET combines technology from CT together with radioisotope imaging to produce images of the working brain. The subject is administered, through inhaling or injection, compounds such as oxygen, water, or glucose that have been bound with positron-emitting isotopes (e.g., ^{15}O and ^{18}F). These radiation-emitting compounds then serve as markers for such physiological measures as cerebral blood flow, blood volume, oxygen extraction, and glucose metabolism. Because these physiological measures tend to be greater in brain regions that are more active, the radioisotopes, in turn, tend to concentrate in these functionally active regions. Positrons are emitted from the radioisotope and they collide with electrons, producing gamma rays, which are recorded by detectors situated around the head. This information is processed by a computer, which can then ascertain the origin of the radioisotopes. The end result is a series of images depicting regional differences in physiological activity within different *slices* of the brain. By having subjects participate in a particular cognitive task during the physiological uptake of the radioisotope, one can then determine the brain regions that participate in that particular cognitive operation. For example, as was demonstrated by early studies that helped validate the PET procedure, the presentation of visual or auditory stimuli produces activation in visual and auditory cortical areas, respectively (e.g., Phelps, Mazziotta, & Huang, 1982). In addition to the activation of sensory cortical areas, specific higher order association cortical areas may become active depending on the nature and complexity of the stimuli or task requirements.

One particularly interesting approach in using PET to study cognition is the subtraction method. Here, subjects undergo a series of PET scans, where for each scan the subject participates in a particular cognitive task, and each successive task differs slightly from the preceding one. For example, Petersen et al. (1988) had subjects participate in the following tasks: (1) visually fixate a point on a screen (i.e., baseline state), (2) passively watch or listen to words presented visually or auditorily, (3) verbally repeat words presented in either modality, and (4) generate and say a use for each presented word (e.g., "eat" is a possible response for the word "cake"). As each successive task tends to add an additional cognitive process, subtracting PET images from successive tasks has the effect of canceling out the activity that is shared or redundant between them, thus highlighting brain regions that participate in the added cognitive process. Petersen et al.'s findings indicate that the inferred cognitive processes of (1) modality-specific passive processing of word codes (i.e., subtracting PET images of task 1 from task 2), (2) verbal motor programming and output (tasks 3–2), and (3) semantic association (tasks 4–3), were associated, respectively, with (1) visual or auditory cortical areas including association regions, (2) sensorimotor cortical areas associated with the mouth, and (3) frontal lobe regions in the left, but not right, hemisphere. Additionally, Wernicke's area in the left hemisphere was activated by auditory but not visual processing of words. As Petersen et al. (1988) note, these findings argue against a serial, single-route model of lexical processing (cf. Geschwind, 1972), and are instead more consistent with multiple-route models of lexical processing that vary with the sensory modality of the linguistic stimulus (however, see Howard et al., 1992). Thus, this example shows how PET can contribute to experimental neuropsychology, such as through the testing of linguistic models.

The neural transmission of information in the brain is dependent on both the passage of electrical currents along neurons as well as neuronal release of chemical substances known as transmitters, that act as chemical messengers between neurons. Another use of PET is to bind radioisotopes to compounds that can act as markers for specific transmitter pathways. Consequently, this type of approach can be used to study the neuropharmacology of normal brain function, and furthermore, it has important clinical implications. For instance, Alzheimer's disease and Parkinson's disease have been linked to the reduced presence of the neurotransmitters acetylcholine and dopamine, respectively, whereas schizophrenia is often associated with an excess of dopamine transmission. Thus, PET holds great promise for further understanding these devastating diseases.

Although the research and clinical applications of PET are plentiful, its use will continue to be limited because of its high cost. In particular, the production of positron-emitting radioisotopes is extremely expensive. Also, there are radiation guidelines that limit the frequency with which a subject or patient can participate in a PET study. Finally, the temporal resolution of PET is in the order of minutes. That is, PET provides a measure of the predominant physiological activity that occurs when a subject repeats a task over a number of minutes. Because the sequence of most cognitive operations occurs in a fraction of a second, researchers who are interested in a finer temporal resolution will need to turn to other techniques such as EEG and magnetoencephalography (MEG), although these techniques have their own limitations.

2. Single Photon Emission Computed Tomography and Cerebral Blood Flow Studies

Functional images of the brain can also be acquired by techniques that measure regional cerebral blood flow through the use of the more accessible single photon–emitting isotopes. This approach has, in turn, been combined with CT technology resulting in SPECT. Although SPECT is most commonly used to measure cerebral blood flow, it is also being applied to neurotransmitter studies. Whereas SPECT is considerably less costly than PET, the trade-off is in less detailed images and physiological information that is less amenable to quantification. Albeit, SPECT is proving to be a valued instrument in clinical and research settings. For instance, in the study of epilepsy, SPECT can be useful in localizing brain regions associated with seizure generation. The neurosurgical removal of such abnormal brain areas is a possible treatment for patients with severe epilepsy who are unresponsive to drug therapy.

Both blood flow and PET studies can even reveal regional brain activity that occurs during different types of *thinking,* in the absence of sensory stimulation or motor responses. This is exemplified by a regional cerebral blood flow study carried out by Roland and Friberg (1985) in which subjects participated in three tasks: (1) "50–3" task, subjects started with a count of 50 and continuously subtracted 3 from the result in their minds; (2) "jingle" task, subjects mentally skipped every second word in a nine-word circular jingle phrase; and (3) "route finding," subjects imagined taking a walk starting from their front door, alternating between turning left and right at each corner. All three types of mental thinking produced considerable cerebral metabolic activity, greater than what was previously found for processing sensory stimuli or producing voluntary movements. Furthermore, all three tasks generated significant increases in the activity of certain frontal lobe areas, suggesting a general involvement of the frontal lobe in organizing mental activity. In contrast to tasks involving sensory stimulation, the three mental tasks showed little or no activity in primary and secondary sensory regions. Instead, modality-specific effects were found in higher order association cortex: activation of auditory association cortex for the *jingle* task, and remote visual association areas for the *route-finding* task. The *50–3* task produced selective activation in a parietal lobe region known as the angular gyrus. Lesions of the angular gyrus in the left hemisphere are known to produce acalculia, the inability to perform mathematical operations.

3. Electroencephalography and Event-Related Potential Techniques

EEG continues to be an important neurophysiological technique that permits the measurement of electrical signals that represent the activity of a large number of brain cells. Typically, this information is recorded using recording electrodes positioned on the scalp. As mentioned above, EEG has excellent temporal resolution, enabling brain activities to be measured in fractions of a second. Where scalp-recorded EEG suffers is in terms of spatial resolution, because it has limited abilities in localizing the brain regions that are responsible for particular electrical signals.

EEG continues to be the primary clinical tool for studying epilepsy. Epileptic patients who are candidates for neurosurgical treatment sometimes have recording electrodes surgically placed directly onto the cortical surface or inserted into the depths of the brain, allowing for more accurate localization of areas that generate seizures. In addition to monitoring seizures, recordings can also be acquired from such patients while they perform perceptual, motor, or cognitive tasks, which may provide insights into the functions of the nonepileptic brain regions.

Because of the precise temporal resolution afforded by EEG, one can essentially create a moving picture of the regional changes in brain activity when subjects perform a particular task. This is achieved using event-related potential (ERP) procedures, in which a subject repeats a task many times over and the EEG signal is averaged across these repeated trials. In short, this acts to enhance the electrophysiological signals that are associated with performing the task, while diminishing the influence of other task-unrelated or background activity. A possible task could be presenting subjects with a successive series of familiar and unfamiliar photographs of faces, and for each photograph subjects respond as to whether they recognize the face. The ERP technique would reveal the precise timing and approximate location of brain regions with recordable activity at each stage of processing: from visual input, through intermediary cognitive stages, to response output.

4. Magnetoencephalography

As a rule, an electrical current will generate a magnetic flux, thus it follows that the tiny currents produced by the brain's neurons also produce magnetic fields. MEG is a technique that measures this biomagnetic information. With MEG, the magnetic flux generated within the brain is detected by superconducting antenna coils connected to extremely sensitive amplifiers known as superconducting quantum interference devices (SQIDs). For EEG, recording electrodes are attached to the scalp, whereas for MEG the antenna coils are permanently positioned within a captor that can be simply lowered over the subject's head. There presently exists MEG systems with captors that contain over 100 recording points and that cover the entire head. One advantage of measuring magnetic fields is that, unlike electrical signals, magnetic fields pass easily through tissue and bone without being distorted. Presently, MEG is still very much a research tool, and like PET, it is extremely expensive and therefore its accessibility is limited.

5. Functional Magnetic Resonance Imaging

MRI techniques have been developed that reveal brain activity through the measurement of changes in blood flow, blood volume, and blood oxygenation (e.g., Belliveau et al., 1991; Kwong et al., 1992). When neurons become more active, they increase their need for oxygen, which results in a regional increase in blood flow and a corresponding increase in the conversion of blood oxyhemoglobin to deoxyhemoglobin. Water molecules produce different radio signals in the presence of oxyhemoglobin and deoxyhemoglobin because these two forms of hemoglobin differ in their magnetic properties. Using high-speed imaging capabilities, it is possible to set MRI parameters to be sensitive to these effects, resulting in a physiological index of neuronal activity. Presently, this technique has a temporal resolution of about 1 s for discerning physiological changes, being superior to that of PET but not as sensitive as EEG and MEG. Because functional MRI can be performed noninvasively (Kwong et al., 1992), individual subjects can participate in an unlimited number of sessions. Consequently, this technique holds great promise for investigations of individual differences. Although functional MRI is presently in its infancy, its future is extremely promising, especially given the current wide-spread use of conventional MRI technology, which in many instances can be adapted to include functional MRI capabilities.

In sum, neuropsychologists now have a wealth of techniques at their disposal to investigate the neuroanatomical and neurophysiological bases of brain functions. Because each approach has its strengths and weaknesses, a comprehensive understanding of brain functioning will depend on appreciating the unique contribution from each approach. For instance, functional imaging techniques are useful for revealing brain regions that *participate* in some function, whereas lesion and brain stimulation studies disclose the areas that are *critical* for a function. It is through such convergence of evidence that relationships between brain anatomy and function will be best understood.

V. MEASURING THE BRAIN: INDIVIDUAL DIFFERENCES

A. Functional Significance of Brain Size

This final section examines whether measurements of brain size or of certain brain structures can be informative in accounting for individual differences in behavioral–functional measures such as intelligence or language organization in the brain. Perhaps the most elementary question in this regard is whether bigger is better. The adult human brain exhibits a remarkable variability in its size, ranging in weight from about 1000 g to 2000 g. Yet, the brains of both eminent scholars and more common individuals show this same variability in brain size (e.g., Gould, 1981). Consequently, there is little evidence for a relationship between brain size and intelligence, and instead, brain size seems to be closely tied to body height and body surface area (Passingham, 1979; Snell, 1891, as cited in Peters, 1988). Because men, on average, are bigger and taller than woman, the relationship between body size and brain size accounts for the reliable sex difference in brain size, whereby male brains are on average about 12% heavier than female brains (e.g., Passingham, 1979). Larger brains do not necessarily contain significantly more neurons than smaller brains since smaller brains may be associated with a greater neuronal packing density rather than a reduction in the number of neurons (Haug, 1987). The advent of MRI provides a means of studying the size of morphometry of the brain or of specific brain structures in living individuals, which, in turn, can be compared with cognitive–behavioral measures in the same individuals. For example, an investigation of healthy young adults found that the area of the inner or midsagittal cortical surface, which is highly correlated with brain weight (F. Aboitiz, personal communication), is unrelated to a variety of cognitive abilities, including linguistic functions, visuoperceptual abilities, memory, manual dexterity, and problem solving (Clarke, 1990). Although such findings suggest that variability in overall brain size is independent of individual differences in cognitive abilities or cortical functional organization, more specific investigations of certain brain structures have revealed relationships between morphometric size and function.

B. Language Areas

Given the striking differences between the left and right cerebral hemispheres for language functions, one might expect to find corresponding anatomical differences between the hemispheres. Just as the left hemisphere is more specialized for language functions than the right for most individuals, a cortical region called the planum temporale is reliably found to be larger in the left than in the right hemisphere in the majority of cases (e.g., Geschwind & Levitsky, 1968). The planum temporale is situated adjacent to the primary auditory cortex, hidden from external view within the crevice-like Sylvian fissure. In the left cerebral hemisphere, it is located within the general region of Wernicke's area. To date, over 500 adult postmortem brains have been examined, and 74% of these exhibit larger left planum temporales than right (see Steinmetz, Volkmann, Jäncke, & Fruend, 1991). Furthermore, this hemispheric difference appears to be present before birth (see Witelson & Kigar, 1988, for review).

The leftward bias in planum temporale measures has been shown to be reduced in left-handers (LeMay & Culebras, 1972; Steinmetz et al., 1991). This finding strengthens the interpretation that the anatomical hemispheric asymmetry of the planum temporale is related to functional hemispheric asymmetries for language, because clinical studies have shown that the incidence of left-hemisphere specialization for language is reduced in left-handers compared to right-handers. Left-hemispheric specialization for speech is found in approximately 96% of right-handers, compared to only 70% of left-handers, with the remaining left-handers having either right-hemisphere or bilateral specialization for speech (Rasmussen & Milner, 1977). In sum, left-handers show reduced hemispheric asymmetry for both language lateralization and planum temporale size.

Although this structure–function relationship is impressive, it is not the case that all individuals with left-hemisphere specialization for language have a larger left than right planum temporale. That is, some 90–95% of the population have left-hemisphere specialization for speech, whereas a left-sided bias in planum temporale size is found in approximately 74% of the cases. One possible explanation for this discrepancy is that the incidence of left-hemisphere language is commonly based on expressive functions of language (i.e., speech output), whereas the planum temporale is probably associated more with receptive language functions (i.e., language comprehension), which seem to be less strikingly lateralized (cf. Witelson & Kigar, 1988). There may also be hemispheric differences at the cellular level that are not reflected in measures of planum temporale size. Recall that differences in neuronal structure were found between Broca's area on the left side and the corresponding region in the right hemisphere (Scheibel, 1990). And yet, unlike the planum temporale, investigations have not found systematic differences in the size of Broca's area in the left and right hemisphere (see Witelson & Kigar, 1988).

C. The Corpus Callosum

Individual differences in a cortical structure known as the corpus callosum have received much attention. The corpus callosum is the principal fiber tract connecting the left and right cerebral hemispheres. Since each cerebral hemisphere is responsible for the motor and sensory functions on the opposite side of the body or sensory space, the corpus callosum is important for unifying this information. Additionally, the corpus callosum has been implicated in participating in such higher cognitive functions as attention (Geschwind, 1965; Kinsbourne, 1975; Levy, 1985; E. Zaidel, 1986), memory (D. Zaidel & Sperry, 1974), semantic processing (Sidtis, Volpe, Holtzman, Wilson, & Gazzaniga, 1981), hemispheric division of labor (Banich & Belger, 1989; Dimond & Beaumont, 1971; Liederman, 1986), and the maintenance of independent processing in the two hemispheres (E. Zaidel, Clarke, & Suyenobu, 1990).

A number of studies have examined whether the cross-sectional area of the corpus callosum differs between males and females, or between left- and right-handed individuals, and the majority of these studies have failed to find significant differences (see Clarke, 1990). It is interesting that there is no sex difference in the size of the corpus callosum given that brain size is on average reliably larger in males than in females (see Peters, 1988 for discussion). Because males and females have corpus callosums that are similar in size, and presumably contain a similar number of neuronal fibers (see Aboitiz, Scheibel, Fisher, & E. Zaidel, 1992), this finding is consistent with the view that the sex difference in brain size is associated more with a sex difference in neuronal cell packing than a difference in total number of neurons (Haug, 1987).

Although overall corpus callosum size does not exhibit reliable group differences, recent investigations have found individual differences in a region of the corpus callosum region known as the isthmus, which is depicted in Figure 3. Different portions of the corpus callosum contain neural fibers that originate from different cortical areas. Anatomical findings suggest that the isthmus contains fibers originating from the left posterior language area and the corresponding region on the right, both of which include the planum temporale (de Lacoste, Kirkpatrick, & Ross, 1985; Pandya & Seltzer,

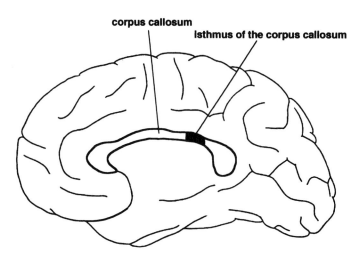

FIGURE 3   Location of the corpus callosum and the isthmus of the corpus callosum as seen from the inner or medial serface of the neocortex. Corpus callosum fibers originate from nearly all cortical areas, and these fibers converge at the point of crossing between the two cerebral hemispheres to form the structure shown in this figure.

1986). Isthmus size may actually depend, in part, on the extent of the asymmetry between left and right planum temporale size. Males who had larger isthmus sizes also tended to have smaller hemispheric differences in planum temporale size, which, in turn, may be associated with greater bilateral representation of language functions (Aboitiz, Scheibel, & E. Zaidel, 1992). This result suggests that when critical language functions are represented in both hemispheres, there may be a greater reliance on interhemispheric communication, and thus the need for a larger isthmus (Aboitiz, Scheibel, & E. Zaidel, 1992; Witelson, 1989). This interpretation is supported by evidence that the isthmus is larger in males who show signs of lefthandedness, and are, in turn, more likely to have bilateral language representation than strongly right-handed males (Clarke, 1990; Denenberg, Kertesz, & Cowell, 1991; Habib et al., 1991; Witelson, 1989). In contrast to males, females do not show a relationship between isthmus size and handedness. Nor do females exhibit an association between isthmus size and right–left planum temporale asymmetries. This is consistent with the view that males and females differ in their cortical organization of language functions (e.g., Kimura, 1987; McGlone, 1980).

VI. CONCLUSION

In summary, individual differences in the functional organization of the brain begin at the microscopic level. Although as adults our brains do not acquire new neurons, the neurons that we do have are likely undergoing constant morphological and neuropharmacological changes as a function of our everyday experiences and mental challenges. The neuroanatomical basis for exceptional reasoning powers, rare musical talents, and other gifted abilities likely lies in the fine-tuned aspects of neuronal microstructure rather than such gross measures as brain size. As was illustrated with brain size, bigger does not necessarily equate with better. A study of corpus callosum size actually found that individuals with larger corpus callosums tended to perform worse on a particular measure of a lateralized verbal auditory task (Clarke, Lufkin, & E. Zaidel, 1993). Although interhemispheric communication is normally beneficial, this may not always be true. Interhemispheric interactions may be detrimental to overall processing if a cerebral hemisphere is not competent for a particular task, yet carries out processing that adversely affects the contributions of the competent hemisphere (Clarke et al., 1993). In other circumstances it is probably advantageous to maximize interhemispheric communication, as may be the case for individuals with language representations in both cerebral hemispheres. Morphometric studies of brain structures seem particularly useful in revealing individual differences in brain organization. This was exemplified by the findings that larger isthmus size and greater equivalence in left and right planum temporale size appear to be neuroanatomical traits that support bilateral language representation. As these findings were observed in males but not females, future studies need to consider effects of sex, and attempt to further clarify the manner and extent to which men's and women's brains differ. Such endeavors will be aided by continued advancements in neuroimaging techniques that allow for precise spatial and temporal identification of cerebral activity.

References

Aboitiz, F., Scheibel, A. B., Fisher, R. S., & Zaidel, E. (1992). Fiber composition of the human corpus callosum. *Brain Research, 598,* 143–153.

Aboitiz, F., Scheibel, A. B., & Zaidel, E. (1992). Morphometry of the Sylvian fissure and the corpus callosum, with emphasis on sex differences. *Brain, 115,* 1521–1541.

Banich, M. T., & Belger, A. (1989). Interhemispheric interaction: How do the hemispheres divide and conquer a task? *Cortex, 26,* 77–94.

Belliveau, J. W., Kennedy, D. N., McKinstry, R. C., Buchbinder, B. R., Weisskoff, R. M., Cohen, M. S., Vevea, J. M., Brady, T. J., & Rosen, B. R. (1991). Functional mapping of the human visual cortex by magnetic resonance imaging. *Science, 254,* 716–719.

Brodmann, K. (1909). *Vergleichende Lokalisationslehre der Grosshirnrinde in ihren Prinzipien dargestellt auf Grund des Zellenbaues.* Leipzig: Barth.

Brun, A. (1983). An overview of light and electron microscopic changes. In B. Reisberg (Ed.), *Alzheimer's disease* (pp. 37–47). New York: Free Press.

Clarke, J. M. (1990). *Interhemispheric functions in humans: Relationships between anatomical measures of the corpus callosum, behavioral laterality effects, and cognitive profiles.* Unpublished doctoral dissertation, University of California at Los Angeles.

Clarke, J. M., Lufkin, R. B., & Zaidel, E. (1993). Corpus callosum morphometry and dichotic listening performance: Individual differences in functional inhibition? *Neuropsychologia, 31,* 547–557.

de Lacoste, M. C., Kirkpatrick, J. B., & Ross, E. D. (1985). Topography of the human corpus callosum. *Journal of Neuropathology and Experimental Neurology, 44,* 578–591.

Denenberg, V. H., Kertesz, A., & Cowell, P. E. (1991). A factor analysis of the human's corpus callosum. *Brain Research, 548,* 126–132.

DeYoe, E. A., & Van Essen, D. C. (1988). Concurrent processing streams in monkey visual cortex. *Trends in Neuroscience, 11,* 219–226.

Diamond, M. C. (1990). Morphological cortical changes as a consequence of learning and experience. In A. B. Scheibel & A. F. Wechsler (Eds.), *Neurobiology of higher cognitive function* (pp. 1–12). New York: Guilford Press.

Dimond, S. J., & Beaumont, G. (1971). Use of two cerebral hemispheres to increase brain capacity. *Nature (London), 232,* 270–271.

Geschwind, N. (1965). Disconnexion syndromes in animals and man. *Brain, 88,* 237–294.

Geschwind, N. (1972). Language and the brain. *Scientific American, 226,* 76–83.

Geschwind, N., & Levitsky, W. (1968). Human brain: Left-right asymmetries in temporal speech region. *Science, 161,* 186–187.

Gould, S. J. (1981). *The mismeasure of man.* New York: Norton.

Habib, M., Gayraud, D., Oliva, A., Regis, J., Salamon, G., & Khalil, R. (1991). Effects of handedness and sex on the morphology of the corpus callosum: A study with brain magnetic resonance imaging. *Brain and Cognition, 16,* 41–61.

Haug, H. (1987). Brain sizes, surfaces, and neuronal sizes of the cortex cerebri: A stereological investigation of man and his variability and a comparison with some mammals (primates, whales, marsupials, insectivores, and one elephant). *American Journal of Anatomy, 180,* 126–142.

Hécaen, H. (1969). Aphasic, apraxic and agnosic syndromes in right and left hemisphere lesions. In P. Wincken & G. Bruyn (Eds.), *Handbook of clinical neurology* (Vol. 4, pp. 291–311). Amsterdam: North-Holland Publ.

Hécaen, H., & Albert, M. L. (1978). *Human neuropsychology.* New York: Wiley.

Howard, D., Patterson, K., Wise, R., Brown, W. D., Friston, K., Weiller, C., & Frackowiak, R. (1992). The cortical localization of the lexicons: Positron emission tomography evidence. *Brain, 115,* 1769–1782.

Hubel, D. H., & Wiesel, T. N. (1962). Receptive fields, binocular interaction and functional architecture in the cat's visual cortex. *Journal of Physiology (London), 160,* 106–154.

Kaas, J. H., Nelson, R. J., Sur, M., Lin, C.-L., & Merzenich, M. M. (1979). Multiple representations of the body within the primary somatosensory cortex of primates. *Science, 204,* 521–523.

Kimura, D. (1963). Right temporal-lobe damage: Perception of unfamiliar stimuli after damage. *Archives of Neurology (Chicago), 8,* 264–271.

Kimura, D. (1987). Are men's and women's brains really different? *Canadian Psychology, 28,* 133–147.

Kinsbourne, M. (1975). The mechanism of hemispheric control of the lateral gradient of attention. In P. M. A. Rabbitt & S. Dornic (Eds.), *Attention and performance V* (pp. 81–97). New York: Academic Press.

Kolb, B., & Whishaw, I. Q. (1990). *Fundamentals of human neuropsychology* (3rd ed.). New York: Freeman.

Kwong, K. K., Belliveau, J. W., Chesler, D. A., Goldberg, I. E., Weisskoff, R. M., Poncelet, B. P., Kennedy, D. N., Hoppell, B. E., Cohen, M. S., Turner, R., Cheng, H.-M., Brady, T. J., & Rosen, B. (1992). Dynamic magnetic resonance imaging of human brain activity during primary sensory stimulation. *Proceedings of the National Academy of Sciences of the U.S.A., 89,* 5675–5679.

LeMay, M., & Culebras, A. (1972). Human brain: Morphological differences in the hemispheres demonstrable by carotid arteriography. *New England Journal of Medicine, 287,* 168–170.

Levy, J. (1985). Interhemispheric collaboration: Single mindedness in the asymmetric brain. In C. T. Best (Ed.), *Hemispheric function and collaboration in the child* (pp. 11–31). New York: Academic Press.

Liederman, J. (1986). Subtraction in addition to addition: Dual task performance improves when asks are presented to separate hemispheres. *Journal of Clinical and Experimental Neuropsychology, 8,* 486–502.

McCarthy, R. A., & Warrington, E. K. (1990). *Cognitive neuropsychology: A clinical introduction.* San Diego: Academic Press.

McFie, J., & Zangwill, O. L. (1960). Visual-constructive disabilities associated with lesions of the left cerebral hemisphere. *Brain, 83,* 243–260.

McGlone, J. (1980). Sex differences in human brain asymmetry: A critical survey. *Behavioral and Brain Sciences, 3,* 215–263.

Milner, B. (1962). Laterality effects in audition. In V. B. Mountcastle (Ed.), *Interhemispheric relations and cerebral dominance* (pp. 177–195). Baltimore, MD: Johns Hopkins University Press.

Milner, B. (1966). Amnesia following operations on the temporal lobes. In C. W. M. Whitty & O. L. Zangwill (Eds.), *Amnesia* (pp. 109–133). London: Butterworth.

Milner, B. (1967). Brain mechanisms suggested by studies of temporal lobes. In F. L. Darley (Ed.), *Brain mechanisms underlaying speech and language* (pp. 122–132). New York: Grune & Stratton.

Mountcastle, V. B. (1957). Modality and topographic properties of single neurons of cat's somatic sensory cortex. *Journal of Neurophysiology, 20,* 408–434.

Ojemann, G., Ojemann, J., Lettich, E., & Berger, M. (1989). Cortical language localization in left, dominant hemisphere. *Journal of Neuroscience, 71,* 316–326.

Pandya, D. N., & Seltzer, B. (1986). The topography of commissural fibers. In F. Lepore, M. Ptito, & H. H. Jasper (Eds.), *Two hemispheres—one brain: Functions of the corpus callosum* (pp. 47–73). New York: Liss.

Passingham, R. E. (1979). Brain size and intelligence in man. *Brain, Behavior and Evolution, 16,* 253–270.

Penfield, W., & Jasper, H. H. (1954). *Epilepsy and functional anatomy of the human brain.* Boston: Little, Brown.

Penfield, W., & Roberts, L. (1959). *Speech and brain mechanisms.* Princeton, NJ: Princeton University Press.

Peters, M. (1988). The size of the corpus callosum in males and females: Implications of a lack of allometry. *Canadian Journal of Psychology, 42,* 313–324.

Petersen, S. E., Fox, P. T., Posner, M. I., Mintun, M., & Raichle, M. E. (1988). Positron emission tomographic studies of the cortical anatomy of single-word processing. *Nature (London), 331,* 585–589.

Phelps, M. E., Mazziotta, J. C., & Huang, S.-C. (1982). Study of cerebral function with positron computed tompography. *Journal of Cerebral Blood Flow Metabolism, 2,* 113–162.

Rassmussen, T., & Milner, B. (1977). The role of early left-brain injury in determining lateralization of cerebral speech functions. *Annals of the New York Academy of Sciences, 299,* 355–369.

Roland, P. E., & Friberg, L. (1985). Localization of cortical areas activated by thinking. *Journal of Neurophysiology, 53,* 1219–1243.

Scheibel, A. B. (1990). Dendritic correlates of higher cognitive function. In A. B. Scheibel & A. F. Wechsler (Eds.), *Neurobiology of higher cognitive function* (pp. 239–270). New York: Guilford Press.

Seldon, H. H. (1985). The anatomy of speech perception: Human auditory cortex. In A. Peters & E. G. Jones (Eds.), *Cerebral cortex: Vol. 4. Association and auditory cortices* (pp. 273–327). New York: Plenum.

Shankweiler, D. (1966). Effects of temporal lobe damage on perception of dichotically presented melodies. *Journal of Comparative and Physiological Psychology, 62,* 115–119.

Sidtis, J. J., Volpe, B. T., Holtzman, J. D., Wilson, D. H., & Gazzaniga, M. S. (1981). Cognitive interaction after staged callosal section: Evidence for transfer of semantic activation. *Science, 212,* 344–346.

Snell, O. (1891). Die Abhängigkeit des Hirngewichtes von dem Körpergewicht und den geistigen Fähigkeiten. *Archiv für Psychiatrie und Nervenkrankheiten, 23,* 436–446.

Steinmetz, H., Volkmann, J., Jäncke, L., & Freund, H.-J. (1991). Anatomical left-right asymmetry of language-related temporal cortex is different in left- and right-handers. *Annals of Neurology, 29,* 315–319.

Ungerleider, L. G., & Mishkin, M. (1982). Two cortical visual systems. In D. J. Ingle, M. A. Goodale, & R. J. W. Mansfield (Eds.), *Analysis of visual behavior* (pp. 549–586). Boston: MIT Press.

Warrington, E., & James, M. (1967). An experimental investigation of facial recognition in patients with unilateral cerebral lesions. *Cortex, 3,* 317–326.

Warrington, E., & Taylor, A. M. (1973). The contribution of the right parietal lobe to object recognition. *Cortex, 9,* 152–164.

Witelson, S. F. (1989). Hand and sex differences in the isthmus and genu of the human corpus callosum. *Brain, 112,* 799–835.

Witelson, S. F., & Kigar, D. L. (1988). Asymmetry in brain function follows asymmetry in anatomical form: Gross, microscopic, postmortem and imaging studies. In F. Boller & J. Grafman (Eds.), *Handbook of neuropsychology* (Vol. 1, pp. 111–142). Amsterdam: Elsevier.

Zaidel, D. W., & Sperry, R. W. (1974). Memory impairment after commissurotomy in man. *Brain, 97,* 263–272.

Zaidel, E. (1985). Language in the right hemisphere. In D. F. Benson & E. Zaidel (Eds.), *The dual brain: Hemispheric specialization in humans.* (pp. 205–231). New York: Guilford Press.

Zaidel, E. (1986). Callosal dynamics and right hemisphere language. In F. Lepore, M. Ptito, & H. H. Jasper (Eds.), *Two hemispheres—one brain? Functions of the corpus callosum* (pp. 435–459). New York: Liss.

Zaidel, E., Clarke, J. M., & Suyenobu, B. (1990). Hemispheric independence: A paradigm case for cognitive neuroscience. In A. B. Scheibel & A. F. Wechsler (Eds.), *Neurobiology of higher cognitive function* (pp. 297–355). New York: Guilford Press.

Zangwill, O. L. (1975). Excision of Broca's area without persistent aphasia. In K. J. Zulch, O. Creutzfeldt, & G. C. Galbraith (Eds.), *Cerebral localization* (pp. 258–263). Berlin & New York: Springer-Verlag.

Zattore, R. J. (1984). Musical perception and cerebral function: A critical review. *Music Perception, 2,* 196–221.

CHAPTER 3

Evolution of the Brain

Harry J. Jerison

I. GENERAL CONSIDERATIONS

There are 40,000 to 50,000 species of vertebrates, each unique in many traits yet sharing "primitive" traits with close and distant relatives. The pattern of unique traits defines each species, and the suite of shared (older, more primitive) traits, depending on the size of the suite, helps define it as a member of a higher taxon: genus, family, and so forth. This is as true for neural traits as it is for other traits that differentiate animal species. All biologists accept the evolutionary dogma that the uniformities in traits across species are due either to common ancestry or to convergent evolution, and that the diversity of species should usually be explained by adaptations to specialized environmental niches.

This chapter emphasizes inferences from allometric analysis of brain–body relations and encephalization, the latter being a complex trait often attributable to convergent evolution. Although the diversity in *organization* of brains is at least as important, especially for understanding the phylogenetic trees, an adequate discussion of the evolution of diversified brain organization requires a more detailed review of comparative anatomy and physiology than is possible in a single chapter, and the conclusions, though important, are almost trivially obvious: Brain structure is appropriate to function, and specialized functions are appropriate to the environment (i.e.,

Neuropsychology

structure and function are *adaptive*). In short, the results are consistent with adaptation as a biological principle (Williams, 1966, 1992). Applied to the sizes (weight, volume, or surface area) of the subsystems in the brain, such as cortical projection areas or thalamic nuclei, this is the principle of *proper mass* (Jerison, 1973).

Despite their simplicity, allometry (the regression of brain size on body size) and encephalization (the residual from that regression) provide more unusual evolutionary insights. Allometry helps us understand the biological role of size; encephalization does the same for understanding neural information-processing capacity and its evolution. It will be enough to review the diversity of organization by citing a few examples, the reports of which are extremely well documented with extensive bibliographies (see, especially, Welker, 1990).

The issues considered in this chapter are also relevant for the evolution of invertebrate nervous systems. The neuron, for example, probably appeared as a specialized cell early in metazoan evolution, more than 600 million years ago (ma), and many of its features are identical in all instances in which it functions in a synaptic nervous system. This is evidently true for small networks of neurons as well as isolated cells. Much of what is known about neural functions as single units and in small networks was learned from giant neurons of horseshoe crabs and from networks of cells in sea slugs and roundworms. From an evolutionist's perspective, however, the features of higher levels of integrated neural activity that are common to vertebrates and invertebrates are analogous ("homoplastic") rather than homologous and resulted from independent evolutionary paths in these major groups of animals (cf. Bitterman, 1988, on "higher order" learning in rats, which he demonstrated as occurring in bees).

A. Brain Structure and Function

Every vertebrate brain is hierarchically organized into forebrain, midbrain or mesencephalon, and hindbrain. The forebrain can be further divided into telencephalon and diencephalon, and hindbrain into rhombencephalon and myelencephalon (Northcutt, 1987). Brain tissue in all animals consists of neurons as information-processing units. and glia and other cells that are, in effect, supporting tissue. Neurons are often specialized with respect to neurotransmitters, shape, and size. Sizes, for example, range from the granule cells of the cerebellum (soma less than 10 μm diameter) to the giant Mauthner cells (soma about 100 μm diameter) that mediate startle responses in fish and in amphibian tadpoles (Korn, 1987; Palay & Chan-Palay, 1987). The full size of a nerve cell includes the arborization of axon and dendrites, which may account for 95% or more of the volume of a neuron, and which varies enormously in pattern both within a brain and between species.

Underlying this diversity there is nevertheless surprising uniformity about principles of nerve action in the transmission of information, which makes it possible to use almost any neuron from any species as a model for neuronal action. There is, furthermore, a uniformity at the level of networks of cells in vertebrate brains, evident even in the neocortex in mammals (Rockel, Hiorns, & Powell, 1980), which encourages one to emphasize information–processing capacity for the brain as a whole as well as in its specialized component systems, such as those for color vision, binocular vision, sound localization, olfaction, and so on.

B. Evolution

The facts of evolution are, first, that it occurred, and, second, that it could occur because of the genotypic and phenotypic diversity both within species and between species (cf. Mayr, 1988). Charles Darwin's great contributions were to recognize the diversity and to explain it by the theory of natural selection. As presently understood, the theory is that given the variety of phenotypes in a species, some individuals will be more successful than others in surviving to produce offspring. Reproduction is the measure of success. The mean of the gene pool of the next generation shifts toward the mean of the successful phenotype. As the environment changes, the characteristics required to be successful change, and there is natural selection of individuals with those characteristics. This is a theory of the origin of species, because there will eventually be enough change in the genotypic population to designate it as a new species.

There is so much support for the theory, in laboratory experiments and from field observations, that one might prefer a stronger word than "theory" to describe Darwin's integration. But there are disagreements among evolutionists, of course, which are sometimes taken incorrectly to be challenges to the credibility of the theory as a whole. The controversies are mainly about the relative importance of selection as opposed to random genetic drift, about the merits of various approaches to determining phylogenetic trees (cladistics), and about the rate of evolutionary change (gradualism versus punctuated equilibria). Dawkins (1987) reviews the evidence and issues in sufficient detail for our purposes; they will be covered only casually as they arise in this chapter. Despite their use and misuse in popular polemics, the controversies are on fairly technical questions and not on the fact of evolution.

The theoretical context for understanding our topic is from the neurosciences and evolutionary theory. Other chapters provide an orientation in the neurosciences, but we probably need a reading list on evolution. I recommend Dawkins (1987) as a nontechnical yet authoritative introduction to modern evolutionary analysis. To avoid terminological tangles, I follow

Carroll (1988) on paleontological and taxonomic issues not related to the brain. For additional background on phylogenetic analysis (cladistics) see Brooks and MacLennan (1991), and on quantitative evolutionary issues see Harvey and Pagel (1991). The evolutionary evidence on the brain is, first, from the fossil record and, second, from the diversity of brain structure and function in living species.

II. THE EVIDENCE

A. Fossil Brains

The fossil record of the brain is from casts ("endocasts") that are molded by the cranial cavity of fossil skulls. Natural endocasts are made by the replacement of soft tissue in the skull by sand and other debris that eventually fossilizes. Artificial endocasts can be made by cleaning the cavity and filling it with a molding compound such as latex, from which plaster casts can be made. Errors in identifying "brain" areas in endocasts of birds and mammals are likely to be nearly the same as in brains when superficial markings rather than histological or physiological evidence are the basis for the identification. Endocasts of some fossil animals are so brainlike in appearance (Figure 1) that they are often referred to as fossil brains.

Figure 1 presents lateral views of the endocast and brain from the same domestic cat, *Felis catus* (Figs. 1A and 1B), and a copy of a natural endocast from a fossil sabretooth (Fig. 1C). The sabretooth is *Hoplophoneus primaevus,* which lived in the South Dakota Badlands during the Oligocene epoch of the Tertiary period, about 30 ma. Although no more than a piece of rock, its endocast is unmistakably a picture of its brain as it was in life; it was clearly appropriate to name its parts as brain areas in Figure 1D, following the nomenclature for cat brains.

There are several lessons to be learned from Figure 1. First, an endocast can provide an excellent picture of the whole brain. This is evident when comparing Figure 1A with Figure 1B: the endocast of the domestic cat provides an excellent picture of external features of its brain and correctly estimates its size. (The estimation from the endocast is as "correct" as that from the brain, which is probably slightly shrunken by fixation.) Second, the convolutional pattern in an endocast may be fairly constant in related species. Thus, despite their separation by 30 million years of felid evolution, the endocasts of the living cat and of the sabretooth (Figs. 1A and 1C) are clearly similar. This lesson is especially important, because convolutions map the way a brain is organized, at least in a general way (Welker, 1990). A third lesson, therefore, is that the felid brain of 30 ma was probably organized in a way similar to that of living felids. Finally, as counterpoint to the lesson of uniformity of organization, there is a lesson of diversity: Two

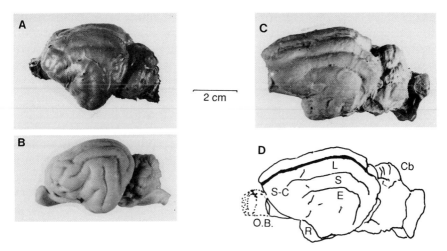

FIGURE 1   Brain and endocasts of felids. (A) Endocast of domestic cat (vol. = 30 ml). (B) Brain of same cat (weight = 29.1 g). (C) Endocast of Oligocene sabretooth, *Hoplophoneus primaevus* of 30 ma (vol. = 50 ml). (D) Tracing of the endocast of *Hoplophoneus* with labels for several structures (Welker, 1990, p. 12): Cb, cerebellum; E, ectosylvian gyrus; L, lateral gyrus; R, rhinal fissure; S, suprasylvian gyrus; S–C, sigmoid and coronal gyral complex (undifferentiated). Both endocasts are rotated about the anterior–posterior axis, exposing the longitudinal fissure (heavily inked in D). The unlabeled gyrus above the lateral gyrus is the lateral gyrus of the right hemisphere.

gyri, the coronal and sigmoid gyral complexes, are differentiated in living domestic cats but are undifferentiated in the sabretooth. Radinsky (1969, 1975) emphasized increases like these in the apparent complexity of the brain in felid evolution and related them to increases in information processing in the expanded areas in later species compared to earlier species, using modern physiological mapping studies to guide his analysis.

The quality of an endocast as a model of the brain differs in different taxa. Endocasts from fish, amphibians, and reptiles (except in very small specimens) are poor models, useful mainly to estimate total brain size after suitable corrections, because the brain fills only a fraction of the cranial cavity. In mammals and birds, on the other hand, the brain actually helps shape the cranial cavity during development, and endocasts are usually excellent pictures of the outside of the brain. Olfactory bulbs, forebrain, and hindbrain are readily identifiable, as are most of the cortical gyri and sulci that are seen when a brain is first removed from the skull. Certain large-brained living mammals, namely, cetaceans, elephants, great apes, and humans, are exceptions to this rule, with little or no impression of their convolutions on their endocasts; even the boundary between cerebrum and cerebellum may be unclear.

Fossils provide other information for understanding brain evolution and for extrapolations to behavior. Body size, for example, estimated from postcranial skeletal data, is used to analyze encephalization of fossil vertebrates. Details of structure, such as the shape of teeth, forelimbs, and hindlimbs, can enable one to analyze feeding habits, gait, and other behavior (e.g., Alexander, 1989; Feduccia, 1993). There is even fossil evidence on social behavior, for example in dinosaurs, which has been reconstructed from the aggregation of fossils, their eggs, and their foot and tail prints (Horner & Gorman, 1988). Perhaps most important for an analysis of brain evolution, there is a fossil record of sensory structures, which is useful in reconstructing the information available to fossil animals. Olfactory bulbs, of course, are visible on the endocast, and their size is related to the evolution of the sense of smell (Jerison, 1990). There are fossil middle ear bones and cochlea important for the analysis of the evolution of hearing (Allin, 1975, 1986); the orientation of the orbits of the eye provides evidence on the evolution of binocular vision (Martin, 1990; pp. 318–323), and the placement of the hyoid bones on fossil humans has been the basis for speculations on the evolution of the voice box and of articulated speech (Lieberman, 1984).

B. The Living Brain

Most of the evolutionary evidence on living brains is from anatomical and physiological studies of brain tracts and regions compared for unique and common features across species. Sarnat and Netsky (1981) is a standard text, but for detailed information one must go to specialized monographs such as Jones and Peters (1990) or Stephen, Baron, and Frahm (1991) and to the primary journals: *Journal of Comparative Neurology, Brain, Behavior and Evolution*, and *Journal für Hirnforschung* (many English articles). There is growing interest in molecular evidence (e.g., on neurotransmitters), and one can anticipate increasing emphasis on that kind of information (e.g., Karten, 1991; MacLean, 1977). I review the comparative literature very selectively and personally, considering only material that has significantly influenced my work (Jerison, 1991).

Braitenberg and Schüz (1991) present a straightforward anatomical monograph, noteworthy for the quantitative analyses of the cerebral cortex of the mouse. Though not specifically concerned with evolutionary issues, they provide exemplars of data necessary for an evolutionary analysis. The most striking facts are on the amount of information-processing machinery in the mouse, with some suggestions on the human brain. There are about 40,000,000 neurons in the half-gram brain of a mouse; more astonishing, there are about 80,000,000,000 synapses in its neocortex. Taking into account the packing density of neurons and synapses, they reached the conclusion that a particular volume of cortex processes the same amount of information, whether it is in a mouse or a human. This is an outstanding uniformity for evolutionary analysis, since it validates the use of brain size as a "statistic" to estimate the total information-processing capacity of a brain.

Uniformity is balanced by diversity. All species differ in the details of the organization of the component systems of their brains. The raccoons and their relatives (family Procyonidae) provide an outstanding example (Johnson, 1990; Welker, 1990). The fish-handling raccoon has a much enlarged forepaw projection area in its somatosensory neocortex, with separate representation in the brain for each of the pads on the forepaw. The coati mundi, kinkajou, and most other procyonids get this kind of information by nosing about, exploring their environment by touching things with the sensory skin around the nostrils. Their neocortical projections from that region are comparably expanded and their forepaw projection areas are much less extensive and not as differentiated as in the raccoon. The conclusion is inescapable that reorganization of the brain, like the differentiation of the behavior that it controls, occurred as part of the speciation of procyonids as they evolved, and that raccoons branched away from the main line by their specialized adaptations in their use of forepaws. Johnson, Kirsch, and Switzer (1982) used data like these for formal cladistic analyses in which the mammalian phylogeny constructed from brain features was found to be essentially the same as that based on a more complete suite of traits.

I depended on the comparative quantitative data laboriously accumulated by Stephen, Frahm, and Baron (1981) on the volumes of many brain structures in "primitive" species represented by insectivores and their relatives and in "advanced" species (primates) for many of my analyses of allometry and encephalization (Figures 2, 3, and 4). Theirs are the most complete data of this sort presently available. In their sample of 76 species there were 26 from the order Insectivora (shrews, moles, and hedgehogs), two Macroscelididae (elephant shrews), three Scandentia (tree shrews), and 45 Primates, of which 18 are from the suborder Prosimii (lemurlike species) and 27 from the suborder Anthropoidea (simian species, including humans). The brain structures are listed in Table 1. These data are especially useful because of the large number of species that are in the sample and the good sample of brain structures on which measurements were taken.

III. QUALITATIVE ANALYSIS

There have been a number of outstanding evolutionary analyses of classic issues in neurobiology, and I describe three of these very briefly to suggest the topics and flavor: Ebbesson (1984), Karten (1991), and Killackey (1990). Ebbesson's "target article," published with open commentary in a forum for ideas and controversy in the neurosciences, provides a superb case history on difficulties in interpreting and reasoning from available anatomical data on the brain. Ebbesson argued that connections are created by a process of "parcellation (segregation–isolation)" that occurs ontogenetically as well as phylogenetically, with originally diffuse and extravagantly proliferating neurons and connections eventually becoming reduced and segregated from one another during the course of development. Northcutt's (1984) commentary was noteworthy, pointing out not only the problems with the data used to support the position but also the semantic and philosophical difficulties: the need for rigorous specification of homologies and homoplasies in using comparative data for cladistic analysis.

Karten (1991) analyzed the origin of neocortex as a uniquely mammalian brain system, pointing out that the neocortex is not functionally unique, because its connections are comparable to those of the *neostriatum* in birds (and even in reptiles). The enlarged neostriatum in birds is homologous with mammalian neocortex. His microscopic analysis of these forebrain systems points to their comparability with respect to information processing, despite the very different ways that the brain is organized in these classes of vertebrates. This agrees with data (see below) that show birds and mammals to be comparable to one another in *grade* of encephalization. Killackey (1990) argued from ontogenetic data on the sequence of appearance of various neocortical regions, making the important point for evolutionists that the detailed organization of the neocortex is established to a significant extent by experience, and the evolution of its organization is, therefore, likely to be difficult to specify with standard genetic models.

Although informed by modern evolutionary theory, with the exception of Northcutt's (1984) commentary, the papers that I have described are traditional in their evolutionary concerns. They develop insight into the origin of neural systems and to the degree of specialization in different species from data on morphology and development and from educated intuition rather than from the rigorous (and sometimes mindless) application of cladistic methodology (cf. Brooks and MacLennan, 1991). They would agree that the nervous system parallels other systems in the body in reflecting adaptations to various environmental niches. Several of them (Killackey, Ebbesson) emphasize the lability of the fate of neural structures, and all are cognizant of the extent to which use determines fate for the circuitry of the brain—that brains can be normal only if they develop in a normal environment (Hebb, 1949; Hubel, 1988).

Comparative brain data have also been used for more formal analyses of relationships, either with the methods of modern cladistics (Johnson et al., 1982, in mammals; Ulinski, 1990b, in reptiles) or with other multivariate methods (Ridet & Bauchot, 1991, in bony fish). The results of these analyses can be summarized in a few sentences. Performing a factor analysis on brain traits in fish helps to clarify issues on the classification of particular groups of fish. The most helpful traits were the size of the olfactory apparatus. The contribution, however, is primarily to taxonomic issues rather than to neurobiology. The cladistic analyses, using only data on brain traits in constructing a species-by-traits matrix, produce essentially the same phylogenetic tree as when a full suite of traits is used. The diversity of species as determined rigorously by a full suite of traits predicts the measured diversity as determined from brain traits. The similarity between *Hoplophoneus* and *Felis catus* in Figure 1 is the expected finding in any comparative analysis of mammalian brains and confirms the taxonomic conclusion that these are relatively closely related species despite their separation by 30 million years of evolution. The brain can serve as well as other organs of the body for evidence on phylogenetic relationships.

IV. QUANTITATIVE ANALYSIS: LIVING VERTEBRATES

Darwin's theory of natural selection emphasized evidence of selection as practiced by animal and plant breeders. The term natural selection implied that nature, like breeders, worked to select the most fit individuals relative to some criterion. In a breeder's case, the criterion might be plumpness, large size, docility, and so forth. Nature had other criteria, and animals well endowed according to those criteria would be more likely to survive to produce more offspring than less well-endowed animals. The unnatural docility of domestic animals suggested some deficit in their brains.

Darwin could explore the relationship by comparing brain size in wild and domesticated populations of animals known to be related to one another. In what was probably his only contribution to neurobiology, Darwin was the first to observe that the brain in domesticated rabbits was smaller than in their wild cousins (1868, Vol. 1, pp. 155–161). This is evidently a general principle on the effect of domestication on brain size (Kruska, 1988). It may even be true for human brain evolution if we think of ourselves as domesticated and our ancestors as savage, or feral, although the available sample size is too small for a clear test. The earliest *Homo sapiens* were the neanderthals, and they were slightly larger brained, on the average, compared to their living conspecifics, that is, to you and me (Falk, 1987).

A. Uniformities in Structure in Living Brains: Allometry

Darwin's publications inspired several generations of comparative neuro-anatomists to provide detailed pictures of the diversity of brains. The effort included studies of brain size and of brain–body relations, some of which stand up under appropriate analysis today. In this tradition, Brodmann (1913) tabulated data on brain surface area in mammals, and his results are included as 33 of the 50 data-points in Figure 2A. The validity of his work is

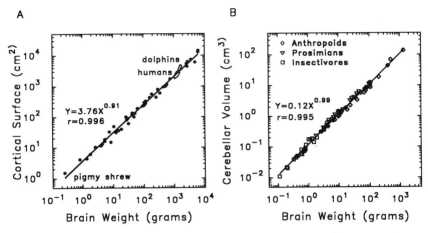

FIGURE 2   (A) Cortical surface area as a function of brain size in fifty species of mammals, including orders Monotremata, Marsupialia, Artiodactyla, Carnivora (including pinnipeds), Cetacea, Perissodactyla, Primates, and Xenarthra. Minimum convex polygons enclose individual human ($N = 20$) and dolphin (*Tursiops truncatus*, $N = 13$) data and indicate within species variability. $Y = 3.76 X^{0.91}$, $r = 0.996$. (B) Cerebellar volume as a function of brain size in 76 species of mammals, $Y = 0.12, 0.79$; $r = 0.995$ (insectivores: 26 Insectivora, 2 Macroscelididae, and 3 Scandentia; primates: 18 Prosimii, 27 Anthropoidea; data from Stephan et al., 1981). (Redrawn from Jerison, 1991, by permission.)

attested to by its consistency with data from more recent studies that used different methods of measurement (Elias & Schwartz, 1971; Ridgway, 1981; Ridgway & Brownson, 1984). A single regression line fits the entire data set remarkably well. It and Figure 2B, which will be discussed later, are examples of uniformities of organization of the brain in mammals.

Analyses such as those in Figure 2 are *allometric,* in that they display the relationship between measures of morphological variables. The relationships displayed in Figure 2 transcend species and are so strong that they appear to reflect a fundamental feature of the body plan (*Bauplan*) of mammals. Evolutionists call shared ancestral features plesiomorphies, and although the term is not usually applied to functional relationships such as those shown in Figure 2, the idea fits. The relationships should be thought of as representing a primitive feature in mammalian evolution.

Because of its unusually diverse sample of species, Figure 2A provides important justification for using total brain size as a statistic that estimates the total neural information-processing capacity of a brain, between species, in the mammals as a class. To understand this further let us consider some candidates for the role of processing unit. A frequent candidate is the cortical column, and its cross section appears to be relatively uniform across species. The neuron is another candidate—and the number of neurons under a given surface area of neocortex is more or less constant across species (Rockel, Hiorns, and Powell, 1980). Finally, the synapse is a candidate. We have the observation by Braitenberg and Schüz (1991) that the number of synapses per unit volume of cortical tissue is constant across species. (Other data in Stephen et al., 1981 indicate that the volume of the cortex is a fixed fraction of the brain.) There are qualifications to these generalizations, but they are reasonable approximations. They reinforce the conclusion about the use of brain size as a statistic.

Figure 2B is another allometric analysis, an example of the many that were derived from Stephan et al. (1981). It demonstrates the uniformity of cerebellar size in mammals—that, independently of species, if you know the size of the brain you can make a very good estimation of the size of the cerebellum. Although this analysis does not have the obvious theoretical significance of Figure 2A, it demonstrates the fundamental orderliness of the construction of the brain. It and the other analyses in Stephan et al. validate the use of brain size as a statistic to estimate the size of other brain structures. To the extent that these other structures can be assigned special functional significance, one may be able to use the data on brain evolution, which are strongest on the measure of gross size, to assess the evolution of brain functions Dunbar (1994), for example, considers a possible role of neocortical evolution in controlling social behavior and uses Stephan's data to support his view. Hofman (1989) and I (Jerison, 1990, 1991) have done the same sort of thing in assessing the evolution of neocortical control. In general, Stephan has emphasized the differences among the species that he examined, but I have been even more impressed by the uniformities. The example in Figure 2B of the relationship between cerebellum and brain size is just one of these. Table 1 summarizes a multivariate analysis of the entire data set: 12 morphological measures in 76 species.

The most important fact in Table 1 is that just two factors were enough to account for all but 1.5% of the variance, and that 86% of the variance is explained by a single "size" factor. The size factor is a "general" factor in the sense that it is strongly represented in all of the brain structures with the exception of the olfactory bulbs, and it is also represented in body weight. The loading of cerebellum on this factor (0.983, accounting for 97% of the variance in cerebellar volume) in conjunction with the even higher loading of total brain weight reflect the high correlation shown in Figure 2B. All of the measures with higher loadings would have produced bivariate graphs like Figure 2B. The mammalian brain hangs together rather well, and when one part is enlarged the rest of the brain tends to be correspondingly enlarged.

The second factor, accounting for 12.7% of the variance, is an olfactory bulb factor. It is represented primarily by the olfactory bulbs, with a modest representation in the parts of the brain that are classic "rhinencephalon"

TABLE 1   Factor Loadings and Percent Variance Explained by Two Principal Components (Factors) in Brain and Body in 76 Species of Mammals[a]

	Factor 1 (General brain size)	Factor 2 (Olfactory bulbs)
Neocortex	0.991	0.059
Total brain weight	0.989	0.137
Diencephalon	0.987	0.144
Basal ganglia	0.987	0.133
Cerebellum	0.983	0.168
Mesencephalon	0.972	0.196
Medulla	0.966	0.224
Hippocampus	0.962	0.239
Schizocortex	0.954	0.274
Body weight	0.939	0.285
Piriform lobe	0.899	0.399
Olfactory bulbs	0.157	0.985
Percent total variance	85.855	12.668

[a] Varimax rotation. Data from Stephan, Frahm, and Baron (1981). From Jerison (1991) by permission.

(piriform lobes, schizocortex, and hippocampus) and in body weight. Factor analyses are notoriously susceptible to artifacts of sampling, and I believe that the high fraction of variance accounted for by the olfactory bulb factor is in a sense such an artifact. Simian primates have much reduced olfactory bulbs whereas insectivores are normal mammals in this regard (Jerison, 1991, and Figure 6, this chapter). The distribution of olfactory bulb size in the entire sample is, therefore, seriously bimodal, which inflates the variance due to this measure and enlarges its fraction of the total variance compared to what would be expected in a more representative sample of mammals. In any case, the important feature of the multivariate analysis is the almost uniformly heavy loadings of the other measures on the "general size" factor.

B. Diversity in Living Brains: Cladistics

Having emphasized uniformities so forcefully, I must warn against underestimating the importance of diversity. All brains are different, and there are major differences both within and between species. Difference in brains within species are often difficult to measure with conventional anatomical and physiological methods, but because the brain is the control system for behavior, behavioral differences are evidence of differences among brains. Differences among species, of course, are much more dramatic.

Welker's (1990) report of the qualitative differences among the procyonids described earlier could be presented as quantitative differences as well, by measuring the amount of tissue in, for example, forepaw and rhinarial projections of the neocortex of procyonids. Differences among orders of mammals or classes of vertebrates are even more striking, but they too have not been quantified, perhaps because they are so obvious. And even when differences are great they may be surprisingly hard to describe quantitatively. One recognizes in an instant that the human brain is an unusual primate brain, for example, yet the analysis of the relative size of its major parts usually shows it to be a perfectly normal primate (or mammalian) brain. In Figure 2 there is nothing other than gross size to distinguish the human data, which fell on or near the regression lines determined for all of the mammals in each sample.

A rigorous, though not really quantitative, analysis of the diversity of organization of the brain has been in the application of cladistic methodology. As indicated earlier, the results of this kind of analysis with brain features are essentially the same as when other morphological features are used in the traits-by-species matrix that provides primary data for the analysis.

A cladistic methodology was applied by Ulinski (1990b), who took as his goal the reconstruction of probable features of the internal anatomy of brains at nodal evolutionary points in the evolution of reptiles, birds, and mammals. His method was, first, to take the results of cladistic classification to determine nodes at which branching occurred when an ancestral species split into two daughter species. Second, he examined the brains of living representatives of the daughter species (or higher taxa). Finally he constructed a hypothetical ancestral brain as a kind of lowest-common-denominator of the brains of the daughter species. The approach can be applied only to nodes in which surviving species from both branches exist. For example, taking living turtles and crocodiles to represent surviving species from the node of the early reptilian branching that led to these species, the ancestral brain can be constructed as having only those features that turtles and crocodiles share. With this procedure Ulinski could suggest various details about the ancestral brain of birds, crocodiles, lizards, and turtles. (From a cladistic perspective birds may be thought of as specialized reptiles derived from dinosaurs.) The nodal point in the history of the mammals, unfortunately (for this approach), is late in a "reptilian" synapsid lineage, represented today only by mammals. The mammal–reptile transition brain could be reconstructed only if synapsids at a reptilian grade of brain evolution had survived, but none have, and for this reason the reconstruction of the brain at the reptile–mammal transition is impossible with Ulinsky's procedure.

It would be possible to temper this conclusion, which is essentially on qualitative internal features of the brain, by analyzing the superficial anatomy using data on fossil endocasts, although such data are sparse for synapsids. Where they exist, in therapsids, they suggest a size pattern comparable to that in living reptiles (Hopson, 1979; Jerison, 1973, 1985). The transition from mammal-like reptiles to mammals is documented in the endocasts, and at present it seems to be reflected primarily as both enlargement of the brain (encephalization) and a major reduction in body size.

In his analysis of mammalian brain evolution, in particular the diversity of organization of somatosensory neocortex, Johnson presents an impressive catalogue of detail on differences, but concludes that "a great many features are constant across all mammals, from platypus to monkey, rat, cat, and sheep" (1990, pp. 432–453). The major variations "include [amount of] multiplication of representations of certain body parts" and details of the representations. He also notes few general trends of organization, but comments that the appearance of "association cortex" intercalated between somatosensory and visual neocortex is haphazard across species, and that its appearance seems "to have something to do with the use of limbs as information-gathering and manipulating organs" (p. 435). Johnson's conclusions are consistent with the notion that the pattern of organization of the brain in a species that differentiates it from other species follows no general principles in the mammals but is part of the specialization of each species. In an earlier cladistic analysis, Johnson et al. (1982) found that the phylogenetic tree in mammals deduced from 15 brain traits was essentially the same as the tree deduced from other traits.

The quantification of diversity depends on the measurement of size. The evolution of brain size in mammals has led to the diversification that was already evident in the data of Figure 2, with species having brains as small as 0.1 g (pigmy shrew) and as large as 8 kg (killer whale). These all evolved from a single species of mammal (according to the monophyly accepted today) that lived more than 200 ma. I will outline that history in the next section, but we must first understand how the diversity of size is analyzed.

C. Allometry and Encephalization

Body size accounts for from 80 to 90% of the variance in brain size, between species, a relationship described by an allometric equation: the regression of the logarithms of brain size on body size. The distance of a species from the regression line is a measure of its encephalization. Because the scales are logarithmic, this distance, or residual, is an encephalization quotient (EQ), the ratio of actual brain size to expected brain size. Encephalization is a characteristic of a species; it is usually meaningless to discuss differences in encephalization within a species.

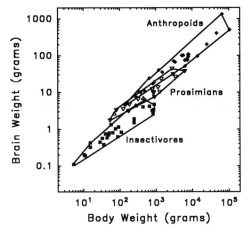

FIGURE 3   Convex polygons to differentiate insectivore, prosimian, and anthropoid data on brain weight and body weight. (Data from Stephan et al., 1981).

Allometry and encephalization do not have to be defined by regression equations and residuals, but most of the recent work on brain evolution involving brain–body allometry uses this approach, which might be called *parametric,* because it involves the estimation of the parameters of a normal probability distribution. Instead of the regression, the data can be described with minimum convex polygons enclosing the data-points of the groups to be compared, but there are presently no quantitative methods to analyze the polygons. Minimum convex polygons described the location of human and dolphin data in Figure 2A, and the brain–body data (Stephan et al., 1981) for the same insectivores, prosimians, and anthropoids as in Figure 2B are graphed in Figure 3 with polygons drawn about each group to compare them with respect to encephalization. As is evident, it is not difficult to distinguish among the groups since there is little overlap. All of the polygons are oriented upward. There is slight overlap between the insectivores and prosimians, and a bit more overlap between prosimians and anthropoids. From Figure 3 one would describe the order of encephalization of these groups as insectivores—least encephalized, prosimians—intermediate, and anthropoids—most encephalized. These data are also described by regression equations in Figure 4.

The work by Stephan's group is especially relevant for evolutionary analysis because of the species they used. They worked with insectivores to represent a primitive grade of brain evolution and to provide an evolutionary perspective on the human brain. The issues are more complex, of course (Cracraft & Eldredge, 1979; Patterson, 1987), but insectivores are reasonable models for the base group from which most placental species evolved

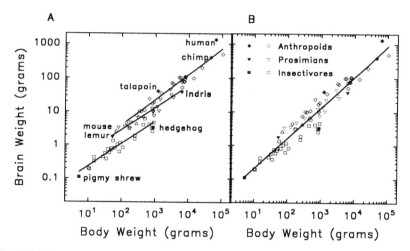

FIGURE 4   The same data as Figure 3 described with the help of regression lines and with some of the species labeled. (A) Separate regressions and correlation coefficients for the three groups: insectivores: $Y = 0.05 \ X^{0.67}$, $r = 0.946$; prosimians: $Y = 0.14 \ X^{0.66}$, $r = 0.960$; anthropoids: $Y = 0.13 \ X^{0.75}$, $r = 0.972$. (B) Combining the data for an overall regression for all 76 species: $Y = 0.05 \ X^{0.91}$, $r = 0.966$. (Redrawn from Jerison, 1991, by permission.)

(Johnson et al., 1982). They resemble the earliest mammals both skeletally (Savage & Long, 1986) and in their endocasts (Jerison, 1990; Kielan-Jaworowska, 1986). although primates are presently a highly encephalized order of mammals, they are also a very ancient order, probably derived during the late Cretaceous period from a species comparable to living insectivores or tree shrews. Comparisons between insectivores and primates are, thus, very appropriate for our topic.

D. A Bit of Theory

Issues in parametric quantification of encephalization as they apply to insectivores and primates are suggested in Figure 4. The two graphs present the same data, fitted by straight lines in different ways. Figure 4A shows the regression of log brain size on log body size computed separately for the three groups; figure 4B is a single regression for all 76 species. The three regression lines in Figure 4A provide the same information as the polygons in Figure 3. But if one is interested in curve fitting all of the regression lines fit remarkably well ($r > 0.94$) despite their different slopes. These slopes on log–log axes are the exponents of the equations written as power functions, and the value of a "true exponent" has been the subject of considerable debate during the past decade. This is where a little theory may help.

The emerging consensus is that an exponent of $\frac{3}{4}$ is the correct value (Martin, 1983). I have quarreled with this view, arguing in favor of a $\frac{2}{3}$ exponent, which has theoretical significance for dimensional analysis of the brain's work in mapping information from the external environment. It is true that empirical analyses of large enough samples of species, or of properly sampled groups of species (Harvey & Pagel, 1991), lead to the $\frac{3}{4}$ exponent when the fit is statistical, but I believe that the theoretical value of $\frac{2}{3}$ is nevertheless correct. The point is that the $\frac{2}{3}$ value is required by the dimensional problem in order to convert data about a volume into data about a surface (the mapping). However, since the conversion is by a physical system that takes up space, one has to take into account the thickness of the map. I have argued that this thickness is estimated by the thickness of neocortex, which is greater in larger brains, varying approximately with the $\frac{1}{9}$ power of body size. The value $\frac{3}{4}$ is approximately the sum of $\frac{2}{3} + \frac{1}{9}$! The theoretical value of $\frac{2}{3}$ which is meaningful for the brain's mapping function, thus leads to an expected empirical value of $\frac{3}{4}$ (0.78, if the value $\frac{1}{9}$ is exactly correct—which is unlikely). For further discussion, see Jerison (1991).

E. Encephalization

The fact of encephalization is evident in the vertical displacement of the lines that are fitted to the three groups (Figure 4A), or of the minimum convex polygons (Figure 3). Since the polygons do not require the dubious assumptions of statistical curve fitting they may be the preferred way to describe encephalization. They are certainly to be preferred if they are adequate for answering questions about whether groups are equal or differ in encephalization.

The degree of encephalization in living vertebrates is summarized in Figure 5. The polygons enclose all of the available data on the indicated classes, and show that one can characterize birds and mammals, jointly, as "higher" vertebrates and reptiles, bony fish, and amphibians as "lower" vertebrates. The polygons do an adequate job.

An analysis of this kind is sufficient to evaluate many of the fossil endocasts with respect to encephalization. Data from a few fossils and some interesting living species were added to the graph; the fossils are easily interpreted with its help. The early fossil mammal and bird are at the lower borders of their respective polygons and would be correctly distinguished from reptiles. Dinosaurs would be diagnosed as reptiles, because they would only extend the reptilian polygon to be equal in size to that of the mammals. There is a place for fancier analysis if a problem requires it. I present a regression analysis later to demonstrate certain facts about neocorticalization (analogous to encephalization but based on the size of the neocortex in mammals rather than the whole brain).

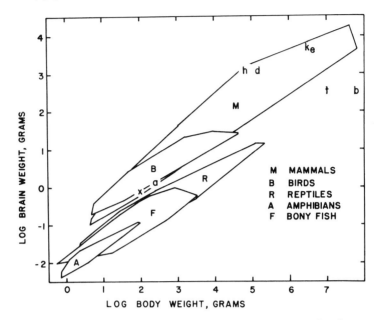

FIGURE 5   Brain–body relations in 623 living vertebrate species enclosed in minimum convex polygons. The samples are 309 mammals (M), 180 birds (B), 46 bony fish (F), 40 amphibians (A), and 48 reptiles (R). Additional data are d, *Tursiops truncatus* (bottlenose dolphin); e, elephant; h, humans; k, *Orcinus orca* (killer whale); two dinosaurs (t, *Tyrannosaurus*, b, *Brachiosaurus*); x, the 150 million yr-old mammal, *Triconodon*; and a, the early bird, *Archaeopteryx*. (From Jerison, 1991, reprinted by permission.)

V. QUANTITATIVE ANALYSIS: FOSSILS

A. Vertebrate History

Vertebrates first appeared during the last half billion (0.5×10^9) yr of the earth's 4.5-billion-yr existence (Schopf, 1992), and Table 2 is a synopsis of their history. For more detail see Carroll (1988) and Savage and Long (1986). Here are some points to remember.

1. The world was very different in the distant past compared to the present. During the Paleozoic era there were times when there was only a single global continent (Pangea), but land masses joined and separated with the passage of time. The global map was significantly different during the Mesozoic, with major masses, Gondwanaland and Laurasia, during the Paleozoic and Mesozoic eras. There were warmer and more stable climates during the Mesozoic, and the continents were drifting toward their present locations. The Cenozoic was more variable in every way, with more diverse and sometimes chilling climates and periods of major mountain building. A

TABLE 2   Synopsis of Vertebrate Evolution

Era	Period and Epoch	Age (Years × 10⁶)	Fauna (first appearance)
Cenozoic	Quaternary		
	Holocene	0.01–	No new megafauna
	Pleistocene	1.8–0.01	*Homo erectus, H. sapiens*
	Tertiary		
	Pliocene	5–1.8	Hominids: *Australopithecus, Homo habilis*
	Miocene	25–5	Hominoids (apes)
	Oligocene	35–25	"Progressive" brains
	Eocene	55–35	Progressive ungulates, Anthropoids
	Paleocene	65–55	Primates[a] and carnivores
Mesozoic	Cretaceous	140–65	Marsupials, placentals
	Jurassic	210–140	Birds, mammal endocast
	Triassic	250–210	Mammals
Paleozoic	Permian	285–250	Primitive dinosaurs
	Carboniferous	360–290	Reptiles
	Devonian	410–360	Bony fish and amphibians
	Silurian	440–410	Jawed fish
	Ordovician	500–440	Jawless fish
	Cambrian	550	First chordates

[a]Primate teeth reported in late Cretaceous deposits. Paleocene primate identification is controversial. There is consensus recognizing early Eocene tarsierlike species, middle Eocene lemurlike species, and recently discovered late Eocene simian species.

burgeoning animal and plant life is evident in fossils from sediments laid down during all of these periods.

2. There were several mass extinctions, the greatest at the end of the Permian and beginning of the Mesozoic. The most famous extinction, attributed to impact by a small asteroid, occurred at the end of the Mesozoic (the K-T, or Cretaceous–Tertiary, boundary) 65 ma. Niches emptied of their otherwise well-adapted organisms that could not survive the environmental catastrophe, could then be filled by suitably adapted birds, mammals, teleost fish, and snakes.

3. Although mammals were present during much of the 185 million yr of the Mesozoic era, all were small bodied, none larger than living cats. They were probably nocturnal in their habits. Only during the Cenozoic did very large mammal species appear, and even today, the average mammalian species is about cat-sized and nocturnal. Humans are giant vertebrates, physically larger and heavier than 90% or more of living species. Anthropoid primates are an unusual group of mammals; the suborder Anthropoidea (monkeys, apes, and humans) are diurnal and are well adapted for color vision.

4. A major environmental event in human history may have been the Pilocene drying of the Mediterranean, about 5 ma, which probably contributed to natural selection among chimpanzeelike primates for a species that became the earliest hominid. Extensive glaciation characterized the Pleistocene epoch and may have driven the evolution of the human species to its present grade.

B. Fossil Brains Revisited

I have reviewed the history of the brain in fish, amphibians, and reptiles as available from the fossil record (Jerison, 1973). The most unusual discovery is that these can all be treated as lower vertebrates in encephalization (Figure 5, above). The exceptions are sharks and the ostrichlike dinosaurs (ornithomimids). A few more of the outstanding discoveries are as follows.

1. From the evidence of small (less than 15 cm long) Carboniferous (350 ma) fossil fish, the diversity in living teleosts was probably foreshadowed by some of the earliest bony fish. They had optic lobes enlarged in ways comparable to those of living fish, such as trout, that feed at or near the surface of the water and rely on visual information.

2. Although sharks and other cartilaginous fish are often considered primitive, they are not primitive with respect to their brains. Sharks are big-brained, overlapping the distributions of relative brain size of the lower vertebrates on the one hand and of birds and mammals on the other (Northcutt, 1987, 1989). There is one uncrushed endocast known in a Permian shark, the earliest evidence of encephalization beyond the grade of living bony fish (Jerison, 1991). The species was comparable in both brain and body size to the living horned shark (*Heterodontus*).

3. Dinosaurs continue to be libeled with the walnut-size brain label despite the evidence to the contrary (Hopson, 1979; Jerison, 1969). Their brains were within the expected size range for reptiles. The *Tyrannosaurus* 404-ml endocast implies a brain in the size range of those of living deer, small for an elephant-sized mammal but impressive for a reptile. The ostrichlike dinosaurs were more encephalized than any living reptile, reaching the level of living birds and mammals.

4. The major transition from water to land in the amphibians more than 350 ma was accomplished without enlargement of the brain, and there has been no enlargement since, if one compares present amphibians with their fossil ancestors. In fact, none of the major shifts in adaptive zones within the several classes of bony fish, within the reptiles, or within the amphibians, excepting only the ornithomimids, were accompanied by measurable encephalization for each class of vertebrates as a whole. These shifts were

presumably accompanied by reorganization of the brain but without measurable changes in gross size. There was and is, of course, considerable diversity in relative brain size within each of the classes of living lower vertebrates, just as there is in birds and mammals, and there has been significant reorganization of the brain across species of lower vertebrates, especially between classes but also within classes as pointed out by Ulinski (1990a). By any standard one must recognize the brain in living reptiles as more specialized than that of fish or amphibians.

5. Of the major lateralization of function in the living human brain, and the recognized lateralization in the brains of many other living species, there is little or no evidence at a gross level. There is no good fossil evidence for such lateralization, though some has been claimed and evidence may yet be forthcoming. The problem is that asymmetries are almost impossible to establish in fossils that are often asymmetrically distorted and partially crushed.

These statements sum up the evidence on brain evolution in about $\frac{3}{4}$ of the vertebrate species. There remains the story of about 8000 species of birds and 5000 species of mammals, in which encephalization is a major feature.

C. Birds and Mammals

The history of the bird brain is not as well known as that of mammals, and the present diversity in brains in birds does not appear to be as dramatic. However, the brain of *Archaeopteryx* was birdlike primarily in filling the cranial cavity and in being larger than in comparable reptiles. There was no *Wulst,* that is, the dorsal enlargement of the forebrain in living birds that functions as equivalent to primary visual cortex in mammals. The next significant evidence in the history of birds is from an Eocene whimbrel-like bird, *Numenius gypsorum,* in which the brain is somewhat smaller than in comparable living birds of its body size, but most dramatically, its forebrain is clearly much smaller so that its optic lobes are more fully exposed than in living birds (Jerison, 1973). Endocasts of later birds are indistinguishable from those of their living relatives.

In their early history the mammals were small, probably nocturnal, insectivorous creatures. Their adaptation for life in nocturnal niches (Crompton, Taylor, & Jagger, 1978; Kemp, 1982) could have been the major selection pressure to explain the "advance" to a mammalian grade of brain morphology and encephalization (Jerison, 1973). The characteristic morphological feature of the brain of living mammals is the presence of neocortex, the six-layered neuronally rich outer covering of the forebrain. Its presence can often be established on an endocast, because a major fissure, the rhinal fissure, is its ventral boundary.

The earliest mammalian brain is known from an Upper Jurassic endocast of *Triconodon mordax,* and is about 150 million yr old. The lateral surface of this endocast is not well enough preserved to indicate whether or not there was a rhinal fissure; therefore, positive evidence on the presence of neo-cortex is not available. In encephalization, however, its brain was compara-ble to that of small-brained living species such as opossums and hedgehogs, in which neocortex is present. It is, therefore, likely that neocortex had appeared at least 150 ma. The best assumption from presently available information is that neocortex is, in fact, part of the suite of traits that characterized the mammals from the beginning of their evolution, at least 50 million yr earlier (Kielan-Jaworowska, 1986).

Mammals in which the endocasts are sufficiently complete to show a rhinal fissure, if present, are about 75 million yr old. They are from a unique assemblage of late Cretaceous mammals from the Gobi desert (Kielan-Jaworowska, 1983, 1984, 1986), which includes early placentals. The most common mammals of the time, the multituberculates, were unrelated to any living species. Superficially, multituberculates probably looked like liv-ing rodents, or insectivores. Their life span as an order was about 120 million yr, between about 150 to 30 ma (Z. Kielan-Jaworowska, personal communication; Savage & Long, 1986), a very long span for a mammalian group. The specimen in which the endocast is best known, *Chulsanbaatar,* weighed no more than about 15 g, a small mammal even for the Mesozoic, and smaller than most living species of mice. There is a suggestion of a rhinal fissure in its endocast, although there is some disagreement about where it is (cf. Jerison, 1990; Kielan-Jaworowska, 1986). Whether or not one can see a rhinal fissure, from its grade of encephalization, it is very likely that neocortex was present in its brain.

D. Neocorticalization

Neocorticalization is a concept in comparative neuroanatomy, which de-scribes, for example, the fact that primates have relatively and absolutely more neocortex than insectivores. There was, of course, no transformation of living insectivores into living primates under natural selection. But there was an evolutionary transformation: The ancestors of living insectivores were members of an order (or other taxon) of mammals that probably included at least one species from which primates evolved. This species has not been identified, but as evolutionists positing a relationship between insectivores and primates as "sister" groups, we have to assume that it existed. Neocorticalization is then understood as part of the differentiation of daughter species from parent species: One daughter species of a fossil insectivore, which had relatively more neocortex than the parent species, was the ancestral primate species. These statements are almost parodies of evolutionary analysis, but they approximate a correct analysis.

The concept of neocorticalization can also be used in another sense, as describing the history of a trait in successive populations of species. If we sample a broad range of species across geological time and determine that later species had relatively more neocortex than earlier species, we could state that neocorticalization had occurred, even though we would not be able to determine its phylogenetic history. Such a discovery would be enough to suggest that there was a selective advantage in an increase in neocortex. The analytic model to be applied might be an elaboration of simple models of phenotypic evolution within lineages (e.g., Lande, 1976). It would require theorizing about selective advantages "above the species level" (Stanley, 1979), about broad evolutionary "landscapes" that are contexts for interaction among species.

Neocorticalization in this sense can be quantified as a feature of the history of mammals. It is more or less evident from a simple inspection of endocasts, but the quantitative effect can only be demonstrated with the help of some statistical analysis. I present such an analysis in Figure 6; a more complete description of the analysis is in Jerison (1990). For the analysis I measured the planar projection of neocortex and olfactory bulbs in 59 species of living and fossil ungulates and carnivores. The sample included 38 Carnivora, 7 Creodonta, 4 Condylarthra, 5 species from extinct South American (neotropical) ungulate orders, 1 Eocene perissodactyl (*Hyrachyus,* an ancestral rhinoceros), and 4 progressive ungulates (artiodactyls). The complete sample consisted of 35 fossil species and 24 living species.

The results were analyzed as neocortical and olfactory bulb quotients, determined by partialling out the effect of body size as is done in EQs. A quotient of 1.0 means that the size was as expected for a species at the centroid, 0.5 means half as big and so on. As presented in Figure 6, the results lead to four conclusions. There is, first, the fact of neocorticalization. Later species tended to have relatively more neocortex than earlier species. This is the meaning of the significantly positive slope of the regression line of the neocortical quotient against geological time.

Second, species from archaic orders (filled data symbols) tended to have less neocortex than species from progressive orders (open data symbols). Thus, three of the four archaic ungulate species, five of the seven archaic carnivore (creodont) species, and four of the five Neotropical ungulate species (also archaic in that their orders are extinct) are below the regression line. Twelve of our 16 "archaic" species thus had less neocortex than would be predicted for their geological age by an unbiased regression analysis. For those who enjoy playing with statistics, a chi-square analysis contrasts this with an expected even split; $\chi^2 = 4$, df $= 1$, $p < .05$.

The third result is in a comparison between progressive and archaic species limited to fossil Carnivora *versus* Credonta and is in two parts. First, the Carnivora points appear generally to be higher than the Credonta. Second, the Carnivora points seem to show more "progress" over time than

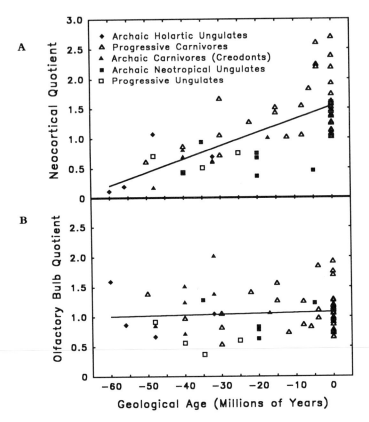

FIGURE 6   (A) Change in relative neocortical surface area (neocortical quotient) as a function of geological age. "Progressive" change noted here (positive slope of regression line) indicates increased neocorticalization over time. Each point is a species (B) Absence of change in relative surface area of the olfactory bulbs as a function of geological age. (Redrawn from Jerison, 1990, by permission.)

do the Credonta. It is not really possible to test the first part properly, because the species are from different geological times, and there is no obvious way to control the time-variable. The second part, however, can be tested by simple regression analysis. The correlation between age and neocortical quotient for 15 Carnivora species was $r = .72$, $p < .01$. For seven Creodonta it was $r = .42$, $p > .05$. Only the Carnivora were demonstrably progressively neocorticalized.

The result is important for evolutionary analysis of the relations between true carnivores and creodonts. The argument is summed up by Carroll (1988) as follows: "Romer (1966) and Jerison (1973) stigmatized the creodonts as archaic and small brained, but Radinsky (1977) demonstrated that relative brain size increased as rapidly among creodonts as it did in the early members of the Carnivora, together with an increase in the extent of the neocortex" (Carroll, 1988, pp. 478–479). The quantitative analysis supports Romer's view as mentioned by Carroll. (My contribution in 1973 was mainly to quote Romer and to provide very limited quantitative data. The present confirmation of our older view is possible because of the additional data collected by Radinsky, which permitted a statistical test.)

The fourth and final conclusion is that unlike neocortex, the olfactory bulbs did not change in relative size with the passage of time. The correlation between the olfactory bulb quotient and geological time was $r = .1$, which is not significantly different from 0. This is an important point because it shows that this approach is fine enough to discriminate between the presence and absence of change. It is also helps quash a myth about what is "primitive" and "progressive" in brain evolution.

On the myth: although careful students (Baron, Frahm, Bhatnagar, & Stephan, 1983; Sarnat & Netsky, 1981) do not make the error, neurobiologists often assume that having large olfactory bulbs is a primitive mammalian trait and that the olfactory bulbs became relatively smaller as the mammals evolved. Figure 6 corrects this error by showing that olfactory bulbs have been a stable feature of the brain in Tertiary carnivores and ungulates. This misconception is a bit of primate chauvinism, as it were. Primates (at least the anthropoids) are neocortical specialists, but they are deficient mammals in olfactory development. A reduced role for olfaction is part of the adaptive mosaic of the adaptive zone of "higher" primates and is not a broad feature of mammalian evolution. Neocorticalization, on the other hand, appeared as a general trend in many mammalian groups and its relative absence in, for example, the insectivores and many marsupials is correctly recognized as a primitive feature in these groups.

VI. CONCLUSIONS

The fossil evidence indicates, first, that there was neocorticalization in mammals and that it can be detected even in samples as small as 15 species of Carnivora. Evolution of the carnivores involved neocorticalization in another sense, in that the two great orders of Tertiary carnivores, namely, Creodonta and Carnivora, differed in the extent of neocorticalization. This could have been a factor in the survival of true carnivores. In any event, the history of neocorticalization indicates that there was almost certainly some benefit derived from the expansion of neocortex. The fossil evidence, therefore, confirms conventional wisdom in neurobiology that it was a progressive thing for mammals to evolve neocortex and (perhaps within limits) more is better.

If our conclusion on neocortex are expected, those on the olfactory bulbs are not. These structures are surprisingly constant features in mammalian brains. There is no reason to have predicted that they would not evolve to large or small size relative to other parts of the brain, depending on the extent of olfactory specializations in particular species. But according to present evidence from fossil brains, the olfactory bulbs have been constant and relatively unchanging features that make a brain a mammal's brain. They are not unusually enlarged in any species; most mammals are olfactory specialists. Evolutionary changes in the olfactory bulbs occurred mainly in a negative way, by reduction. The reduced state of olfactory bulbs in humans and other primates (and their complete absence in some cetaceans) merely reflects the extremes of diversity that are possible as the brain evolved to control the activities of mammals in the variety of niches in which they function.

One general conclusion or inference at this point. From these and related data it seems likely that encephalization in mammals was driven by neocorticalization. One mammalian trend was toward enlarged neocortex, and since neocortex is a fairly fixed fraction of total brain size (Jerison, 1991) the enlargement of the brain was presumably correlated with the increased size of neocortex. We can note, also, that neocortical function is deeply involved with cognitive functions—knowledge of "reality." Expanded neocortex would be associated with more elaborate cognition, a major suggestion about the evolution of mind.

It would be appropriate to look more closely at neocortical functions and assume that the evolutionary advantage conferred by these functions was the engine driving *progressive* brain evolution in mammals. But it would be a mistake to make much of such an idea of progress. It is true that neocorticalized species are more prevalent now than in the distant past. It must also be true that some fitness is associated with this aspect of the brain's evolution. But there are many successful living species that are at a very ancient grade of mammalian neocorticalization. Hedgehogs in Europe and opossums in America are outstanding examples, because they are so fit in the evolutionary sense. They may litter our highways because of their "stupidity" in refusing to yield the right of way to cars and trucks, but the litter is part of the evidence of their reproductive success. And they manage this at a grade of neocorticalization and encephalization that some mammalian species reached 150 ma.

The analysis of neocorticalization suggests that comparable advances occurred in birds with the expansion of their forebrains (Karten, 1991). It is certainly true that the avian forebrain is much enlarged compared to that of reptiles, and the grade of encephalization in birds is probably related to forebrain enlargement.

But the final conclusion must be that animals do not live by brains alone. The majority of living vertebrates get along with about as much brain as was present in their earliest ancestors. Adaptation to one's niche can be accomplished in many ways, and to adapt behaviorally by brain enlargement is expensive energetically. The brain is profligate in its use of energy, and almost any other solution to an adaptational problem is less costly. And yet, in those groups that adopted encephalization as an adaptive strategy, there was evidently a real gain in fitness associated with that strategy. Encephalization appeared in many very distantly related species of birds and mammals. It is a general rather than specific adaptation for increased total information-processing capacity. It is sometimes considered as the brain-correlate of intelligence. If that is true, it must mean that there are many intelligences that evolved, because encephalization is an overall sum of enlargements contributed to by differential enlargement of regions within the brain.

Acknowledgments

I thank Elizabeth Adkins-Regan, Donald A. Dewsbury, Alan C. Kamil, and Roger K. R. Thompson, colleagues in the Division of Comparative Psychology of the American Psychological Association, for valuable advice on documenting the literature on cladistics.

References

Alexander, R. McN. (1989). *Dynamics of dinosaurs and other extinct giants.* New York: Columbia University Press.

Allin, E. F. (1975). Evolution of the mammalian middle ear. *Journal of Morphology, 147,* 403–438.

Allin, E. F. (1986). The auditory apparatus of advanced mammal-like reptiles and early mammals. In N. Hotton, III, P. D. MacLean, J. J. Roth, & E. C. Roth (Eds.), *The evolution and ecology of mammal-like reptiles* (pp. 283–294). Washington, DC: Smithsonian Institution Press.

Baron, G., Frahm, H. D., Bhatnagar, K. P., & Stephan, H. (1983). Comparison of brain structure volumes in Insectivora and Primates. III. Main olfactory bulb (MOB). *Journal für Hirnforschung, 24,* 551–558.

Bitterman, M. E. (1988). Vertebrate-invertebrate comparisons. In H. J. Jerison & I. L. Jerison (Eds.), *Intelligence and evolutionary biology* (pp. 251–276). Berlin & New York: Springer-Verlag.

Braitenberg, V., & Schüz, A. (1991). *Anatomy of the cortex: Statistics and geometry.* New York & Berlin: Springer-Verlag.

Brodmann, K. (1913). Neue Forschungsergebnisse der Grosshirnrindenanatomie mit besonderer Berucksichtung anthropologischer Fragen. *Verhandlungen der 85ste Versammlung Deutscher Naturforscher und Aerzte in Wien,* pp. 200–240.

Brooks, D. R., & MacLennan, D. A. (1991). *Phylogeny, ecology, and behavior: A research program in comparative biology.* Chicago: University of Chicago Press.

Carroll, R. L. (1988). *Vertebrate paleontology and evolution.* New York: Freeman.

Cracraft, J., & Eldredge, N. (Eds.), (1979). *Phylogenetic analysis and paleontology.* New York: Columbia University Press.

Crompton, A. W., Taylor, C. R., & Jagger, J. A. (1978). Evolution of homoeothermy in mammals. *Nature (London), 272,* 333–336.

Darwin,.C. (1868). *The variation of animals and plants under domestication*. London: Murray/New York: Orange Judd & Co.

Dawkins, R. (1987). *The blind watchmaker*. New York: Norton.

Dunbar, R. I. M. (1993). Coevolution of neocortex size, group size and language in humans. *Behavioral and Brain Sciences, 16,* 681–735.

Ebbesson, S. O. E. (1984). Evolution and ontogeny of neural circuits. *Behavioral and Brain Sciences, 7,* 321–366.

Elias, H., & Schwartz, D. (1971). Cerebro-cortical surface areas, volumes, lengths of gyri and their interdependence in mammals, including man. *Zeitschrift für Saugertierkunde, 36,* 147–163.

Falk, D. (1987). Hominid paleoneurology. *Annual Review of Anthropology, 16,* 13–30.

Feduccia, A. (1993). Evidence from claw geometry indicating arboreal habits of *Archaeopteryx*. *Science, 259,* 790–793.

Harvey, P. H., & Pagel, M. D. (1991). *The comparative method in evolutionary biology*. Oxford & New York: Oxford University Press.

Hebb, D. O. (1949). *The organization of behavior: A neuropsychological theory*. New York: Wiley.

Hofman, M. A. (1989). On the evolution and geometry of the brain in mammals. *Progress in Neurobiology, 32,* 137–158.

Hopson, J. A. (1979). Paleoneurology. In C. Gans, R. G. Northcutt, & P. Ulinski (Eds.), *Biology of the reptilia* (Vol. 9, pp. 39–146). London & New York: Academic Press.

Horner, J. R., & Gorman, J. (1988). *Digging dinosaurs* (1st Perennial Library Edition). New York: Harper & Row.

Hubel, D. H. (1988). *Eye, brain, and vision*. New York: Freeman.

Jerison, H. J. (1969). Brain evolution and dinosaur brains. *American Naturalist, 103,* 575–588.

Jerison, H. J. (1973). *Evolution of the brain and intelligence*. New York: Academic Press.

Jerison, H. J. (1985). Issues in brain evolution. *Oxford Surveys in Evolutionary Biology, 2,* 102–134.

Jerison, H. J. (1990). Fossil evidence on the evolution of the neocortex. In E. G. Jones & A. Peters (Eds.) *Cerebral cortex* (Vol. 8A, pp. 285–309). New York: Plenum.

Jerison, H. J. (1991). *Brain size and the evolution of mind*. (59th James Arthur Lecture on the Evolution of the Human Brain). New York: American Museum of Natural History.

Johnson, J. I. (1990). Comparative development of somatic sensory cortex. In E. G. Jones & A. Peters (Eds.), *Cerebral cortex* (Vol. 8B. pp. 335–449). New York: Plenum.

Johnson, J. I., Kirsch, J. A. W., & Switzer, R. C. (1982). Phylogeny through brain traits: Fifteen characters which adumbrate mammalian geneology. *Brain, Behavior and Evolution, 20,* 72–83.

Jones, E. G., & Peters, A. (Eds.). (1990). *Cerebral cortex* (Vols. 8A & 8B). New York: Plenum.

Karten, H. J. (1991). Homology and evolutionary origins of the 'neocortex.' *Brain, Behavior and Evolution, 38,* 264–272.

Kemp, T. S. (1982). *Mammal-like reptiles and the origin of mammals*. London & New York: Academic Press.

Kielan-Jaworowska, Z. (1983). Multituberculate endocranial casts. *Paleovertebrata, Montpellier, 13*(1–2), 1–12.

Kielan-Jaworowska, Z. (1984). Evolution of the therian mammals in the Late Cretaceous of Asia. Part VI. Endocranial casts of eutherian mammals. *Paleontologica Polonica,* No. 46-1984, pp. 151–171.

Kielan-Jaworowska, Z. (1986). Brain evolution in Mesozoic mammals in J. A. Lillegraven (Ed.), *G. G. Simpson Memorial Volume. Contributions to Geology,* University of Wyoming, Special Paper *3,* 21–34.

Killackey, H. P. (1990). Neocortical expansion: An attempt toward relating phylogeny and ontogeny. *Journal of Cognitive Neuroscience, 2,* 1–16.

Korn, H. (1987). The Mauthner Cell. In G. Adelman (Ed.), *Encyclopedia of neuroscience* (Vol. 2, pp. 617–619). Boston, Basel, & Stuttgart: Birkhaeuser.

Kruska, D. (1988). Mammalian domestication and its effect on brain structure and behavior. In H. J. Jerison & I. Jerison (Eds.), *Intelligence and evolutionary biology* (pp. 211–250). Berlin & New York: Springer-Verlag.

Lande, R. (1976). Natural selection and random genetic drift in phenotypic evolution. *Evolution (Lawrence, Kansas), 30,* 314–334.

Lieberman, P. (1984). *The biology and evolution of language.* Cambridge, MA: Harvard University Press.

MacLean, P. D. (1977). Why brain research on lizards? In N. Greenberg & P. D. MacLean (Eds.), *Behavior and neurology of lizards.* Bethesda, MD: National Institutes of Mental Health.

Martin, R. D. (1990). *Primate origins and evolution: A phylogenetic reconstruction.* London: Chapman & Hall.

Mayr, E. (1988). *Toward a new philosophy of biology.* Cambridge, MA: Harvard University Press.

Northcutt, R. G. (1984). Parcellation: The resurrection of Hartsoeker and Haekel. *Behavioral and Brain Sciences, 7,* 345. (Commentary on Ebbesson, 1984).

Northcutt, R. G. (1987). The evolution of the vertebrate brain. In G. Adelman (Ed.), *Encyclopedia of neuroscience* (Vol. 2, pp. 415–418). Boston, Basel, & Stuttgart: Birkhaeuser.

Northcutt, R. G. (1989). Brain variation and phylogenetic trends in elasmobranch fishes. *Journal of Experimental Zoology, Supplement, 2,* 83–100.

Palay, S. L., & Chan-Palay, V. (1987). Neuron. In G. Adelman (Ed.), *Encyclopedia of neuroscience* (Vol. 2, pp. 812–815). Boston, Basel, & Stuttgart: Birkhauser.

Patterson, C. (Ed.). (1987). *Molecules and morphology in evolution: Conflict or compromise?* Cambridge: Cambridge University Press.

Radinsky, L. B. (1969). Outlines of canid and felid brain evolution. In C. R. Noback & W. Montagna, (Eds.), *The primate brain* (pp. 209–224). New York: Appleton.

Radinsky, L. B. (1975). Evolution of the felid brain. *Brain, Behavior and Evolution, 11,* 214–254.

Radinsky, L. B. (1977). Brains of early carnivores. *Paleobiology, 3,* 333–349.

Ridet, J. M., & Bauchot, R. (1991). Analyse quantitative de l'encéphale des Téléostéens: Caractères évolutifs et adaptifs de l'encéphalization. III. Analyze multivarieé des indices encéphaliques. *Journal für Hirnforschung, 33,* 383–393.

Ridgway, S. H. (1981). Some brain morphometrics of the Bowhead whale. In T. F. Albert (Ed.), *Tissues, structural studies, and other investigations on the biology of endangered whales in the Beaufort Sea* (Final Report to the Bureau of Land Management, U.S. Dept. of Interior, Vol. 1, pp. 837–844). College Park: University of Maryland.

Ridgway, S. H., & Brownson, R. H. (1984). Relative brain sizes and cortical surfaces of odontocetes. *Acta Zoologica Fennica, 172,* 149–152.

Rockel, A. J., Hiorns, R. W., & Powell, T.P.S. (1980). The basic uniformity in structure of the neocortex. *Brain, 103,* 221–244.

Romer, A. S. (1966). *Vertebrate paleontology* (3rd ed.). Chicago: University of Chicago Press.

Sarnat, H. B., & Netsky, M. G. (1981). *Evolution of the nervous system* (2nd ed.). London & New York: Oxford University Press.

Savage, R. J. G., & Long, M.R. (1986). *Mammal evolution: An illustrated guide.* London: British Museum (Natural History).

Schopf, J. W. (Ed.). (1992). *Major events in the history of life.* Boston: Jones & Bartlett.

Stanley, S. M. (1979). *Macroevolution: Pattern and process.* San Francisco: Freeman.

Stephan, H., Baron, G., & Frahm, H. D. (1991). *Insectivora: With a stereotaxic atlas of the hedgehog brain.* New York: Springer-Verlag.

Stephan, H., Frahm, H., & Baron, G. (1981). New and revised data on volumes of brain structures in insectivores and primates. *Folia Primatologica, 35,* 1–29.

Ulinski, P. S. (1990a). The cerebral cortex of reptiles. In E. G. Jones & A. Peters (Eds.), *Cerebral cortex* (Vol. 8A, pp. 139–215). New York: Plenum.

Ulinski, P. S. (1990b). Nodal events in forebrain evolution. *Netherlands Journal of Zoology, 40,* 215–240.

Welker, W. I. (1990). Why does cerebral cortex fissure and fold? A review of determinants of gyri and sulci. In E. G. Jones & A. Peters (Eds.), *Cerebral cortex* (Vol. 8B, pp. 1–132). New York: Plenum.

Williams, G. C. (1966). *Adaptation and natural selection.* Princeton, NJ: Princeton University Press.

Williams, G. C. (1992). *Natural selection: Domains, levels, and challenges.* New York: Oxford University Press.

CHAPTER 4

Neuropsychology of Perceptual Functions

Michael C. Corballis

I. INTRODUCTION

Until recently, perception has been the poor relation in neuropsychology. Ever since the 1860s, when Broca demonstrated the special role of the left cerebral hemisphere in the production of speech, language has been the topic of major focus, with memory not far behind. Language has had a special status, not only because of its asymmetrical representation in the brain, but also because it seems to set humans apart from other species. Moreover, as human beings we really cannot do without it, whereas we can at least cope without sight or hearing. Perception by contrast seems relatively mundane. Our perceptual capacities are probably very similar to those of the other primates, and therefore do not distinguish us in any special way. Moreover it was once thought that perceptual processes did not require very much explaining. Once the mechanics of the eye or ear had been worked out, there seemed little else one needed to know.

It has taken quite a long time to learn just how wrong this is. Recordings of the responses of single cells in the brain to light falling on the retina show that over half of the primate brain is involved in one way or another with visual perception (Blakemore, 1991), and some 32 distinct cortical areas associated with vision have so far been identified (Van Essen, Anderson, & Felleman, 1992). We are visual animals. Rather less is known about the auditory perceptual system, but it is beginning to emerge that it, too, is highly complex (e.g., Bregman, 1990). However, most of this chapter will be about vision, for that is what we know most about in terms of neuropsychology.

Although language is often regarded as the pinnacle of human intellect, setting us apart from all other species, I think it can now be fairly argued that perception is at least as complex. Modern computational theories can probably make a better stab at parsing a written paragraph than at parsing the visual world. Perception *seems* easy because it is done so effortlessly, and this in turn is presumably because it evolved over a much longer period of time than it took human language to emerge. What is interesting about language is not so much that it is computationally complex, but rather that it appears to have properties unique to itself that set it apart from perception and nonlinguistic thought. The processes of perception are by contrast relatively invisible, woven so tightly into the nervous system that we hardly know they are there. We are much more aware of the world we perceive than of the mechanisms by which we perceive it.

II. NEUROPSYCHOLOGY OF VISION

A. Early Processing

Visual processing of course begins at the retina, but we need not be too concerned with retinal processing because visual defects that occur at this level are the province of optometry rather than neuropsychology. From the retina, the main visual pathway courses through the optic chiasm to the lateral geniculate nucleus (LGN) of the thalamus, and thence, via the so-called optic radiations, to the striate area of the occipital cortex, also known as the primary visual cortex, or V1. There is also a pathway from the retina to the superior colliculi, a pair of nuclei in the upper brain stem.

Retinotopic mapping is preserved along these pathways, so that damage to the optic radiations or to V1 produces a *scotoma* (or *visual field defect*)—the inability to see objects in the corresponding region of the visual field. The nature of the projections through the optic chiasm is such that the visual hemifield to one side of visual fixation is projected to the visual cortex on the opposite side (see Figure 1). Unilateral damage to the visual cortex therefore results in *hemianopia,* or a visual field defect that affects the contralateral side of space.

In some cases, however, patient with visual field defects following unilateral damage to the optic radiations or to V1 exhibit what is known as *blindsight* (see Weiskrantz, 1986). The patient may deny the existence of objects placed in the blind field, but may be able to reach for them quite accurately, and may even be able to perform simple discriminations, such as distinguishing a circle from a cross. This residual vision, interesting because

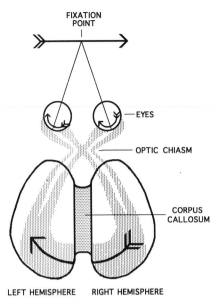

FIGURE 1 Schematic representation of how the two visual hemifields map onto the contralateral sides of the brain. The stippled areas show how the neural projections proceed from the retina to the visual cortex.

it seems to be inaccessible to consciousness, may depend on the pathway from the retina to the superior colliculus. There is evidence that the superior colliculus in turn projects to other visual areas, notably area V5 in the prestriate cortex (discussed below), bypassing the primary visual cortex.

B. Magno and Parvo Systems

In the Primate visual system, there is a distinction to be drawn between two subsystems, known as *parvocellular* and *magnocellular* (Livingstone & Hubel, 1988)—or magno and parvo for short. These names derive from cell types in the LGN, which consists of six layers. The two inner layers are known as the magnocellular layers because the cells there are large, whereas the outer four layers are known as parvocellular because the cells there are small (Latin scholars will understand). The magno system is primarily concerned with the perception of motion and the rapid detection of visual events. It is colorblind and highly sensitive to luminance contrast and stereoscopic depth, but provides only poor spatial resolution. The parvo system, which is well developed only in Primates, has high spatial resolution and is sensitive to color but insensitive to motion and depth. It may have evolved primarily to allow close scrutiny of stationary objects, as when we view paintings in an art gallery.[1]

The distinction between the two systems can be demonstrated perceptually in interesting ways. Composing stimuli in which all surfaces are of equal luminance, varying only in color, effectively neutralizes the magno system. Such "equiluminance" arrays are seen has having no depth and little figure-ground organization. Perception of motion is also substantially impaired if the moving patterns are defined in equiluminant arrays (Cavanagh, Boeglin & Favreau, 1985; Ramachandran & Gregory, 1978).

In V1, the parvo system seems to be divided into two subsystems, represented in different layers of cells, known as *blobs* and *interblobs*—these names are derived from the shapes of the cells. Blobs are color-coded but insensitive to stimulus orientation, whereas interblobs are sensitive to orientation but relatively insensitive to color. This illustrates a further parsing of the visual input, with separate channels for color and orientation. The tripartite distinction between magno, parvo-blob, and parvo-interblob is maintained in separate layers of cells in the projections beyond V1 (Livingstone & Hubel, 1988).

Figure 2 summarizes in diagrammatic form the main divisions of the visual system as they are currently known.

C. The Prestriate Areas

The prestriate areas are anterior to the striate cortex (V1) in the neighboring occipital and temporal regions. These also contain retinotopic maps and process the visual input in further specialized ways. The following overview of the anatomy and physiology of these areas is based primarily on work on the rhesus monkey, but the organization of these areas in the human brain is probably very similar—or at least similar enough to provide insights into the nature of visual disorders that arise from damage to prestriate areas in humans.

Figure 2 shows in schematic form the various interconnections between the prestriate areas: V2 and V3 are in the occipital lobe adjacent to V1, and V3 is also in the occipital lobe. Areas V4 and V5 are in the posterior temporal lobe. Note that V5 receives input from the superior colliculus

---

[1] The properties of the magno and parvo systems can actually be traced to two different kinds of cells in the retina itself (in the retinal ganglion layer). *Type A* cells, also known as *parasol ganglion cells,* comprise about 10% of the population of ganglion cells, and have large dendritic fields that give them their parasol-like appearance. They are insensitive to differences in color but have relatively high sensitivity to contrast, and respond to the onset and/or offset of stimulation. *Type B* cells, or *midget ganglion cells,* have small dendritic fields, and comprise about 80% of retinal ganglion cells. They have relatively low sensitivity to contrast, respond for the duration of a stimulus, and most are sensitive to differences in color.

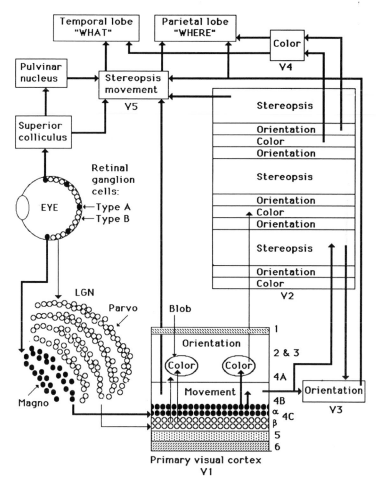

FIGURE 2   Schematic representation of the visual system, illustrating the distinction between the magno and parvo systems, and the various cortical and subcortical areas involved
and the connections between them. (Adapted from Carlson, 1991, and Livingstone & Hubel,
1988.)

(which may explain blindsight, as we saw earlier). As the figure shows,
these areas are each dedicated to rather different aspects of the visual input.
This complex system of interconnected areas, each with specific functions,
makes it clear that visual perception is not simply a matter of relaying a
retinotopic image to higher brain centers, to be "viewed" by some inner
eye. Rather, the image is disassembled, with different aspects—color, motion, depth, orientation, movement—analyzed in different areas in somewhat "modular" fashion. Because of this, damage to specific areas can give
rise to rather specific perceptual deficits.

Area V4, for example, is specialized for the analysis of color (represented by the parvo-blob system). Damage to a corresponding area in humans may account for the disorder known as *achromatopsia,* in which the patient sees objects as lacking in color, as though in a black-and-white film. This is not the same as colorblindness due to abnormalities in the eye, even though patients with achromatopsia cannot perform standard tests of color vision (Damasio, Yamada, Damasio, Corbett, & McKee, 1980; Mollon, New-combe, Polden, & Ratcliff, 1980).

Again, V5 on the posterior bank of the superior temporal sulcus seems to be specialized for the analysis of motion (magno system). This may explain reports of so-called motion blindness after damage to the posterior temporal lobe. One patient with this disorder complained that when she poured tea the stream of liquid appeared frozen. Crossing the street was a hazard, because cars seemed suddenly "there" without having moved. The world was reduced to a series of stills (Hess, Baker, & Zihl, 1989).

It is however comparatively rare to find these disorders occurring in isolation, presumably because cerebral damage is unlikely to affect a single specialized area. For example, achromatopsia commonly occurs in conjunction with *prosopagnosia,* which is an inability to recognize familiar faces (this will be discussed later), probably because the cortical areas responsible for color and face processing are close to one another.

D. Beyond the Prestriate Areas: What versus Where?

Based on his research with hamsters, Schneider (1969) distinguished two fundamental aspect of visual perception: The perception of *what* things are, he suggested, depends on the projections via the LGN to the visual cortex, whereas the perception of *where* things are depends on the retino-collicular system. Evidence from research with monkeys, however, has suggested that there may also be a distinction between "what" and "where" systems within the cortex itself (Ungerleider & Mishkin, 1982). Beyond the prestriate areas, there is a bifurcation of the visual pathways, with one system leading to the parietal lobe and the other to the inferior temporal cortex. The parietal system appears to be involved primarily with the "where" of perception, the inferior temporal lobe with the "what." It may well be that the parietal "where" system is connected to the retino-collicular one, since the superior colliculus projects to area V5 of the prestriatal system, bypassing the primary visual cortex, and V5 in turn projects to the parietal lobe.

The distinction between "what" and "where" has interesting implications for perception generally, and for the neuropsychology of perception in particular. The "what" system presumably evolved to enable us to recognize objects independently of where they are located in space. This would surely have survival value to a foraging animal, because prey, predators, or other objects of interest might appear in any location. Conversely, the "where" system presumably has to do with navigation and reaching, allowing us to know where things are independently of what they are. This system would enable us to walk around in an environment in which nothing was familiar, and to pick things up and examine them. In broad terms, temporal and parietal lesions produce deficits consistent with this division.

1. Parietal Deficits

An interesting syndrome that follows bilateral damage to the occipitoparietal regions in humans, and that reflects difficulties to do with spatial location, is *Balint's syndrome* (Damasio, 1985). It comprises three symptoms. One is *optic apraxia,* characterized by a deficit in visually guided reaching, even though the patient can see and recognize the object to be reached for. Another is *ocular ataxia,* a deficit in visual scanning in which the patient is unable to systematically scan an array of objects, or maintain fixation, or direct an eye movement toward a particular object. The third symptom is known as *simultanagnosia,* which is the inability to perceive more than one object at a time. Here, the patient can name objects if presented singly, but if the examiner holds up two objects, such as a comb and a pen, the patient identifies only one and seems not to notice the other. Simultagnosia is sometimes observed independently of Balint's syndrome. It is then defined as the inability to provide the theme of a picture despite the fact that individual figures in the picture are identified (Wolpert, 1924).

The parietal lobe also plays a role in covert visual attention; that is, in our ability to attend to an object in some location, say to the left or right of visual fixation, without actually looking directly at it. In particular, patients with unilateral damage to the parietal lobe often have difficulty disengaging visual attention from objects in the ipsilateral visual field. A patient with a right parietal lesion, for example, will find it difficult to disengage attention from an object in the right visual field and direct it toward an object in the left visual field (corresponding to the damaged right side) (Posner, Walker, Friedrich, & Rafal, 1984).

This deficit may underlie the phenomenon of *visual extinction,* in which patients with unilateral occipito-parietal lesions can identify a single object falling anywhere in the visual field, but if two objects are presented simultaneously, one in each visual field, the patients disregard the one in the field contralateral to the site of the lesion. This may well result from the failure to disengage attention from the object in the visual field corresponding to the intact side. There is some suggestion that extinction is more common following right- and left-hemispheric damage, although the evidence for this is not unequivocal (Bisiach & Vallar, 1988).

A more striking phenomenon still is *hemineglect,* in which patients with unilateral brain lesions ignore stimuli on the side of space ipsilateral to the

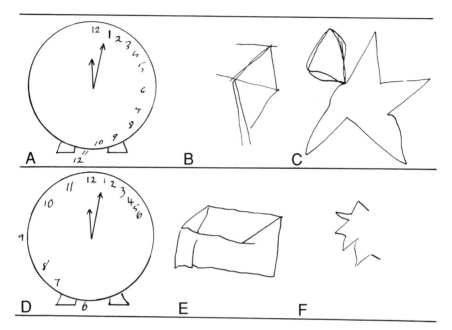

FIGURE 3 Examples of hemineglect in patients' attempts to draw a clock, a cube, and a star. A–C were drawn by patients with posterior right-sided tumors, whereas D–F were drawn by patients with left-sided tumors—D by a patient with a posterior tumor, E by a patient with an anterior tumor, and F by a patient with a (subcortical) tumor of the basal ganglia. (Figure kindly supplied by Dr. J. A. Ogden.)

lesion. Unlike hemianopia, visual hemineglect applies to one side of space rather than to one visual field (defined in relation to the point of visual fixation); in attempting a crossword puzzle, for example, a patient with hemineglect may fill in the clues on only one side of the grid, even though there is no restriction on where to look. Patients with visual hemineglect may also ignore objects on the neglected side of *imagined* scenes (Bisiach & Luzzatti, 1978; Bisiach, Luzzatti, & Perani, 1979).

Although hemineglect has been reported following unilateral damage to a wide range of cortical and even subcortical areas (including the superior colliculus—Rizzolatti & Gallese, 1988), it is most commonly associated with parietal lesions (Bisiach & Vallar, 1988). It is also much more frequently observed following right-sided than left-sided damage. A curious exception to this was reported by Ogden (1985), who found an equal incidence in patients with left- and right-sided damage (due in most cases to tumors), although the neglect was more severe among the right-lesioned group (see Figure 3 for illustrations). Ogden also found that most of the patients in the left-damaged group had frontal lesions, whereas most of those in the right-damaged group had posterior lesions.

There is still no general agreement as to the mechanisms underlying hemineglect. One possibility is that it is attentional, and again it has been related to the failure (described earlier) to disengage attention from the side of space ipsilateral to the lesion (Posner et al., 1984). Reviews and critiques of various theories are provided by Bisiach and Vallar (1988), who favor the view that hemineglect is caused by a disorder of conscious representation on one side of space, and by Rizzolatti and Gallese (1988), who relate hemineglect to an inability to organize movements toward one side of space. There may in fact be different *kinds* of hemineglect, each dependent on different brain areas. Mesulam (1990), for example, suggests that damage to the posterior parietal lobe is responsible for perceptual hemineglect, whereas damage to the motor prefrontal area may produce hemineglect in orienting and exploring. Unilateral damage to another area, the cingulate gyrus, may produce a more emotional form of hemineglect, in which objects on the neglected side of space are subjected to emotional denial, or lose their meaning.

At this point it is worth commenting briefly on the role of consciousness in perception. The parietal attentional system seems to operate without conscious awareness, perhaps precisely because it is concerned with the directing of attention to *unattended* stimuli. Conscious awareness of visual input seems to depend rather on the geniculo-striatal pathway, leading on to the inferior occipital regions. Thus blindsight results when the input bypasses the geniculo-striatal system to reach the intact localization system in the parietal lobe; conversely, hemineglect is probably the result of damage to this localizational system itself. In both cases there is a lack of awareness (Graves & Jones, 1992).

2. The Agnosias

Agnosia is the general term for the inability, due to brain damage, to recognize previously familiar objects. At the highest level, then, it may be regarded as a deficit of the "what" system. Object recognition may also fail because of disruption to an earlier stage of processing, and we need to distinguish the agnosias from the sorts of deficits, referred to above, that result from visual field defects, or even from damage to the prestrite areas of the visual cortex; indeed these lower order deficits are sometimes known as "pseudoagnosias" (Shallice, 1988).

Discounting the pseudoagnosias, Lissauer (1890) drew a distinction between *apperceptive agnosia,* which is a failure to construct an internal representation of an object, and *associative agnosia,* which is a failure to understand its meaning. Apperceptive agnosia is well illustrated by the work of Warrington and her colleagues, who have described patients with right posterior lesions who have difficulty recognizing common objects viewed from unconventional angles, or presented as silhouettes or as projected shadows

(Warrington & James, 1988; Warrington & Taylor, 1973, 1978). These patients perform normally on tests of sensory and perceptual discrimination, and have no difficulty identifying objects shown in conventional orientations in nondegraded fashion.

In associative agnosia, the patient is able to perceive objects as objects, but cannot name them or demonstrate their use.[2] For example, associative agnosics have no difficulty with tasks that the apperceptive agnosic finds difficult, such as coloring in the individual objects drawn in overlapping fashion, or in copying drawings, but they cannot identify the objects in question (see Hécaen, Goldblum, Masur, & Famier, 1974; McCarthy & Warrington, 1986). Associative agnosias typically result from lesions to the inferior occipitotemporal regions, as one might expect if they are essentially disorders of the "what" system.

E. Hemispheric Differences

Although the left-hemispheric specialization for language has dominated research on cerebral asymmetry, John Hughlings Jackson speculated as early as 1864 that if "expression" resided in one hemisphere, then it might well be asked whether "perception—its corresponding opposite" might reside in the other. There is in fact considerable evidence that there is at least a right-hemispheric advantage for many nonverbal perceptual functions, even if this does match the rather absolute quality of the left-hemispheric dominance for speech. We have already seen, for example, that extinction and hemineglect may occur more often following right-sided than left-sided brain damage, suggesting a right-hemispheric advantage in attentional function.

Hemispheric differences are often studied by comparing the perceptual responses to stimuli in the two visual hemifields, since each hemifield (regardless of which *eye* one is viewing with) projects to the primary visual cortex on the opposite side (see Figure 1). The subjects fixate a point, and stimuli are flashed to one or other side of that point. The flash is brief, typically less than about 180 ms, so that the subjects do not have time to move their eyes in the direction of the flash. Studies of normal subjects suggest that the right hemisphere (or left visual half-field) may be superior to the left in a wide range of even quite elementary perceptual functions, including judgments of depth (Durnford & Kimura, 1971), lightness

---

[2] In cases where the patient cannot name a visual object but can demonstrate its use, the disorder is termed *optic aphasia* rather than apperceptive agnosia. The optic aphasic is typically able to name objects felt with the hand, however, implying that the problem is visual rather than semantic (Shallice, 1988). The information reaches the semantic system via the tactual modality. Optic aphasia was first described by Freund (1889).

(Davidoff, 1975), color (Davidoff, 1976), and curvature (Longden, Ellis, & Iversen, 1976).

There is also evidence that the two cerebral hemispheres may process in qualitatively different ways. This is cleverly illustrated in experiments by D. Zaidel (1990). She took pictures of faces, viewed frontally, and moved their internal features about systematically, so that the nose might appear where the eye should be, or the mouth where the nose should be. These pictures of mutilated faces were then shown to two split-brain patients, using a special contact lens device (the Z lens) that restricted viewing to a single visual hemifield, and thus to a single hemisphere. The patients were then asked to point to various features, such as nose, eyes, mouth, and so forth. When viewing with the left hemisphere, they pointed accurately to the features themselves, even though they were misplaced. When viewing with the right hemisphere, however, they pointed to the locations where the features *should* have been.[3] These observations illustrate a recurring theme in studies of hemispheric asymmetry, namely, that the left hemisphere operates in an analytic, piecemeal sort of way, the right hemisphere in a more holistic, configurational manner. D. Zaidel argues that the distinction in her studies stems from the way in which information about faces is stored in memory, but there is also evidence that the two modes of operation apply to perceptual processing itself (Bradshaw & Nettleton, 1981).

Right-hemispheric specialization may also apply to higher order visual functions. An example is *mental rotation,* the act of imagining an object turning around so that it is pictured in a different orientation (Shepard & Metzler, 1971). Evidence that mental rotation is primarily right hemispheric has come from the testing of patients with unilateral brain damage (Ratcliff, 1979), from brain activity as assessed by regional cerebral blood flow (Deutsch, Bourbon, Papanicolaou, & Eisenberg, 1988), and from the study of a split-brained person (Corballis & Sergent, 1988, 1989).

We also saw earlier that one measure of apperceptive agnosia is the inability to recognize objects viewed from unusual angles, and that this also typically results from damage to the right rather than to the left parietal regions (see also Humphreys & Riddoch, 1984, 1985; Shallice, 1988). It is tempting to suppose that the deficit is actually one of mental rotation. As evidence against this, Farah and Hammond (1988) described a patient with a right posterior lesion who was unable to carry out mental rotation, but easily able to recognize rotated objects.

It has also been claimed that, unlike apperceptive agnosia, associative

---

[3] D. Zaidel also showed these two patients Magritte's painting, *The Rape,* (see Figure 4) in which the nude torso of a female figure is presented as a face, with breasts as eyes, navel as nose, pubic area as mouth, and again the right hemisphere responded by location and the left in terms of the parts themselves.

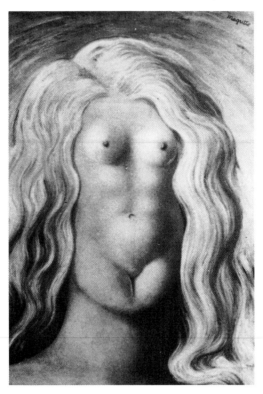

FIGURE 4   René Magritte's painting *The Rape*. When D. Zaidel (1990) showed this to two commissurotomized subjects under unilateral viewing conditions, both hemispheres of each subjects recognized it as a face. However their right hemispheres could not identify the anomalous parts, whereas their left hemispheres recognized the parts for what they actually were. (Reprinted with permission from H. Torczyner, 1979, *Magritte: Ideas and Images*. New York: Abrams).

agnosia typically results from lesions to the posterior *left* hemisphere (Warrington & Taylor, 1978). However this may depend on the type of associative agnosia. Farah (1991) has suggested that *pure alexia,* which is the inability to read words as wholes, and *prosopagnosia,* which is the inability to recognize previously familiar people by their faces alone may both be regarded as extreme forms of associative agnosia. Alexia typically results from left-sided lesions, prosopagnosia from right-sided or bilateral lesions (Young, 1988). In a survey of 99 published cases of associative agnosia, Farah observed that, with two dubious exceptions, agnosia for objects always occurred in conjunction with either alexia or prosopagnosia or both, but never with neither, and alexia and prosopagnosia never occurred together without additional signs of object agnosia. Moreover, alexia tended to be associated with agnosia for manufactured objects or other objects that are clearly composed of parts, whereas prosopagnosia tended to be associated with agnosia for natural objects, such as animals or vegetables, that involve subtle distinctions of shape and are distinguished perhaps in a more holistic fashion.

This brings us back to the idea that the left hemisphere processes in a partwise, analytical manner, and the right hemisphere in a more holistic fashion. In the context of the representation of objects, Farah's observations may yield clues about the evolution of cerebral asymmetry, and indeed of the human mind. The holistic way of representing and processing objects may be evolutionarily old, the result of selective pressure to represent aspects of the natural environment that are stable over time. However, humans have uniquely created manufactured environments that forever change and that increasingly dominate our perceptual world. Representation of this world required a different kind of system, one that could be rapidly applied to novel structures. This was solved by developing a small vocabulary of standardized internal shapes that could be assembled to provide a representation of an unlimited set of objects, just as a child might use a Lego® set to construct acceptable (though crude) models of a wide variety of common objects. These standardized shapes might take the form of *generalized cones,* as proposed by Marr (1982)—also dubbed "geometric ions" or *geons* by Biederman (1987). As Biederman points out, this scheme resembles language, in which an unlimited variety of meanings can be expressed by generating combinations of units (phonemes) drawn from a limited vocabulary. This generative, syntactic mode of object representation, like language, is primarily left-hemispheric, and is probably uniquely human (Corballis, 1991, 1992).[4]

III. NEUROPSYCHOLOGY OF AUDITION

Within the auditory modality, the main emphasis has been on the perception of speech or speech sounds, which lies beyond the scope of this chapter. However, some of the visual deficits described above do have their auditory counterparts.

A. Extinction and Hemineglect

Extinction can be manifest in both vision and audition; that is, presented with two sounds, one on each side, patients with unilateral lesions may ignore the one on the same side as the lesion. For example, De Renzi,

---

[4] The two modes are essentially complementary, and neither is superior to the other. For example, the generative mode might represent a prototypical automobile, but could not capture the subtle distinction between different makes, for which the other, more holistic mode is necessary.

Gentillini, and Pattacini (1984) tested extinction in unilaterally brain-damaged patients by having them point to sounds produced on two sound generators, one on each side. Although the incidence of extinction was the same following left or right damage, extinction lasted longer following right damage. Auditory extinction was largely independent of visual extinction, and CT scans suggested that auditory extinction may have been due to the encroachment of lesions onto the auditory pathways, suggesting that its basis may have been perceptual rather than attentional.

Hemineglect, too, may be manifest in the auditory modality. Altman, Balonov, and Deglin (1979) studied patients after unilateral electroconvulsive shock therapy, and found that after right-sided shock they tended to localize leftward sounds as though they came from the right. In some cases the patient would engage in conversation with a person on the left as though that person were on the right, even looking in that direction![5] There were no such distortions of sound localization following left-sided shock, suggesting that auditory neglect, like visual neglect, generally follows malfunction of the right hemisphere (see also Bisiach, Cornacchia, Sterzi, & Vallar, 1984).

B. Auditory Agnosias

Examples of auditory analogues to the visual agnosias come most obviously from the verbal domain. For example, so-called pure word deafness, which typically follows damage to the left temporal lobe, may be regarded as a higher order auditory deficit in which the patient has normal hearing, can talk, read, and write normally, and can perceive and understand nonverbal environmental sounds, but cannot perceive spoken words (e.g., Hemphill & Stengel, 1940; Klein & Harper, 1956). Superficially, at least, this seems analogous to pure alexia, although it may simply reflect a failure to track the rapid shifts in frequency that characterize spoken consonants, rather than a failure to perceptually construct a higher order sequential pattern (Ellis & Young, 1988). A better analogy may come from a rare deficit that has been called *word-meaning deafness,* which resembles pure word deafness except that patients with this disorder are able to repeat back words or phrases that they cannot understand (see Ellis & Young, 1988, for examples and discussion), whereas those with pure word deafness cannot. This seems to be a difficulty at the level of mapping the sound onto stored meaning, and might therefore be considered a form of associative agnosia.

There are also rare examples of auditory agnosia for nonspeech sounds, and Vignolo (1969) even suggested that these might be divided into apper-

[5] The disposition to treat sounds on one side as though they come from the other has also been called *alloacusis* (Diamond & Bender, 1965).

ceptive and associative types. For instance, a man classified as having associative auditory agnosia following right-hemispheric damage had specific
difficulty recognizing common environmental sounds, although the localization of sounds and the perception of speech were normal (Spreen, Benton,
& Fincham, 1965; see also Albert, Sparks, Stockert, & Sax, 1972).

C. Amusia

Brain damage may also lead to impairments in the perception of music.
Because there is much more variability in musical than in verbal ability in
the normal population, musical deficits may be hard to detect, and have not
received the attention that language deficits have. Even so, so-called amusia
has been recognized since Knoblauch coined the term in 1888.[6] As with
aphasia, it is possible to roughly distinguish *receptive amusia,* associated with
posterior lesions, from *expressive amusia,* associated with anterior lesions
(Henson, 1985).

Milner (1962) administered the Seashore Test of Musical Talent to patients with unilateral temporal lobe lesions, finding that those with right-
sided lesions were impaired on the discrimination of timbre and on memory
for tones. Shankweiler (1966) later reported that right temporal lobectomy
impaired recognition of melodies, whereas left temporal lobectomy did not.
In a review, Zatorre (1984) concluded that where deficits in aspects of
musical perception have been observed, they have nearly always followed
damage to the right temporal lobe, although there is also evidence that
damage to the right frontal lobe may impair the processing of melodic
sequences (Shapiro, Grossman, & Gardner, 1981).

Most of the research on the neuropsychology of musical perception has
not focused on the brain areas involved within the cerebral hemispheres, but
rather on the differences between the hemispheres, the subject to which I
now turn.

D. Hemispheric Differences

The main technique used to investigate hemispheric differences in auditory
perception in normal subjects is dichotic listening (Kimura, 1961). The
technique is similar to that used to test for extinction, but the purpose is
different. Different sounds are played simultaneously into the two ears, and
any advantage accruing to one ear over the other in the identification or
detection of sounds is taken as evidence that the contralateral hemisphere is
the more specialized.[7] By far the majority of studies have focused on speech

---

6 Perhaps in deference to Queen Victoria's famous utterance: "We are not amused."

7 The explanation as to why dominance of one ear should imply a dominance of the contralateral hemisphere is not fully resolved.

and speech sounds, which typically give rise to a right-ear advantage, implying left-hemispheric specialization.

However there have also been studies showing a left-ear (or right-hemispheric) advantage, for various nonverbal auditory perceptual tasks, such as perception of environmental sounds (Curry, 1967) and vocal nonverbal sounds (King & Kimura, 1972), as well as of several aspects of music, including melody (Kimura, 1964), pitch (Blumstein & Cooper, 1974), timbre (Kallman & Corballis, 1975), and harmony (Gordon, 1970; Sidtis, 1984). However it should not be thought that the right hemisphere has simply "commandeered" all musical function. Other dichotic-listening studies show the *left* hemisphere to be dominant for the perception of rhythm (e.g., Gordon, 1978; Robinson & Solomon, 1974), and in a review of the evidence, Peretz and Morais (1988) conclude that the left-hemispheric component is more marked the more complex the temporal structure. Studies of unilateral temporal lobe lesions have also suggested that identification of familiar tunes is impaired by left-sided rather than right-sided damage (Zatorre, 1989). Moreover, Bever and Chiarello (1974) reported that the left-ear advantage[8] in the recognition of melodies was reversed in musically trained subjects, and suggested that musically sophisticated subjects may adopt a more analytic way of processing music that is dependent on the left hemisphere, whereas those untrained in music tend to adopt a more holistic, right-hemispheric strategy. Although subsequent evidence on the effect of musical training has been equivocal (Zatoree, 1984), the idea that lateral asymmetries may depend on processing strategies rather than on fixed specialization for different components has received considerable support (Bradshaw & Nettleton, 1981; Peretz & Morais, 1988; Zatorre, 1984).

This may well tie in with the idea, introduced earlier, that the left hemisphere in humans is specialized for a generative, partwise mode of representation, whereas the right hemisphere preserves a more holistic, subtle form of representation that goes back much further in evolution (Corballis, 1991, 1992). The generative mode may be applied to music as to language and the representation of objects, especially among skilled musicians; indeed Lerdahl and Jackendoff (1983) have proposed a generative grammar of tonal music that parallels that of language. Recent evidence suggests that, in professional musicians, music is not simply a right-hemispheric analogue of speech; rather, the brain circuits involved in music resemble those involved in language and lie close to them. For example, the frontal areas involved in musical performance appear to be immediately above Broca's area in the left hemisphere, and even in perceptual aspects the activated areas of the left hemisphere outnumbered those of the right hemisphere (Sergent, Zuck, Terriah, & MacDonald, 1992). Finally, it should be noted that amusia in

[8] This result was obtained with monaural rather than dichotic presentation.

professional musicians is typically associated with aphasia, although the *type* of amusia is not necessarily predictable from the type of aphasia (Brust, 1980).

IV. OTHER MODALITIES

Extinction and hemineglect are also manifest in other sensory modalities. In one interesting study, for example, patients with right-hemispheric damage attempted to identify different odors presented simultaneously to each nostril. One might have predicted extinction for the odor presented to the ipsilesional *right* nostril since the olfactory pathways are not crossed. Instead, however, extinction occurred for the odors presented to the contralesional *left* nostril (Bellas, Novelly, Eskenazi, & Wasserstein, 1988). The authors argued that this implied a defective representation of the side of space represented by the damaged right hemisphere, rather than reduced sensory input.

In testing for neglect, patients are routinely assessed for both visual and tactile neglect, in part to differentiate between *extrapersonal* neglect, in which environmental objects on one side are neglected, and *personal* neglect, in which one side of the patient's own body is neglected (Bisiach & Vallar, 1988). Patients with personal neglect may become untidy and dirty on one side of the body, sometimes even neglecting to clothe it; this may reflect neglect in several modalities, including visual, somesthetic, and motor, although case studies also show that neglect of visual and tactile stimuli may be dissociated (Perani, Vallar, Cappa, Messa, & Fazio, 1987).

Unilateral lesions sometimes produce what is known as *allesthesia,* or *allochiria,* in which a tactile stimulus on one side of the body is referred to the symmetrical location on the other side—a condition analogous to alloacusis in the auditory modality. Again, it has been claimed that this more commonly follows right- than left-hemispheric lesions (Critchley, 1953).

Cerebral asymmetries may be manifest in somesthetic as well as visual and auditory tasks. For example, there is evidence that the blind are better at reading Braille with the left hand than the right, despite the verbal nature of the task. This has been attributed to the greater spatial precision of the right hemisphere (see Harris, 1980, for a review). Varney and Benton (1975) have also shown the left hand to be the more accurate in determining the orientations of rods pressed against the palm.

V. CONCLUDING REMARKS

This review has been necessarily brief, and has skipped over some controversial issues. For example, I have treated the neuropsychology of vision as though vision were simply a matter of processing from the retina onward, with different circuits and brain areas dedicated to different aspects of the visual input. Thus magno is distinguished from parvo, color from motion, what from where, and left-hemispheric from right-hemispheric. The myriad of different pathways and specialized centers serve to dismantle the visual scene and scatter it about the brain. This raises what has come to be called the "binding" problem: How is it all put back together again?

It is possible that this question is an improper one, based on a false view of how perception works. It implies that there is some location in the brain where the percept is finally formed from all of its scattered parts. The act of perception may consist rather of the totality of activity in the brain. If this is so, the percept does not need to be "reassembled"; rather, different brain areas simply provide different information about the perceived world. The binding problem may be solved, not by spatial reassembly, but by a temporal code, a synchronization of oscillatory activity that signals temporary conjunctions between attributes that make up a perceived object (e.g., Hummel & Biederman, 1992).

It is also worth noting that there are descending as well as ascending pathways in the perceptual systems, which probably serve to filter and modify forward processing (Van Essen et al., 1992). It has even been suggested that the descending pathways may play the more prominent role. Brown (1991), for example, has argued that the sequence of events in the perceptual act is somewhat the reverse of what is generally assumed. In his scheme of things, the visual percept, for example, originates in the brain stem, proceeds to the limbic system of the brain where it makes contact with personal memories, then to the parietal lobe where it is interpreted in three-dimensional space coordinates, and *finally* to the visual cortex where perceived objects are exteriorized. This may be a willful departure from accepted doctrine to make a point, but nevertheless serves to correct the impression that perception is a one-way flow from the sensory receptors inwards.

I have also adopted what may be seen as a heavy "localizational" stance, in which different brain areas are seen as performing discretely different functions. By and large, this approach has served neuropsychology quite well, because deficits are often quite specific and can be dissociated from one another, even if they also often co-occur. Moreover, neurophysiological evidence does suggest specialized pathways for different perceptual functions, especially within the visual system. Even so, theory is often at the mercy of method, and this review has leaned rather heavily on neurophysiology and on psychological techniques designed to differentiate function (e.g., between hemispheres) rather than to reflect integrated brain activity. The concept of parallel distributed processing (Rumelhart, McClelland, & the PDP Research Group, 1986), popular in recent psychological theorizing, emphasizes a more holistic approach in which "representations" (if they can be said to exist at all) are distributed throughout the neural network. Taken to its extreme this would imply that one cannot localize functions in the brain at all. Whether psychological functions are localized or distributed may be largely a matter of grain; psychological functions may be grossly localized, but distributed at a more fine-grained level. Functional imaging techniques such as positron emission tomography (PET) scanning and functional magnetic resonance imaging (MRI) may also provide a more holistic view of the brain mechanisms involved in perception than has emerged from single-cell recordings.

Finally, although we are getting increasingly detailed anatomical and physiological maps, especially of the visual pathways in the brain, and increasingly sophisticated accounts of perceptual deficits following circumscribed brain lesions, there is a long way to go in putting it all together into a coherent theory.

References

Albert, M. L., Sparks, R., Stockert, T., & Sax, D. (1972). A case study of auditory agnosia: Linguistic and nonlinguistic processing. *Cortex, 8,* 427.

Altman, J. A., Balonov, L. J., & Deglin, V. L. (1979). Effects of unilateral disorder of the brain hemisphere function in man on directional hearing. *Neuropsychologia, 17,* 295–301.

Bellas, D. N., Novelly, R. A., Eskenazi, B., & Wasserstein, J. (1988). The nature of unilateral neglect in the olfactory sensory system. *Neuropsychologia, 26,* 45–52.

Bever, T., & Chiarello, R. (1974). Cerebral dominance in musicians. *Science, 185,* 537–539.

Biederman, I. (1987). Recognition-by-components: A theory of human image understanding. *Psychological Review, 94,* 115–147.

Bisiach, E., Cornacchia, L., Sterzi, R., & Vallar, G. (1984). Disorders of perceived auditory lateralization after lesions of the right hemisphere. *Brain, 107,* 37–52.

Bisiach, E., & Luzzatti, C. (1978). Unilateral neglect of representational space. *Cortex, 14,* 129–133.

Bisiach, E., Luzzatti, C., & Perani, D. (1979). Unilateral neglect, representational schema, and consciousness. *Brain, 102,* 609–618.

Bisiach, E., & Vallar, G. (1988). Hemineglect in humans. In F. Boller & J. Grafman (Eds.), *Handbook of neuropsychology* (Vol. 1). Amsterdam: Elsevier.

Blakemore, C. (1991). Computational principles of the cerebral cortex. *Psychologist, 14,* 73.

Blumstein, S., & Cooper, W. E. (1974). Hemispheric processing of intonation contours. *Cortex, 10,* 146–158.

Bradshaw, J. L., & Nettleton, N. C. (1981). The nature of hemispheric specialization in man. *Behavioral and Brain Sciences, 4,* 51–91.

Bregman, A. S. (1990). *Auditory scene analysis: The perceptual organization of sound.* Cambridge, MA: MIT Press.

Brown, J. (1991). *Self and process.* New York: Springer-Verlag.

Brust, J. C. M. (1980). Music and language: Musical alexia and agraphia. *Brain, 103,* 367–392.

Carlson, N. R. (1991). *Physiology of behavior* (4th ed.). Boston: Allyn & Bacon.

Cavanagh, P., Boeglin, J., & Favreau, O. E. (1985). Perception of motion in equiluminous kinematograms. *Perception, 14,* 151–162.

Corballis, M. C. (1991). *The lopsided ape.* New York: Oxford University Press.

Corballis, M. C. (1992). On the evolution of language and generativity. *Cognition, 44,* 197–226.

Corballis, M. C., & Sergent, J. (1988). Imagery in a commissurotomized patient. *Neuropsychologia, 26*, 13–26.

Corballis, M. C., & Sergent, J. (1989). Mental rotation in a commissurotomized subject. *Neuropsychologia, 27*, 585–597.

Critchley, M. (1953). *The parietal lobes*. London: Hafner Press.

Curry, F. K. W. (1967). A comparison of left-handed and right-handed subjects on verbal and nonverbal listening tasks. *Cortex, 3*, 343–352.

Damasio, A. R. (1985). Disorders of complex visual processing: Agnosias, achromatopsia, Balint's syndrome, and related difficulties of orientation and construction. In M.-M. Mesulam (Ed.), *Principles of behavioral neurology*. Philadelphia: Davis.

Damasio, A. R., Yamada, T., Damasio, H., Corbett, J., & McKee, J. (1980). Central achromatopsia: Behavioral, anatomical, and physiological aspects. *Neurology, 30*, 1064–1071.

Davidoff, J. B. (1975). Hemispheric differences in the perception of lightness. *Neuropsychologia, 13*, 121–124.

Davidoff, J. B. (1976). Hemispheric sensitivity differences in the perception of color. *Quarterly Journal of Experimental Psychology, 28*, 387–394.

De Renzi, E., Gentilini, M., & Pattacini, F. (1984). Auditory extinction following hemispheric damage. *Neuropsychologia, 22*, 733–744.

Deutsch, G., Bourbon, T., Papanicolaou, A. C., & Eisenberg, H. M. (1988). Visuospatial tasks compared via activation of regional cerebral blood flow. *Neuropsychologia, 26*, 445–452.

Diamond, S. P., & Bender, M. B. (1965). On auditory extinction and alloacusis. *Transactions of the American Neurological Association, 90*, 154–157.

Durnford, M., & Kimura, D. (1971). Right hemisphere specialization for depth perception reflected in visual field differences. *Nature (London), 231*, 394–395.

Ellis, A. W., & Young, A. W. (1988). *Human cognitive neuropsychology*, London: Erlbaum.

Farah, M. J. (1991). Patterns of co-occurrence among the associative agnosias: Implications for visual object representation. *Cognitive Neuropsychology, 8*, 1–19.

Farah, M. J., & Hammond, K. M. (1988). Mental rotation and orientation-invariant object recognition: Dissociable processes. *Cognition, 29*, 29–46.

Freund, C. S. (1889). Ueber optische Aphasie und Seelenblindheit. *Archiv für Psychiatrie und Nervenkrankheiten, 20*, 276–297, 371–416.

Gordon, H. (1970). Hemispheric asymmetries in the perception of musical chords. *Cortex, 6*, 387–398.

Gordon, H. (1978). Left-hemisphere dominance for rhythmic elements in dichotically-presented melodies. *Cortex, 14*, 58–70.

Graves, R. E., & Jones, B. S. (1992). Conscious visual perceptual awareness vs. nonconscious visual spatial localization examined with normal subjects using possible analogues of blindsight and neglect. *Cognitive Neuropsychology, 9*, 487–508.

Harris, L. J. (1980). Which hand is the "eye" of the blind?—a new look at an old question. In J. Herron (Ed.), *Neuropsychology of left-handedness*. New York: Academic Press.

Hécaen, H., Goldblum, M. C., Masur, M. C., & Ramier, A. M. (1974). Une nouvelle observation d'agnosie d'objet. Déficit de l'association ou de la catégorisation, spécifique de la modalité visuelle. *Neuropsychologia, 12*, 447–464.

Hemphill, R. E., & Stengel, E. (1940). A study on pure word deafness. *Journal of Neurology, Neurosurgery and Psychiatry, 3*, 251–262.

Henson, R. A. (1985). Amusia. In J. A. M. Frederiks (Ed.), *Handbook of clinical neurology* (Vol. 1, pp. 483–490). New York: Elsevier.

Hess, R. H., Baker, C. L., & Zihl, J. (1989). The "motion-blind" patient: Low-level spatial and temporal filters. *Journal of Neuroscience, 9*, 1628–1640.

Hummel, J. E., & Biederman, I. (1992). Dynamic binding in a neural network for shape recognition. *Psychological Review, 99*, 480–517.

Humphreys, G. W., & Riddoch, M. J. (1984). Routes to object constancy: Implications from neurological impairments of object constancy. *Quarterly Journal of Experimental Psychology, 36A*, 385–415.

Humphreys, G. W., & Riddoch, M. J. (1985). Author's correction to "Routes to object constancy." *Quarterly Journal of Experimental Psychology, 37A*, 493–495.

Jackson, J. H . (1864). Clinical remarks on cases of defects of expression (by words, writing, signs, etc) in diseases of the nervous system. *Lancet, 2*, 457.

Kallman, J., & Corballis, M. C. (1975). Ear asymmetry in reaction time to musical sounds. *Perception and Psychophysics, 17*, 368–370.

Kimura, D. (1961). Cerebral dominance and the perception of verbal stimuli. *Canadian Journal of Psychology, 15*, 166–171.

Kimura, D. (1964). Left-right differences in the perception of melodies. *Quarterly Journal of Experimental Psychology, 16*, 355–358.

King, F. L., & Kimura, D. (1972). Left-ear superiority of dichotic perception of vocal nonverbal sounds. *Canadian Journal of Psychology, 26*, 111–116.

Klein, R., & Harper, J. (1956). The problem of agnosia in the light of a case of pure word deafness. *Journal of Mental Science, 102*, 112–120.

Lerdahl, F., & Jackendoff, R. (1983). *A generative theory of tonal music*. Cambridge, MA: MIT Press.

Lissauer, H. (1890). Ein Fall von Seelenblindheit nebsteinen Betrag zur Theorie derselben. *Archiv für Psychiatrie und Nervenkrankheiten, 21*, 222–270.

Livingstone, M. S., & Hubel, D. H. (1988). Segregation of form, color, movement, and depth: Anatomy, physiology, and perception. *Science, 240*, 740–749.

Longden, K., Ellis, C., & Iversen, D. (1976). Hemispheric differences in the perception of curvature. *Neuropsychologia, 14*, 195–202.

Marr, D. (1982). *Vision*. San Francisco: Freeman.

McCarthy, R. A., & Warrington, E. K. (1986). Visual associative agnosia: A clinico-anatomical study of a single case. *Journal of Neurology, Neurosurgery and Psychiatry, 49*, 1233–1240.

Mesulam, M.-M. (1990). Large-scale neurocognitive networks and distributed processing for attention, language, and memory. *Annals of Neurology, 28*, 597–613.

Milner, B. (1962). Laterality effects in audition. In V. B. Mountcastle (Ed.), *Interhemispheric relations and cerebral dominance*. Baltimore, MD: Johns Hopkins University Press.

Mollon, J. D., Newcombe, F., Polden, P. G., & Ratcliff, G. (1980). On the presence of three cone mechanisms in a case of total achromatopsia. In G. Verriest (Ed.), *Color vision deficiencies* (Vol. 5). Bristol: Hilger.

Ogden, J. A. (1985). Anterior-posterior interhemispheric differences in the loci of lesions producing visual hemineglect. *Brain and Cognition, 4*, 59–75.

Perani, D., Vallar, G., Cappa, S. F., Messa, C., & Fazio, F. (1987). Aphasia and neglect after subcortical stroke: A clinical/cerebral perfusion correlation study. *Brain, 110*, 1211–1229.

Peretz, I., & Morais, J. (1988). Determinants of laterality for music: Towards an information-processing account. In K. Hugdahl (Ed.), *Handbook of dichotic listening* (pp. 323–358). New York: Wiley.

Posner, M. I., Walker, J. A., Friedrich, F. J., & Rafal, R. D. (1984). Effects of parietal injury on covert orienting of visual attention. *Journal of Neuroscience, 4*, 1863–1874.

Ramachandran, V. S., & Gregory, R. L. (1978). Does colour provide input to human motion perception? *Nature (London), 275*, 55–56.

Ratcliff, R. (1979). Spatial thought, mental rotation, and the right cerebral hemisphere. *Neuropsychologia, 17*, 49–54.

Rizzolatti, G., & Gallese, V. (1988). Mechanisms and theories of spatial neglect. In F. Boller & J. Grafman (Eds.), *Handbook of neuropsychology* (Vol. 1). Amsterdam: Elsevier.

Robinson, G., & Solomon, D. (1974). Rhythm is processed by the speech hemisphere. *Journal of Experimental Psychology, 102*, 508–511.

Rumelhart, D. E., McClelland, J. L., & the PDP Research Group. (1986). *Parallel distributed processing: Explorations in the microstructure of cognition: Vol. 1. Foundations.* Cambridge, MA: MIT Press/Bradford Books.

Schneider, G. E. (1969). Two visual systems. *Science, 163,* 895–902.

Sergent, J., Zuck, E., Terriah, S., & MacDonald, B. (1992). Distributed neural network underlying musical sight-reading and keyboard performance. *Science, 257,* 106–109.

Shallice, T. (1988). *From neuropsychology to mental structure.* Cambridge: Cambridge University Press.

Shankweiler, D. (1966). Effects of temporal-lobe damage on perception of dichotically presented melodies. *Journal of Comparative and Physiological Psychology, 7,* 115–119.

Shapiro, B. E., Grossman, M., & Gardner, H. (1981). Selective processing deficits in brain damaged populations. *Neuropsychologia, 19,* 161–169.

Shepard, R. N., & Metzler, J. (1971). Mental rotation of three-dimensional objects. *Science, 171,* 701–703.

Sidtis, J. J. (1984). Music, pitch perception, and the mechanisms of cortical hearing. In M. S. Gazzaniga (Ed.), *Handbook of cognitive neuroscience* (pp. 91–114). New York: Plenum.

Spreen, O., Benton, A. L., & Fincham, R. (1965). Auditory agnosia without aphasia. *Archives of Neurology (Chicago), 13,* 84.

Torczyner, H. (1979). *Magritte: Ideas and images.* New York: Abrams.

Ungerleider, L. G., & Mishkin, M. (1982). Two cortical visual systems. In D. J. Ingle, M. A. Goodale, & R. J. W. Mansfield (Eds.), *Analysis of visual behavior.* Cambridge, MA: MIT Press.

Van Essen, D. C., Anderson, C. H., & Felleman, D. J. (1992). Information processing in the primate visual system: An integrated systems approach. *Science, 255,* 419–423.

Varney, N. R., & Benton, A. L. (1975). Tactile perception of direction in relation to handedness and familial handedness. *Neuropsychologia, 13,* 449–454.

Vignolo, L. (1969). Auditory agnosia: A review and report of recent evidence. In A. L. Benton (Ed.), *Contributions to clinical neuropsychology.* Chicago: Aldine.

Warrington, E. K., & James, M. (1988). Visual apperceptive agnosia: A clinico-anatomical study of three cases. *Cortex, 24,* 13–32.

Warrington, E. K., & Taylor, A. M. (1973). The contribution of the right parietal lobe to object recognition. *Cortex, 9,* 152–164.

Warrington, E. K., & Taylor, A. M. (1978). Two categorical stages of object recognition. *Perception, 7,* 695–705.

Weiskrantz, L. (1986). *Blindsight.* Oxford: Clarendon Press.

Wolpert, I. (1924). Die Simultanagnosie: störung der gesamtauffassung. *Zeietschrift für die gesamte Neurologie und Psychiatrie, 93,* 397–415.

Young, A. W. (1988). Functional organization of visual recognition. In L. Weiskrantz (Ed.), *Thought without language* (pp. 78–107). Oxford: Clarendon Press.

Zaidel, D. W. (1990). Long-term semantic memory in the two cerebral hemispheres. In C. Trevarthen (Ed.), *Brain circuits and functions of the mind: Essays in honor of R. W. Sperry* (pp. 266–280). Cambridge: Cambridge University Press.

Zatorre, R. J. (1984). Musical perception and cerebral function: A critical review. *Music Perception, 2,* 196–221.

Zatorre, R. J. (1989). Effects of temporal neocortical excisions on musical processing. *Contemporary Musical Review, 4,* 255–266.

CHAPTER 5

Neuropsychology of Attention

Marcel Kinsbourne

I. INTRODUCTION

The control of behavior is divided into *selection* and *processing*. All motile organisms, when foraging for food and while seeking to evade predators, continually have to decide which target to approach and from which to withdraw. In behaviorally simple species such selections for action are "hard-wired" into the nervous system and depend rigidly on stimulus characteristics. This is also largely the case in the young of behaviorally more complex species. Neuronal predisposition controls the earliest choices that infants make, but during neurological maturation humans become increasingly able to override these control selection priorities when, in view of experience, this would be adaptive. In species such as humans, which are generously equipped with sense receptors, the environment offers so many concurrent opportunities for information processing that rigorous selection is required to safeguard the individual from being immobilized into helplessness by a flood of competing response demands. Selective attention and response mechanisms systematically assure definitive decision and action and avoid behavioral impasse. Selection is made on both the input and the output side. Selective attention directs the receptors and their connected central processors toward specified features in the environment or in memory, and directs response mechanisms toward the selected goal.

Neuropsychology

In parallel with guiding responses, attention causes the target to stand out as figure against a less differentiated ground. The ground consists of the background field in the selected modality, the current states of the other sense modalities, and some sense of the self that is doing the observing.

Abnormal selective attending can be caused by impairment in the mechanism of attending in a particular cognitive domain, degrading its attentional priority with respect to all eliciting circumstances. It can also result from any dysfunction that distorts response priorities in a given context, and thereby biases the individual's attentional focus; the disadvantaged content attracts attention only within abnormally limited boundary conditions, whereas competing content more frequently becomes the focus of attention. Finally, the scope of selective attending can be limited by diminished attentional capacity.

A. The Mechanism of Attention

What highlights any one of a multitude of inputs or enables them all to be supplanted by an imagined or anticipated target? Two contrasting approaches attempt to answer this question. One relies on a serial, hierarchical model of brain organization. Represented inputs are scanned by an attentional mechanism, as it were an internal eye (Kosslyn, 1980), which picks out the target and brings it into attention by transport to a consciousness module. However, in view of the many inadequacies of the serial model of the "centered brain" (e.g., Dennett & Kinsbourne, 1992; Kinsbourne, 1982, in press-c), an uncentered parallel model is preferred. This model is more consistent not only with the bidirectional connectivity of the cerebrum, but also with the demonstrably heterarchical organization of perceptual (Freeman, 1991), orientational (Stein & Meredith, 1993), and motor (Kupferman, 1993) circuitry. Parallel circuitry might implement attention by activating (and perhaps multiplexing) the representation of the selected content (array, shape, feature or fragment). As we shall see, neuropsychological disorders of attention, notably unilateral neglect, are more readily understood in terms of dysfunction in reciprocal interactions in a self-organizing network, than as reflecting a lesion of, or misinformation of, supervisory equipment.

In order to contribute to the perceptual background, representations must be activated beyond some threshold value. Within the neural network those representations that are selected are further activated (Norman & Shallice, 1985) by maximizing their input by orienting sensitive receptors surfaces toward it, or by some internal means, such as a "spotlight" (e.g., Crick & Koch, 1990) of ascending activation. So activated, they enjoy a competitive advantage with respect to selection for action (Allport, 1989). They also become more likely to contribute their contents to the field of awareness, that is, to the contents of the individual's consciousness. According to the "dominant focus" model, this is because they become more apt to entrain in (e.g., co-oscillate with) the prevailing pattern of activation in the brain ("dominant focus"; Kinsbourne, 1988).

What selects a cell assembly that represents a given stimulus for activation? Norman and Shallice postulate dedicated "supervisory" machinery, which imposes the organization in question, and attribute this activity at least in part to the prefrontal lobes. But rather than crediting prefrontal neurons with superior and more comprehensive overview, they can be thought of as bringing posteriorly located representations under the control of motivational and experiential variables, enabling the latter to override selection based on the innately predetermined influence of stimulus salience alone. Thus orbitofrontal lesions are associated with diminished impulse control (i.e., impaired ability to inhibit dominant responses) when these are inexpedient in the longer term. Medial prefrontal lesions diminish the influence of motivation on goal-directed behavior. Dorsolateral prefrontal lesions impair planning, which requires attention to potential outcomes, and self-monitoring (Fuster, 1989).

B. Selective Attention in Cognitive Development

When selective attention is disordered, the patient can no longer freely select a *focus* for attention, within a modality or along a spatial axis. He may find it difficult to *sustain* attention on a particular class of targets when others compete, or conversely to *detach* attention from its current focus in favor of other targets. Again, he may be unable to *divide* attention between two or more mental representations, which may be reflected in failure both on divided attention tasks, and on problems that require several considerations to be entertained simultaneously.

The normal newborn human is subject to all these limitations. Immature attending is characterized by its rigidly specified perceptual priorities, its stereotyped patterning, and its very limited capacity. The stimuli that prevail in the competition to capture the attention of young infants are described as being positioned high on the perceptual hierarchy. They include bright colors, particularly reds, discontinuities in brightness, and conjoint movement. Intermittent stimuli are favored over steady ones both in sight and sound. Facelike patterns appear to have innately determined precedence. In searching a visual display, young children are unsystematic and redundantly tied to salient elements (Vurpillot, 1968). Attentional capacity, in terms of number of entries that can be maintained in working memory, expands gradually from an initial load of one unit only (Case, Kurkland, & Goldberg, 1982).

What develops in attentional development is the ability to detach attention from the more salient features, and to differentiate out and recombine elements of the major response synergisms (Gibson, 1969). These modifications of the basic plan are products of the maturation of superimposed control systems. However, though overlaid, the basic plan remains, as is demonstrable in extreme conditions. Even mature subjects retain color and shape better from briefly exposed displays than from the less salient attributes of orientation and sequence. Again, although the normal adult does not exhibit overt motor overflow, when she exerts maximal force with one muscle group, the other muscles that participate in the synergism are measurably activated. The individual can exert maximal effort when the muscular contractions are patterned so as to involve synergic rather than antagonistic muscle groups (Berntson & Torello, 1977).

The stereotyped nature of immature attending is well exemplified in the asymmetrical tonic neck response (ATNR). Its presence in early infancy, and even in premature and anencephalic infants implicates brain stem mechanisms. The child turns head and eyes to one side, stretching the ipsilateral arm in that direction as if pointing, extends the ipsilateral leg in that direction (although this is not an option for the young infant), while she reciprocally flexes the contralateral limbs. This selective orienting response is deployed as a whole: the infant cannot yet selectively inhibit some part of this synergism, turn eyes without turning head, look without pointing, and so forth. Fine gradations of opponent interaction are generally not obtained in young children. The child can squeeze a balloon only with full force, that is, in an all-or-nothing grip. He does not yet have the inhibitory capability needed to graduate his grip. The agonist muscle group is fully activated, but the antagonist group fails to hold it in check. Similar problems in the fine tuning of the grip are reinstated by certain premotor frontal lobe lesions.

The origins of laterality can be detected in the organization of neonatal patterns of orienting and responding. The spontaneous ATNR is grossly skewed to the right in most newborns, environmental stimulation being held constant (Gesell, 1938). Furthermore, the child with right-biased ATNR is the child who holds an object in his grasp longer with his right hand (Caplan & Kinsbourne, 1976), reaches out with the right arm (Hawn & Harris, 1983), and ultimately exhibits right-hand preference (Viviani, Turkewitz, & Karp, 1978). (A few newborns do not show this rightward bias: offspring of non-right-handed parents [Liederman & Kinsbourne, 1980] and infants stressed at birth [Turkewitz, 1987].) The ATNR findings indicate that the reciprocal lateral orienting facilities, though opposite, are not equal in their potency. In early infancy, even before the left frontal eye fields, which direct eyes and head rightward, have become functional, comparable centers in the brain stem more forcefully direct attention rightward than their opponents direct it to the left. This bias can be reinstated and further amplified after lateralized cerebral damage in adults, as will become apparent when the mechanism of *unilateral neglect* is considered.

The ability to withhold responding can be impaired at diverse levels of organization from motor to cognitive. In the grasp response, a prefrontal release sign, the patient cannot restrain a grasping movement toward the source of a touch on the back of the hand. In utilization behavior, the patient automatically imitates what the examiner does (Lhermitte, 1983). Impulse control at the cognitive level is notably deficient in the so-called pseudo-psychopathic syndrome of right prefrontal lobe damage (Stuss & Benson, 1986), as well as in confusional states (Mesulam, 1985).

The cognitive analogue of the ability to graduate motor response is inhibiting response to attractive stimuli, which is implemented by the behavioral inhibition system (Gray, 1982), namely septohippocampal and orbital prefrontal circuitry, and controlled by monoamine neuromodulators. The ability to restrain responding, delay gratification, and wait emerges gradually over the years during which prefrontal lobe development proceeds (Welsh & Pennington, 1988) and monoamine circuitry matures. In developmental disinhibitory psychopathologies such as attention deficit disorder (ADD), conduct disorder, and primary psychopathy, this brain system is defective, though more probably underactivated than undeveloped. The ability to sustain attention in the face of attractive distractors is a closely allied orbitofrontal function that is both a developmental and an individual variable. Correspondingly, inattention to activities that are not intrinsically reinforcing is, with impulsivity, the major hallmark of ADD.

When the relevant circuitry is intact but underactivated, the behavioral deficit is potentially reversible. ADD offers an instructive instance, a deficit of catecholamine production, which can be reversed by use of catecholamine agonist drugs. Unilateral neglect, on the other hand, cannot currently be reversed chemically, but it is amenable to maneuvers that increase right-brain activation level, presumably by activating compensatory mechanisms. Whether these can also be activated chemically remains to be determined.

C. Outward or Self-Focus of Attention

Attention can be directed either outward to the environment or inward as self-focus. Most people attend outwardly most of the time (Duval & Wicklund, 1972), particularly those with extraverted personality. In externalizing or internalizing psychopathology, attending may be unduly external or self-referential, respectively. The individual's self-regulation counteracts fluctuations in internal state by readjusting it toward some reference value (Carver & Scheier, 1981). When the deviations from the reference value are extreme, the requisite internal focus may exclude attention to mundane external problems of living. When internal states are grossly deviant, as perhaps in autism and schizophrenia, the amount of self-focus they elicit may be so great as to cause maladaptive inattention to external change.

Self-focus is necessarily referenced to bodily sensations. Neuropsychological considerations suggest that attention to individual body parts is, like externally directed attention, a vector resultant of the interaction of laterally oriented opponent processors (Kinsbourne, in press-a). Only the lateral extremes of the body (and left much more than right) appear to be subject to selective unawareness (neglect of person).

D. Capacity Limitations

Humans are well known to be limited in maximal rate of information transmission, a limitation that is particularly severe in young children, the mentally retarded, the very elderly, and the demented. Even the normal adult finds it difficult to disengage attention from an existing train of thought or an incorrect solution to a problem. What is the brain basis of this limitation? The issue is usually shelved by appealing to a metaphorical limited resource, an inherently circular concept (Navon, 1984), a hypothetical source of energy that can be carved up in diverse ways by an (equally hypothetical) "resource allocation" mechanism (e.g., Norman & Bobrow, 1975). The subjective sensation of "effort" attaches to a performance in proportion to the resources that it engages (Kahneman, 1973). But no brain-based store for such thought fuel has been discovered. Nor is it strictly the case that a unitary limitation on information transmission exists. When two tasks are combined, in a dual-task paradigm, the extent of the limitation on overall performance depends systematically on *neuropsychological* aspects of the particular tasks that are being combined (Kinsbourne & Hicks, 1978).

The cerebral network itself is the resource. The extent to which a mental operation interferes with a concurrent unrelated task is not only a function of how much network (resource) the task engages, but also where in the network, relative to each other, the "generators" of the functions required for each task are located. The more complex a mental operation is, and the less compatible the mental operations are with innate predispositions, the more of the network will the operations occupy (e.g., Haier et al., 1992), and therefore the more likely there is to be overlap with the territory utilized by a concurrent set of computations. This will be relatively severe if the two mental operations are represented close together in "cerebral functional space" (Kinsbourne, 1981; Kinsbourne & Hicks, 1978), that is, in relatively richly connected areas of cortex. But it can be minimal if the tasks are represented relatively far apart in cerebral functional space.

The depleted cerebral cortex of the demented, and to a lesser extent of the normally aging individual is effectively more connected, to the extent that inhibitory neurons that surround actively computing areas with inhibition to protect them from cross-talk have dropped out. Patients with Alzheimer's disease are disproportionately impaired on tests of divided attention (Nebes & Brady, 1989). Elderly people are notoriously deficient in dual-task performance (Salthouse, Rogan, & Prill, 1984). Inability to exert attentional effort leaves patients in acute confusional states unable to concentrate, because they are at the mercy of the ever-changing flux of salient stimuli ("pathologically riveted to distractors" Mesulam, 1985).

E. Sustained Attention

Failure to sustain attention to signals or to the performance of a task is not necessarily a failure of the neural basis of attending. Thus a patient will fail to sustain attention although directed to do so either if the requisite circuitry is ineffective, or if he is not motivated to comply.

There is clinical evidence for an anteriorly located right-hemisphere system for sustained attention (Whitehead, 1991), and "impersistence" (Fisher, 1956) is a consequence of its impairment. Asked to maintain a posture, such as outstretched arms, the patient quickly flags. Right prefrontal and superior parietal blood flow is activated when normal subjects performed a visual and a tactile vigilance task (Pardo, Fox, & Raichle, 1991). When, in contrast to these simple signal detection tasks, rapidly presented complex signals are analyzed, then the anterior cingulate gyrus is also activated. However, neither neuropsychological nor neuroimaging findings point to dysfunction in these cortical regions in the frequently encountered ADD. Instead, the indications are of bilateral prefrontal underactivation, especially in the orbitofrontal cortex. This localization would fit known facts of brain organization if, in ADD, the machinery of attention is intact, but underused. ADD is therefore presented here as an example of disordered influence of limbic circuitry over attending, rather than of a deficit in attending itself.

II. ATTENTION DEFICIT DISORDER

Though necessary, the participation of right prefrontal and superior parietal cortex is not sufficient to ensure attentive behavior across all situations. Unless the task is inherently attention attracting (novel, enjoyable, immediately rewarded), its sustained performance requires additional support from incentive motivation, with circuitry to be found in the mesolimbic and mesocortical dopaminergic projections, originating in area A10 of the ventral tegmentum (Glowinsky, Tassin, & Thierry, 1984; King, 1986). Spontaneous exploratory behavior depends on the integrity of the ventral tegmentum and can be manipulated by use of dopamine (DA) agonists and DA blockers. Such behavior in animals may correspond to so-called sensation seeking or novelty seeking, and this is thought to depend on reactivity of this midbrain DA system. When resting DA transmission is low, sensation seeking may be at a maximum. Under such circumstances only directly motivating (novel or rewarded) stimuli capture attention, and the individual finds it difficult to resist attractive distractors and to delay gratification. Stimulus salience exerts control on the attention of school-aged ADD children, but not normal children (Kinsbourne, 1990), and ADD children are comparable to younger normal children in this respect (Amin, Douglas, Mendelson, & Dufresne, 1993). When resting DA transmission is temporarily increased by a DA agonist such as dextroamphetamine or methylphenidate, the ADD patient finds it possible to persist in tasks that call for incentive motivation—the ability to work for delayed reward.

The postulate that prefrontal cortex is underactivated in ADD (e.g., Evans, Gualtieri, & Hicks, 1986; Heilman, Voeller, & Nadeau, 1991) relies on behavioral analogies between the effects of prefrontal lesions and ADD symptoms. It finds some support from studies of cerebral metabolism (Lou, Henriksen, & Bruhn, 1984; Zametkin et al., 1990). Neuropsychological testing (Chelune, Ferguson, Koon, & Dickey, 1986; Shue & Douglas, 1992) only weakly and inconstantly uncovers impaired performance on classical tests of dorsolateral prefrontal function (Wisconsin Card Sorting Test, Stroop Test), as would be expected if the dysfunction is primarily mediobasal. The findings are somewhat reliable on tests of response inhibition (Barkley, Grodzinsky, & Du Paul, 1992). But we have found reliable impairments in verbal fluency, a left prefrontal function, both when comparing ADD children with controls and when comparing ADD children on placebo to themselves appropriately medicated. Evidence for prefrontal dysfunction in another disinhibitory psychopathology, conduct disorder, is reviewed by Moffit (1993).

A. Disorders of the Mechanism of Attending

There is no cerebral locus where damage impairs the ability to attend selectively regardless of the nature of the target. Instead, lesions in different locations counteract the selection for attending of particular categories or physical attributes of stimuli. For instance, the cat normally is more attentive to auditory than visual cues when these coincide. After bilateral temporal lobe excisions, which leave auditory acuity intact, the cat now is guided by a visual cue, which prevails over the auditory cue, conditioned to a conflicting response. Correspondingly, children with developmental auditory receptive impairment ("cortical deafness") exhibit striking impairment in selective auditory attention, resulting in widely variable audiometric thresholds.

Unawareness of deficit (anosognosia) has been related to impaired attention to the body part in question. Like deficits in selective attention, anosognosias are specific and do not involve the patient's full set of disabilities. A neglect patient may be aware of hemiplegia and deny hemianopia, or the reverse. He may deny a gross paralysis, but complain of a mild aphasia, or minor joint pains. There is no centralized mechanism for the appreciation of personal malfunction. There are distributed neural systems, and injury to any one of them may result in corresponding anosognosia for the domain of specialization. Lesions that impair material- or location-specific attention injure central networks with the same specialization. This applies particularly to a set of often dramatic syndromes of attention impairment to stimuli in the various modalities as well as movement—but only in a given direction. These are syndromes of unilateral neglect of space and of person.

B. The Lateral Axis in Behavior

Readiness to orient, explore, or act in a particular direction is normally determined by contingencies and plans, but not by the identity of the spatial coordinate. In the bisymmetrical vertebrate nervous system, each half-brain controls contralaterally targeted behavior. A unilateral brain lesion can selectively disturb this ability to distribute attention with roughly equal facility to either side, be it of distal (visual or acoustic) or proximal (touch) or even personal (kinesthetic) space. The data permit a choice between two possibilities. One is that attention, like sensorimotor control, distributes between body halves and between the two sides of egocentric space. The assumption that each hemisphere houses a module that caters to attention within contralateral space, as in the term "hemispatial neglect" (Heilman & Valenstein, 1979), still appears in some texts (Mesulam, 1985). But data from both animal and human neglect studies favor the alternative formulation, that lateral attending is *directionally* organized.

III. NEGLECT IN PERCEPTION

Severe neglect of the left results in failure to observe, explore, and respond to stimuli from the left side of extrapersonal space. The patient's neglect is also object centered; he reads only the extreme right words or letters of a text, eats only from the right side of the plate, regardless of where these displays are located. If the patient ambulates he fails to avoid left-sided obstacles. The patient describes only the right side of imaged scenes (Bisiach & Luzzatti, 1978). Auditorily, the patient displaces the source of a sound rightward (Bisiach, Cornacchia, Sterzi, & Vallar, 1984), retrieves little from the left ear channel in dichotic listening, and tends to forget what is picked up from that side (Heilman, Watson, & Shulman, 1974). In tactile neglect a touch may be referred to the intact (mirror image) body part (allesthesia). In each modality, left neglect is more striking if there is stimulation to the right of the intended target, because attention is actively drawn toward the right extreme of any display (Kinsbourne, 1970b, 1977, 1987). In animal models of neglect this manifests as ipsilesional circling (Wise & Holmes, 1986). Conversely, if the right side of space is featureless, some exploration of the left side becomes possible (Eglin, Robertson, & Knight, 1989). As indexed by bias in line bisection, neglect is minimized if the task is carried out in the dark (Hjaltason & Tegner, 1992), but a bias in exploratory eye movements remains (Hornak, 1992). Many investigations have supported the proposition that attention in visual neglect is not intact ipsilesionally and impaired contralesionally, with a sharp midline discontinuity, but dwindles progressively along a right-to-left gradient (reviewed by Kinsbourne, 1993).

Patients rarely exhibit visual neglect in the upward (Posner, Cohen, & Rafal, 1982) or downward (Butter, Evans, Kirsh, & Newman, 1989; Rapcsak, Cimino, & Heilman, 1988) direction. Physiological studies suggest that vertical movement is programmed by laterally paired control centers, and it may require bisymmetrical lesions of an unusual distribution to result in altitudinal neglect. Altitudinal neglect has not been reported in personal space, and the possibility of neglect in the front–back (ventral–dorsal) axis of the body seems not to have been considered.

Bodily sensation is withdrawn from the left limbs, and notably the left hand, with a gradient of increased ignoring and disowning from shoulder to fingers (Bisiach, Meregalli, & Berti, 1990). The patient fails to complain of the left-sided disability, and denies its existence when confronted with its manifestations. Bizarre distributions centering on the neglected limb are amply documented in the literature (Critchley, 1955; Weinstein & Kahn, 1952). These are resistant to reasoned refutation, even though the patient is thoroughly rational in other respects. This demonstrates the "anisotropic" nature of thought processes. The patient entertains contradictory beliefs, showing that not all thought processes are necessarily able to interact. In other words, their organization in the brain is not isotropic.

A. Neglect in Movement

The pattern with neglect seldom initiates action contralesionally. For this the label disorder of "intention" (Valenstein & Heilman, 1981) is correct but too restrictive, because automatic action in the same direction is also reduced, including movements that are not only unintended but even outside awareness, such as patterns of saccades surveying pictures or print (Ishiai, Furukawa, & Tsukagoshi, 1989). This deficit may be of the same general nature as the perceptual restriction. Preceding a movement the brain projects its expected outcome in a representation (Jeannerod, 1990). If the representation is right-biased, then the movement will be judged to have been accomplished if its outcome conforms to expectation on the right. This may be why neglect patients are unaware of their failure to launch movements contralesionally and claim to have, for instance, moved their left arm when they actually moved the right or neither (a manifestation of *allochiria*). Rizzolatti and Camarda (1987) go further in describing neglect as a modular property intrinsically linked to premotor activity. The correlation between sensory and motor neglect is quite imperfect, however.

Tegner, Levander, and Caneman (1990) so arranged a line-bisection display as to pit the direction of exploratory eye movements against the direction of manual response. Some subjects showed right-biased exploration, though this necessitated leftward hand movement. Some subjects showed the reverse pattern. Some vacillated between the two strategies.

B. Frames of Representation in Neglect

Neglect is usually conceived as implicating viewer-centered representations of the outside world, consistent with rivalry between input projected to each hemisphere. However, if lateral position and visual half field of stimulation are deconfounded by having the patient tilt his head 180°, then neglect of a left-located stimulus can be demonstrated, although perceived and neglected stimuli both enter the same half-field and hemisphere (Calvanio, Petrone, & Levine, 1987; Ladavas, 1987). Bellas, Novelly, Eskenazi, and Wasserstein (1988) were able to elicit olfactory neglect. Although the olfactory tracts differ from all other cranial nerve pathways in being uncrossed, it was input to the left nostril, projecting to the left hemisphere, that was neglected in patients with right parietal disease.

Neglect has also been shown at an object-centered level of representation for the reading of words printed backward. Patients persisted in "backward" (i.e., leftward) word completion, although the substituted letters had been presented on the right (Baxter & Warrington, 1983; Hillis & Caramazza, 1991). The interplay between the two half-brains in the control of lateral attending takes place regardless of hemisphere of stimulus entry, and operates even when the display is abstracted from the physical orientation of its source.

C. Dissociations in Neglect

Individual variation in the relative severity of neglect across modalities and between perception and movement is richly documented. The extrapersonal neglect syndromes also dissociate from the syndromes of bodily neglect (e.g., Guarglia & Antonnucci, 1992). These multiple dissociations contradict the proposition that neglect results from the injury of a particular mechanism or circuit. Instead, the attentional bias reflects a characteristic way in which multiple circuits malfunction when unilaterally lesioned (Kinsbourne, 1974; Rizzolatti & Camarda, 1987). The exact clinical phenotype depends on the particular pattern according to which these circuits are injured in the specific case. One consequence of the variability of neglect phenotypes is frequent discrepancy in the outcomes of particular procedures when they are applied to different patients.

D. Neglect Due to Lateral Hypoactivation

Neglect is far more frequent and more often severe with right-hemisphere damage than with left (Hécaen, 1962). Causative lesions are usually retro-rolandic, involving the inferior parietal lobule, and when subcortical, involve thalamus or basal ganglia (Vallar & Perani, 1987), but there is much variability in whether neglect will result from a lesion in a given location. Only large hemisphere lesions engender clinical neglect. Significant hemisphere hypoactivation appears to distinguish those lesions, cortical or subcortical, that cause neglect from those that do not. Perhaps the cell assemblies that act as opponent processors are multiplexed across wide areas of cortex, and neglect becomes clinically evident only if much of this territory is destroyed. However, neglect has a striking tendency to recover. Perhaps farflung, relatively ineffective representations gain activation over time, analogous to the remarkable short-term effect of a simple activating maneuver: caloric irrigation.

Silberpfennig's (1941) empirical finding that cold irrigation contralesionally or warm irrigation ipsilesionally temporarily restores attentional balance in neglect patients has been verified both for space (Rubens, 1985) and person (Cappa, Sterzi, Vallar, & Bisiach, 1987). Even somatoparaphrenia, the disowning of a body part, temporarily remits (Bisiach, Rusconi, & Vallar, 1991; Rode et al., 1991). Vestibular stimulation enhances cerebral blood flow and therefore cerebral activation (Friberg, Öberg, Roland, Paulsen, & Lassen, 1985). Manipulating the position of the body axis while holding the eyes still also modifies neglect (Karnath, Schenkel, & Fischer 1991) as does optokinetic stimulation (Pizzamiglio, Frasca, Guariglia, Incoccia, & Antonucci, 1990). Restricting sensory stimulation of the intact hemisphere by occluding the contralateral eye (and the prepotent crossed optic pathway) has accelerated neglect recovery in nonhuman primates (Deuel & Collins, 1983) and human patients (Butter & Kirsh, 1992). On theoretical grounds, activating a hemisphere cognitively by imposing a task for which it is specialized (Kinsbourne, 1970a) should manipulate the severity of neglect (Kinsbourne, 1970b) and has been shown to do so (Heilman & Watson, 1978). Cuing maneuvers that direct attention leftward can assist in the performance of particular tasks (Butter, Kirsh, & Reeves, 1990; Riddoch & Humphreys, 1983), but have not been shown to correct the more disabling lack of automatic response toward the left.

A case reported by Costello and Warrington (1987) dramatically illustrated the theory-based prediction that imposing lateralized tasks should induce unilateral hemisphere arousal (Kinsbourne, 1970a). The patient neglected the left when reading, and the right when doing a visuospatial task. Callosally sectioned patients show mild left neglect when the left hemisphere is engaged, and even right neglect when the right hemisphere is engaged (Heilman, Bowers, & Watson, 1984; Kashiwagi, Kashiwagi, Nishikawa, Tanabe, & Okuda, 1990; Plourde & Sperry, 1984). Each hemisphere also completes incomplete figures into contralateral space (C. Trevarthen & M. Kinsbourne, unpublished, cited in Trevarthen, 1974). Unilateral electroshock induces transient left neglect when applied to the right hemisphere, but the reverse was not observed (Altman, Balonov, & Deglin, 1979).

E. Is Neglect a Disorder of Attention or Representation?

Neglect patients exhibit gross limitations in where they attend. They do not look over to the contralesional side or act or react in that direction. Moreover, the tendency of the neglect patient to seek out and fixate the right extreme of a display is an obvious attentional bias.

Other findings are less obviously attentional. Automatic response to left-sided stimulation in left neglect is also deficient. Indeed, volition can to some extent overcome the rightward bias, while the bias remains profound at the automatic level. Premotor covert attentional shifts are also biased (Posner, Walker, Friedrich, & Rafal, 1984).

Neglect occurs even with displays that are so brief as to preclude an attentional shift (Kinsbourne & Warrington, 1962; Warrington, 1962). When forms or words are briefly exposed to intact areas of neglected patients' visual fields, they respond only to right-sided features (and confabulate or "fill-in" the left in disregard of what is actually there). The same occurs in visual imagery as in visual stimulation; the patient images and reports only right-sided features (Bisiach & Luzzatti, 1978; Bisiach, Luzzatti, & Perani, 1979). Even hallucinations are limited to the intact visual field in neglect patients. To accommodate such findings within an attentional framework one must locate the attentional problem at the level of representation, not only at the level of overt behavior.

A modularity theorist might suppose that each hemisphere houses a module for contralateral hemispatial attention. In neglect, one module attending within opposite hemispace is disabled. The preponderance of left neglect would be due to disconnection of input that impinges on the right hemisphere from the left-sided language centers (Geschwind, 1965). But neglect is demonstrable within both hemispaces, the left side of the stimulus being neglected regardless of its location relative to the midline. Each module therefore would have to be responsible for the awareness of one side of any display, regardless of where it is located within the visual field, a curiously post hoc idea.

If one discards paired noninteractive modules but retains hierarchical brain organization, one could posit a bias in the sweep of inner "eye" that scans the passively represented input for attentional purposes (Kosslyn, 1980). The input itself, or the image, is fully represented, but the inner monitor sweeps only to one side, just as receptor orientation to external objects is laterally biased. But such a monitor must itself be guided by a model, and how is that model monitored? An infinite regress is avoided if one discards the distinction between the attending monitor and the attended representation, using the alternative parallel brain model and the concept of a self-organizing network.

If selective attending is implemented by enhancing the activation of the chosen representation, then neglect teaches us that the two half-brains activate the cell assemblies that represent stimuli disposed along the lateral plane in a complementary fashion. Each hemisphere contributes activation to that part of the representation that is induced by contralateral segments of the stimulus. By graduated change in this dynamic interaction, the normal individual can attend selectively to either side or any intermediate part of a thing at will. In neglect the component of the cell assembly that represents the contralesional section of the stimulus is underactivated. Contralesional contents is therefore not experienced and does not trigger action.

When a section of a familiar shape is missing at its contralesional extreme, there is nothing in awareness that signals its absence. In the absence of contradictory information, the shape is perceived as an intact whole, the objectively missing portion being "imaginatively completed" (e.g., Kinsbourne & Warrington, 1962). The contralesional extremity of the input is the loser when representations compete for the control of behavior. The percept is formed by interaction between ipsilesional information and expectancy. There is indeed an abnormality of representation in unilateral neglect, namely one that interferes with the means by which we selectively attend.

IV. REPRESENTATIONS AND CONSCIOUSNESS

External change induces correlated patterned neural activity, qualified by the traces of prior experience and by prevailing internal states. This activity is said to "represent" the external change, though for the brain it does not represent the corresponding experience, it *is* that experience. The level of activation of the cell assemblies that do the representing determines the probability that their contents will be included in awareness (Kinsbourne, in press-b), as well as the probability that these contents will be the topic of ongoing responding. When one is conscious of a stimulus and responds to it, it is not to be assumed that the awareness is a condition of the response, or even that the awareness precedes the response in time (Velmans, 1991). Rather, the awareness and the behavior independently reflect the prevailing brain state: The response, (third person), what the brain state causes, and the experience, (first person), what it is like for a brain to be in that state. In disordered attention, awareness and behavior both suffer, but they do so in parallel rather than through a casual sequence.

V. CONCLUSIONS

Brain-based disorders of attention distort the individual's ability to select percepts, images, memories, or actions. Representations of a given category, or a given location, suffer a competitive disadvantage, or specific eliciting and sustaining variables, such as motivation and reinforcement history, lose efficacy. The patient thus makes selections that, though maladaptive, are constrained by the brain dysfunction.

References

Allport, A. (1989). Visual attention. In M. I. Posner (Ed.), *Foundations of cognitive science* (pp. 631–682). Cambridge, MA: MIT Press.

Altman, J. A., Balonov, I. J., & Deglin, V. L. (1979). Effects of unilateral disorder of the brain hemisphere function in man on directional hearing. *Neuropsychologia, 17,* 295–301.

Amin, K., Douglas, V. I., Mendelson, M. J., & Dufresne, J. (1993). Separable/integral classification by hyperactive and normal children. *Development and Psychopathology, 5,* 415–431.

Barkley, R. A., Grodzinsky, G., & Du Paul, G. J. (1992). Frontal lobe function in attention deficit disorder with or without hyperactivity: A review and research report. *Journal of Abnormal Child Psychology, 20,* 163–188.

Baxter, D. M., & Warrington, E. K. (1983). Neglect dysgraphia. *Journal of Neurology, Neurosurgery and Psychiatry, 46,* 1073–1078.

Bellas, D. N., Novelly, R. A., Eskenazi, & Wasserstein, J. (1988). The nature of unilateral neglect in the olfactory sensory system. *Neuropsychologia, 26,* 45–52.

Bernston, G. G., & Torello, M. W. (1977). Expression of Magnus tonic neck reflexes in distal muscles of prehension in normal adults. *Physiology and Behavior, 19,* 585–587.

Bisiach, E., Cornacchia, L., Sterzi, R., & Valler, G. (1984). Disorders of perceived auditory lateralization after lesions of the right hemisphere. *Brain, 107,* 37–52.

Bisiach, E., & Luzzatti, C. (1978). Unilateral neglect of representational space. *Cortex, 14,* 129–133.

Bisiach, E., Luzzatti, C., & Perani, D. (1979). Unilateral neglect, representational schema and consciousness. *Brain, 102,* 609–618.

Bisiach, E., Meregalli, S., & Berti, A. (1990). Mechanisms of production control and belief fixation in human visuospatial processing: Clinical evidence from unilateral neglect and misrepresentation. In M. L. Commons, R. J. Herrnstein, S. M. Kosslyn, & D. B. Mumford (Eds.), *Models of behavior: Computational and clinical approaches to pattern recognition and concept formation* (pp. 3–21). Hillsdale, NJ: Erlbaum.

Bisiach, E., Rusconi, M. L., & Vallar, G. (1991). Remission of somatoparaphrenic delusion through vestibular stimulation. *Neuropsychologia, 29,* 1029–1031.

Butter, C. M., Evans, J., Kirsh, N., & Newman, D. (1989). Altitudinal neglect following traumatic brain injury: A case report. *Cortex, 25,* 135–146.

Butter, C. M., & Kirsh, N. (1992). Combined and separate effects of eye patching and visual stimulation on unilateral neglect following stroke. *Archives of Physical and Medical Rehabilitation, 73,* 1133–1139.

Butter, C. M., Kirsh, N., & Reeves, G. (1990). The effect of lateralized dynamic stimuli on unilateral spatial neglect following right hemisphere lesions. *Restorative Neurology and Neuroscience, 2,* 39–46.

Calvanio, R., Petrone, P. N., & Levine, D. N. (1987). Left visual spatial neglect is both environment-centered and body-centered. *Neurology, 37,* 1179–1183.

Caplan, P. J., & Kinsbourne, M. (1976). Baby drops the rattle: Asymmetry of duration of grasp by infants. *Child Development, 47,* 532–536.

Cappa, S., Sterzi, R., Vallar, G., & Bisiach, E. (1987). Remission of hemineglect and anosognosia during vestibular stimulation. *Neuropsychologia, 25,* 775–782.

Carver, C. S., & Scheier, M. F. (1981). *Attention and self-regulation: A control theory approach to human behavior.* New York: Springer-Verlag.

Case, R., Kurkland, M., & Goldberg, J. (1982). Operational efficiency and the growth of short term memory. *Journal of Experimental Child Psychology, 33,* 386–404.

Chelune, C. J., Ferguson, W., Koon, R., & Dickey, T. O. (1986). Frontal lobe disinhibition in attention deficit disorder. *Child Psychiatry and Human Development, 16,* 221–234.

Costello, A., & Warrington, E. K. (1987). The dissociation of visual neglect and neglect dyslexia. *Journal of Neurology, Neurosurgery and Psychiatry, 50,* 1110–1116.

Crick, F., & Koch, C. (1990). Towards a neurobiological theory of consciousness. *Seminars in the Neurosciences, 2,* 263–275.

Critchley, M. (1955). Personification of paralyzed limbs in hemiplegics. *British Medical Journal, 30,* 284.

Dennett, D. C., & Kinsbourne, M. (1992). Time and the observer: the where and when of consciousness in the brain. *Behavioral and Brain Sciences, 15,* 183–247.

Deuel, R. K., & Collins, R. C. (1983). Recovery from unilateral neglect. *Experimental Neurology, 81,* 733–748.

Duval, S., & Wicklund, R. A. (1972). *A theory of objective self-awareness.* New York: Academic Press.

Eglin, M., Robertson, L. C., & Knight, R. T. (1989). Visual search performance in the neglect syndrome. *Journal of Cognitive Neuroscience, 1,* 372–385.

Evans, R. W., Gualtieri, C. T., & Hicks, R. E. (1986). A neuropathic substrate for stimulant drug effects in hyperactive children. *Clinical Neuropharmacology, 9*(3), 264–281.

Fisher, M. (1956). Left hemiplegia and motor impersistence. *Journal of Nervous and Mental Disorders, 123,* 201–218.

Freeman, W. J. (1991). Insights into processes of visual perception from studies in the olfactory system. In L. R. Squire, N. M. Weinberger, G. Lynch, & J. L. McGaugh (Eds.), *Memory: Organization and locus of change* (pp. 35–48). New York: Oxford University Press.

Friberg, L., Öberg, T. S., Roland, P. E., Paulsen, O. B., & Lassen, N. A. (1985). Focal increase of blood flow in the cerebral cortex of man during vestibular stimulation. *Brain, 108,* 609–623.

Fuster, J. M. (1989). *The prefrontal cortex.* New York: Raven Press.

Geschwind, N. (1965). Disconnexion syndromes in animals and man. *Brain, 88,* 585–644.

Gesell, A. (1938). The tonic neck reflex in the human infant. *Journal of Pediatrics, 13,* 455–464.

Gibson, E. J. (1969). *Principles of perceptual learning and development.* New York: Appleton-Century-Crofts.

Glowinsky, J., Tassin, J. P., & Thierry, A. M. (1984). The mescocortical-prefrontal dopaminergic neurons. *Trends in Neuroscience, 9,* 415–418.

Gray, J. A. (1982). *The neuropsychology of anxiety.* New York: Oxford University Press.

Guarglia, C., & Antonnucci, G. (1992). Personal and extrapersonal space: A case of neglect dissociation. *Neuropsychologia, 30,* 1001–1009.

Haier, R. J., Siegel, B. V., MacLachlan, A., Soderling, E., Lottenberg, S., & Buchsbaum, M. S. (1992). Regional glucose metabolic changes after learning a complex visuospatial/motor task: A positron emission tomographic study. *Brain Research, 570,* 134–143.

Hawn, P. R., & Harris, L. J. (1983). Hand differences in grasp duration and reaching in two- and five-months old infants. In G. Young, S. J. Segalowitz, C. M. Carter, & S. E. Trehub (Eds.), *Manual specialization and the developing brain* (pp. 331–348). New York: Academic Press.

Hécaen, H. (1962). Clinical symptomatology on right and left hemisphere lesions. In V. B. Mountcastle (Ed.), *Interhemispheric relations and cerebral dominance* (pp. 215–243). Baltimore, MD: Johns Hopkins University Press.

Heilman, K. M., Bowers, D., & Watson, R. T. (1984). Pseudoneglect in a patient with partial callosal disconnection. *Brain, 107,* 519–532.

Heilman, K. M., & Valenstein, E. (1979). Mechanisms underlying hemispatial neglect. *Annals of Neurology, 5,* 166–170.

Heilman, K. M., Voeller, K.K.S., & Nadeau, S. E. (1991). A possible pathophysiological substrate of attention deficit-hyperactivity disorder. *Journal of Child Neurology, 6,* 576–581.

Heilman, K. M., & Watson, R. T. (1978). Changes in the symptoms of neglect induced by changes in task strategy. *Archives of Neurology (Chicago), 35,* 47–49.

Heilman, K. M., Watson, R. T., & Schulman, H. M. (1974). A unilateral memory defect. *Journal of Neurology, Neurosurgery and Psychiatry, 37,* 790–793.

Hillis, A. E., & Caramazza, A. (1991). Deficit to stimulus-centered letter shape representations in a case of "unilateral neglect." *Neuropsychologia, 29,* 1223–1240.

Hjaltason, H., & Tegner, R. (1992). Darkness improves line bisection in unilateral spatial neglect. *Cortex, 28,* 353–358.

Hornak, J. (1992). Ocular exploration in the dark by patients with visual neglect. *Neuropsychologia, 30,* 547–552.

Ishiai, S., Furukawa, T., & Tsukagoshi, H. (1989). Visuospatial processes of line bisection and the mechanism underlying unilateral spatial neglect. *Brain, 112,* 1485–1502.

Jeannerod, M. (1990). The representation of the goal of an act and its role in the control of goal-directed movements. In E. L. Schwartz (Ed.), *Computational neuroscience* (pp. 352–368). Cambridge, MA: MIT Press.

Kahneman, D. (1973). *Attention and effort.* Englewood Cliffs, NJ: Prentice-Hall.

Karnath, H. O., Schenkel, P., & Fischer, B. (1991). Trunk orientation as the determining factor of the "contralateral" deficit in the neglect syndrome and as the physical anchor of the internal representation of body orientation in space. *Brain, 114,* 1997–2014.

Kashiwagi, A., Kashiwagi, T., Nishikawa, T., Tanabe, H., & Okuda, J. (1990). Hemispatial neglect in a patient with callosal infarction. *Brain, 113,* 1005–1023.

King, R. (1986). Motivational diversity and mesolimbic dopamine: A hypothesis concerning temperament. *Emotion: Theory, Research and Experience, 3,* 363–380.

Kinsbourne, M. (1970a). The cerebral basis of lateral asymmetries in attention. *Acta Psychologica, 33,* 193–201.

Kinsbourne, M. (1970b). A model for the mechanism of unilateral neglect of space. *Transactions of the American Neurological Association, 95,* 143–145.

Kinsbourne, M. (1974). Lateral interactions in the brain. In M. Kinsbourne & W. L. Smith (Eds.), *Hemispheric disconnection and cerebral function* (pp. 239–259). Springfield, IL: Thomas.

Kinsbourne, M. (1977). Hemineglect and hemisphere rivalry. In E. A. Weinstein & R. A. Friedland (Eds.), *Hemi-inattention and hemisphere specialization* (pp. 41–49). New York: Raven Press.

Kinsbourne, M. (1981). Single-channel theory. In D. H. Holding (Ed.), *Human skills* (pp. 65–89). Chichester, Sussex: Wiley.

Kinsbourne, M. (1982). Hemispheric specialization and the growth of human understanding. *American Psychologist, 37,* 411–420.

Kinsbourne, M. (1987). Mechanisms of unilateral neglect. In M. Jeannerod (Ed.), *Neuro-

physiological and neuropsychological aspects of spatial neglect (pp. 69–86). Amsterdam: North-Holland Publ.

Kinsbourne, M. (1988). Integrated field theory of consciousness. In A. J. Marcel & E. Bisiach (Eds.), *Consciousness in contemporary science* (pp. 239–256). Oxford: Oxford University Press.

Kinsbourne, M. (1990). Testing models for attention deficit-hyperactivity disorder in the behavioral laboratory. In M. Kinsbourne & C. K. Conners (Eds.), *Diagnosis and treatment of attention deficit disorders* (pp. 51–70). Munich: MMW Press.

Kinsbourne, M. (1993). Orientational bias model of unilateral neglect: Evidence from attentional gradients within hemispace. In I. H. Robertson & J. C. Marshall (Eds.), *Unilateral neglect: Clinical and experimental studies.* New York: Erlbaum.

Kinsbourne, M. (in press-a). Awareness of one's own body: A neuropsychological hypothesis. In J. Bermudez, A. J. Marcel, & N. Eilan (Eds.), *The body and the self.* Cambridge: Bradford Books/MIT Press.

Kinsbourne, M. (in press-b). What qualifies a representation for a role in consciousness? In J. D. Cohen & J. W. Schooler (Eds.), *Scientific approaches to the question of consciousness.* Hillsdale, NJ: Erlbaum.

Kinsbourne, M., & Hicks, R. E. (1978). Functional cerebral space: A model for overflow, transfer and interference effects in human performance. In J. Requin (Ed.), *Attention and performance VII* (pp. 345–362). Hillsdale, NJ: Erlbaum.

Kinsbourne, M., & Warrington, E. K. (1962). A variety of reading disability associated with right hemisphere lesions. *Journal of Neurology, Neurosurgery and Psychiatry, 25,* 334–339.

Kosslyn, S. M. (1980). *Image and mind.* Cambridge, MA: Harvard University Press.

Kupferman, I. (1993). The generation of motor patterns. *Current Directions in Psychological Research, 4,* 126–129.

Ladavas, E. (1987). Is the hemispatial deficit produced by right parietal lobe damage associated with retinal or gravitational coordinates? *Brain, 110,* 167–180.

Lhermitte, F. (1983). Utilization behavior and its relation to lesions of the frontal lobes. *Brain, 106,* 237–255.

Liederman, J., & Kinsbourne, M. (1980). Rightward motor bias of newborns depends on parental right-handedness. *Neuropsychologia, 18,* 579–584.

Lou, H. C., Henriksen, L., & Bruhn, P. (1984). Focal cerebral hypoperfusion in children with dysphasia and/or attention deficit disorder. *Archives of Neurology (Chicago), 41,* 825–892.

Mesulam, M.-M. (1985). Attention, confusional states and neglect. In M.-M. Mesulam (Ed.), *Principles of behavioral neurology* (pp. 125–168). Philadelphia: Davis.

Moffit, T. (1993). The neuropsychology of conduct disorder. *Development and Psychopathology, 5,* 135–151.

Navon, D. (1984). Resources—a theoretical soup stone? *Psychological Review, 91,* 216–234.

Nebes, R. D., & Brady, C. B. (1989). Focused and divided attention in Alzheimer's disease. *Cortex, 25,* 305–315.

Norman, D. A., & Bobrow, D. G. (1975). On data-limited and resource-limited processes. *Cognitive Psychology, 7,* 44–64.

Norman, D. A., & Shallice, T. (1985). Attention to action: Willed and automatic control of behavior. In R. J. Davidson, G. E. Schwartz, & D. Shapiro (Eds.), *Consciousness and self-regulation:* Advances in research and theory (Vol. 4, pp. 1–18). New York: Plenum.

Pardo, J. V., Fox, P. T., & Raichle, M. E. (1991). Localization of a human system for sustained attention by positron emission tomography. *Nature (London), 349,* 61–64.

Pizzamiglio, L., Frasca, R., Guariglia, C., Incoccia, C., & Antonucci, G. (1990). Effect of optokinetic stimulation in patients with visual neglect. *Cortex, 26,* 535–540.

Plourde, G., & Sperry, R. W. (1984). Left hemisphere involvement in left spatial neglect from right-sided lesion-a commissurotomy study. *Brain, 107,* 95–106.

Posner, M. I., Cohen, Y., & Rafal, R. D. (1982). Neural systems control of spatial orienting. *Philosophical Transactions of the Royal Society of London. Series B, 298,* 187–198.

Posner, M. I., Walker, J. A., Friedrich, F. J., & Rafal, R. D. (1984). Effects of parietal injury on covert orienting of attention. *Journal of Neuroscience, 7,* 1863–1874.

Rapcsak, S. Z., Cimino, C. R., & Heilman, K. M. (1988). Altitudinal neglect. *Neurology, 38,* 277–281.

Riddoch, M. J., & Humphrey, G. (1983). The effect of cueing on unilateral neglect. *Neuropsychologia, 21,* 589–599.

Rizzolatti, G., & Camarda, R. (1987). Neural circuits for spatial attention and unilateral neglect. In M. Jeannerod (Ed.), *Neurophysiological and neuropsychological aspects of spatial neglect* (pp. 289–314). Amsterdam: North-Holland Publ.

Rode, G., Charles, N., Perenin, M. T., Vighetto, A., Trillet, M., & Aimond, G. (1991). Partial remission of hemiplegia and somatoparaphrenia through vestibular stimulation in a case of unilateral neglect. *Cortex, 28,* 203–208.

Rubens, A. B. (1985). Caloric stimulation and unilateral neglect. *Neurology, 35,* 1019–1024.

Salthouse, T. A., Rogan, J. D., & Prill, K. (1984). Division of attention: Age differences on a visually presented memory test. *Memory & Cognition, 12,* 613–620.

Shue, K. L., & Douglas, V. I. (1992). Attention deficit hyperactivity disorder and the frontal lobe syndrome. *Brain and Cognition, 20,* 104–124.

Silberpfennig, J. (1941). Contributions to the problem of eye movements. III. Disturbances of ocular movements with pseudohemianopsia in frontal tumors. *Confinia Neurologica, 4,* 1–13.

Stein, B. E., & Meredith, M. A. (1993). *The merging of the senses.* Cambridge, MA: MIT Press.

Stuss, D. T., & Benson, D. F. (1986). *The frontal lobes.* New York: Raven Press.

Tegner, R., Levander, M., & Caneman, G. (1990). Apparent right neglect in patients with left visual neglect. *Cortex, 26,* 455–458.

Trevarthen, C. (1974). Functional relations of disconnected hemispheres with the brain stem, and with each other: Monkey and man. In M. Kinsbourne & W. L. Smith (Eds.), *Hemisphere disconnection and cerebral function* (pp. 187–207). Springfield, IL: Thomas.

Turkewitz, G. (1987). Psychobiology and developmental psychology: The influence of C. Schneirla on human developmental psychology. *Developmental Psychology, 20,* 369–375.

Valenstein, E., & Heilman, K. M. (1981). Unilateral hypokinesia and motor extinction. *Neurology, 31,* 445–448.

Vallar, G., & Perani, D. (1987). The anatomy of spatial neglect in humans. In M. Jeannerod (Ed.), *Neurophysiological and neuropsychological aspects of spatial neglect* (pp. 235–258). Amsterdam: North-Holland Publ.

Velmans, M. (1991). Is human information processing conscious? *Behavioral and Brain Sciences, 14,* 651–726.

Viviani, J., Turkewitz, G., & Karp, E. (1978). A relationship between laterality of functioning at 2 days and at 7 years of age. *Psychonomic Science, 12,* 189–192.

Vurpillot, E. (1968). The development of scanning strategies and their relation to visual differentiation. *Journal of Experimental Child Psychology, 6,* 632–650.

Warrington, E. K. (1962). Completion of visual forms across hemianopic field defects. *Journal of Neurology, Neurosurgery and Psychiatry, 25,* 208–217.

Weinstein, E. A., & Kahn, R. L. (1952). *Denial of illness.* Springfield, IL: Thomas.

Welsh, M. C., & Pennington, B. F. (1988). Assessing frontal lobe functioning in children: Views from developmental psychology. *Developmental Neuropsychology, 4,* 199–230.

CHAPTER 6

Brain and Language

Harry A. Whitaker
Helen J. Kahn

About 5000 years ago, physicians to the Egyptian pharaohs of the Old Kingdom compiled an epitome that represented the medical knowledge of the period. Among the maladies which could not be treated by liniments, ointments, or prosthetic devices was the loss of speech that followed severe skull fractures of the temporal bone. A cuneiform tablet dating from about the sixteenth century B.C. describes the expressive aphasia of the Hittite King Mursilis, following an apoplectic attack that probably was a stroke. The observations continued to accumulate through the Greek, Roman, and Christian eras, although hardly in any systematic form. An interesting seventeenth century compilation of early aphasia cases is found in Wepfer (1690). The eighteenth century Swedish naturalist Carl Linnaeus accurately described anomia following brain damage. By the beginning of the nineteenth century, although there was no real knowledge of the functional neuroanatomy of the brain, it was well understood that various brain injuries or diseases may cause expressive or receptive language disorders, isolated impairments of reading or writing, or in polyglots, the loss of one language but not others (Benton & Joynt, 1960). It was not until the end of the nineteenth century however that a coherent model of the brain organization of language had emerged from research in neurology and psychology.

The relationship between brain and language continues to dominate neuroscience, as has been the case since the latter half of the nineteenth century.

Neuropsychology

For example, the cover of the third and latest edition of the most successful contemporary text in neuroscience, Kandel, Schwartz, and Jessell's, *Principles of Neural Science,* (1991), shows a positron emission tomography (PET) scan image of "three areas in the left brain that are metabolically active during a language task" (p. 3). The picture of an iridescent blue skull and brain showing three superimposed bright yellow spots that mark the active language sites is certainly quite captivating, much as was Pierre Paul Broca's demonstration in 1861 of the lesion in the left posterior frontal lobe that had rendered his patient "Tan" unable to speak (Broca, 1861a,b). The first issue of the new journal, *Human Brain Mapping,* launched in 1993, contains six articles, three of which focus on functional maps of language processes. Several journals are presently devoted exclusively to the subject of brain and language relations: *Brain and Language,* the *Journal of Neurolinguistics,* and *Aphasiology;* dozens of other journals in linguistics, psychology, and medicine carry articles on brain and language in almost every issue. There are, of course, many books on the subject, among the more useful contemporary ones are by Caplan (1987, 1992), Coltheart, Sartori, and Job (1987), von Euler, Lundberg, and Lennerstrand (1989), Galaburda (1989), Grodzinsky (1990), Howard and Franklin (1988), and Plum (1988).

I. BRAIN AND LANGUAGE SYSTEMS: THE CLASSICAL MODEL

Living organisms of the same species tend not to be identical, which means, in the simplest terms, that biological classification is a statistical enterprise; for that reason, the relationships between human language and human brain are plural. It appears that they are also quite complex, although it is reasonably accurate to conclude that for the majority of adult human beings, most of the necessary and probably all of the sufficient neural substrates for language are to be found in the left hemisphere. The typically asymmetric distribution of language functions in the brain is perhaps the most important component of the concept of hemispheric dominance or specialization. However, the lateralization of language seems to be neither consistent nor unidirectional across different linguistic levels, and much of the evidence is, to say the least, controversial. Some valuable contemporary treatments of the lateralization problem may be found in Segalowitz (1983), Hellige (1993), and Efron (1990). Although the evidence to support the asymmetric distribution of language functions in the brain is not easily subsumed under a single model of laterality, it is virtually certain that language is differentially distributed in the left and right hemispheres in any person, and thus the minimum criterion for localization is met: some components of language are "in" some parts of the brain and not "in" others. Thus, we are confident that language functions are lateralized and from this we logically conclude that they are localized as well. The evidence also strongly suggests that language functions are differentially distributed within their proper hemisphere, usually the left. Goodglass and Kaplan (1983) observed that "distinct configurations of language abnormality keep recurring, each in conjunction with a lesion of a different zone in the peri-Sylvian region of the left hemisphere" (p. 74), which is to say that the accumulated evidence over the past 130+ years unequivocally points to a statistical correlation between certain syndromes of aphasia and lesions of certain geographic areas in the left hemisphere. For general clinical purposes, as well as to provide a first generalization about the human brain, we speak of Broca's area and Broca's aphasia, or Wernicke's area and Wernicke's aphasia, or the arcuate fasciculus and conduction aphasia and similar links. Although there are limits to these generalities as well as certain questions about how one incorporates them into experimental research designs, a brief review of the classical aphasia taxonomy is a useful introduction to modern studies of the neuropsychology of language (i.e. neurolinguistics).

A. Core Syndromes

Broca's aphasia refers to a complex of language disorders that fall under the rubric of language output or production problems. Other terms used in the past for a very similar symptom–complex have been (efferent) motor aphasia, expressive aphasia, or verbal aphasia (Goodglass & Kaplan, 1983). The several lesions frequently associated with Broca's aphasia are in the left posterior inferior frontal lobe (Broca's area), the inferior anterior parietal lobe above the Sylvian fissure, the insula and the white matter deep to those three cortical regions. Lesions producing Broca's aphasia are typically fairly large. The impairments in language functions that identify an aphasic syndrome differ somewhat according to the test battery being employed; thus the *Western Aphasia Battery* (Kertesz, 1982), does not always agree with the *Boston Diagnostic Aphasia Examination* (BDAE) (Goodglass & Kaplan, 1983), nor do these two with others. Nonetheless, one usually recognizes a selection of the following language impairments as part and parcel of the syndrome of Broca's aphasia: effortful (nonfluent) speech production, short phrases with pauses in between, sound segment errors of repetition or ordering or omission or addition, errors of syntax (grammar) as in the omission of function words, written language similar to spoken language, relatively better preserved comprehension and reading ability, difficulty with word-finding or naming (anomia), and a self-awareness of the aphasic impairment. The typical interpretation is that large, more anterior lesions will compromise language production more than comprehension systems, an interpretation which in gross measure corresponds to interpreting left hemisphere posterior inferior frontal and anterior inferior parietal brain as the most probable cortical language output sites.

Wernicke's aphasia is in some respects opposite to Broca's aphasia, in that it is a complex of language impairments related mostly to input or the reception of language. Previously used terms for similar impairments are syntactic aphasia, receptive aphasia, sensory aphasia, or acoustic aphasia. The characteristic left-hemisphere sites in which fairly large lesions give rise to Wernicke's aphasia extend from the superior and middle temporal lobe back to the occipital lobe and inferior parietal-temporal lobe in the vicinity of the supramarginal and angular gyri. A selection of the following language impairments would likely lead to a diagnosis of Wernicke's aphasia: fluent speech output with relatively long phrases, the substitution of one word for another or one sound for another (paraphasias), the appearance of neologisms or jargon aphasia, impaired auditory comprehension of speech, and, frequently, impaired reading as well, impaired word-finding or naming, grammatical or syntactic errors often resulting from improper use of or addition of extraneous function words, and, in distinct contrast to the expressive aphasias, an unawareness of aphasic deficit.

Conduction aphasia is, conceptually, a simpler form of aphasia; its primary distinguishing characteristic is an impairment in repetition out of proportion to the relatively preserved comprehension of language and relatively preserved fluency of output. There may be various other language impairments accompanying the repetition impairment, such as errors in the sound segments, agrammatism, or anomia. Although many authors use the term conduction aphasia, the syndrome has also been referred to as central aphasia and as afferent motor aphasia. In keeping with the classical model's notion that information flow moves from the temporal lobe to the frontal through the arcuate fasciculus, which is a fiber tract that connects the two lobes, lesions to the arcuate fasciculus were thought to be responsible for conduction aphasia.

In the classical literature the core aphasic syndromes, Broca's, Wernicke's, and conduction aphasia reflected the then-prevailing view point that the essential language cortex was peri-Sylvian. The fourth core syndrome, anomia, known also as nominal aphasia, semantic aphasia, or amnesic aphasia, differs in one very significant way from all other classical syndromes: no specific localization was proposed. On the contrary, anomia was thought to arise from any changes to any language cortex, whether from a small lesion or a distortion caused by a space-occupying lesion elsewhere or from some other alteration in structure or physiology. Anomia is characterized by the prominence of word-finding difficulties, out of all proportion to other language deficits; reading and writing may be variably preserved but auditory comprehension is usually good and the anomic aphasic patient is usually quite fluent. A fifth classical core syndrome, alexia with agraphia, follows from a lesion in the angular gyrus, which is located just posterior to the supramarginal gyrus. The angular gyrus bridges temporal, occipital, and parietal language cortices, an anatomic convergence that was thought to be the substrate for the multivalent nature of reading and writing (i.e., visual, tactile, and acoustic input coupled to both articulatory and gestural output) (Geschwind, 1965). Although an isolated problem with reading and writing with relatively well-preserved speech and hearing was rare, it had been described following lesions to the angular gyrus. More typical for posterior cortical lesions, speech and hearing are affected, usually in the form of a mild to moderate anomia (Goodglass & Kaplan, 1983).

B. Transcortical Aphasias

An interesting class of syndromes was based upon the notion that one could disconnect the peri-Sylvian language region from the brain centers for other cognitive processes as well as from the peripheral motor and sensory systems (Geschwind, 1965); the idea of the preservation of the speech–language core led to the construction of the concept of the transcortical aphasias. The term transcortical was intended to suggest that the faculty of repetition requires use of all three cortical regions of the language core, namely the temporo-parieto-frontal cortex that surrounds the fissure of Sylvius.

Transcortical sensory aphasia was attributed to the isolation of the posterior speech area from the rest of brain (Goodglass & Kaplan, 1983) having the effect of creating a variant of Wernicke's aphasia in which repetition is strikingly preserved, in fact, often so well preserved that the patient may repeat long and complex sentences without understanding them. There is typically a fluent, often paraphasic speech, an anomia, and usually an echolalia. The effect of the presumed disconnection was explained thus: "The isolation of this portion of the speech system, however, prevents any interaction between the knowledge, intention and the perceptions of the rest of the brain and those of the isolated speech mechanism" (Goodglass & Kaplan, 1983, p. 91). The location of the lesion responsible for transcortical sensory aphasia has always been in contention with some looking to an inferior posterior temporal lesion and others finding, surprisingly, a mesial posterior temporal and mesial occipital lesion.

On the other hand, transcortical motor aphasia, also known as dynamic aphasia, arose from a disconnection at the front-end of the speech area, which had the effect of separating speech processing from the brain mechanisms of initiation of action. Patients with transcortical motor aphasia find it difficult to start talking but once started were relatively intact. The lesion site was variously ascribed to the mesial face of the anterior left frontal lobe, in the region of the supplementary motor cortex, or to lesions along the lateral aspect of the left frontal lobe. As in transcortical sensory aphasia, repetition is intact; the main problem is one of initiating speech and in "organizing responses in conversation" (Goodglass & Kaplan, 1983, p. 94), although seriatim speech and naming (e.g., numbers, days of the week, etc.) is intact. There is little anomia and the patient usually responds to prompting. A third transcortical syndrome had been identified: on rare occasions, the peri-Sylvian speech areas may be totally isolated, front and back, a situation that occasionally results from the degenerative processes associated with Pick's Disease or from lesions associated with carbon monoxide poisoning; in either event, the outcome is referred to as mixed transcortical aphasia (or, the "isolation of the speech area") in which a quasi-automatic repetition and echolalia are most prominent in a framework of few other intact language functions except for preserved articulatory fluency (H. Whitaker, 1976).

C. Other Disconnection Syndromes

In pure word deafness (auditory agnosia) the auditory comprehension of language is lost, although the ability to hear other sounds is relatively intact. Speech output, reading, and writing are relatively unaffected. The causative lesion destroys the primary auditory cortex (Heschl's gyrus) in the dominant hemisphere and the subcortical input fibers beneath Heschl's gyrus that would have brought information in from the auditory association areas of the non-dominant right hemisphere into Wernicke's area; this lesion leaves much of the superior and middle temporal lobe intact (Wernicke's area) with the result that the patient cannot recognize speech sounds as speech nor repeat them, but otherwise does not exhibit the symptoms of a Wernicke's aphasia. Pure alexia is an analogous disconnection, but in this case the lesion destroys the dominant hemisphere's visual association cortex and as well the callosal fibers that bring information in from the right or non-dominant visual association areas; the effect is that visual stimuli are not recognized as words, though they can be seen. In principle, there are output disconnection syndromes, too. For example, aphemia, also known as sub-cortical motor aphasia, is described as an isolated disorder of articulation in which auditory comprehension, reading, and writing remain intact, and pure agraphia is an isolated disorder of writing where the other language functions remain intact.

From the foregoing it is clear that the classical model of language and brain relationships is grounded in an anatomical concept of a core speech–language system surrounding the fissure of Sylvius and consisting of at least four centers: the superior-posterior temporal lobe (Wernicke's area), the supramarginal gyrus with surrounding cortex, the angular gyrus, and the inferior-posterior frontal lobe (Broca's area). The four centers are connected by pathways between them as well as pathways to the periphery. Although not clearly neuroanatomically specified, the core speech–language system also interfaces with surrounding cortex in which higher level cognitive processes are found. Lesions in specific parts of this core, according to the classical model, caused specific syndromes; lesions that disconnect the core from other brain areas leave the core functions intact while affecting either more peripheral or more high-level central language functions.

II. MODERN NEUROLINGUISTICS: A DEPARTURE FROM THE CLASSICAL MODEL

Since the 1960s, research in neurolinguistics has veritably bloomed. The classical model, with its syndrome localization referred to above, survived these new research efforts fairly well into the 1970s, but much less so to the present time. Several lines of research development contributed to its de facto demise. One challenge came from the increasing use of linguistics in the analyses of aphasia, originally introduced by Henry Hécaen, Alexander Luria, Harold Goodglass, John Marshall, Harry Whitaker, and others in the 1950s and 1960s; this led to descriptions of aphasia based on linguistic levels—phonological, morphological, syntactic, and semantic—which often cut across the traditional syndrome boundaries as they cut across the geography of these syndromes. For example, linguistically similar phonological impairments may show up in Wernicke's, Broca's, or conduction aphasia (Blumstein, Baker, & Goodglass, 1977): or, for example, similar syntactic deficits (agrammatism) may be seen in a variety of expressive or receptive aphasic disturbances (Kean, 1985); or, for example, reading disorders could be broken down into graphemic–phonological problems, semantic problems, morphological problems, and connections between the levels, which led to a whole new classification of the dyslexias (Caplan, 1987, 1992). Thus the first challenge to the classical model of the nineteenth century was based on the fact that it represented too simplistic a view of the structure of human language.

A. Language and the Right Hemisphere

A second challenge, which was actually a very early one that only recently has been adequately developed, came from the realization that the right hemisphere makes an important contribution to language processing, a fact not at all captured in the classical model. John Hughlings Jackson, a British neurologist whose work spanned the late nineteenth century to the early part of the twentieth century, was among the first to recognize the participation of the right hemisphere in language processing. His ideas about the right hemisphere were largely ignored during his lifetime, perhaps because the neurolinguistic debates at the end of the nineteenth century were mostly concerned with focal localization of function. According to Jackson, the left hemisphere was particularly implicated in the more volitional aspects of language, whereas both hemispheres contributed to automatic language (Jackson, 1915), thus explaining the frequently observed preservation of many automatic language functions even in severe aphasia after major left-hemisphere lesions. Today, Jackson's distinction approximately corresponds to the concept of automatic versus effortful processing, a concept that still resists an adequate brain model (H. A. Whitaker, 1983). In the 1960s, Jon Eisenson (1962) stated that the right hemisphere was implicated in "extra-ordinary language function" (p. 49); his observation could be illustrated by the following example: The spouse of an expressive aphasic patient (classical Broca's aphasia) explains that the patient "understands everything" although by BDAE criteria, the patient has moderate deficits in auditory comprehension (not unusual for a Broca's aphasic), is unable to match spoken words with their pictured representations, and cannot follow one- or two-step commands. A second patient, reportedly nonphasic by the same BDAE criterion (a right-hemisphere lesion in approximately the same location as the first, aphasic patient), makes few errors on the same test items of the BDAE. Yet this patient's family comments that she has great difficulty following a conversation, often makes remarks inappropriate or irrelevant to the topic, and in general seems to miss the point. The family wonders how well the patient really does understand speech, in spite of the nonphasic test report. What would explain this disparity between the two accounts? The first patient (left-hemisphere lesion) understands the pragmatics of language use but has difficulty with the individual linguistic elements. The second patient (right-hemisphere lesion) can process the linguistic elements of language, but is unable to successfully use such information in conversational contexts. Recent reports support Eisenson's (1962) observation: Patients with right-hemisphere lesions have more difficulty in synthesizing information in a coherent manner, because they are unable to use the contextual elements of language, that is, their deficit is in the actual "use" of language with respect to the specific communication situation (e.g., following a conversation, grasping the plot of a novel, or a telephone interaction) (Gardner, Brownell, Wapner, & Michelow, 1983; Joanette, Goulet, & Hannequin, 1990; Wapner, Hamby, & Gardner, 1981).

The possibility, then, that the right hemisphere makes a contribution to language, albeit an indirect one, raises another issue. Where must the lesion be located in the right hemisphere to produce such a deficit? If lesions in the left hemisphere can produce specific deficits in language, then it would stand to reason that functional localization would also be a feature of right-hemisphere organization. Unfortunately, the answer to this question is still somewhat vague. Although researchers seem to have pinpointed the presence of language deficits from right hemisphere lesions, they have been less successful in providing the evidence necessary to show the localization of these deficits; right-lesioned experimental subject groups have been small, and there have been few attempts to select patients with similar lesion locations (Ross, 1981; Joanette et al., 1990).

B. The Challenge to Localizing Language in the Brain

A third challenge to the classical model directly addressed the notion of localization itself, a question debated since the 1820s confrontations that pitted Franz Joseph Gall against Jean Pierre Marie Flourens, and Flourens against Jean-Baptiste Bouillaud. A classic centers-and-pathway model, which had directly incorporated the then-prevailing associationist psychology model of the late nineteenth century, has been increasingly seen as inadequate. Our knowledge of brain neuroanatomy and physiology is now sophisticated enough to realize that, for example, the model that auditory processing originates in the temporal lobe, then passes word recognition information from there through the arcuate fasciculus to the frontal lobe, where articulatory output processing occurs, cannot be right; or, for example, the model that reading only involves processing in the angular gyrus does not square with the functional neuroanatomical facts derived from computerized tomography (CT) and magnetic resonance imaging (MRI) lesion studies, from electrical stimulation of the brain (ESB) studies, nor from electroencephalography (EEG), positron emission tomography (PET), single photon emission computed tomography (SPECT) and regional cerebral blood flow rCBF functional studies. First, we assume today that there is a great deal of parallel processing in the brain (which was never considered in the classical model to begin with), and second we realize from physiological studies that information passes in both directions across those structures called the arcuate fasciculus. Also at odds with the classical view is the realization that discrete regions of the brain participate in multiple rather than single functions, as revealed by studies of electrical stimulation of the brain (Ojemann, 1983). It has also been shown in recent work that many other parts of the left hemisphere itself, parts never implicated in the classical model, are directly involved in primary language processing: the insula, the mesial posterior temporal and mesial occipital lobes, the mesial superior frontal and mesial anterior superior parietal lobes, the superior parietal lobe, the inferior lateral temporal lobe and, perhaps most significantly of all, many subcortical nuclei including the caudate, putamen, globus pallidus, and even the cerebellum (Damasio & Damasio, 1992; Ojemann & Whitaker, 1978). The classic model, based as it was upon the geographically distinct regions corresponding to Broca's and Wernicke's areas, the supramarginal and angular gyri, and the pathways between them, simply cannot reflect the anatomic diversity of the left hemisphere's language system.

III. IMAGING: THE BRAIN AT WORK

In addition to the many areas of the left hemisphere that modern research has shown to be implicated in language processing, there is also the difficult question of comparing a model comprising functional systems that involve separate, distributed anatomical sites versus a model comprising punctate localized functional units (more in line with the classical model). One advantage that the classical approach had was a consistent experimental methodology: the clinico-pathological correlation method (lesion studies) tends to produce results that can be interpreted in the same way. Today, however, the different research methodologies have led, so far, to different conclusions. For example, PET studies of language processing invariably reveal multiple sites that are concurrently active during individual language tasks (Posner, Petersen, Fox, & Raichle, 1990). Although there is no doubt that multiple sites do reliably increase their metabolism during specific language tasks, it is not yet certain that the language task is the only thing that influences the change in metabolism. The subtraction method used in most PET studies has recently come under fire (Demonet, Wise, & Frackowiak, 1993) for the same reasons that it was rejected by cognitive psychology many years ago: the method requires the assumption of a constant baseline measure against which the experimental measures are subtracted. Unfortunately, there is little reason to believe that baseline values are the same from moment to moment in these experiments. Another criticism of the PET studies is that, in most studies only the "peaks" of metabolic activity are recorded and thus shown as experimental data, however, it is now known that there are "troughs" in other regions of the cortex (a decrease in metabolic activity) that are also statistically correlated with the dependent measures of the experiment. If metabolism goes up and down at the same time but in different brain regions, all correlated with the experimental task, it is difficult to see how one might interpret changes in metabolism in terms of cognitive variables.

PET studies and EEG studies (the latter measuring another equally physiologically relevant parameter of brain function during language tasks) both clearly show right-hemisphere changes in activity in homologous cortical locations to the left-hemisphere sites during all language tasks, even the most simple naming tasks. One could conclude from this data that there is much more to the right hemisphere's contribution to language than superficially tapped by the lesion studies referred to above. Or, recalling that when the right hemisphere sustains focal lesions in the very same locations that are metabolically or electrically (or, magnetically) active in PET and EEG studies that there are *no* aphasic sequelae, one might wonder if both PET and EEG reflect other brain processes—physiological or motoric or sensorial for example—in which language tasks are embedded. The fact that the left-hemisphere PET changes are often larger than the right-hemisphere PET changes in a language task seems a weak basis on which to assume that the change in metabolism exclusively or even primarily reflects language processing.

There are nearly insurmountable difficulties in localizing electrical changes in the brain with the commonly used evoked potential (EP) or readiness potential techniques; in the majority of reported studies to date, one simply cannot tell whether the activity recorded by the left parietal electrode is coming from the left parietal lobe or somewhere else, for reasons having to do with the generation of electrical fields within the skull. This localizing problem has, fortunately, been solved by vastly increasing the number of electrodes in the array (Tucker, in press), although this alternative is beyond the capability of many EEG labs at present. We expect that future research using large electrode arrays will notably contribute to our understanding of the physiological systems involved in language processing and in particular their geographic location. Should the EP data correlate well with the PET data (cognitively, physiologically, and geographically) we further expect that some of the current puzzles of language localization will find some answers.

The current puzzles are indeed difficult. Virtually any modern neuroscientist would argue that language processes make use of systems in the brain, in other words, that different geographical regions, cortical and subcortical, participate collectively in language use. Against this view one must contrast some very impressive data derived from studying brain-damaged patients who have sustained very small focal lesions of the left hemisphere and who exhibit very specific language task deficits, for example, an impairment in the derivational morphology of English words shown as a deficit in processing affixes such as -ity, -ness, -tion, resulting from a small lesion to the supramarginal gyrus (Kehoe & Whitaker, 1973). Against the view of distributed systems, one must also contrast the electrical stimulation data derived during neurosurgery, where the application of a small current to a tiny area of cerebral cortex can interrupt from one to five highly specific but different tasks (such as naming pictures, mimicking oro-facial gestures, reading words, recalling words from memory, etc.), but when the electrode is moved a half a centimeter away on the same gyrus, there are no effects of stimulation at all. Perhaps in the final analysis what is needed to resolve these sometimes conflicting data about the brain mechanisms of language is a better cognitive model that is able to properly interpret and integrate anatomical and physiological data.

References

Benton, A. L., & Joynt, R. L. (1960). Early description of aphasia. *Archives of Neurology (Chicago), 3,* 205–221.

Blumstein, S., Baker, E., & Goodglass, H. (1977). Phonological factors in auditory comprehension in aphasia. *Neuropsychologia, 15,* 19–30.

Broca, P. P. (1861a). Perte de la parole. *Bulletin de la Societe d'Anthropologie, 2,* 235–238.

Broca, P. P. (1861b). Remarques sur le siège de la faculté du langage articulé. *Bulletin de la Société Anatomique de Paris, 36,* 330–357.

Caplan, D. (1987). *Neurolinguistics and linguistic aphasiology.* Cambridge: Cambridge University Press.

Caplan, D. (1992). *Language: Structure, processing and disorders.* Cambridge, MA: MIT Press.

Coltheart, M., Sartori, G., & Job, R. (Eds.). (1987). *The cognitive neuropsychology of language.* London: Erlbaum.

Damasio, A., & Damasio, H. (1992). Brain and language in mind and brain. Readings from *Scientific American* Magazine. NY: W. H. Freeman. pp. 54–65.

Demonet, J. F., Wise, R., & Frackowiak, R. S. J. (1993). Language functions explored in normal subjects by positron emission tomography: A critical review. *Human Brain Mapping, 1,* 39–47.

Efron, R. (1990). *The decline and fall of hemispheric specialization.* Hillsdale, NJ: Erlbaum.

Eisenson, J. (1962). Language and intellectual modifications associated with right cerebral damage. *Language and Speech, 5,* 49–53.

Galaburda, A. (Ed.). (1989). *From reading to neurons.* Cambridge, MA: MIT Press.

Gardner, H., Brownell, H., Wapner, W., & Michelow, D. (1983). Missing the point: The role of the right hemisphere in the processing of complex linguistic materials. In E. Perecman (Ed.), *Cognitive processing in the right hemisphere.* (pp. 169–191). New York: Academic Press.

Geschwind, N. (1965). Disconnexion syndromes in animals and men. *Brain, 88,* 237–294, 585–644.

Goodglass, H., & Kaplan, E. (1983). *The assessment of aphasia and related disorders* (2nd ed.). Philadelphia: Lea & Febiger.

Grodzinsky, Y. (1990). *Theoretical perspectives on language deficits.* Cambridge, MA: MIT Press.

Hellige, J. (1993). *Hemispheric asymmetry: What's right and what's left.* Cambridge, MA: Harvard University Press.

Howard, D., & Franklin, S. (1988). *Missing the meaning? A cognitive neuropsychological study of the processing of words by an aphasic patient.* Cambridge, MA: MIT Press.

Jackson, J. H. (1915). On the nature of the duality of the brain. *Brain, 38,* 80–103.

Joanette, Y., Goulet, P., & Hannequin, D. (1990). *Right hemisphere and verbal communication.* New York: Springer-Verlag.

Kandel, E. R., Schwartz, J. H., & Jessell, T. M. (1991). *Principles of neural science* (3rd ed.). New York: Elsevier.

Kean, M.-L. (Ed.). (1985). *Agrammatism.* New York: Academic Press.

Kehoe, W., & Whitaker, H. A. (1973). Lexical structure disruption in aphasia: A case study. In H. Goodglass & S. Blumstein (Eds.), *Psycholinguistics and aphasia* (pp. 267–279). Baltimore, MD: Johns Hopkins University Press.

Kertesz, A. (1982). *Western aphasia battery and test manual.* New York: Grune & Stratton.

Ojemann, G. A. (1983). Brain organization for language from the perspective of electrical stimulation mapping. *Behavioral and Brain Sciences, 2,* 189–203.

Ojemann, G. A., & Whitaker, H. A. (1978). Language localization and variability. *Brain and Language, 6,* 239–260.

Plum, F. (Ed.). (1988). *Language, communication and the brain.* New York: Raven Press.

Posner, M. I., Petersen, S. E., Fox, P. T., & Raichle, M. E. (1990). Localization of cognitive operations in the human brain. *Science, 240,* 1627–1631.

Ross, E. (1981). The Aprosodias: Functional-anatomical organization of the affective components of language in the right hemisphere. *Archives of Neurology (Chicago), 38,* 561–569.

Segalowitz, S. (1983). *Two sides of the brain: Brain lateralization explored.* Englewood Cliffs, NJ: Prentice-Hall.

Tucker, D. (in press). Spatial sampling of head electrical fields: The geodesic electrode net. *Electroencephalography and Clinical Neurophysiology.*

von Euler, C., Lundberg, I., & Lennerstrand, G. (Eds.). (1989). *Brain and reading*. London: Macmillan.

Wapner, W., Hamby, S., & Gardner, H. (1981). The role of the right hemisphere in the apprehension of complex linguistic materials. *Brain and Language, 25,* 144–159.

Wepfer, J. J. (1690). *Observationes medico-practicae de affectionis capitis internis et externis* (1st ed.). Schaffhausen: J. A. Ziegler. (New edition in 1727 by G. M. Wepfer).

Whitaker, H. (1976). Isolation of the language area. In H. Whitaker and H. A. Whitaker (Eds.), *Studies in neurolinguistics* (Vol. 1). New York: Academic Press.

Whitaker, H. A. (1983). Towards a brain model of automatization. In R. Magill (Ed.), *Memory and control of action* (pp. 199–214). Amsterdam: North-Holland Publ.

CHAPTER 7

Emotion and the Brain
A Distributed Modular Network Mediating Emotional Experience

Kenneth M. Heilman

I. INTRODUCTION

The purpose of this chapter is to explore the neural basis of emotional experience. We will first briefly review the classical feedback and central nervous system (CNS) theories. We will also discuss the more recent revisions of these theories. We will then advance a distributed modular network theory.

II. FEEDBACK THEORIES

Emotional feelings or experiences are unlike traditional sensory experiences because they do not rely directly on the physical characteristics of the external stimulus and may even occur in the absence of an external stimulus (e.g., memory-induced emotional experiences). Therefore, according to the feedback theory, emotional feelings or experience require afferent input into the brain, and this afferent activity has to be induced by efferent activity. Efferent activity, either muscular or visceral, is a part of emotional expression. However, efferent activity may not only be important for emotional expression, but feedback of this expression to the brain may also be at least in part responsible for emotional experience. The two major feedback theories are the facial and visceral theories.

A. Facial Feedback Hypothesis

Darwin (1972) noted that the free expression of an emotion intensifies the emotion but the repression of an emotional expression softens the emotional experience. "He who gives violent gesture increases his rage" Darwin thought that the means by which we express emotions is innate. Izard (1977) and Ekman, Sorenson, and Friesen (1969) performed cross-cultural studies of facial emotional expression and provide support for Darwin's hypothesis that emotional expression may be innate. Tomkins (1962, 1963) thought that the sensory receptors in the face become active during emotional expression and this activity fed back to the brain. He felt that it is the self-perception of facial expression that induces emotional experience. Laird (1974) found that facial expressions changed the quality of emotional experience, providing support for Tomkins's hypothesis. There are many unresolved problems with the facial feedback theory. Although one's experience of emotion may be intensified or diminished by altering one's facial expression, there is little to suggest that the valence of emotion can be changed by altering ones facial expression. One can also express one emotion while feeling another. It remains possible, however, that the innervatory pattern of voluntary facial gestures are different than those that occur naturally. Patients with pseudobulbar palsy may express strong facial emotions that they are not feeling (Poeck, 1969; Sackheim et al., 1982). It is possible however that these patient's brain lesions also interrupt feedback to the brain. There are other patients who have reduced facial mobility from peripheral neurological diseases, such as myasthenia gravis, who report emotional feelings. Although facial expressions may embellish emotions as Darwin suggested, this influence may not stem from feedback from facial muscles but may be mediated totally within the CNS by associative networks.

B. Visceral Feedback

William James (1890/1950) proposed that emotion-provoking stimuli induce changes in the viscera and that the self-perception of these visceral changes produce emotional experience. James also noted that there were cerebral forms of emotion that did not require bodily changes or the perception of these changes (e.g., pleasure).

The visceral feedback model of James was challenged by Cannon (1927), who argued that the separation of the viscera from the brain as occurs with cervical spinal cord injuries does not eliminate emotional experience. Hohmann (1966) studied patients with spinal cord injuries and found that patients with either high or low spinal cord transections did experience emotions as predicted by Cannon but that patients with lower lesions reported stronger emotions than those with higher lesions, providing some support for the visceral feedback theory. In addition, the vagus nerve is a primarily visceral afferent nerve, and spinal cord transections would not interfere with this nerve's ability to provide the brain with feedback from the viscera.

Because Cannon thought that the same visceral response occurs with different emotions, feedback of these visceral responses could not account for the variety of emotions that we experience. Ax (1953), however, demonstrated that different bodily reactions can be associated with different emotions. What has not been demonstrated is that feedback of these different body reactions can induce different emotional experiences.

Cannon also thought that the viscera have insufficient afferent input to the brain to be important in inducing emotional experience. Using a heartbeat detection paradigm, Katkin, Morrell, Goldband, Bernstein, and Wise (1982) found that some normal subjects can accurately detect their heartbeats. The subjects who had the strongest emotional responses to negative slides as determined by self-report were the subjects who were able to detect their own heartbeat (Hantas, Katkin, & Blasovich, 1982). In summary, Cannon's critiques failed to refute the visceral feedback theory of emotional experience.

For visceral feedback to occur, the brain must be able to activate the viscera and autonomic nervous system (ANS). We use the term *feed forward* to refer to the brain's ability to activate the ANS and various viscera. In humans, the neocortex plays a critical role in the analysis and interpretation of various stimuli (see Heilman, Bowers, & Valenstein, 1993, for a review). Therefore, there must be descending neural systems that enable the cortex to control the ANS and the endocrine system, which in turn would influence the viscera such as the heart. The ANS has two components: the sympathetic and parasympathetic. Sympathetic nerves originate in the spinal cord in the intermediolateral section. These sympathetic neurons receive projections from the hypothalamus as well as from cells in the ventral pons and medulla. The ventral lateral medulla also receive projections from the hypothalamus including the periventricular and lateral nuclei. The hypothalamus receives projections from many limbic and paralimbic areas, including the amygdala. The most important parasympathetic nerve is the vagus. The vagus originates in the dorsal motor nucleus situated in the brain stem and projects to the viscera such as the heart. The amygdala not only projects to the hypothalamus but also sends direct projections to the nucleus of the solitary tract and the dorsal motor nucleus of the vagus. In this manner the amygdala may directly influence the parasympathetic system. The amygdala not only projects to the neocortex but also receives neocortical input. Whereas the amygdala may be the most important part of the limbic system to influence ANS and viscera, stimulation of other areas including the insula and orbitofrontal cortex can also induce autonomic and visceral changes.

In humans, most of the stimuli that induce emotional behavior must first be analyzed and interpreted by the neocortex (stimulus appraisal). The stimuli that induce emotion also cause changes in the ANS and viscera. The amygdala, insula, and orbitofrontal cortex are probably areas that are critical for transcoding the knowledge gained by the neocortex to changes of the ANS and viscera.

In regard to feedback, the major nerve that carries visceral afferent information back to the brain is the vagus. Vagal afferents terminate in the medulla, primarily in the nucleus of the solitary tract. This nucleus then projects to the central nucleus of the amygdala. The central nucleus of the amygdala projects to other amygdala nuclei and the insula. It has been demonstrated that stimulation of the vagus nerve produces excitation of the insula and amygdala. The amygdala and insula project to several neocortical areas, including the temporal, parietal, and frontal lobes.

Luria and Simernitskaya (1977) thought that the right hemisphere may be more important than the left in perceiving changes in the viscera. However, there have not been many studies on asymmetry of visceral perception. Of the few studies, Davidson, Horowitz, Schwartz, and Goodman (1981) gave a variety of tapping tests to normal individuals to assess whether the right or left hand was more influenced by heartbeat. They found that the left hand was more influenced by heart rate than the right hand, suggesting the right hemisphere may be superior at detecting heartbeat. Unfortunately, this left-hand superiority in the detection of heartbeat has not been replicated by other investigators. In the future, further studies will have to be performed on normal subjects and on brain-impaired subjects to determine which hemisphere is dominant for autonomic perception and what portions of the hemisphere are important for receiving and interpreting this visceral information.

Although many of Cannon's objections to the visceral feedback theory could be refuted, there are still observations for which the visceral feedback theory cannot account. Perhaps the most important of these are those of Marañon (1924) who injected epinephrine into subjects and then inquired as to the nature of the emotion felt by these subjects. Epinephrine does not flow from the blood into the brain. That is, it does not cross the blood–brain barrier. Epinephrine, however, does cause the heart to beat more rapidly and has many other effects on the ANS and viscera. However, Marañon found that injections of epinephrine were not associated with emotional experience but rather "as if" feelings.

Schachter and Singer (1962) also injected epinephrine into experimental subjects. Schachter and Singer reported that pharmacologically induced visceral activation did not produce an emotion unless this arousal was accompanied by a cognitive set. Based on studies of pharmacological arousal and cognitive set, Schachter proposed the cognitive-arousal attribution theory of emotions. According to Schachter and Singer's theory, the experience of emotion involves specific cognitive attributions superimposed upon a state of diffuse physiological arousal.

Whereas Schachter and Singer's study suggested that visceral feedback together with central mediated cognition are important for emotional experience, observations in the clinic suggest that patients may experience emotions even in the absence of a cognitive set. For example, patients with complex partial seizures may have emotional experiences, such as fear, as part of their seizure. Autonomic and visceral changes may be associated with partial seizures and the patient's being aware that they are having a seizure also may induce a cognitive set. However, in many epileptic patients the emotional experience is often the first symptom. Therefore, in these patients, cognitive set may come after the experience rather than prior to the experience. Schachter and Singer's cognitive arousal attribution theory cannot account for these clinical observations. Even in the absence of cognitive set, focal activation in the CNS can induce emotion.

III. CENTRAL THEORIES

A. Diencephalic

Walter Cannon (1927) proposed one of the first central theories of emotion. According to Cannon, afferent stimuli enter the brain and are transmitted to the thalamus. The thalamus activates the hypothalamus. The hypothalamus can in turn activate the endocrine system and ANS. These systems induce the physiological changes in the viscera. According to Cannon, the visceral activation induced by the endocrine system and the ANS are primarily adaptive and aid in the survival of the organism. Instead of the viscera feeding back to the cortex, as suggested by James, Cannon posited that it was the hypothalamus that activates the cortex, and it was this cerebral activation that was responsible for emotional experience. Cannon thought that the cortex normally exerts inhibitory control on the hypothalamus, and the loss of this inhibition was responsible for a loss of the appropriate emotional control, as seen in sham rage. Cannon, however, did not suggest a critical role for the cortex in the interpretation of stimuli. Whereas some stimuli may induce emotion without cortical interpretation, there is overwhelming evidence that in humans the neocortex is critical for interpreting the meaning of many stimuli, especially those stimuli that are complex. For example, verbal and written stimuli may engender strong emotions. These stimuli need phonological, lexical, and semantic processing that are mediated primarily by the left hemisphere. Hearing emotional prosody or seeing emotional faces may also induce an emotion. The right hemisphere appears to be dominant in processing these stimuli. Lesions of the left or right hemisphere, therefore, may interfere with the interpretation of these complex stimuli. For a more detailed discussion of the cortical role in interpreting emotional stimuli, see Heilman, Bowers, and Valenstein (1993).

B. Limbic System

Not only did Cannon's diencephalic model fail to account for how humans experience emotion in response to complex stimuli, it also failed to explain how humans can experience a variety of emotions.

Whereas the neocortex and hypothalamus may influence each other, many of the connections between these areas are indirect. The medial and basolateral aspects of the human cerebral hemispheres contain structures that have reciprocal connections between the neocortex and hypothalamus. It has been posited that these structures play a critical role in emotional experience. The first to draw attention to this system was Paul Broca (1878) who used the term *limbique* to describe a group of anatomically related structures on the medial wall of the cerebral hemisphere. After Bard (1934) demonstrated that the hypothalamus was important in mediating rage, Papez (1937) posited that a circuit in the limbic lobe was important in mediating emotion. The medial or Papez circuit consists of the mammillary bodies of the hypothalamus that project via the mammillothalamic tract to the anterior thalamus, which in turn projects to the cingulate gyrus. The cingulate gyrus projects to the hippocampus, and the hippocampus projects back to the mammillary bodies via the fornix. Yakovlev (1948) described a basolateral circuit that includes the orbitofrontal cortex, which projects to the anterior temporal cortex via the uncinate fasiculus. The anterior temporal cortex projects to the amygdala and the amygdala projects to the dorsomedial nucleus of the thalamus, which projects back to the orbitofrontal cortex. As previously mentioned, portions of the basolateral circuit, such as the amygdala, also have connections with the hypothalamus. This basolateral circuit together with the medial circuit was designated as the limbic system by MacLean (1952).

Klüver and Bucy (1937) bilaterally ablated the anterior temporal lobe of monkeys, including both the hippocampus, which is part of Papez circuit, and the amygdala, which is part of the Yakovlev circuit. This ablation also included visual association cortex. Following the anterior temporal lobe ablation, animals demonstrated a complex behavioral disorder, including a loss of fear for humans. Subsequent studies have revealed that lesions of the hippocampus as well as structures in the Papez circuit were more likely to account for memory loss than changes in emotional experience or behavior. Although the loss of fear may have been related to the animals' visual agnosia (induced by ablation of the visual association cortex), Weiskrantz (1956) demonstrated that ablation of the amygdala alone can induce a change in fear behavior.

Iwata, LeDoux, Meeley, Arneric, and Reis (1986) revived and modified Cannon's central hypotheses. It appears that the sensory portions of the thalamus, such as the medial geniculate body (auditory thalamus), send projections to the amygdala. Iwata et al. (1986) classically conditioned animals to adversive stimuli (foot shock associated with a tone). Thereafter, when animals heard this tone, they responded as if they were shocked. Even though bilateral lesions of the auditory cortex had no effect on the animals' behavioral response to these conditioned tones, bilateral lesions of the inferior colliculus or medial geniculate interfered with this conditioned response. In contrast, lesions of these conditioned animals' hypothalamus interfered with the autonomic response but not with these animals' behavioral response to the conditioned stimuli. Behavioral fear response appeared to be mediated by a system that projects from the amygdala to the midbrain.

Since emotional experience cannot be studied in animals, the system important for mediating conscious awareness has not been elucidated by these animal studies. These studies on conditioned fear also cannot account for other types of emotional experience such as happiness or joy. Although humans may develop conditioned emotional responses to simple stimuli, for the most part, the stimuli that induce human emotions are complex stimuli that must be processed by the cortex. Therefore, to understand how the human brain mediates emotional experience, we must turn to studies of humans.

IV. DIMENSIONAL ORGANIZATION OF EMOTIONS

William James (1890/1950) wondered whether the brain contains specialized emotional systems or if emotions were mediated by systems that were not devoted. In the former case (devoted systems), there would be a special system for fear, anger, happiness, and so on. This would imply that each emotion was uniquely mediated. In the latter case, the neural apparatus that mediates one emotion may not only play a role in other emotions but also may also mediate even nonemotional functions.

This latter view (nondevoted systems) is consistent with the *dimensional* or *component* view of emotion favored by many cognitive emotional theorists. The dimensional view was perhaps initiated by Wundt (1903), who proposed that emotional experiences vary in three dimensions: quality, activity, and excitement. More recently, Osgood, Suci, and Tannenbaum (1957) performed factor analyses on verbal assessments of emotional judgements and found that the variance could be accounted for by three major dimensions: valence (positive/negative, pleasant/unpleasant), arousal (calm/

excited), and control or dominance (in control/out of control). One may use this type of multidimensional scale to redefine emotions. For example, fear would be unpleasant and high arousal; out of control and sadness could be unpleasant and low arousal. Studies on normal subjects using a variety of techniques (Greenwald, Cook, & Lang, 1989) have supported this dimensional view. Frijda (1987) also explored the cognitive structure of emotion and found that "action readiness" was an important component.

Heller (1990) suggested that a dimensional view of emotional experience may be of aid in understanding how human brains mediate emotion. We propose that conscious experience of emotion is mediated by an anatomically distributed modular network. This network contains three major modules, one that determines valence, another that controls arousal, and a third that mediates motor activation with approach or avoidance behaviors. In the next section we will describe the portions of the brain that may mediate valence, arousal, and motor activation.

A. Valence

Goldstein (1948) observed that patients with left-hemisphere lesions and aphasia often appeared anxious, agitated, and sad. Goldstein called this behavioral syndrome the *catastrophic reaction*. Gianotti (1972) studied 160 patients with strokes of either the right or left hemisphere. He also noted that patients with left-hemisphere lesions had a catastrophic reaction. He thought that this response was a normal response to the serious cognitive (e.g., aphasia) and physical deficits (e.g., hemiparesis) that these patients sustained. Babinski (1914), Hécean, Ajuriaguerra, and de Massonet (1951) and Denny-Brown, Meyer, and Horenstein (1952) noticed that patients with right-hemisphere lesions often appeared either inappropriately indifferent or even euphoric. Gianotti (1972) also confirmed these observations and suggested that these patients' indifference may be related to the denial of illness or anosognosia that often is associated with right-hemisphere lesions.

Whereas the patient's psychological response to their own illness may account for some of the emotional asymmetries observed between patients with right- and left-hemisphere lesions, there are several additional observations that a psychological reactive theory cannot explain. Prior to epilepsy surgery, patients undergo selective hemispheric anesthesia (Wada test) to determine which hemisphere is dominant for speech and language. Terzian (1964) and Rossi and Rosadini (1967) studied the emotional reactions of patients recovering from selective hemispheric barbiturate-induced anesthesia. Right carotid injection were associated with euphoria and barbiturate injections into the left carotid artery were associated with catastrophic reactions.

Because the Wada test is a diagnostic test that only causes transient hemiparesis and aphasia, it would appear unlikely that this procedure would cause a reactive depression. In addition, we have seen right-hemisphere-damaged patients who appear to be indifferent but do not demonstrate anosognosia or verbally explicit denial of illness. We do not know if these patients' propensity to be indifferent about their illness is related to a general emotional flattening or if they have a mild form of anosognosia (anosodiaphoria) and their indifference is related to their reduced awareness or a defective evaluation of their disabilities.

The depression associated with left-hemisphere lesions is seen most commonly in patients with nonfluent aphasia who have anterior perisylvian lesions (Benson, 1979; Robinson & Sztela, 1981). Hughlings Jackson (1932) noted that left-hemisphere lesions induced deficits of propositional language and nonfluent aphasics could not express themselves using propositional language but nevertheless expressed their feelings by using expletives and by using emotional intonations of simple repetitive utterances. Hughlings Jackson postulated that it was the right hemisphere that was mediating this affective speech. This right-hemisphere emotional speech postulate was supported by the observations of Tucker, Watson, and Heilman (1977) and Ross and Mesulam (1979), who reported that right-hemisphere-damaged subjects lost their ability to express emotional prosody. Because left-hemisphere-lesioned aphasic patients are unable to express themselves using propositional speech, they may rely more on right-hemisphere nonpropositional affective communication systems. Therefore, they may intone their speech more heavily and use more emotional facial expressions. Because these left-hemisphere-damaged patients may have a greater need to use these expressive emotional systems, they may appear to be highly emotional. In contrast, patients with right-hemisphere disease may have more difficulty than patients with left-hemisphere disease in expressing emotional faces and emotional speech prosody. Therefore, when compared to left-hemisphere-damaged patients, they may appear to be indifferent.

Although defects of emotional expression may account for some of the behavior observations by Goldstein (1948), Babinski (1914), and Gainotti (1972), they cannot explain the results of Gasparrini, Satz, Heilman, and Coolidge (1978), who administered the Minnesota Multiphasic Personality Inventory (MMPI) to a group of left- and right-hemisphere-damaged patients. The left- and right-hemisphere-damaged groups were balanced for cognitive and motor defects. Although the MMPI is widely used to assess emotional experience, this inventory does not require emotionally intoned speech or facial expressions. Gasparrini et al. (1978) found that whereas patients with left-hemisphere disease showed a marked elevation of the depression scale, patients with right-hemisphere disease did not. These results demonstrate that the right–left differences in emotional behavior cannot be attributed to emotional expressive disorders or to severity of deficit.

Starkstein, Robinson, and Price (1987) also studied emotional changes associated with stroke. They found that about one third of stroke patients were depressed and that the depression was associated with both left frontal and left caudate lesions. The closer to the frontal pole the lesion was located the more severe the depression. Many of the patients with left-hemisphere lesions and depression were also anxious. In contrast to these left-hemisphere-damaged patients, in the acute poststroke period, patients with right frontal lesions were often indifferent or even euphoric.

Not all investigators agree that after stroke there is more depression with left- than right-hemisphere lesions (House, Dennis, Warlow, Hawton, & Molyneux, 1990). Milner (1974) could not replicate the emotional symmetries found in prior reports of Wada testing.

Several groups of investigators have studied patients with primary depression using physiological imaging. In general, these investigations have noted a decrease of activation in the left frontal lobe as well as the left cingulate gyrus (Bench et al., 1992; Phelps, Mazziotta, Baxter, & Geiner, 1994). However, Drevets and Raichle (1992) found evidence for increased activity in the left prefrontal cortex, amygdala, basal ganglia, and thalamus.

Davidson, Schwartz, Saron, Bennett, and Goldman (1979) and Tucker (1981) studied normal subjects using electrophysiological techniques. Their studies have also suggested that the frontal region of each hemisphere makes asymmetric contributions to affective regulations such that greater right than left activation is associated with negative moods and greater left than right activation is associated with positive moods. Unfortunately, it is not known how the right and left hemisphere may influence emotional valence. Although Fox and Davidson (1984) suggest that positive and negative emotions are related to approach (left hemisphere) and avoidance (right hemisphere) behaviors, this approach–avoidance model does not explain how the two hemispheres are differently organized, such that they make opposite contributions to mood. This approach–avoidance theory does not explain how other emotions are mediated and it also does not explain the role of other areas in the brain such as the limbic system. Whereas Fox and Davidson (1984) posited interhemispheric inhibition, Tucker and Williamson (1984) think the abnormal moods associated with frontal lesions are related to intrahemispheric rather than interhemispheric disinhibition. Tucker and Williamson think that hemispheric valence asymmetries may be related to asymmetrical control of neuropharmacological systems, with the left hemisphere being more cholinergic and dopaminergic and the right hemisphere being more noradrenergic than the left. Based on positron emission tomography (PET) studies, Robinson and Starkstein (1989) reported that pharmacologic changes in the two hemispheres may be different after stroke. Whereas the right-hemisphere stroke appears to increase serotonergic receptor binding, left-hemisphere stroke lowers serotonergic binding. The lower the serotonergic binding, the more severe the depression. Although neuro-transmitter systems may have a profound influence on mood, and changes in these systems may induce either euphoria or dysphoria, the mechanism by which the pharmacological changes induce mood remain unknown. We will confine our discussion to the anatomic and physiological models of emotion.

B. Arousal

Arousal is defined both behaviorally and physiologically. Whereas an aroused organism is alert and prepared to process stimuli, an unaroused organism is comatose and not prepared to process stimuli. Physiologically, arousal has many definitions. In the CNS, arousal usually refers to the excitatory state or the propensity of neurons that discharge when appropriately activated. Peripherally, arousal usually refers to activation of the sympathetic nervous system and such viscera as the heart. Peripheral arousal has been previously discussed.

Arousal and attention are intimately linked and appear to be mediated by a cortical limbic reticular network (Heilman, 1979; Mesulam, 1981; Watson, Valenstein, & Heilman, 1981). We will provide an overview of this network but for details, one should refer to the original articles or see Heilman, Watson, and Valenstein (1993). Much of what we know about this network comes from studies of monkeys and patients with discrete brain lesions. In humans, inferior parietal lobe lesions are most often associated with disorders of attention and arousal (Critchley, 1966; Heilman, Valenstein, & Watson, 1983). Temporoparietal ablations in monkeys are also associated with attentional disorders (Heilman, Pandya, & Geschwind, 1970; Lynch, 1980). Recordings from neurons in the parietal lobes of monkeys appear to support the postulate that the parietal lobe is important in attention. Unlike neurons in the primary sensory cortex, the rate of firing of these "attentional" neurons appears to be associated with the significance of the stimulus to the monkey, such that important stimuli are associated with higher firing rates of these neurons than unimportant stimuli (see Bushnell, Goldberg, & Robinson, 1981; Lynch, 1980).

Sensory information projects from the thalamus to the primary sensory cortex. Each of the primary sensory cortices (e.g., visual, tactile, auditory) project only to their association cortices. Each of these modality-specific association areas converge upon polymodal areas such as the frontal cortex (periarcuate, prearcuate, and orbitofrontal) and both banks of the superior temporal sulcus (Pandya & Kuypers, 1969). These polymodal convergence areas project to the supramodal inferior parietal lobe (Mesulam, Van Hesen, Pandya, & Geschwind, 1977). The determination as to whether the stimulus is novel may be mediated by the modality-specific sensory association cortex. However, stimulus significance requires knowledge as to both the meaning of the stimulus and the motivational state of the organism. The motivational state is dependent upon biological needs and long-term goals. Portions of the limbic system monitor the internal milieu, and limbic input into regions important in determining stimulus significance may provide information about immediate biological needs. In contrast, the frontal lobe has been demonstrated to play a major role in goal-oriented behavior and set development (Damasio & Anderson, 1993; Stuss & Benson, 1986) and frontal input into the attentional-arousal systems may provide information about goals that are not motivated by immediate biological needs. The temporoparietal region not only has strong connections with both the limbic system (i.e., cingulate gyrus) and the prefrontal cortex but also contains representations important in determining the meaning of stimuli.

Mesencephalic reticular formation (MRF) stimulation in animals induces behavioral arousal (increased alertness) and is associated with encephalographic desynchronization, a physiological measure of central arousal (Moruzzi & Magoun, 1949). Whereas bilateral lesions of the MRF induce coma, unilateral lesions cause ipsilateral hemispheric hypoarousal (Watson, Heilman, Miller, & King, 1974). The polymodal and supramodal cortex we discussed not only play a role in determining stimuli significance but also modulate arousal by influencing the MRF. For example, when the dorsolateral frontal lobe or temporoparietal areas are stimulated, the animal demonstrates an arousal response (Segundo, Naguet, & Buser, 1955). The exact means by which these cortical areas influence the MRF and the MRF influences the cortex remain unknown. There are at least three possible means by which the MRF may influence cortical processing. Shute and Lewis (1967) described as ascending cholinergic reticular formation. The nucleus basalis, which receives input from the reticular formation, has cholinergic projections to the cortex, and these cholinergic projections appear to be important for increasing neuronal responsivity (Sato, Hata, Hagihara, & Tsumoto, 1987). Alternatively, the MRF may influence the cortex through its projections to the thalamus. Steriade and Glenn (1982) demonstrated that certain thalamic nuclei, such as the centralis lateralis and paracentralis, project to widespread cortical regions and these thalamic nuclei can be activated by stimulation of the MRF. The third possible mechanism to account for cortical arousal involves the nucleus reticularis. This thin nucleus envelops the thalamus and projects to the sensory thalamic relay nuclei. Physiologically, this thalamic nucleus inhibits thalamic relay of sensory information (Scheibel & Scheibel, 1967). When cortical limbic networks determine a stimulus is important; corticofugal projections may inhibit the nucleus reticularis and allow the thalamus to relay sensory input to the cortex.

Changes in the level of activity of the peripheral ANS often mirror arousal changes in the CNS. Arousal of the ANS is often associated with hand sweating. Using the galvanic skin response (GSR), which changes with hand sweating, as a measure of peripheral arousal, Heilman, Schwartz, and Watson (1978) presented nociceptive stimuli (electric shock) to right-temporoparietal-damaged subjects who were emotionally indifferent and demonstrated that patients with right-hemisphere lesions had a reduced arousal response when compared to normal subjects and left-hemisphere-damaged controls. Morrow, Vrtunski, Kim, and Boller (1981) and Schrandt, Tranel, and Damasio (1989) also found that right-hemisphere-damaged patients had a reduced GSR to emotional stimuli. In contrast, when compared to normal subjects, patients with left-hemisphere lesions appear to have a greater autonomic response (Heilman et al., 1978; Schrandt et al., 1989). Using changes in heart rate as a peripheral measure of arousal, Yokoyama, Jennings, Ackles, Hood, and Boller (1987) obtained similar results to those obtained using GSR. In regard to measures of central arousal, patients with right-hemisphere lesions have more delta and theta EEG activity over their nonlesioned left hemisphere than patients with left-hemisphere lesions have over their right hemisphere (Heilman & Van Den Abell, 1979). When neurons become aroused, they increase their metabolic rate. Using physiological imaging, Perani, Vallar, Paulesu, Alberoni, and Fasio (1993) found that in cases of right-hemisphere stroke there was also metabolic depression of the left hemisphere. Unfortunately, left-hemisphere-damaged control patients were not reported.

The mechanisms underlying the asymmetrical reduction of arousal with right- versus left-hemisphere lesions are unknown. Because lesions restricted to the right hemisphere could not directly interfere with the left hemisphere's corticofugal projections to the reticular systems or the reticular system's corticopedal influence of the cortex, one would have to propose that the right hemisphere's control of arousal may be related to the right hemisphere's privileged communication with the reticular activating system. For example, the bilateral arousal defects associated with right-hemisphere lesions may be related to a loss of the right hemisphere's corticofugal influence on the reticular formation. Alternatively, the right hemisphere may play a dominant role in computing stimulus significance. The increased arousal associated with left-hemisphere lesions also remains unexplained but may be related to the loss of some type of inhibitory control mediated by the left hemisphere. This control may be mediated either transcallosally or directly on the reticular systems.

C. Motor Activation and Approach Avoidance

Whereas some emotions do not call for action (e.g., sadness, satisfaction) others do (e.g., anger, fear, joy, surprise). In regard to those emotions that are associated with action, this action may be toward the stimulus (approach) or away from the stimulus (avoidance). For example, fear and disgust may be associated with avoiding behavior and joy and anger with approach behavior.

Pribram and McGuiness (1975) used the term activation to denote the physiological readiness to respond to stimuli. It has been posited that motor activation or intention is mediated by a network that includes the cerebral cortex, basal ganglia, and limbic system. The dorsolateral frontal lobe appears to be the center of this motor preparatory network (Watson, Miller, & Heilman, 1978; Watson et al., 1981). Recordings from cells in the frontal region reveal neurons that have enhanced activity when the animal is presented with a stimulus that is meaningful and predicts movement. Activity in these cells precede the movement (Goldberg & Bushnell, 1981). The dorsolateral frontal lobes receive input from limbic areas such as the cingulate gyrus and from posterior cortical association areas that are both modality specific and polymodal. Whereas input from thee posterior neocortical areas may provide the frontal lobes information about the stimulus or its meaning, the limbic system may provide information as to the organism's motivational state. The dorsolateral frontal lobe has nonreciprocal connections with the basal ganglia (caudate), which in turn projects to the globus pallidus (internal segment), then the thalamus, and eventually projects back to the cortex (Alexander, DeLong, & Strick, 1986). The dorsolateral frontal lobes also have extensive connections with the intralaminar nuclei of the thalamus (central median and parafasicularis) as well as direct input into premotor areas. The intralaminar nuclei may gait motor activation by their influence on the basal ganglia, especially the putamen, or by influencing the thalamic portion of motor circuits (ventralis lateralis pars oralis). Not surprisingly, lesions of the dorsolateral frontal lobe, the cingulate gyrus, the basal ganglia, the intralaminar nuclei, or the ventrolateral thalamus may all cause akinesia or inability to activate the motor systems. For a more detailed discussion of this intentional network, please see Heilman, Watson, and Valenstein (1993).

Studies in patients with focal brain damage as well as studies in normal subjects suggest that the right hemisphere plays a special role in motor activation or intention. For example, Coslett and Heilman (1989) demonstrated that right-hemisphere lesions are more likely to be associated with contralateral akinesia than those of the left hemisphere. Simple reaction times (RT) are in part the time it takes to activate motor systems. Howes and Boller (1975) measured RT of the hand ipsilateral to a hemispheric lesion and demonstrated that right-hemisphere lesions were associated with slower RT than left-hemisphere lesions. Heilman and Van Den Abell (1979) measured RT of normal subjects who received warning stimuli directed to either their right or left hemisphere. They found that warning stimuli delivered to the right hemisphere reduced RT more than warning stimuli delivered to the left hemisphere.

The portions of the brain that mediate approach–avoidance behavior have not been entirely elucidated. Denny-Brown and Chambers (1958) suggested that, whereas the frontal lobes mediate avoidance behavior, the parietal lobes mediate approach behaviors. They also suggested that these approach–avoidance behaviors may be reciprocal, such that a loss of one behavior may release the other behavior. Therefore, since the frontal lobes mediate avoidance behavior, frontal lobe dysfunction would cause inappropriate approach behaviors. In support of Denny-Brown and Chambers' postulate, one can see patients with frontal lesions who demonstrate manual grasp reflexes, visual grasp reflexes, rooting and sucking responses, magnetic apraxia, and utilization behaviors. One also can see patients who have defective response inhibition. All these behaviors are characterized by aberrant approach. Unfortunately, the area within the frontal lobes that when damaged causes approach behaviors has not been entirely elucidated. Animals with frontal lesions show an increase of aggressive behavior (Fuster, 1989). This aggressiveness in monkeys with frontal lesions has been attributed to an inability to use previously learned avoidance behaviors (Brody & Rosvold, 1952). Patients with left dorsolateral frontal lesions are also prone to hostility and anger (Grafman, Vance, Weingartner, Salazar, & Amin, 1986).

In contrast to the manual grasp response associated with frontal lesions, patients with parietal lesions may demonstrate a palmar avoiding response. Patients with parietal lesions may fail to move or have a delay in moving their arms, head, and eyes toward a part of the space that is opposite the parietal lesion. Patients with parietal lesions may even deviate their eyes, head, and arms toward ipsilateral hemispace. Unlike patients with frontal lesions who cannot withhold their response to stimuli, patients with parietal lesions may not be able to respond to stimuli (neglect). The aberrant approach behavior seen with frontal lesions and the avoidance responses seen with parietal lesions are both more commonly seen after right- than after left-hemispheric lesions, suggesting that not only would the right hemisphere be overall dominant for activation, but may be dominant also for mediating these approach–avoidance behaviors.

V. OVERVIEW

Although emotional experience may be induced by conditioned stimuli, most emotional behavior and experiences are induced by complex stimuli that may be verbal or nonverbal, visual, auditory, or even tactile. The cerebral cortex of humans has complex modular systems that analyze these stimuli, develop precepts, and interpret meaning. The portions of the brain that process emotional stimuli depend upon the modality and mode of the stimulus. The determination of valence is based upon whether or not the stimulus is beneficial (positive) or detrimental (negative) to the well-being of the person or the person's family or society. The right frontal lobe appears to be important in the mediation of emotions with negative valence and the left frontal lobe in the mediation of emotions with positive valence. Depending upon the nature of the stimulus, some positive and some negative emotions are associated with high arousal (e.g., joy and fear) and others with low arousal (e.g., satisfaction and sadness). The right parietal lobe appears to be important in mediating arousal response and the left appears to inhibit the arousal response. Similarly, some positive and negative emotions are associated with motor activation and others are not. For example, whereas anger may be associated with motor activation, sadness may not. The dorsolateral frontal lobes appear to be important in motor activation, with the right frontal appearing to be dominant. Some emotions are not only associated with motor activation but this activation is associated with either approach or avoidance behaviors. Whereas approach behaviors may be mediated by the parietal lobes (especially the right), avoidance behaviors may be mediated by the frontal lobes.

The cortical and subcortical areas we have discussed have rich connections. For example, intrahemispherically, the frontal and parietal areas are densely connected, and the right and left hemispheres are connected by the neocommisures. In addition, these neocortical areas also contain rich connections with the limbic system, basal ganglia, and reticular system. Therefore, the valence arousal and activation systems we have discussed are interconnected and form a modular network.

We posit that emotional experience depends upon the patterns of neural activation in the modular system we have discussed. Although some of this neural activity is sequential (i.e., stimulus appraisal precedes arousal or activation), emotional experience requires that multiple regions be simultaneously activated or inhibited. Even in the absence of an eliciting stimulus, emotions can be experienced. Under these conditions, the modular networks we have posited also become activated. Although we have proposed that emotional experience is primarily a CNS process, we also believe that the feedback systems we have discussed may also influence emotional experience.

Although we are now beginning to learn how the brain may mediate emotional experience, there remains much to be learned. We hope the preliminary hypotheses put forth in the chapter will have heuristic value and stimulate more research on the biology of emotional experience.

References

Alexander, G. E., DeLong, M. R., & Strick, P. L. (1986). Parallel organization of functionally segregated circuits linking basal ganglia and cortex. *Annual Review of Neuroscience, 9,* 357–381.

Ax, A. F. (1953). The physiological differentiation between fear and anger in humans. *Psychosomatic Medicine, 15,* 433–442.

Babinski, J. (1914). Contribution à l'étude des troubles mentaux dans l'hemisplegic organique cérébrale (anosognosie). *Revue Neurologique, 27,* 845–848.

Bard, P. (1934). Emotion: I. The neuro-humoral basis of emotional reactions. In C. Murchison (Ed.), *Handbook of general experimental psychology.* Worchester, MA: Clark University Press.

Bench, C. J., Friston, K. J., Brown, R. G., Scott, L. C., Frackowiak, R. S., & Dolan, R. J. (1992). The anatomy of melancholia focal abnormalities of blood flow in major depression. *Psychological Medicine, 22,* 607–615.

Benson, D. F. (1979). Psychiatric aspects of aphasia. In D. F. Benson (Ed.), *Aphasia, alexia, and agraphia.* New York: Churchill-Livingstone.

Broca, P. P. (1878). Anatomic comparée des enconvolutions cérébrales: Le grand lobe limbique et al scissure limbique dans la seire des mammifères. *Revue Anthropologique, 1,* 385–498.

Brody, E. G., & Rosvold, H. E. (1952). Influence of prefrontal lobotomy on social interaction in a monkey group. *Psychosomatic Medicine, 14,* 406–415.

Bushnell, M. C., Goldberg, M. E., & Robinson, D. L. (1981). Behavioral enhancement of visual responses in monkey cerebral cortex: I. Modulation of posterior parietal cortex related to selected visual attention. *Journal of Neurophysiology, 46,* 755–772.

Cannon, W. B. (1927). The James-Lange theory of emotion: A critical examination and an alternative theory. *American Journal of Psychology, 39,* 106–124.

Coslett, H. B., & Heilman, K. M. (1989). Hemihypokinesia after right hemisphere strokes. *Brain and Cognition, 9,* 267–278.

Critchley, M. (1966). *The parietal lobes.* New York: Hafner.

Damasio, A. R., & Anderson, S. W. (1993). The frontal lobes. In K. M. Heilman & E. Valenstein (Eds.), *Clinical neuropsychology.* 3rd ed. New York: Oxford University Press.

Darwin, C. (1972). *The expression of emotion in man and animals.* London: Murray.

Davidson, R. J., Horowitz, M. E., Schwartz, G. E., & Goodman, D. M. (1981). Lateral differences in the latency between finger tapping and heart beat. *Psychophysiology, 18,* 36–41.

Davidson, R. J., Schwartz, G. E., Saron, C., Bennett, J., & Goldman, D. J. (1979). Frontal versus parietal EEG asymmetry during positive and negative affect. *Psychophysiology, 16,* 202–203.

Denny-Brown, D., & Chambers, R. A. (1958). The parietal lobe and behavior. *Research Publications—Associations for Research in Nervous and Mental Disease, 36,* 35–117.

Denny-Brown, D., Meyers, J. S., & Horenstein, S. (1952). The significance of perceptual rivalry resulting from parietal lesions. *Brain, 75,* 434–471.

Drevets, W. C., & Raichle, M. E. (1992). Neuroanatomic circuits in depression. *Psychopharmacology Bulletin, 28,* 261–274.

Ekman, P., Sorenson, E. R., & Freisen, W. V. (1969). Pancultural elements in facial displays of emotions. *Science, 164,* 86–88.

Fox, N. A., & Davidson, R. J. (1984). Hemispheric substrates for affect: A developmental model. In N. A. Fox & R. J. Davidson (Eds.), *The psychobiology of affective development.* Hillsdale, NJ: Erlbaum.

Frijda, N. H. (1987). Emotion, cognitive structure, and action tendency. *Cognition and Emotion, 1,* 115–143.

Fuster, J. (1989). *The prefrontal cortex* (2nd ed.). New York: Raven Press.

Gainotti, G. (1972). Emotional behavior and hemispheric side of lesion. *Cortex, 8,* 41–55.

Gasparrini, W. G., Satz, P., Heilman, K. M., & Coolidge, F. L. (1978). Hemispheric asymmetries of affective processing as determined by the Minnesota multiphasic personality inventory. *Journal of Neurology, Neurosurgery and Psychiatry, 41,* 470–473.

Goldberg, M. E., & Bushnell, B. C. (1981). Behavioral enhancement of visual responses in monkey cerebral cortex: II. Modulation in frontal eye fields specifically to related saccades. *Journal of Neurophysiology, 46,* 773–787.

Goldstein, K. (1948). *Language and language disturbances.* New York: Grune & Stratton.

Grafman, J., Vance, S. C., Weingartner, H., Salazar, A. M., & Amin, D. (1986). The effects of lateralized frontal lesions on mood regulation. *Brain, 109,* 1127–1140.

Greenwald, M. K., Cook, E. W., & Lang, P. J. (1989). Affective judgment and psychophysiological response: Dimensional co-variation in the evolution of pictorial stimuli. *Journal of Psychophysiology, 3,* 51–64.

Hantas, M., Katkin, E. S., & Blasovich, J. (1982). Relationship between heartbeat discrimination and subjective experience of affective state. *Psychophysiology, 19,* 563.

Hécaen, H., Ajuriagerra, J., & de Massonet, J. (1951). Les troubles visuoconstuctifs par lesion parieto-occipitale droit. *Encephale, 40,* 122–179.

Heilman, K. M. (1979). Neglect and related disorders. In K. M. Heilman & E. Valenstein (Eds.), *Clinical neuropsychology.* New York: Oxford University Press.

Heilman, K. M., Bowers, D., & Valenstein, E. (1993). Emotional disorders associated with neurological disease. In K. M. Heilman & E. Valenstein (Eds.), *Clinical neuropsychology.* 3rd ed. New York: Oxford University Press.

Heilman, K. M., Pandya, D. N., & Geschwind, N. (1970). Trimodal inattention following parietal lobe ablations. *Transactions of the American Neurological Association, 95,* 259–261.

Heilman, K. M., Schwartz, H., & Watson, R. T. (1978). Hypoarousal in patients with the neglect syndrome and emotional indifference. *Neurology, 28,* 229–232.

Heilman, K. M., Valenstein, E., & Watson, R. T. (1983). Localization of neglect. In A. Kertesz (Ed.), *Localization in neurology* (pp. 471–492). New York: Academic Press.

Heilman, K. M., & Van Den Abell, T. (1979). Right hemispheric dominance for mediating cerebral activation. *Neuropsychologia, 17,* 315–321.

Heilman, K. M., Watson, R. T., & Valenstein, E. (1993). Neglect and related disorders. In K. M. Heilman & E. Valenstein (Eds.), *Clinical neuropsychology.* 3rd ed. New York: Oxford University Press.

Heller, W. (1990). Neuropsychology of emotion: Developmental patterns and implications for psychopathology. In N. L. Stein, B. Leventhal, & T. Trabasso (Eds.), *Psychological and biological approaches to emotion.* Hillsdale, NJ: Erlbaum.

Hohmann, G. (1966). Some effects of spinal cord lesions on experimental emotional feelings. *Psychophysiology, 3,* 143–156.

House, A., Dennis, M., Warlow, C., Hawton, K., & Molyneux, A. (1990). Mood disorders after stroke and their relation to lesion location. *Brain, 113,* 1113–1129.

Howes, D., & Boller, F. (1975). Evidence for focal impairment from lesions of the right hemisphere. *Brain, 98,* 317–332.

Hughlings Jackson, J. (1932). In J. Taylor (Ed.), *Selected writings of John Hughlings Jackson.* London: Hodder & Stoughton.

Iwata, J., LeDoux, J. E., Meeley, M. P., Arneric, S., & Reis, D. J. (1986). Intrinsic neurons in the amygdaloid field projected to by the medial geniculate body mediate emotional responses conditioned to acoustic stimuli. *Brain Research, 383,* 195–214.

Izard, C. E. (1977). *Human emotions.* New York: Plenum.

James, W. (1950). *The principles of psychology* (Vol. 2). New York: Dover Publications. (Original work published 1890)

Katkin, E. S., Morrell, M. A., Goldband, S., Bernstein, G. L., & Wise, J. A. (1982). Individual differences in heartbeat discrimination. *Psychophysiology, 19,* 160–166.

Klüver, H., & Bucy, P. C. (1937). "Physic blindness" and other symptoms following bilateral temporal lobe lobectomy in rhesus monkeys. *American Journal of Physiology, 119,* 352–353.

Laird, J. D. (1974). Self-attribution of emotion: The effects of expressive behavior on the quality of emotional experience. *Journal of Personality and Social Psychology, 29,* 475–486.

Luria, A. R., & Simernitskaya, E. G. (1977). Interhemispheric relations and the functions of the minor hemisphere. *Neuropsychologia, 15,* 175–178.

Lynch, J. C. (1980). The functional organization of posterior parietal association cortex. *Behavioral and Brain Sciences, 3,* 485–534.

MacLean, P. D. (1952). Some psychiatric implications of physiological studies on frontotemporal portion of limbic system (visceral brain). *Electroencephalography and Clinical Neurophysiology, 4,* 407–418.

Marañon, G. (1924). Contribution à l'étude de l'action emotive de l'adrenaline. *Revue Française d'Endocrinologie, 2,* 301–325.

Mesulam, M. M. (1981). A cortical network for directed attention and unilateral neglect. *Annals of Neurology, 10,* 309–325.

Mesulam, M. M., Van Hesen, G. W., Pandya, D. N., & Geschwind, N. (1977). Limbic and sensory connections of the inferior parietal lobule (area PG) in the rhesus monkey: A study with a new method for horseradish peroxidase histochemistry. *Brain Research, 136,* 393–414.

Milner, B. (1974). Hemispheric specialization: Scope and limits. In F. O. Schmitt & F. G. Worden (Eds.), *The neurosciences: Third study program.* Cambridge, MA: MIT Press.

Morrow, L., Vrtunski, P. B., Kim, Y., & Boller, F. (1981). Arousal responses to emotional stimuli and laterality of lesions. *Neuropsychologia, 19,* 65–71.

Moruzzi, G., & Magoun, H. W. (1949). Brainstem reticular formation and activation of the EEG. *Electroencephalography and Clinical Neurophysiology, 1,* 455–473.

Osgood, C., Suci, G., & Tannenbaum, P. (1957). *The measure of meaning.* Urbana: University of Illinois.

Pandya, D. M., & Kuypers, H. G. J. M. (1969). Cortico-cortical connections in the rhesus monkey. *Brain Research, 13,* 13–36.

Papez, J. W. (1937). A proposed mechanism of emotion. *Archives of Neurology and Psychiatry, 38,* 725–743.

Perani, D., Vallar, G., Paulesu, E., Alberoni, M., & Fasio, F. (1993). Left and right hemisphere contributions to recovery from neglect after right hemisphere damage. *Neuropsychologia, 31,* 115–125.

Phelps, M. E., Mazziotta, J. C., Baxter, L., & Geiner, R. (1984). Positron emission tomographic study of affective disorders: Problems and strategies. *Annals of Neurology, 15,* (Suppl.), S149–S156.

Poeck, K. (1969). Pathophysiology of emotional disorders associated with brain damage. In P. J. Vinken & G. W. Bruyn (Eds.), *Handbook of neurology* (Vol. 3). New York: Elsevier.

Pribram, K. H., & McGuiness, D. (1975). Arousal, activation and effort in the control of attention. *Psychological Review, 182,* 116–149.

Robinson, R. G., & Starkstein, S. (1989). Mood disorders following stroke: New findings and future directions. *Journal of Geriatric Psychiatry, 22,* 1–15.

Robinson, R. G., & Sztela, B. (1981). Mood change following left hemisphere brain injury. *Annals of Neurology, 9,* 447–453.

Ross, E. D., & Mesulam, M. M. (1979). Dominant language functions of the right hemisphere? Prosody and emotional gesturing. *Archives of Neurology (Chicago), 36,* 144–148.

Rossi, G. S., & Rosadini, G. (1967). Experimental analysis of cerebral dominance in man. In C. Millikan & F. L. Darley (Eds.), *Brain mechanisms underlying speech and language.* New York: Grune & Stratton.

Sackheim, H. A., Greenberg, M. S., Weiman, A. L., Gur, R. C., Hungerbuhler, J. P., & Geschwind, N. (1982). Hemispheric asymmetry in the expression of positive and negative emotions: neurologic evidence. *Archives of Neurology (Chicago), 39,* 210–218.

Sato, H., Hata, Y., Hagihara, K., & Tsumoto, T. (1987). Effects of cholinergic depletion on neuron activities in the cat visual cortex. *Journal of Neurophysiology, 58,* 781–794.

Schacter, S., & Singer, J. E. (1962). Cognitive, social, and physiological determinants of emotional state. *Psychological Review, 69,* 379–399.

Scheibel, M. E., & Scheibel, A. B. (1966). The organization of the nucleus reticularis thalami: A Golgi study. *Brain Research, 1,* 43–62.

Scheibel, M. E., & Scheibel, A. B. (1967). Structural organization of nonspecific thalamic nuclei and their projection toward cortex. *Brain, 6,* 60–94.

Schrandt, N. J., Tranel, D., & Damasio, H. (1989). The effects of total cerebral lesions on skin conductance response to signal stimuli. *Neurology, 39*(Suppl. 1), 223.

Segundo, J. P., Naguet, R., & Buser, P. (1955). Effects of cortical stimulation on electrocortical activity in monkeys. *Neurophysiology, 1B,* 236–245.

Shute, C.C.D., & Lewis, P. R. (1967). The ascending cholinergic reticular system, neocortical olfactory and subcortical projections. *Brain, 90,* 497–520.

Starkstein, S. E., Robinson, R. G., & Price, T. R. (1987). Comparison of cortical and subcortical lesions in the production of poststroke mood disorders. *Brain, 110,* 1045–1059.

Steriade, M., & Glenn, L. (1982). Neocortical and caudate projections of intralaminar thalamic neurons and their synaptic excitation from the midbrain reticular core. *Journal of Neurophysiology, 48,* 352–370.

Stuss, D. T., & Benson, D. F. (1986). *The frontal lobes.* New York: Raven Press.

Terzian, H. (1964). Behavioral and EEG effects of intracarotid sodium amytal injections. *Acta Neurochirugica, 12,* 230–240.

Tomkins, S. S. (1962). *Affect, imagery, consciousness: Vol. 1. The Positive Affects.* New York: Springer.

Tomkins, S. S. (1963). *Affect, imagery, consciousness: Vol. 2. The Negative Affects.* New York: Springer.

Tucker, D. M. (1981). Lateral brain function, emotion and conceptualization. *Psychological Bulletin, 89,* 19–46.

Tucker, D. M., Watson, R. T., & Heilman, K. M. (1977). Affective discrimination and evocation in patients with right parietal disease. *Neurology, 17,* 947–950.

Tucker, D. M., & Williamson, P. A. (1984). Asymmetric neural control in human self-regulation. *Psychological Review, 91,* 185–215.

Watson, R. T., Heilman, K. M., Miller, B. D., & King, F. A. (1974). Neglect after mesencephalic reticular formation lesions. *Neurology, 24,* 294–298.

Watson, R. T., Miller, B. D., & Heilman, K. M. (1978). Nonsensory neglect. *Annals of Neurology, 3,* 505–508.

Watson, R. T., Valenstein, E., & Heilman, K. M. (1981). Thalamic neglect: The possible role of the medial thalamus and nucleus reticularis thalami in behavior. *Archives of Neurology (Chicago), 38,* 501–507.

Weiskrantz, L. (1956). Behavioral changes associated with ablation of the amygdaloid complex in monkeys. *Journal of Comparative Physiology and Psychology, 49,* 381–391.

Wundt, W. (1903). *Grundriss der Psychologie.* Stuttgart: Engelmann.

Yakovlev, P. I. (1948). Motility, behavior and the brain: Stereodynamic organization and neural coordinates in behavior. *Journal of Nervous and Mental Disease, 107,* 313–335.

Yokoyama, K., Jennings, R., Ackles, P., Hood, P., & Boller, F. (1987). Lack of heart rate changes during an attention-demanding task after right hemisphere lesions. *Neurology, 37,* 624–630.

CHAPTER 8

Neuropsychology of the Prefrontal Cortex

Jordan Grafman

I. INTRODUCTION

The prefrontal cortex occupies approximately one-third of the entire cerebral cortex in humans. This proportion is much greater than that seen in other species. In fact, when proportionality is taken into account, the prefrontal cortex occupies over 200% more cortical space in humans compared to monkeys (Stuss & Benson, 1986). The magnitude of this evolutionary development is dramatic and without precedence elsewhere in the brain. This dramatic growth of the prefrontal cortex in humans reinforces its importance in our evolutionary survival.

The prefrontal cortex does not fully mature until around 15 yrs of age (Stuss, 1992). In the adult brain, the right frontal pole is enlarged in comparison with the left frontal pole. Other areas of the prefrontal cortex appear grossly symmetrical.

The cortical morphology of the prefrontal cortex is quite similar to other areas of cortex in terms of the number of layers, with the exception of the granular layer of cortex, which appears to be absent (Petrides and Pandya, in press). The columnar organization observed in posterior regions of cortex also reappears in the prefrontal cortex. As with other cortices, the prefrontal cortex was assigned regional numbers by Brodmann, and they are still used today as conventional landmarks. Petrides and Pandya have recently attempted to unify animal and human cortical anatomical mapping into a single landmark system (Petrides and Pandya, in press). The prefrontal cortex can also be grossly divided into dorsolateral, medial, and orbitofrontal regions. These gross divisions are the most typically used landmarks when describing the location of lesions in patients.

Several neurotransmitter- and peptide-labeled systems project to the prefrontal cortex (Cohen & Servan-Schreiber, 1992). Receptors exist for neurotransmitters such as serotonin, dopamine, and acetylcholine. The exact role of transmitter levels in the expression of higher cognitive processes remains unknown.

The basic electrophysiological properties of single cells and neural assemblies located in the prefrontal cortex appear compatible with those seen in neural networks in posterior cortex. However, there is a greater tendency of neurons in the prefrontal cortex to fire in the absence of environmental stimuli both in preparation for a response and, apparently, to temporarily keep information active until a response is required, than neurons in posterior cortex (Uylings, Van Eden, De Bruin, Corner, & Feenstra, 1990).

The prefrontal cortex has extensive connections with other cortical association areas as well as midline deep structures such as the basal ganglia, thalamus, basal forebrain, and entorhinal cortex.

Because of its extensive connections with other brain regions, the functioning of the prefrontal cortex is affected by many neurological diseases including those resulting in focal (e.g., stroke, tumor, penetrating head injury) and diffuse (e.g., degenerative dementias) lesions (Stuss & Benson, 1986). Many psychiatric disorders are caused by dysfunction in brain structures that are part of, or project to, the prefrontal cortex (Weinberger, 1993).

Thus, the prefrontal cortex is most prominent in humans, matures late in development, has a similar morphology when compared to other cortical regions, extensive connectivity, and has some idiosyncratic features related to the functional properties of its neurons. It is also involved in many neurological disorders. Given these characteristics, it might be logical to infer that the prefrontal cortex plays some integrative role in cognitive functioning. One way to discover its role in cognitive functioning is to examine the effects of frontal lobe lesions or dysfunction on higher cognitive processes in humans. Those findings are summarized next.

II. THE EFFECTS OF BRAIN DAMAGE IN PREFRONTAL CORTEX ON HIGHER COGNITIVE FUNCTIONS

Various neurological disorders may impair prefrontal cortex functioning and therefore also affect higher cognitive functions (Shallice, 1988). In general, the methods used to study such patients are primarily group designs.

Single-case study designs have only rarely been applied with patients with frontal lobe lesions (Shallice, 1988). In these rare cases, the studies tend to primarily be descriptive but provide many ideas for hypothesis testing.

The domains of higher cognitive functioning that have been examined in patients with prefrontal lesions include concept formation and shifting (S. W. Anderson, Damasio, Jones, & Tranel, 1991; Arnett et al., in press; Cicerone & Lazar, 1983; Delis, Squire, Bihrle, & Massman, 1992; Grafman, Litvan, Gomez, & Chase, 1990; Milner, 1963; Mountain & Snow, 1993; Owen, Roberts, Polkey, Sahakian, & Robbins, 1991; Robinson, Heaton, Lehman, & Stilson, 1980), reasoning (Golding, 1981; F. C. Goldstein & Levin, 1991), planning (L. H. Goldstein, Bernard, Fenwick, Burgess, & McNeil, 1993; Grafman & Hendler, 1991; Karnath, Wallesch, & Zimmermann, 1991), insight (Janowsky, Shimamura, & Squire, 1989a; Shallice & Evans, 1978), and associative learning (Janowsky, Shimamura, Kritchevsky, & Squire, 1989; Janowsky, Shimamura, & Squire, 1989b; Lang et al., 1988; Parkin, Dunn, Lee, O'Hara, & Nussbaum, 1993; Petrides, 1985, 1990; Schacter, 1987; A. Shimamura, Gershberg, Jurica, Mangels, & Knight, 1992). Patients with prefrontal lobe lesions routinely perform worse than controls in these domains. However, this is a slightly misleading statement because only a handful of tests have been extensively used. These include the Wisconsin Card Sorting Test (concept formation and shifting), Category Test (conceptual reasoning), Raven Progressive Matrices Test (visuospatial reasoning), Trail Making Test (set shifting), a variety of Tower of Hanoi-type tasks (planning), and verbal and nonverbal fluency tasks. Many of these tasks have been administered to large numbers of patients as part of standardized batteries. Some, like the Tower of Hanoi, have caught on as a potential measure of planning behavior and are slowly being incorporated into the assessment of patients with frontal lesions. If one delves deep enough into the literature, one can find the Wason Card Selection task and related traditional measures from the reasoning literature being used too (Stuss, Eskes, & Foster, in press). Unfortunately, there has been relatively little work in understanding why patients with prefrontal lobe lesions fail on these tasks. Even less effort has been committed to fitting the results into a theoretical construct of higher cognitive functions that is something more than a glorified black box. However, there are some notable exceptions to this rather negative viewpoint and they will be introduced in a subsequent section.

A. Subject Selection

Much has been written about the poor performance of patients with focal lesions (e.g., strokes, tumors, penetrating missile wounds) in the frontal lobes on tests of higher cognitive functions (Stuss & Benson, 1986). In general, on most tests of reasoning and problem solving, patients with nonfrontal lesions perform equal or better to patients with focal prefrontal lesions (Stuss & Benson, 1986). However, investigators may have difficulty avoiding a bias in subject selection in these comparisons. For example, patients with marked language or visuospatial disorders (due to posterior lesions) are usually excluded from such studies, and sometimes the total lesion volume size is not easily computed or equated for across groups. Caveats aside, the general finding of prefrontal patient impairment on tests of higher cognitive functions (HCF) appears to be durable.

Of course, cognitive neuroscience approaches to brain mapping encourage the parcellation of prefrontal cortex into distinctive information-processing networks. There is some certainty that the orbitofrontal and medial prefrontal cortices are concerned with social cognition, regulation of mood, and aspects of supervisory attention (Grafman, Vance, Weingartner, Salazar, & Amin, 1986; Stuss Gow, & Hetherington, 1992). There is also sufficient evidence to indicate that the dorsolateral prefrontal cortex subserves reasoning and concept-formation functions (Stuss et al., in press). Newer research using the techniques of functional imaging has indicated that even finer distinctions in representation are possible (Frith, Friston, Liddle, & Frackowiak, 1991; Rueckert et al., 1994). For example, Petrides has recently demonstrated a dissociation between two types of memory processes that are subserved by prefrontal cortex (Petrides, Alivisatos, Evans, & Meyer, 1993; Petrides, Alivisatos, Meyer, & Evans, 1993).

III. PATIENTS WITH DEGENERATIVE DISORDERS

The information-processing components of a functional activity are hypothesized to be represented in distributed neural systems. Such systems may include local neural networks in cortex, basal ganglia, thalamic nuclei, the cerebellum, and midbrain. Given this topographical distribution and the contribution of many local information-processing networks to performing a human activity, it is likely that damage to any part of the system will affect a functional activity. By studying patients with damage to a structure distant from but connected to the prefrontal cortex, we may learn about how the information-processing components stored in prefrontal cortex interact with other regional brain functions (see Chapter by Koss, this volume). Since degenerative brain disorders such as Parkinson's disease (Cummings, 1993; Pascual-Leone et al., 1993), progressive supranuclear palsy (Grafman, Litvan, Gomez, and Chase, 1990), Huntington's disease (Cummings, 1993), multiple sclerosis (Arnett et al., 1994), and cerebellar atrophy (Grafman, Litvan, et al., 1992; Pascual-Leone et al., 1993) include damaged structures that directly or indirectly project to (or receive projections from) the prefrontal cortex, it should be instructive to test those patients on instruments similar to those used with patients with prefrontal lesions (Bogousslavsky et al., 1988; Cummings, 1993; Laplane et al., 1989). The bottom line is that patients with subcortical degenerative disorders clearly demonstrate some of the same kinds of deficits that patients with prefrontal focal lesions show. In general, the findings are subtler in patients with subcortical degenerative disorders. For example, patients with Parkinson's disease (PD) are thought to have difficulty on tasks requiring reasoning or planning because the basal ganglia structures affected by PD are responsible for setting an internally guided context (based on previous situational experience and practice) that biases which knowledge stored in the prefrontal is selected for response execution (Cummings, 1993).

IV. THE EFFECTS OF PREFRONTAL DAMAGE ON SUBJECT RESPONSE

It has been sufficiently demonstrated that prefrontal lobe damage or dysfunction leads to several kinds of characteristic errors in task performance. These errors include perseveration, embellishment, and confabulation. *Perseveration* can be defined as the inappropriate repetition of a behavior (Daigneault, Braun, & Whitaker, 1992). Perseverative behavior can be observed when the patient draws, writes letters or words, and in interpersonal communication. *Embellishment* can be defined as the inappropriate addition of details to a subject's response when such details were not required nor appeared in the stimulus set given to the subject. *Confabulation* can be defined as a fabricated response where, in most cases, the patient is unaware that they are reporting invented information (Stuss, 1978).

These three error-types are responsible for the poor performance of patients with prefrontal lesions on numerous tests. Other related error-types include inappropriate set-shifting (i.e., abandonment of an appropriate response set), stuck-in-set behavior, poor recognition of the meaning of social cues, disinhibition, impulsiveness, and response bias. A comprehensive classification of errors committed by patients with prefrontal lesions is lacking. It is currently unknown whether error-types overlap in their definition and how domain-specific they may be. Error analysis is an accepted methodology for investigators concerned with knowledge representation (Heckhausen and Beckmann, 1990). For example, models of reading often include a number of component processes along with their buffers. By adapting an error analysis strategy, investigators have been able to argue for component-specific deficits in some patients (Shallice, 1988). Although there is always some debate over the specificity of such findings, the general methodology appears to have gained widespread acceptance within the cognitive neuropsychological literature. There is no a priori reason to think why this approach could not be extended to patients with prefrontal lobe lesions if we could identify the appropriate components to study.

V. MODELS OF PREFRONTAL LOBE FUNCTIONS

Although studies of patients with prefrontal lobe lesions have appeared in the scientific literature since the late nineteenth century, theory and model building in this area has primarily occurred within the last 20 yr (Grafman, 1989). Some of the reasons for this lateness in theory development have to do with the few standardized and experimental instruments that have been used to test patients with prefrontal lobe lesions, the lack of a cognitive framework for many of the behaviors exhibited by patients with prefrontal lobe dysfunction, and the lack of animal models that could be easily applied to humans. For the most part, these problems have been overcome in the last two decades, although there is still no general agreement on the form that symbolic representational systems subserved by prefrontal cortex would take (Grafman, 1989). Nevertheless, there are several prominent theories that have come to dominate and facilitate scientific investigation in this area. They are reviewed next.

A. Working Memory

It has been known since the middle of the nineteenth century that sub-regions of the left frontal cortex subserve speech and motor output functions and that these areas are connected to posterior language areas to form a dynamic system for repetition and production of words and speech sounds (Shallice, 1988). Direct damage to the anterior areas affected language production, whereas a lesion causing a disconnection between the posterior and anterior language systems resulted in word repetition or auditory–verbal short-term memory deficits—both of which interfered with ongoing memory. In the early 1970s, Alan Baddeley (1986) referred to the normal operations of this system as a *working memory*. He argued that this system was composed of several input and output language components as well as a rehearsal loop that linked components. Baddeley's conceptual notion of working memory has sustained and replaced the older term *short-term memory* in the psychology and animal neuroscience literature. There is some evidence that an analogous area of the right hemisphere is concerned with spatial or non-verbal working memory.

In addition to these working memory systems, it has also been known that there was a region of prefrontal cortex just anterior to the premotor area devoted to the voluntary control of eye movements. This region is called the frontal eye field (Guitton, Buchtel, & Douglas, 1985). Each hemisphere has space devoted to this operation.

On the basis of behavioral and electrophysiological studies in monkeys, Goldman-Rakic was able to relate Baddeley's notion of working memory to neural activity (Goldman-Rakic, Bates, & Chafee, 1992). She found that certain cells in the prefrontal cortex would fire only during the interval between stimulus offset and the probe onset. It had been known for some time that in humans, an event-related slow wave appears during the same interval and gradually increased in amplitude as the appearance of the expected probe gets closer in time (Ruchkin, Johnson, Grafman, Canoune, & Ritter, 1992). This slow wave was also related to the type of stimulus and required probe response (Singh & Knight, 1990). Goldman-Rakic concluded that this activity indicated that the frontal lobes were needed to keep information that was no longer available in the environment in an active or working memory state so that it could be used for subsequent responses (Sawaguchi & Goldman-Rakic, 1991). Goldman-Rakic's recent work now suggests that for visual stimuli, this working memory activity in the prefrontal cortex can be retinotopically specified (Funahashi, Bruce, & Goldman-Rakic, 1993).

Although Goldman-Rakic's description of working memory centers on the maintenance of visual stimuli in representational memory and is less cognitively based than Baddeley's work or prior work on language production and aphasia, these three approaches can be tied together to suggest that there is a form of representation in the prefrontal cortex that allows for the activation of information no longer in the immediate sensory environment (Perrides, 1991a,b; Jonides et al., 1993; Paulesu, Frith, & Frackowiak, 1993). Goldman-Rakic has suggested that the information being held active is actually stored in posterior cortex and the role of the prefrontal cortex is merely to keep it activated during a rehearsal interval.

B. Temporal Encoding

There are a number of results in the psychological literature to indicate that temporal encoding of an event (i.e., the order and timing of a sequence of individual events) is stored separately from its content (e.g., phonology, form, or meaning) (Della Malva, Stuss, D'Alton, & Willmer, 1993; Dennett & Kinsbourne, 1992). There is also evidence that patients with prefrontal lesions have great difficulty in encoding the exact order in which stimuli were presented to them, although they may have normal recognition and even recall of a list of stimuli (McAndrews & Milner, 1991; Milner, Petrides, & Smith, 1985; A. P. Shimamura, Janowsky, & Squire, 1990; Smith & Milner, 1988; Wilkins, Shallice, & McCarthy, 1987). Furthermore, Fuster has determined that a subset of cells in the prefrontal cortex is extremely sensitive to the temporal properties of stimuli (Fuster, 1989). He has elaborated his findings into a theory that claims that the prefrontal cortex is uniquely specified for the temporal encoding of information (Fuster, 1989).

If temporal encoding and working memory are reliable theoretical constructs, then it can be argued that the prefrontal cortex not only keeps information that is no longer in the environment active, but is very concerned with constructing a memory for the timing and sequence of such information.

C. Affect and Social Cognition

Patients with prefrontal lesions almost always have problems in interpersonal interactions that have been hard to conceptualize (Stuss et al., 1992). One of the oldest and most widely cited cases was a railroad worker named Gage who suffered an accidental penetrating missile wound to the frontal lobes while at work (Stuss et al., 1992). Gage's co-workers thought that after recovering from his penetrating head injury, "he was no longer Gage." His personality had changed and he was less respectful and predictable when compared to what he had been like before his injury. Gage later moved to Chile in South America and paradoxically appeared able to work steadily for the time he lived there. Thus, although Gage's personality changed by all accounts following his injury, the changes were not completely disabling. Patients diagnosed with schizophrenia have also been found to have abnormal prefrontal lobe functioning that may account for some of their negative symptoms that adversely affect their social functioning (Weinberger, 1993).

D. Moral Judgment

Damasio and his co-workers have offered a possible explanation for some of the abnormal changes in personality and mood state seen in patients with prefrontal lobe lesions (Damasio, Tranel, & Damasio, 1990, 1991; Eslinger, Grattan, Damasio, & Damasio, 1992; Grattan & Eslinger, 1992; Saver & Damasio, 1991; Tranel, Anderson & Benton, in press). They argued that the lesion, most often in the orbito- or medial-frontal cortex, disconnects the prefrontal cortex from limbic system structures that mediate the affective valence or sensation that humans use to appreciate the meaning of social-emotional expression and help us decide how to respond to certain social demands. They demonstrated this decision-making impairment by measuring autonomic responsivity to certain emotion-evoking stimuli in a small group of patients with orbitofrontal lesions. They found that their patients, unlike controls, showed no responsivity when asked to merely covertly observe emotion–evoking stimuli. However, their autonomic responsivity was no different than controls when asked to overtly respond to the stimuli.

Thus, in addition to impaired working memory and temporal encoding, prefrontal lobe patients may also suffer from a diminished autonomic sensitivity to socially relevant stimuli under certain conditions.

E. Supervisory Attention and Planning and the Prefrontal Cortex

Norman and Shallice have proposed a model of attention that they hoped would explain why patients with frontal lobe lesions were so distractable (Norman and Shallice, 1980, 1986). They proposed that the frontal lobes were highly concerned with the internal *control* of behavior (Duncan, 1990). They suggested that behavioral control could be implemented via one of two attentional mechanisms: a *contention scheduler* and a *supervisor* (Norman and Shallice, 1986). The *contention scheduler* was a mechanism by which environmental information would directly and automatically activate stored knowledge (Shallice has variously described such stored knowledge as scripts, schemas, or memory operation packets). This knowledge, when activated, presumably would guide the expression of specific sequences of behaviors while inhibiting the activation of both related and unrelated behaviors (Klouda & Cooper, 1990; Miller, 1992).

The *supervisory attention* mechanism allowed for the overriding of automatically generated behaviors in the case when an event occurring in the environment or an internally generated idea requires more immediate processing. A simple example of this might occur in the following scenario. You are walking to work. You are taking the same route as always, obeying pedestrian rules. While you are crossing a street on your route, you remember you had an appointment downtown. At this point, you might *interrupt* your normal routine to pause and decide whether you need to call and cancel your appointment. You decide to first call work from a public telephone to inquire whether the person you had your meeting with had called. All the thoughts and subsequent actions that occurred following your memory of an appointment would be dependent on the expression of the supervisory attention system (rather than environmental contingencies) in the Norman and Shallice model.

Norman and Shallice's model implies that without the development of a supervisory attention mechanism, the immediate environment would manipulate the response repertoire of an animal with few opportunities to override preprogrammed behavior (Eslinger, Warner, Grattan, & Easton, 1991; Lhermitte, 1983, 1986; Lhermitte, Pillon, Serdaru, 1986; Shallice, Burgess, Schon, & Baxter, 1989). Therefore, the homeostasis between the world and its sensory imposition on the brain and the symbolic world of the individual is conserved by the prefrontal cortex (Shallice & Burgess, 1991).

Although it is only briefly mentioned in their writings, Norman and Shallice note that their proposed attentional mechanisms primarily activate stored knowledge that is unique to the frontal lobes (Shallice, 1988). The neuroanatomical concomitants of their attentional model is unspecified but some have argued that the longitudinal white matter fibers that project from the prefrontal cortex to other cortical and subcortical regions and the cingulate gyrus would be prime candidate structures by which attentional commands would be carried out.

It is tempting to view the various forms of attention as euphemistic for some as yet unspecified set of processes. On the other hand, connectionist modelers have discussed how a pattern of inhibitory and facilitatory mechanisms could mimic an attentional process (Kimberg & Farah, 1993). In any case, the Norman and Shallice model of attention and the prefrontal cortex has been highly influential.

Thus, patients with prefrontal lesions suffer from impaired working memory, temporal encoding, and a diminished autonomic sensitivity to socially relevant stimuli, which under certain conditions would impair their ability to exercise control over their behavior—particularly if the control is based upon internal mental states rather than environmental demands (Alivsatos, 1992).

F. Summary of Current Models and What They Are Able to Explain

Most of the current models of prefrontal lobe functions, including those reviewed above and others, suggest that the main function of the prefrontal cortex is to manipulate in some manner information stored elsewhere in the cerebral cortex and brain. Whether the process being referred to is working memory, attention, or serial encoding, they all appear to be dependent upon an as-yet-unseen marionette operator. This notion should give you pause. After all, since no other area of cerebral cortex has been anointed this function, it would represent a radical departure from current thinking about representational networks.

That is, it suggests that there may be two fundamentally different kinds of representations in the cerebral cortex. One kind of representation, the symbolic one, is currently captured by the notion of a lexicon or associative memory system that would be contained within the boundaries of a local neural network (Goel and Grafman, 1993; submitted). Thus, our knowledge of a word or picture is stored within a particular neural network and that increasing damage to that network (from a local brain lesion or degenerative process) would make it increasingly difficult to both retrieve and make use of that knowledge (usually based upon some metric like similarity, frequency, or familiarity). This kind of symbolic representation can be contrasted with one that represents operations rather than symbols. Operations are algorithms that manipulate stored knowledge. The current conventional presumption is that these operator algorithms are stored in local neural networks within the prefrontal cortex. They would manipulate knowledge stored in temporal, parietal, and occipital cortex as well as subcortical structures. The operations referred to include the aforementioned working memory, attention, and temporal encoding processes.

This proposal of two distinctive kinds of representation is attractive to many researchers, yet there are at least two risky assumptions associated with it. It implies that we have captured all aspects of knowledge within the realm of the posterior cortex. It also implies that there should be a fundamental difference in the neuroanatomy and molecular biology of the frontal and posterior cortices.

Of course, there is also the question of how much of normal and impaired human behavior can these models explain and predict. In the case of patients with frontal lobe lesions, they all carry "shotgun" type explanatory power that attempts to account for a large number of cognitive and behavioral deficits on the basis of a single type of operator failure.

I have criticized these approaches in the past because each fails to account in detail for most of the cognitive deficits exhibited by patients with prefrontal lobe lesions and almost none provide a rich cognitive architecture that can be tested (Grafman, 1989).

There is an alternative approach to understanding the functions of the prefrontal cortex. That is to suppose that it serves a function similar to that of other regions of cerebral cortex. In other words, there may not be a need to assign nonsymbolic operations to the prefrontal cortex but instead to propose what kind of symbolic representations might be stored there. This is a more parsimonious approach than the dual-representational approach described above. Of course, the cerebral cortex is not laid out in a haphazard fashion and to argue for a kind of representation that would be stored in prefrontal cortex, one must also put that representation into the broader context of representational knowledge and evolutionary development (remember that in humans, the prefrontal cortex has reached its apogee and is clearly the area of cortex that has shown the greatest proportional development across species).

VI. EVOLUTIONARY COGNITIVE ARCHITECTURAL PERSPECTIVES

The most parsimonious approach to building a model of the cognitive architecture of knowledge stored in the prefrontal cortex would be to adapt an architecture similar to that used in other representational domains (Johnson-Laird, 1983). Thus, items in such an architecture would be interrelated on the basis of similarity, frequency, category membership, association values, and so on (Johnson-Laird, 1983). The more related an item was to another item in any one of the metrics, the more likely that such items would be neighbors in a psychological space. The boundaries encompassing such psychological space would probably be fuzzy to accommodate cognitive plasticity. This approach was used by D. Zaidel (1987; 1994) to determine the nature of the conceptual organization in the left and right hemispheres of normal subjects as well as of split-brain patients.

Within these cognitive architectures, a *unit* of knowledge represents a *single* assembly of information such as an edge, word, meaning, form, location in space, or syntactic frame. Across cognitive-processing components there appears to be an evolutionary trend from components in which knowledge units are representing a single aspect or feature of a stimulus event and can be activated for brief periods of time (such as an "edge detector") to units that represent a *series of events* that are activated for longer durations of time (such as a syntactic frame). This trend is also apparent phylogenetically with lower species dominated by information-processing components in which the units of representation are weighted towards the singular aspects of events with rapid onset and offset times, whereas higher species are dominated by components in which units of representation are weighted towards the sequential aspects of events with long duration onset and offset times. This evolutionary development in knowledge representation would, of course, allow for *single units* of memory that store a *structured event complex* (SEC). This SEC contains information relevant to the consequences of past and current behavior by virtue of its storing events that have occurred in the past and will occur in the future. This representation would store both the theme and boundaries of events and not simply re-represent the other features of event series, such as words, sentences, or visual features, which it would be temporally bound to for any given situation (Singer, 1993; Singer et al., 1993).

Within this conception of the evolution of knowledge representation, linguistic terms that indicate future and past tense and qualify the consequences of current behavior emerged. This ability to store single units of memory representing thematic and temporal aspects of event series would give humans a distinct advantage over animals who were much more prone to respond to single environmental events without being aware of, or able to conceptualize, the consequences of their actions. Furthermore, this kind of thematic memory unit, when activated, would link the event currently underway to events already in the past and events yet to come. These units could be learned on the basis of experiencing external events and the generation of "internal thought." It is this kind of unitized *thematic* knowledge that may be stored in the prefrontal cortex.

I will develop the idea of this kind of thematic memory unit, its relationship with other cognitive processes, and how its reality could underlay many, if not all, of the higher cognitive function models described above. I call this unit the *managerial knowledge unit* (MKU), a type of SEC (Grafman, Sirigu, Spector, & Hendler, 1993).

VII. DEVELOPMENT AND DECLINE OF STRUCTURED EVENT COMPLEXES AND THE MANAGERIAL KNOWLEDGE UNIT

Children are able to adequately process simple events and remember them—even remembering aspects of those events related to their contingencies. Can children adequately store and process large-scale knowledge units such as the ones we propose are stored in prefrontal cortex? Children show impatience when participating in extended event series (e.g., eating at a restaurant), have a difficult time expressing knowledge about such event series, and are unable to solve complex problems requiring the use of plans (Welsh & Pennington, 1992).

There is evidence that the prefrontal cortex does not mature until the teenage years and perhaps matures more slowly than other cortical association areas (Diamond & Doar, 1989; Diamond, Zola-Morgan, & Squire, 1989). Given these observations, we suspect that there are two basic possibilities governing the development of the SEC. In the first case, the brain may be unprepared to store large series of events as a single unit until the teenage years. Young children might be able to store simple contingencies, procedural rules, and develop simple skills (the primitive SEC antecedents of the MKU) but more complex cognitive knowledge would be developed slowly over time. The second possibility is that the child can develop even a large series of events as a single MKU in early childhood, but the number of such memories would be limited until the teenage years.

By the time a child becomes a young adult, the prefrontal cortex would be stocked with SECs, many of which would qualify as MKUs. These memories would allow us to express and understand schematic knowledge in the form of plans, themes, and other complex event series. In turn, there is some evidence that the prefrontal cortex is particularly affected by the aging process (Craik, Morris, Morris, & Loewen, 1990; Salmon et al., 1991).

The structure of the MKU and the functional architecture to which it belongs is next described.

VIII. STRUCTURE AND FUNCTIONAL ARCHITECTURE OF THE STRUCTURED EVENT COMPLEX AND MANAGERIAL KNOWLEDGE UNIT

There is general agreement that the thematic and serial aspects of knowledge cannot be easily captured by current models of semantic or sentence knowledge. Instead, frames, scripts, maps, schemas, general knowledge units, thematic knowledge, cases, and plans have all been proposed as theoretical psychological structures that store the meaning of series of events in memory (Allen, Hendler, & Tate, 1990; J. R. Anderson, 1993; Bower & Morrow, 1990; Goel & Grafman, 1994b; Grafman, 1989; Halford, 1992; Hammond, 1989; Holland, Holyoak, Nisbett, & Thagard, 1986; Johnson-Laird, 1983; Langley & Drummond, 1990; Riesbeck & Schank, 1989; R. Schank & Abelson, 1977; R. C. Schank, 1982). It has not been clear whether these memories represent a distributed network of event knowledge or have unique properties that require a distinctive form of storage (A. P. Shimamura, Janowsky, & Squire, 1991).

Patients with prefrontal lobe lesions often perform well on tasks requiring word and sentence processing and have relatively good immediate memory yet consistently fail on tasks designed to examine reasoning and planning (Stuss et al., in press). They also have problems with the serial ordering of information. Could their deficits be explained by an impairment in accessing memories containing thematic serial knowledge? The logic used to explain the cognitive deficits of patients with cortical lesions in posterior cortex relies upon conceptualizing damage to various knowledge stores (Shallice, 1988). For example, agnosic patients may have difficulty recognizing objects because their cortical lesions directly affect a neural network that stores an aspect of the object (e.g., its name, its use, or its form). This logic can be adapted for understanding the cognitive deficits of patients with frontal lobe lesions. That is, the lesion affects neural networks that subserve knowledge specific to event series. If this is the case, then specifying the nature of that knowledge and its cognitive architecture should help us solve the riddle of the functions of the prefrontal cortex.

The only model that reflects this approach is one offered by Grafman and his colleagues (Grafman, 1989; Grafman et al., 1993; Grafman, Thompsen-Putnam, Sunderland, & Weingartner, 1991). As noted above, they have labeled these hypothetical prefrontal cortical knowledge structures the MKU. The MKU was considered an evolved form of the SEC. The SEC, in its more primitive form, might be a series of motor actions or a sentence frame. In its more complex form, the SEC would take on the format of an MKU—representing a cognitive plan or theme. We have argued that one of the achievements of human brain development was to be able to store single events together within a single memory unit. This would allow a single memory unit to evoke the present (the event being currently carried out or processed), the past (events previously experienced but no longer in working memory), and the future (events to be processed or experienced as part of the series of events but not currently in working memory). This linkage would enable a person to anticipate the consequences of their current or past actions. Predictability certainly helps survival rates. So instead of a simple associative relationship across individuated events stored in memory, the individuated events would now be stored *together* as a simple memory unit-in effect, creating the kind of memory that could store themes, scripts, plans, and the like in parallel with other features of the event series (object knowledge, procedures, etc.).

What might an individual MKU represent? Grafman et al. (1993) have proposed three levels of MKU representation. The most *abstract* level would contain nonspecified events such as a beginning, setting, subject intention, subject actions, resolution of intentional action, departure from a setting, and ending. This level of MKU representation would allow people to rationalize their most ambiguous experiences by placing them within the constraints afforded by this abstract MKU structure. The next level of MKU representation would be the *context-free* level, which would have greater specifications regarding the MKU events. For example, eating dinner would be a context-free MKU since its events could be acted out or perceived in a variety of contexts. The last level would be a *context-dependent* level and could only be appropriately acted out in a certain context(s). For example, behaviors appropriate to eating at an elegant French restaurant.

At each of these levels, the individual MKU is composed of a series of thematic event features that rerepresent the actual experience of a person. Of course, event boundaries can range on a continuum from fuzzy to sharp. For example, when does a bill payment event begin and end? Does it begin when you ask for the bill or when you receive it? Does it end when you pay the bill or when you receive your receipt? Somehow the neural networks concerned with storing event series must obey certain symbolic or environmental rules in order to parse these boundaries. Perhaps the role of sustained attentional processes is to set event and event-series boundaries. Relatively rapid shifts of attention would bias information to be stored as a simple unit (e.g., object form), whereas sustained attention would bias information to be stored as an MKU (e.g., a behavioral series concerned with eating). Why are our behaviors so predictable? The rigidity of an event series is unknown. That is, whether the order of events in an MKU must be total (rigidly ordered) or partial (or can be both) also remains to be determined.

The assumption that Grafman et al. (1993) made was that SECs and MKUs are activated during the perception of event series, during their expression, and even during their verbal description. Thus, SECs and MKUs can be activated in real or in "compressed" time.

Grafman et al. also suggest that the MKU has different forms (Grafman, 1989; Grafman et al., 1993). For example, there should be an MKU that has primarily linguistic properties (lists or scripts) and one that has primarily imagistic properties (visual scenes).

If an individual MKU is simply another kind of memory unit, it should be part of a representational network that has characteristics or properties that resemble other cognitive architectures. Therefore, MKU units would be related to each other within a local neural network devoted to its representation on the basis of frequency, similarity, or association value. They could also be stored within a network in a distributed fashion. Furthermore, it would not be surprising if SECs and MKUs had some sort of categorical organization, such that social and nonsocial knowledge might be distinctively stored with more specific categorical distinctions nested within these broader ones. Interactive activation and inhibition between MKUs could operate under the same constraints as those proposed for lexical stores. Thus, "errors" in behavior should be due to a lack of inhibition.

Why is it important to specify the cognitive architecture of these structures? If MKUs are stored in prefrontal cortex, then damage to the prefrontal cortex would, in some systematic way, disable the cognitive architecture. A blueprint of a cognitive architecture should also indicate the number of ways that such an architecture might conceivably fail (i.e., its stress points).

Besides the effort by Grafman, very little in the way of architectural specification has occurred, partly because most other investigators attempting to understand the functions of the prefrontal cortex simply do not believe that the prefrontal cortex subserves such a symbolic architecture (Grafman, in press).

IX. SUMMARY

If Grafman is correct, then the road to understanding the functions of the prefrontal cortex may be shorter than previously thought because methods to understand cognitive architectures and their content are available. Furthermore, MKUs may be the units of thematic knowledge that underlie our ability to plan, reason out actions, and conceptualize situations. If Grafman's approach is incorrect, then the way knowledge is stored in the prefrontal cortex represents a dramatic departure from the way neuropsychologists have described knowledge stores in posterior cortex. If investigators adapt this latter approach, then they should be required to specify predictions about patient failure that go beyond simple unidimensional descriptions.

X. MORE COMMENTS ON METHODOLOGY

In many of the neuropsychological studies cited above, the patients' deficits were based upon whether they misordered stimuli during recognition or problem solving, whether they perseverated in their responses, and whether deficits occurred in novel or overlearned situations. The question that researchers must answer is whether this kind of error analysis is sufficient or whether a more detailed error analysis would be useful (Mayer, Reed,

Schwartz, Montgomery, & Palmer, 1990; Schwartz, Mayer, Fitzpatrick, DeSalme, & Montgomery, 1993; Schwartz, Reed, Montgomery, Palmer, & Mayer, 1991). Many of the tasks used in such studies are tasks that were not originally designed to evaluate the patient with prefrontal lobe lesions. Can we design tasks that are targeted to the deficits exhibited by these patients? Can such tasks be designed without a comprehensive cognitive model? Finally, which patients should be used to study the prefrontal cortex? Clearly, patients with focal lesions relatively limited to the cerebral cortex would be ideal research subjects. However, many patients studied in the past were premorbidly ill or had large lesions that included the prefrontal cortex but extended to subcortical and other cortical regions (e.g., in closed head injury [Baddeley & Wilson, 1988; Ross, Graham, & Adams, 1993]). A careful description of patients that are selected for research studies that includes their lesion location and premorbid history must be adhered to for advances in our knowledge of the functions of the prefrontal cortex to be made.

XI. CONCLUSIONS

The prefrontal cortex occupies a predominant position in human cortical space. We are privileged as humans to have a large prefrontal cortex, yet we know relatively little about its functions. Can we fully understand a semi-modular yet distributed whole-brain network without this piece of the puzzle? Not likely. Understanding the functions of the prefrontal cortex remains the great challenge of cognitive neuroscience as we turn toward the twenty-first century. An understanding of its function(s) will help us solve one of the great mysteries of life, how the brain parses the environmental and symbolic world in order for us to optimally represent information.

Acknowledgment

I would like to acknowledge Angela Sirigu, Lee Spector, Jim Hendler, Paolo Nichelli, Vinod Goel, and Irene Litvan for their help in stimulating the ideas contained in the chapter.

References

Alivsatos, B. (1992). The role of the frontal cortex in the use of advance information in a mental rotation paradigm. *Neuropsychologia, 30*(2), 145–159.
Allen, J., Hendler, J., & Tate, A. (Ed.). (1990). *Readings in Planning.* San Mateo: Morgan Kaufmann.
Anderson, J. R. (1993). Problem solving and learning. *American Psychologist, 48*(1), 35–44.
Anderson, S. W., Damasio, H., Jones, R. D., & Tranel, D. (1991). Wisconsin card sorting test performance as a measure of frontal lobe damage. *Journal of Clinical and Experimental Neuropsychology, 13*(6), 909–922.
Arnett, P. A., Rao, S. M., Bernadin, L. J., Grafman, J., Yetkin, F. Z., & Lobeck, L. (1994).

Relationship between frontal lesions and Wisconsin card sorting test performance in patients with multiple sclerosis. *Neurology, 44*(3), 420–424.

Baddeley, A. (1986). Working Memory. Oxford: Oxford University Press.

Baddeley, A., & Wilson, B. (1988). Frontal amnesia and the dysexecutive syndrome. *Brain and Cognition, 7,* 212–230.

Bogousslavsky, J., Ferrazzini, M., Regli, F., Assal, G., Tanabe, H., & Delaloye-Bischof, A. (1988). Manic delirium and frontal-like syndrome with paramedian infarction of the right thalamus. *Journal of Neurology, Neurosurgery and Psychiatry, 51,* 116–119.

Bower, G. H., & Morrow, D. G. (1990). Mental models in narrative comprehension. *Science, 247,* 44–48.

Cicerone, K. D., & Lazar, R. M. (1983). Effects of frontal lobe lesions on hypothesis sampling during concept formation. *Neuropsychologia, 21*(5), 513–524.

Cohen, J. D., & Servan-Schreiber, D. (1992). Context, cortex, and dopamine: A connectionist approach to behavior and biology in schizophrenia, *99*(1), 45–77.

Craik, F. I. M., Morris, L. W., Morris, R. G., & Loewen, E. R. (1990). Relations between source amnesia and frontal lobe functioning in older adults. *Psychology and Aging, 5*(1), 148–151.

Cummings, J. L. (1993). Frontal-subcortical circuits and human behavior. *Archives of Neurology (Chicago), 50*(8), 873–880.

Daigneault, S., Braun, C. M. J., & Whitaker, H. A. (1992). Early effects of normal aging on perseverative and non-perseverative prefrontal measures. *Developmental Neuropsychology, 8*(1), 99–114.

Damasio, A. R., Tranel, D., & Damasio, H. (1990). Individuals with sociopathic behavior caused by frontal damage fail to respond autonomically to social stimuli. *Behavioural Brain Research, 41,* 81–94.

Damasio, A. R., Tranel, D., & Damasio, H. C. (1991). Somatic markers and the guidance of behavior: Theory and preliminary testing. In H. S. Levin, H. M. Eisenberg, & A. L. Benton (Eds.), *Frontal lobe function and dysfunction* (pp. 217–229). New York: Oxford University Press.

Delis, D. C., Squire, L. R., Bihrle, A., & Massman, P. (1992). Componential analysis of problem-solving ability: Performance of patients with frontal lobe damage and amnesic patients on a new sorting test. *Neuropsychologia, 30*(8), 683–697.

Della Malva, C. L., Stuss, D. T., D'Alton, J., & Willmer, J. (1993). Capture errors and sequencing after frontal brain lesions. *Neuropsychologia, 31*(4), 363–372.

Dennett, D. C., & Kinsbourne, M. (1992). Time and the observer: The where and when of consciousness in the brain. *Behavioral and Brain Sciences, 15*(2), 183–247.

Diamond, A., & Doar, B. (1989). The performance of human infants on a measure of frontal cortex function, the delayed response task. *Developmental Psychobiology, 22*(3), 271–294.

Diamond, A., Zola-Morgan, S., & Squire, L. R. (1989). Successful performance by monkeys with lesions of the hippocampal formation on AB and object retrieval, two tasks that mark developmental changes in human infants. *Behavioral Neuroscience, 103*(3), 526–537.

Duncan, J. (1990). Goal weighting and the choice of behavior in a complex world. *Ergonomics, 33*(10/11), 1265–1279.

Eslinger, P. J., Grattan, L. M., Damasio, H., & Damasio, A. R. (1992). Developmental consequences of childhood frontal damage. *Archives of Neurology (Chicago), 49*(7), 764–769.

Eslinger, P. J., Warner, G. C., Grattan, L. M., & Easton, J. D. (1991). "Frontal lobe" utilization behavior associated with paramedian thalamic infarct. *Neurology, 41*(3), 450–452.

Frith, C. D., Friston, K., Liddle, P. F., & Frackowiak, R. S. J. (1991). Willed action and the prefrontal cortex in man: A study with PET. *Proceedings of the Royal Society of Medicine, Series B, 244,* 241–246.

Funahashi, S., Bruce, C. J., & Goldman-Rakic, P. S. (1993). Dorsolateral prefrontal lesions and oculomotor delayed-response performance: Evidence for mnemonic "scotomas." *Journal of Neuroscience, 13*(4), 1479–1497.

Fuster, J. M. (1989). *The prefrontal cortex: Anatomy, physiology, and neuropsychology of the frontal lobe* (2nd ed.). New York: Raven Press.

Goel, V., & Grafman, J. (1993). Modularity and the prospects of a cognitive neuroscience of central systems. *Proceedings of the 15th Annual Conference of the Cognitive Science Society, Boulder, Colorado.* 481–486.

Goel, V., & Grafman, J. (1994). Can there be a cognitive neuroscience of human problem solving. (submitted for publication).

Golding, E. (1981). The effect of unilateral brain lesions on reasoning. *Cortex, 17*(1), 31–40.

Goldman-Rakic, P. S., Bates, J. F., & Chafee, M. V. (1992). The prefrontal cortex and internally generated motor acts. *Current Opinion in Neurobiology, 2,* 830–835.

Goldstein, F. C., & Levin, H. S. (1991). Question-asking strategies after severe closed head injury. *Brain and Cognition, 17*(1), 23–30.

Goldstein, L. H., Bernard, S., Fenwick, P. B. C., Burgess, P. W., & McNeil, J. (1993). Unilateral frontal lobectomy can produce strategy application disorder. *Journal of Neurology, Neurosurgery and Psychiatry, 56,* 274–276.

Grafman, J. (1989). Plans, actions, and mental sets: Managerial knowledge units in the frontal lobes. In E. Perecman (Ed.), *Integrating theory and practice in clinical neuropsychology* (pp. 93–138). Hillsdale, NJ: Erlbaum.

Grafman, J. (in press). Competing theories of frontal lobe function. In F. Boller & J. Grafman (Eds.), *Handbook of neuropsychology,* (Volume 9) Amsterdam: Elsevier.

Grafman, J., & Hendler, J. (1991). Planning and the brain. *Behavioral and Brain Sciences, 14*(4), 563–564.

Grafman, J., Jonas, B., & Salaar, A. (1990). Wisconsin card sorting test performance based on location and size of neuroanatomical lesion in Vietnam veterans with penetrating brain injuries. *Perceptual and Motor Skills, 71,* 1120–1122.

Grafman, J., Jonas, B., & Salazar, A. (1992). Epilepsy following penetrating head injury to the frontal lobes: Effects on cognition. In P. Chauvel, A. V. Delgado-Escueta, E. Halgren, & J. Bancaud (Eds.), *Frontal lobe seizures and epilepsies* (pp. 369–378). New York: Raven Press.

Grafman, J., Litvan, I., Gomez, C., & Chase, T. (1990). Frontal lobe function in progressive supranuclear palsy. *Archives of Neurology (Chicago), 47,* 553–558.

Grafman, J., Litvan, I., Massaquoi, S., Stewart, M., Sirigu, A., & Hallett, M. (1992). Cognitive planning deficit in patients with cerebellar atrophy. *Neurology, 42*(8), 1493–1496.

Grafman, J., Sirigu, A., Spector, L., & Hendler, J. (1993). Damage to the prefrontal cortex leads to decomposition of structured event complexes. *Journal of Head Trauma Rehabilitation, 8*(1), 73–87.

Grafman, J., Thompsen-Putnam, K., Sunderland, T., & Weingartner, H. (1991). Script generation as an indicator of knowledge representation in patients with Alzheimer's disease. *Brain and Language, 40*(3), 344–358.

Grafman, J., Vance, S. C., Weingartner, H., Salazar, A. M., & Amin, D. (1986). The effects of lateralized frontal lesions on mood regulation. *Brain, 109,* 1127–1148.

Grattan, L. M., & Eslinger, P. J. (1992). Long-term psychological consequences of childhood frontal lobe lesion in patient DT. *Brain and Cognition, 20,* 185–195.

Guitton, D., Buchtel, H. A., & Douglas, R. M. (1985). Frontal lobe lesions in man cause difficulties in suppressing reflexive glances and in generating goal-directed saccades. *Experimental Brain Research, 58,* 455–472.

Halford, G. S. (1992). Analogical reasoning and conceptual complexity in cognitive development. *Human Development, 35,* 193–217.

Hammond, K. J. (1989). *Case-Based Planning: Viewing Planning as a Memory Task.* Boston: Academic Press.

Heckhausen, H., & Beckmann, J. (1990). Intentional action and action slips. *Psychological Review, 97*(1), 36–48.

Holland, J. H., Holyoak, K. J., Nisbett, R. E., & Thagard, P. R. (1986). *Induction: Processes of Inference, Learning, and Discovery.* Cambridge: The MIT Press.

Janowsky, J. S., Shimamura, A. P., Kritchevsky, M., & Squire, L. R. (1989). Cognitive impairment following frontal lobe damage and its relevance to human amnesia. *Behavioral Neuroscience, 103*(3), 548–560.

Janowsky, J. S., Shimamura, A. P., & Squire, L. R. (1989a). Memory and metamemory: Comparisons between patients with frontal lobe lesions and amnesic patients. *Psychobiology, 17*(1), 3–11.

Janowsky, J. S., Shimamura, A. P., & Squire, L. R. (1989b). Source memory impairment in patients with frontal lobe lesions. *Neuropsychologia, 27*(8), 1043–1056.

Johnson-Laird, P. N. (1983). *Mental Models: Towards a Cognitive Science of Language, Inference, and Consciousness.* Cambridge: Harvard University Press.

Jonides, J., Smith, E. E., Koeppe, R. A., Awh, E., Minoshima, S., & Mintun, M. A. (1993). Spatial working memory in humans as revealed by PET. *Nature (London), 363,* 623–625.

Karnath, H. O., Wallesch, C. W., & Zimmermann, P. (1991). Mental planning and anticipatory processes with acute and chronic frontal lobe lesions: A comparison of maze performance in routine and non-routine situations. *Neuropsychologia, 29*(4), 271–290.

Kimberg, D. Y., & Farah, M. J. (1993). A unified account of cognitive impairments following frontal lobe damage: The role of working memory in complex, organized behavior. *Journal of Experimental Psychology: General, 122*(4), 411–428.

Klouda, G. V., & Cooper, W. E. (1990). Information search following damage to the frontal lobes. *Psychological Reports, 67*(2), 411–416.

Lang, W., Lang, M., Uhl, F., Kornhuber, A., Deecke, L., & Kornhuber, H. H. (1988). Left frontal lobe in verbal associative learning: A slow potential study. *Experimental Brain Research, 70,* 99–108.

Langley, P., & Drummond, M. (1990). Toward an Experimental Science of Planning. In *Proceedings of the Workshop on Innovative Approaches to Planning, Scheduling, and Control* (pp. 109–114). San Mateo: Morgan Kaufmann.

Laplane, D., Levasseur, M., Pillon, B., Dubois, B., Baulac, M., Mazoyer, B., Tran Dinh, S., Sette, G., Danze, F., & Baron, J. C. (1989). Obsessive-compulsive and other behavioral changes with bilateral basal ganglia lesions. *Brain, 112,* 699–725.

Lhermitte, F. (1983). "Utilization behavior" and its relation to lesions of the frontal lobes. *Brain, 106*(2), 237–255.

Lhermitte, F. (1986). Human autonomy and the frontal lobes. Part II. Patient behavior in complex and social situations: The "Environmental Dependency Syndrome." *Annals of Neurology, 19*(4), 335–343.

Lhermitte, F., Pillon, B., & Serdaru, M. (1986). Human autonomy and the frontal lobes. Part I. Imitation and utilization behavior: A neuropsychological study of 75 patients. *Annals of Neurology, 19*(4), 326–334.

Mayer, N. H., Reed, E., Schwartz, M. F., Montgomery, M., & Palmer, C. (1990). Buttering a hot cup of coffee: An approach to the study of errors of action in patients with brain damage. In D. E. Tupper & K. D. Cicerone (Eds.), *The neuropsychology of everyday life: Assessment and basic competencies* (pp. 259–284). Boston: Kluwer Academic Publishers.

McAndrews, M. P., & Milner, B. (1991). The frontal cortex and memory for temporal order. *Neuropsychologia, 29*(9), 849–859.

Miller, L. A. (1992). Impulsivity, risk-taking, and the ability to synthesize fragmented information after frontal lobectomy. *Neuropsychologia, 30*(1), 69–79.

Milner, B. (1963). Effects of different brain lesions on card sorting. *Archives of Neurology (Chicago), 9*(7), 90–100.

Milner, B., Petrides, M., & Smith, M. L. (1985). Frontal lobes and the temporal organization of memory. *Human Neurobiology, 4,* 137–142.

Mountain, M. A., & Snow, W. G. (1993). Wisconsin card sorting test as a measure of frontal pathology: A review. *Clinical Neuropsychologist, 7*(1), 108–118.

Norman, D. A., & Shallice, T. (1980). *Attention to Action: Willed and Automatic Control of Behavior* (No. CHIP 99). Center for Human Information Processing, University of California—San Diego La Jolla, California.

Norman, D. A., & Shallice, T. (1986). Attention to action: Willed and automatic control of behavior. In R. J. Davidson, G. E. Schwartz, & D. Shapiro (Eds.), *Consciousness and Self-Regulation: Advances in Research and Theory* (pp. 1–18). New York: Plenum.

Owen, A. M., Roberts, A. C., Polkey, C. E., Sahakian, B. J., & Robbins, T. W. (1991). Extra-dimensional versus intra-dimensional set shifting performance following frontal lobe excisions, temporal lobe excisions, or amygdalo-hippocampectomy in man. *Neuropsychologia, 29*(10), 993–1006.

Parkin, A. J., Dunn, J. C., Lee, C., O'Hara, P. F., & Nussbaum, L. (1993). Neuropsychological sequelae of Wernicke's encephalopathy in a 20-year-old woman: Selective impairment of a frontal memory system. *Brain and Cognition, 21*(1), 1–19.

Pascual-Leone, A., Grafman, J., Clark, K., Stewart, M., Massaquoi, S., Lou, J.-L., & Hallett, M. (1993). Procedural learning in Parkinson's disease and cerebellar atrophy. *Annals of Neurology, 34*(4), 594–602.

Paulesu, E., Frith, C. D., & Frackowiak, R. S. J. (1993). The neural correlates of the verbal component of working memory. *Nature (London), 362,* 342–345.

Petrides, M. (1985). Deficits on conditional associative-learning tasks after frontal- and temporal-lobe lesions in man. *Neuropsychologia, 23*(5), 601–614.

Petrides, M. (1990). Nonspatial conditional learning impaired in patients with unilateral frontal but not unilateral temporal lobe excisions. *Neuropsychologia, 28*(2), 137–149.

Petrides, M. (1991a). Monitoring of selections of visual stimuli and the primate frontal cortex. *Proceedings of the Royal Society of London, Series B, 246,* 293–298.

Petrides, M. (1991b). Functional specialization within the dorsolateral frontal cortex for serial order memory. *Proceedings of the Royal Society of Medicine, Series B, 246,* 299–306.

Petrides, M., Alivisatos, B., Evans, A. C., & Meyer, E. (1993). Dissociation of human mid-doroslateral from posterior dorsolateral frontal cortex in memory processing. *Proceedings of the National Academy of Sciences of the U.S.A., 90,* 873–877.

Petrides, M., Alivisatos, B., Meyer, E., & Evans, A. C. (1993). Functional activation of human prefrontal cortex during the performance of verbal working memory tasks. *Proceedings of the National Academy of Sciences of the U.S.A., 90,* 878–882.

Petrides, M., & Pandya, D. N. (in press). Comparative architectonic analysis of the human and the macaque frontal cortex. In F. Boller & J. Grafman (Eds.), *Handbook of neuropsychology.* (Vol. 9). Amsterdam: Elsevier.

Riesbeck, C. K., & Schank, R. C. (1989). *Inside Case-Based Reasoning.* Hillsdale, NJ: Lawrence Erlbaum Associates, Inc.

Robinson, A. L., Heaton, R. K., Lehman, R. A. W., & Stilson, D. W. (1980). The utility of the Wisconsin card sorting test in detecting and localizing frontal lobe lesions. *Journal of Consulting and Clinical Psychology, 48*(5), 605–614.

Ross, D. T., Graham, D. I., & Adams, J. H. (1993). Selective loss of neurons from the thalamic reticular nucleus following severe human head injury. *Journal of Neurotrauma, 10*(2), 151–165.

Ruchkin, D. S., Johnson, R., Jr., Grafman, J., Canoune, H., & Ritter, W. (1992). Distinctions and similarities among working memory processes. *Cognitive Brain Research, 1*(1), 53–66.

Rueckert, L., Appollonio, I., Grafman, J., Jezzard, P., Johnson, R., Jr., LeBihan, D., & Turner, R. (1994). MRI functional activation of left frontal cortex during covert word production. *Journal of Neuroimaging, 4*(2), 67–70.

Salmon, E., Maquet, P., Sadzot, B., Degueldre, C., Lemaire, C., & Franck, G. (1991). Decrease of frontal metabolism demonstrated by positron emission tomography in a population of healthy elderly volunteers. *Acta Neurologica Belgica, 91*(5), 288–295.

Saver, J. L., & Damasio, A. R. (1991). Preserved access and processing of social knowledge in a patient with acquired sociopathy due to ventromedial frontal damage. *Neuropsychologia, 29,* 1241–1249.

Sawaguchi, T., & Goldman-Rakic, P. S. (1991). D1 dopamine receptors in prefrontal cortex: Involvement in working memory. *Science, 251,* 947–950.

Schacter, D. L. (1987). Memory, amnesia, and frontal lobe dysfunction. *Psychobiology, 15*(1), 21–36.

Schank, R., & Abelson, R. (1977). *Scripts, plans, goals, and understanding: An inquiry into human knowledge structures.* Hillsdale, NJ: Erlbaum.

Schank, R. (1982). *Dynamic memory: A theory of reminding and learning in computers and people.* Cambridge: Cambridge University Press.

Schwartz, M. F., Mayer, N. H., FitzpatrickDeSalme, E. J., & Montgomery, M. W. (1993). Cognitive theory and the study of everyday action disorders after brain damage. *Journal of Head Trauma Rehabilitation, 8*(1), 59–72.

Schwartz, M. F., Reed, E. S., Montgomery, M., Palmer, C., & Mayer, N. H. (1991). The quantitative description of action disorganization after brain damage: A case study. *Cognitive Neuropsychology, 8*(5), 381–414.

Shallice, T. (1988). *From neuropsychology to mental structure.* Cambridge: Cambridge University Press.

Shallice, T., & Burgess, P. (1991). Higher order cognitive impairments and frontal lobe lesions. In H. S. Levin, H. M. Eisenberg, & A. L. Benton (Eds.), *Frontal lobe function and dysfunction* (pp. 125–138). New York: Oxford University Press.

Shallice, T., Burgess, P. W., Schon, F., & Baxter, D. M. (1989). The origins of utilization behaviour. *Brain, 112,* 1587–1598.

Shallice, T., & Evans, M. E. (1978). The involvement of the frontal lobes in cognitive estimation. *Cortex, 14,* 294–303.

Shimamura, A., Gershberg, F. B., Jurica, P. J., Mangels, J. A., & Knight, R. T. (1992). Intact implicit memory in patients with frontal lobe lesions. *Neuropsychologia, 30,* 931–937.

Shimamura, A., Janowsky, J. S., & Squire, L. R. (1990). Memory for the temporal order of events in patients with frontal lobe lesions and amnesic patients. *Neuropsychologia, 28,* 803–813.

Shimamura, A., Janowsky, J. S., & Squire, L. R. (1991). What is the role of frontal lobe damage in memory disorders. In H. S. Levin, H. M. Eisenberg, & A. L. Benton (Eds.), *Frontal lobe function and dysfunction* (pp. 173–198). New York: Oxford University Press.

Singer, W. (1993). Neuronal representations, assemblies, and temporal coherence. *Progress in Brain Research, 95,* 461–474.

Singer, W., Artola, A., Engel, A. K., Konig, P., Kreiter, A. K., Lowel, S., & Schillen, T. B. (1993). Neuronal representations and temporal codes. In T. A. Poggio & D. A. Glaser (Eds.), *Exploring brain functions: Models in neuroscience* (pp. 179–194). London: Wiley.

Singh, J., & Knight, R. T. (1990). Frontal lobe contribution to voluntary movements in humans. *Brain Research, 531,* 45–54.

Smith, M. L., & Milner, B. (1988). Estimation of frequency of occurrence of abstract designs after frontal or temporal lobectomy. *Neuropsychologia, 26,* 297–306.

Stuss, D. T. (1978). An extraordinary form of confabulation. *Neurology, 28,* 1166–1172.

Stuss, D. T. (1992). Biological and psychological development of executive functions. *Brain and Cognition, 20,* 8–23.

Stuss, D. T., & Benson, D. F. (1986). *The frontal lobes*. New York: Raven Press.

Stuss, D. T., Eskes, G. A., & Foster, J. K. (in press). Experimental neuropsychological studies of frontal lobe functions. In F. Boller & J. Grafman (Eds.), *Handbook of neuropsychology* (Vol. 9). Amsterdam: Elsevier.

Stuss, D. T., Gow, C. A., & Hetherington, C. R. (1992). "No longer gage": Frontal lobe changes and emotional changes. *Journal of Consulting and Clinical Psychology, 60,* 349–359.

Tranel, D., Anderson, S. W., & Benton, A. (in press). Development of the concept of "executive function" and its relationship to the frontal lobes. In F. Boller & J. Grafman (Eds.), *Handbook of Neuropsychology* (Volume 9) Amsterdam: Elsevier.

Uylings, H. B. M., Van Eden, C. G., De Bruin, J. P. C., Corner, M. A., & Feenstra, M. G. P. (Ed.). (1990). *The Prefrontal Cortex: Its Structure, Function, and Pathology*. Amsterdam: Elsevier.

Weinberger, D. R. (1993). A connectionist approach to the prefrontal cortex. *Journal of Neuropsychiatry, 5,* 241–253.

Welsh, M. C., & Pennington, B. F. (1992). Assessing frontal lobe functioning in children: Views from developmental psychology. *Developmental Neuropsychology, 4,* 199–230.

Wilkins, A. J., Shallice, T., & McCarthy, R. (1987). Frontal lesions and sustained attention. *Neuropsychologia, 25,* 359–365.

Zaidel, D. W. (1987). Hemispheric asymmetry in long-term semantic relationships. *Cognitive Neuropsychology, 4,* 321–332.

Zaidel, D W. (1994). Worlds apart: Pictorial semantics in the left and right cerebral hemispheres. *Current Directions in Psychological Science, 3,* 5–8.

CHAPTER 9

Neuropsychology of Movement Sequencing Disorders and Apraxia

Eric A. Roy
Paula A. Square

Apraxia is a disorder affecting the ability to pantomime or execute previously familiar, intimate gestures, following brain damage. Familiar, well-known gestures involving the use of objects (e.g., brushing teeth [transitive gestures]) or interpersonal communication (e.g., wave good-bye [intransitive, representational gestures]) and novel, meaningless hand gestures (intransitive, nonrepresentational gestures) are both affected. Identifying apraxia typically involves noting the occurrence of particular types of performance errors. One of the most well known is termed a body–part–as–object error in which the hand is used as if it were the object (e.g., the extended index finger representing a toothbrush, see Haaland and Flaherty [1984] for a discussion of other body–part–as–object errors). An impairment in gesturing cannot be termed apraxia, however, if it results from a basic motor problem (e.g., a hemiparesis), a difficulty in language comprehension, an impairment in recognizing the object with which the gesture is associated, or from dementia (Poeck, 1986; Roy & Square, 1985).

Much of the work on apraxia points to the importance of damage to the left hemisphere, particularly the parietal, prefrontal, and supramarginal areas. This hemisphere is thought to subserve a praxis system used to control gestural movements with both hands, as damage to this hemisphere, especially in the parietal area, produces apraxia bilaterally (e.g.,

Neuropsychology

183

Kimura, 1982; Liepmann, 1913). Unimanual expressions of apraxia that usually affect the left hand arise primarily in the context of a right hemiparesis or callosal damage. In the first instance, the apraxia is thought to arise because the motor area in the right hemisphere controlling the left hand is disconnected from the praxis system in the left hemisphere (Geschwind, 1975). However, D. Zaidel and Sperry (1977) have studied a group of patients with callosal damage (split-brain patients) and have found left-hand apraxia only to verbal commands (ideomotor apraxia), not in pantomime, imitation, or object handling.

Indeed, a considerable number of studies have subsequently questioned the sole executive role of the left hemisphere in apraxia. Some researchers have implicated the importance of the right hemisphere, particularly the prefrontal area (e.g., Kimura, 1982; Kolb & Milner, 1981), whereas others have suggested that each hemisphere may have its own "action system" such that damage to either hemisphere may give rise to apraxia in the contralateral hand (e.g., Pilgrim & Humphreys, 1991).

Several different types of apraxia have been identified (see Rothi & Heilman, 1985; Roy, 1978, 1982, 1985), although the two most well-known types are ideational and ideomotor apraxia. The distinction between these two apraxias is largely based on the pattern of performance when pantomiming as opposed to imitating gestures (see Roy, 1982, for other distinctions). In the pantomime condition the patient demonstrates how to perform a gesture to verbal command (e.g., salute) or use an object (e.g., a hammer), although the tool, in the case of *transitive* gestures (e.g., tool use) is not actually manipulated. In the imitation condition the patient attempts to imitate the gesture demonstrated by the examiner. In ideational apraxia performance is impaired when pantomiming but not when imitating the gesture. With ideomotor apraxia both pantomime and imitation performance are impaired.

This distinction in the pattern of performance is thought to reflect differences in the integrity of memory structures used in programming the movements in gesturing. In ideational apraxia these engrams are thought to be destroyed. The patient's performance, then, is impaired in the pantomime condition when these memory structures must be accessed but not in the *imitation* condition when visual gestural information is available in the examiner's demonstration. In ideomotor apraxia these memory structures are thought to be intact. The posterior brain areas thought to subserve these structures (supramarginal gyrus) as well as processes involved in the analysis of visual gestural information (occipital lobe) are thought to be disconnected from the more anterior brain areas responsible for movement control. Thus, the patient's performance is impaired both when pantomiming and imitating gestures.

9   Movement Sequencing Disorders and Apraxia   **185**

I. MODELS OF APRAXIA

A number of approaches have been developed to understand apraxia (Duffy & Duffy, 1990; Rothi, Ochipa, & Heilman, 1991; Roy, 1983a, 1983b). An approach developed by Roy (1983a, 1983b; Roy & Square, 1985) proposes that apraxia may result from disruption to one of two systems involved in the generation and control of movement: a *conceptual system* and a *production system*. The conceptual system affords the knowledge base for gesturing and includes three types: knowledge of objects and tools which act upon objects, knowledge of actions (e.g., hammering) into which objects and tools may be incorporated, and knowledge of the serial order of actions. The production system is concerned with the generation and control of movement. Link between these systems permit the conceptual system to drive the production system in a "top-down" fashion. Attention is required at key choice points in the unfolding action to ensure that successive actions in the sequence are the intended ones. Between these key choice points control is exerted by action programs that do not demand attention for their execution. These programs are generalized in the sense that they can be applied to any one of a number of effectors to produce the desired action. For example, one can write a letter of the alphabet with the pen held in the mouth, the hand, or between the toes. Although these programs control the general spatiotemporal pattern of the actions they represent, the details of movement are controlled at a lower level through the operation of muscle synergies and coordinative structures.

Although the production system may be directed in a top-down mode from the conceptual system, control may also be exerted from the bottom up through links between the environment and actions. *Perceptual referents* (visual and tactual features of objects and tools that relate to their functions) and *contextual referents* (the time or place in which actions are performed) provide environmental information relevant to action. If the performer does not attend at the key choice points alluded to above, unintended actions may be induced through the intrusion of this environmental information. The environment then can direct the selection of actions to be performed.

The production system, then, is composed of a number of parallel systems in which control can migrate from one level to another. Performing actions involves a delicate balance between the attention-demanding processes of higher levels and the more autonomous operations subserved at lower levels.

Based on this approach it is possible to envisage that apraxia and movement sequencing disorders might involve disruptions to the conceptual or production system or both. Disruptions to the conceptual system are typically reflected in aberrations to one or more of the knowledge components.

Evidence for production disorders is sought through studies of the characteristics of apractic performance. The pattern of errors observed under various performance conditions and qualitative analyses of movement control are of particular importance in these investigations.

II. DISRUPTIONS TO THE CONCEPTUAL SYSTEM

Three approaches to the study of apraxia have identified disruptions in the conceptual system. One approach focuses on impairments in the patient's ability to recognize features of the tool or object or the movement involved in the gesture. A second approach stresses impairments in *comprehension* either of the gesture itself or the verbal command used to elicit it. The third approach argues that the problem in apraxia may involve a memory disorder that affects the patient's ability to select the appropriate gesture.

A. Recognition Impairments

In this approach it is argued that the difficulty with gesturing may arise from the patient not recognizing important features of the appropriate gesture or the structural characteristics of the tool or object used. Pilgrim and Humphreys (1991) described a patient who could accurately pantomime a gesture associated with a particular object when requested to do so on verbal command but was unable to pantomime the gesture correctly when the stimulus to movement was the actual object. This case, they argued, demonstrated a disruption in a direct link between the structural characteristics of the object and the action or gesture with which it was associated.

A somewhat similar dissociation between modalities used to elicit a gesture was identified by Ochipa, Rothi, and Heilman (1990). In this case, patients were able to pantomime accurately to verbal command but were unable to imitate the same gesture when demonstrated by the examiner. A disruption in the visual analysis of the movement attributes of a gesture is implicated in these patients.

Heilman, Rothi, and their colleagues have completed a series of studies (Heilman, Rothi, & Valenstein, 1982; Ochipa, Rothi, & Heilman, 1992; Rothi, Heilman, & Watson, 1985; Rothi, Mack, & Heilman, 1986) that have examined gesture recognition. In one study (Heilman et al., 1982), they compared apractic and nonapractic patients with either anterior or posterior lesions to the left hemisphere. Two recognition tasks were involved, one requiring the patient to correctly identify the target gesture among several demonstrated by the examiner on videotape, and the other requiring the patient to identify the correct gesture from among several performed by the examiner.

The nonapractic patients were able to perform the recognition tasks without error. There was, however, an interesting dissociation between the anterior and posterior apractic patients. Despite being equally impaired on an apraxia test, the anterior apractics were able to identify the target gesture correctly on both recognition tests, whereas the posterior apractics were unable to do so. These findings led to the notion that there may be two forms of ideomotor apraxia associated with either anterior or posterior damage to the left hemisphere. With posterior damage, Heilman argued that apraxia results from a disruption to *visuokinesthetic (memory) engrams,* which impairs the patient's ability to correctly recognize the target gestures. The preserved ability at *gesture recognition* in the anterior apractics suggested to Heilman that these engrams were intact but were functionally disconnected from the anterior motor control regions used to generate the gestural movements.

Wang and Goodglass (1992) examined pantomime recognition and apraxia in groups of anterior and posterior aphasic patients. Performance on a battery of gesture tests revealed a clear relationship between impairments in gesture recognition, gesture production, and imitation of gestures, supporting Heilman's earlier findings. In contrast to Heilman's observations, comparisons between patients with posterior lesions and those with anterior lesions revealed no differences in this relationship, indicating that recognition deficits do not arise only with posterior lesions.

Roy (1983a, 1983b) also examined the ability of apractic patients to recognize errors in performance. In this study (Roy, 1983a) the patients were presented with an object. They then viewed four different pantomimes and were asked to indicate which one was appropriate for demonstrating how the object is used. One pantomime was the correct gesture, and the other was a completely inappropriate movement. A third involved a spatial error in which the gesture was demonstrated in an inappropriate location on the body, whereas the fourth involved a *body-part-as-object* error (e.g., the extended index finger represents the toothbrush). In comparing the performance of apractic and nonapractic patients, Roy observed that both groups noticed that the appropriate pantomime was in fact correct and the completely inappropriate gesture was not. For the other two pantomimes, both groups indicated that the pantomime with the spatial movement error was not correct. For the body-part-as-object pantomime, however, the nonapractics recognized that it was incorrect, whereas the apractics endorsed it as being appropriate for the object.

Because the apractic patients frequently make both spatial and body-part-as-object errors, the difference in recognition of these errors led Roy to suggest they may arise from disruptions in different component systems. The inability of the apractic patients to recognize the body-part-as-object pantomime as being incorrect suggests that these errors may arise from a disruption in the conceptual system. The fact that these patients were able to accurately identify the spatial error suggests that this type of error may arise from a disruption in the production system.

Building on this work by Roy (1983a, 1983b) and their own studies (e.g., Rothi et al., 1985, 1986) Ochipa et al. (1992) compared Alzheimer's patients with ideomotor apraxia to those without apraxia on a series of recognition tasks, two of which required the patient to select a tool that could be used to complete a particular action. In one task the patient had to select the appropriate tool (e.g., a hammer) from among 11 others to complete a partially finished action (e.g., a nail partially driven into a piece of wood). In the other task the appropriate tool was not presented. Rather several tools, one of which shared structural–functional features with the appropriate tool, were presented and the subject had to select the most appropriate alternate tool (e.g., a shoe) to permit completion of the task. Analyses revealed significantly poorer performance for the apractic patients.

Ochipa et al. (1992) termed the disorder on these tasks a conceptual apraxia. This type of apraxia leads to errors referred to as *content errors,* where the patient uses a tool inappropriately although the movement itself may be performed well (e.g., using a toothbrush as a spoon). These errors are contrasted with production errors involving poor performance of the target movement most often in ideomotor apraxia. The presence of these two types of errors confirms Roy's notions of disruptions in conceptual (i.e., content errors) or production (production errors) systems as underlying apraxia.

The tool selection tasks employed by Ochipa et al. (1992) assess what Roy (1983a, 1983b) referred to as knowledge of object function, whereas the gesture recognition tests used by Heilman (e.g., Heilman et al., 1982) and Roy (1983b) tap into knowledge of action (Roy, 1983a). Knowledge of serial order, the third component of the conceptual system, has been examined in studies by Poeck (1983), where patients were required to place a series of action picture cards in an order that would correctly depict the sequence necessary to complete a task (e.g., making a cup of coffee). Analyses revealed that patients with ideational apraxia but not those with ideomotor apraxia performed poorly on this conceptual sequencing task. From these findings Poeck reasoned that this conceptual disorder contributed significantly to the movement problems observed in ideational apraxia.

In considering these studies it seems that the adequate performance on the various recognition tasks require not only intact knowledge components but also an ability to analyze the critical features associated with the visual gestural information and the tools and objects present. In the original model Roy (1983a, 1983b) included both of these aspects as part of the conceptual system. In fact, it would appear that two separate modules or systems are involved here, a sensory-perceptual system employed in analyzing visual gestural and tool and object information and a *conceptual system,* which incorporates knowledge components that provide an interpretation for the output from the sensory-perceptual system. The predicted effects of disruptions to these systems will be examined in the last section of the chapter.

B. Comprehension and Apraxia

Some of the earliest accounts of apraxia attributed the disorder to some disruption in language function due to the co-incidence of apraxia and aphasia (e.g., Square-Storer, Roy, & Hogg, 1990). Liepmann (1913) argued strongly against this attribution as he reported several cases where apraxia was not accompanied by a marked aphasia. Goodglass and Kaplan (1963) conducted one of the first systematic studies of this relationship. In a group of 20 mild to moderate aphasics the correlations between severity of aphasia and apraxia proved not to be significant. Other studies following up on this seminal work have used larger numbers of aphasic patients, involving a variety of aphasia types, and have examined both overall severity of aphasia and disorders of specific speech and language functions (e.g., naming, comprehension).

There is compelling evidence for the co-occurrence of apraxia with aphasia (e.g., Kertesz, Ferro, & Shewan, 1984; Square-Storer et al., 1990). This relationship led some to argue that left-hemisphere damage results in a generalized disturbance to express or comprehend "symbols" in any modality (see Duffy & Duffy, 1990). Much of this work has demonstrated that aphasics exhibit impairments in both pantomime expression and comprehension that are correlated with aphasic deficits, particularly those affecting comprehension (e.g., Duffy & Duffy, 1990; Gainotti, 1980; Gainotti & Lemmo, 1976).

Several investigators have looked closely at the relationship between verbal comprehension and apraxia. Kertesz and Hooper (1982) examined the performance of a large number of left-hemisphere-damaged patients on the Western Aphasia Battery. Performance on the apraxia subtest was poorest in those patients classified as global aphasics and the score on this subtest was most highly correlated with the comprehension score. De Renzi (De Renzi, Faglioni, Lodesani, & Vecchi, 1983; De Renzi, Motti, & Nichelli, 1980) and Gainotti and Lemmo (1976) have also noted a relationship between comprehension and apraxia. However, D. Zaidel & Sperry (1977) ruled out lack of comprehension as the main cause of left hand ideomotor apraxia in split-brain patients.

Work by Poeck (Lehmkuhl, Poeck, & Willmes, 1983), who looked more closely at the modality (e.g., verbal command versus imitation) used in performing gestures, found that the global aphasics, the patients with the poorest auditory comprehension scores, were as impaired at imitating gestures as they were at pantomiming them from verbal command. These findings suggest that the gestural impairment in these patients does not arise from a deficit in comprehending the command per se. One would have expected poorer performance in the verbal command condition. Rather, some more global impact of comprehension deficits is implied in that the patients with the poorest comprehension scores exhibit rather global deficits in gestural performance.

More recently Alexander, Baker, Naeser, Kaplan, and Palumbo (1992) found that the global and Wernicke's aphasics exhibited the most severe apraxia and, consistent with Poeck's finding, were just as impaired imitating as pantomiming gestures. A closer comparison of these modalities revealed that performance to verbal command (pantomime) was consistently poorer than imitation regardless of the patient's comprehension score. It would seem, then, that poor auditory comprehension cannot explain the impaired gestural performance in these patients. Nevertheless, a correlation analysis across all the aphasic patients revealed a significant relationship between comprehension and apraxia scores on both pantomime and imitation. Alexander et al. (1992) argue that this relationship reveals some more global comprehension factor that transcends language to which both auditory and gestural comprehension may relate. Disruption to this factor will affect both auditory and gestural comprehension, which in turn will affect speech and praxis.

A number of investigators argue that the co-occurrence of aphasic deficits and apraxia arises more from the proximity of their neuroanatomical centers than from any common symbolic or comprehension deficit underlying each (e.g., De Renzi et al., 1980, 1983; Kertesz et al., 1984; Lehmkuhl et al., 1983). Further, several studies indicate that apraxia and aphasia are dissociable (e.g., Square-Storer et al., 1990). Nevertheless, there is enough evidence to warrant more careful investigations of how speech and language deficits relate to impairments in gestural comprehension and expression.

C. Memory Disorder

Work by De Renzi (1985; De Renzi & Luchelli, 1988) has revealed that patients with left-hemisphere damage often have greater difficulty in performing gestures to verbal command than when imitating the examiner. These patients, De Renzi argued, have a problem with internally generating gestures from memory affecting processes such as response selection. Some work by Roy (Roy, Square-Storer, Hogg, & Adams, 1991; see Roy et al., 1993, for a review) has replicated these findings across a variety of gestures. In this study (Roy et al., 1991), stroke patients with left-hemisphere damage or right-hemisphere damage and normal adults performed several types of limb gesture involving both single gestures (e.g., comb hair) and more complex, multiple gestures (e.g., knock and open door), as well as axial or whole body gestures. Not only did the left-hemisphere-damaged patients perform significantly fewer correct gestures, but the modality effect described by De Renzi was also observed. The left–hemisphere–damaged patients were significantly less accurate in performing all of the gesture types to command as opposed to imitation. These findings demonstrate the generality of the modality effect, revealing that left-hemisphere damage compromises the ability to generate a gesture from memory, regardless of the movement system involved (i.e., axial or limb) or the complexity of the gesture.

Roy and his colleagues have also examined the role of memory in the performance of gestural sequences. In one of their initial studies (Roy, 1981) groups of left- and right-hemisphere-damaged patients performed a sequence of four movements on a sequencing board. The four movements in the sequence were presented as a series of pictures, each depicting the action to be performed at each position in the sequence. Each trial involved two phases: the *perceptual* phase, in which the pictures were present continually throughout performance, and the *memory* phase, in which the pictures were removed and the patient performed the sequence from memory. The number of trials to achieve the learning criterion of five consecutive correct sequences was determined for each of these phases for each subject.

In the perceptual phase, the left-hemisphere-damaged patients learned the sequence in the same number of trials as the patients with right-hemisphere damage. In the memory phase, however, the left-hemisphere-damaged patients required significantly more trials. Analyses of various types of error in each phase mirrored these results on trials to criterion. Only in the memory phase did the left-hemisphere-damaged patients make significantly more errors than did those with right-hemisphere damage.

Work by Jason (1983, 1985, 1986) has provided further support for the role of memory in movement sequencing. In these studies, left- and right-hemisphere-damaged patients performed various gestural sequencing tasks. In one study (Jason, 1983) the patients performed gestural sequences under two conditions. In the first condition (Sequence 1), the sequence of four hand postures was demonstrated and the patient performed them from memory. The focus was on learning the sequence with the criterion being number of trials needed to reach three consecutive correct trials. In the other condition (Sequence 2), the patients imitated the sequence performed by the examiner by successively copying each gesture as it was demonstrated. The time interval between each gesture was controlled by a metronome, such that the intervals became successfully shorter over a series of trials. Performance was reflected as the shortest interresponse interval before the patient made an error copying a gesture. On Sequence 1 the left-hemisphere-damaged patients required significantly more trials to learn the sequence and made significantly more errors than did the right-hemisphere-damaged patients. On Sequence 2, which placed no demands on memory, there were no performance differences between the brain-damaged groups. In concert with Roy's (1981) initial findings, these data suggested that the impairment in sequencing with left-hemisphere damage appears only when the sequence must be generated from memory.

This effect of memory in movement sequencing has been examined in greater depth in more recent work by Roy (Roy, Square-Storer, & Adams, 1992; Roy, Square-Storer, Adams, & Friesen, 1989). Several factors were investigated in these studies: the length of the sequence (two, three or four movements), the motor system involved (limb or oral nonverbal movements), and the modality in which the sequence was performed. In one condition the sequence placed no demands on memory. A series of pictures depicted the sequence of movements to be performed. The other two conditions did place demands on memory requiring patients to perform the sequence to imitation or to verbal command. In the imitation condition, the sequence was demonstrated by the examiner, whereas in the command condition the movement sequence was described verbally (e.g., slide, turn, point) to the patient. These two conditions were included to compare a visuospatial (imitation) with a linguistic (verbal command) representation.

Several phases of testing were involved. In the first phase, the movements were demonstrated according to the modality condition involved. In the command condition, for example, the movement associated with each verbal label was presented. Following this demonstration, the patient was required to perform five consecutive repetitions of each single movement. In the second phase, the individual movements were presented in a random order and the patient performed each. The patient had to achieve a criterion of 80% correct in order to progress on to the third phase, performing the movement sequence. In this last phase, seven trials of the sequence were performed and the patient had to achieve a criterion of at least two correct sequences before moving on to the next higher sequence length. If the patient achieved this criterion, another movement was added and the three phases repeated for the next sequence length.

In this study, groups of right- and left-hemisphere-damaged patients and normal controls performed these gestural tasks. Performance was examined in terms of the longest sequence attained and the percentage of correct sequences performed. The former measure was the longest sequence in which the subject met the criterion of at least two correct sequences in the third phase of testing. The results revealed a group by modality effect. In the picture condition, no differences were observed among the three groups. For the two memory conditions, however, the left-hemisphere-damaged patients performed more poorly than the other two groups. Significantly fewer left-hemisphere-damaged patients achieved a sequence length of four, and they made a significantly lower percentage of correct sequences. The right-hemisphere-damaged and control groups were not significantly different. This effect was present for both the limb and oral gestures.

In accord with previous work (Jason, 1983; Roy, 1981), impairments in sequencing were apparent for the left-hemisphere-damaged patients only when the tasks placed demands on memory. These findings provide new insights into the role of memory in movement sequencing, however. First, relative to the right-hemisphere-damaged patients, those with left-hemisphere damage were impaired in both the verbal and imitation conditions, suggesting that the left-hemisphere-damaged patients are equally impaired regardless of whether the information in memory is visuospatial (imitation condition) or linguistic (command condition). Secondly, the left-hemisphere-damaged patients were impaired in these memory conditions for both the oral and limb sequences, suggesting that this impairment in generating sequences from memory is common to both movement systems. Finally, comparisons of performance across the last two phases of testing indicates the specific nature of this impairment in generating movements from memory.

In the second phase of testing, the patient was required to perform a sequence of sorts in that each individual movement had to be performed when prompted. In the imitation and command conditions, demands were placed on memory as the patient had to generate each individual movement from memory. The left-hemisphere-damaged patients were not impaired on these tasks. These patients were also not impaired in the third phase of testing, providing the task placed no demands on memory (picture condition). These patients, then, seem able to select the appropriate response from memory as long as they do not need to generate a series of movements (phase 2 performance), and they can perform the sequence of movements providing there is no need to select the movements from memory (picture modality in the third phase). Only when these two demands (response selection and movement sequencing) are conjointly required in the task do the left-hemisphere-damaged patients exhibit an impairment.

One of the problems with many of these studies is that little attention has been paid to the temporal aspects of sequencing reflecting response preparation and programming. These more precise measures may reveal deficits in movement sequencing with left-hemisphere damage even when the task places no demands on memory. Recent work by Harrington and Haaland (1991, 1992), which has examined these measures in a task requiring the performance of sequences of increasing length supports this contention. Interresponse times and movement time increased more with sequence length in patients with left-hemisphere damage, particularly those with ideomotor apraxia, implicating deficits in the temporal organization of a sequence. Possibly these findings reflect a disruption at a different "level of programming" (Harrington & Haaland, 1991) than that involved when the sequencing task places demands on memory. The disruptions observed at this level may involve more the production system to which we now turn.

III. DISRUPTIONS TO THE PRODUCTION SYSTEM

The production system is concerned with the generation and control of movement in gesturing. A number of studies have examined various dimensions of gesture production in apraxia, including the impact of movement complexity and deficits in fine motor control, the nature and pervasiveness of movement sequencing deficits across movement systems, and impairments in the coordination of movement components. Research pertaining to each of these dimensions will now be examined.

A. Impairments to Fine Motor Control

One of the errors characteristic of apraxia is poorly controlled or clumsy-looking movements (Rothi & Heilman, 1985). This observation led Heilman (1975) to argue that part of the deficit in apraxia may involve an impairment in fine motor control. Performance on a finger-tapping task was used by Heilman to reflect this impairment. In comparing groups of apractic and nonapractic left-hemisphere patients he observed a significant difference in tapping performance with the apractic patients tapping less frequently.

Kimura (1979) also examined fine motor control in apraxia using a somewhat different measure. In this task the patients were required to rotate a screw on a bolt as rapidly as possible. Comparisons were made between left- and right-hemisphere-damaged patients and the relationships between movement sequencing, praxis, and fine motor control were examined. Analyses revealed that in both patient groups performance on the screw rotation task was impaired only on the hand contralateral to the damaged hemisphere. For the left-hemisphere-damaged patients, impairments in this fine motor task were unrelated to deficits in praxis and movement sequencing. These findings led Kimura to argue that impairments in fine motor control are independent of and do not contribute to apraxia and deficits in movement sequencing.

Haaland, Porch, and Delaney (1980) compared apractic and nonapractic patients with left-hemisphere damage on a series of motor tasks involving simple repetitive movements such as finger tapping to more complex tasks such as maze coordination and grooved pegboard. They found that the apractic patients were impaired relative to those without apraxia only on the more complex movements. From these results Haaland et al. (1980) suggest that the movement problem underlying apraxia is not one involving poor control of simple movements but rather arises from deficits in sensorimotor integration reflected in performance on the more complex tasks.

In general, these studies reveal that motor performance deficits following lateralized brain damage are most commonly observed in the contralesional hand on a variety of tasks, including simple repetitive tapping and movement steadiness (e.g., Kimura, 1979; Roy, Clark, Aigbogun, & Square-Storer, 1992; Vaughan & Costa, 1962; Wyke, 1968), and more complex pegboard and maze coordination tasks (Haaland et al., 1980). Ipsilesional hand impairments have also been observed. These impairments are important in understanding the neurobehavioral bases of motor performance because they indicate the impact that damage to one hemisphere has on performance with both hands. It would appear that ipsilesional impairments are observed on more complex tasks, such as grooved pegboard and maze coordination, which require a series of movements or which place heavy demands on sensorimotor integration (see Haaland & Yeo, 1989, for a review) but not on simple repetitive tasks, such as finger tapping. Ipsilesional impairments may not have been observed in these tasks, however, because of the rather gross performance measures, such as tapping rate, that have been used. Indeed, a number of studies examining manual asymmetries in tapping have demonstrated that other measures (e.g., intertap variability, time inflexion and extension in the tap cycle) are more sensitive reflections of tapping performance than tapping rate (e.g., Peters, 1980; Todor & Smiley, 1985). Ipsilesional impairments in simple repetitive tasks such as finger tapping, then, may become apparent when these other measures reflecting consistency or variability are used.

Accordingly, Roy, Clark et al. (1992) examined tapping rate and variability in groups of stroke patients with left- or right-hemisphere damage and a group of age-matched normal adults. The task involved tapping as rapidly as possible for a 10-s period over a series of 10 trials. Tapping performance was measured in terms of rate (mean intertap interval) and variability (variability of intertap intervals). The brain-damaged patients used the ipsilesional hand as the contralesional hand was paralyzed in the majority of cases. The normal controls tapped with both hands, half beginning with the right. The brain-damaged patients were also examined on a limb apraxia battery. The results indicated no differences in the rate of tapping between the controls and either group of brain-damaged patients. The left-hemisphere-damaged patients exhibited significantly greater tapping variability, however.

Why might only left-hemisphere damage affect tapping variability? This measure would appear to reflect the demands for rather precise and consistent phasing or sequencing of muscle activation in terms of either timing (duration) or magnitude (force). As such, it may be a more sensitive reflection of tapping performance than the mean intertap interval. Because damage to the left hemisphere is frequently associated with difficulty in making transitions among movements in a sequence (Kimura, 1979; Roy, 1981; Wyke, 1968; and see below), damage to this hemisphere may impair the patients' ability to generate a consistent sequence of agonist–antagonist muscle activations. This variability may lead to variability in the amplitude of the movements, which in turn would result in variability in intertap intervals.

In order to examine this hypothesis the tapping task must be modified to enable a more direct examination of the flexion–extension movements themselves. At this point, these movements relate only to the opening and closing of a switch. A more analogous measure would provide a clearer view of the phases in the tap cycle. The task should also be modified so as to measure the electromyographic activity and force exerted in tapping. Other studies that have examined electromyographic activity in patients with brain damage have provided valuable clues to the nature of the motor impairment.

A recent pilot study using these kinematic, kinetic, and electromyographic measures (Roy, Clark, & Square-Storer, 1989) found that relative to the normal patients the left-hemisphere-damaged patients again demonstrated more variable intertap intervals. A closer look at the tapping movements revealed that the left-hemisphere-damaged patients exhibited greater force and force variability in both the flexion and extension phases of the tap cycle. These preliminary findings suggest that the observed difference between these groups in intertap variability relates to less consistency in the magnitude of muscle activation.

How do these impairments in tapping performance relate to apraxia? All of the left-hemisphere damaged patients were impaired on this measure of tapping performance. However, only two patients exhibited limb apraxia, and they were no more impaired on the tapping task than the nonapractics. This disorder in the consistency of movement in this fine motor task, then, appears to be independent of apraxia.

B. Complexity of Movement

Work by Kimura and Archibald (1974) suggested that disruptions to gesturing seen with left-hemisphere damage arose only for more complex gestures involving multiple movements. In this study, left- and right-hemisphere-damaged patients performed various meaningless hand gestures either as single gestures or in a sequence. The left-hemisphere-damaged patients were impaired relative to the right-hemisphere-damaged patients only when performing the sequences.

More recent work (e.g., De Renzi et al., 1980, 1983; Kimura, 1982; Kolb & Milner, 1981) has shown that left-hemisphere damage may impair performance of both single gestures and more complex gestural sequences, but which of these tasks is affected depends on the intrahemispheric location of the lesion. Kimura (1982) observed that relative to patients with right-hemisphere damage those with left-hemisphere damage to the parietal area were impaired in performing both single and multiple hand postures. More anterior damage was associated with impairments in multiple but not single hand postures.

De Renzi (De Renzi et al., 1980, 1983) found that left-hemisphere-damaged patients were equally impaired in performing single or multiple hand gestures. Analyses of the effects of intrahemispheric location of the lesion within the left hemisphere revealed that parietal damage impaired performance regardless of movement complexity. Damage to the frontal area appeared not to impair performance of either single or multiple gestures.

Kolb and Milner (1981) found that only left-hemisphere-damaged patients were impaired in performing limb gestures. Single limb gestures were most impaired in the patients with parietal damage. Sequencing of limb gestures was impaired with both frontal and parietal damage, although parietal damage led to more severe deficits.

All of this work has pointed to the importance of left-hemisphere damage in gestural performance. Roy et al. (1991) have shown that right-hemisphere damage may affect performance of hand gestures depending on their complexity. In the part of their study relevant to this discussion, patients imitated gestures demonstrated by the examiner that increased in complexity from single intransitive to single transitive to sequences of two or three intransitive gestures (e.g., salute and wave). Patients with left-hemisphere damage were impaired on all the gestures and the degree of this impairment increased with complexity. The right-hemisphere-damaged patients, on the other hand, were not impaired on any of the tasks except the most complex one, the three-gesture sequence. Complexity, then, served to increase the impairment in patients with left-hemisphere damage but served to elicit the impairment in those with right-hemisphere damage.

A more recent investigation by Roy, Square-Storer & Adams (1992, see Section II.C. Memory Disorders for details) confirmed the importance of movement complexity. Left- and right-hemisphere-damaged patients performed movement sequences that increased in the number of movement elements from two to four. They attempted seven trials at each sequence length. One measure of performance was the proportion of patients able to achieve a criterion of at least two correct sequences at a given sequence length. Another was the percentage of errors made at each sequence length. Relative to the right-hemisphere-damaged patients the proportion of left-hemisphere-damaged patients who achieved criterion was significantly smaller for the three and four movement sequences. Also, the percentage of errors was greater for the left-hemisphere-damaged patients at all sequences, but this difference increased with the length of the sequence.

Movement complexity to this point has referred to the number of movement elements in a sequence. An alternate interpretation is one that focuses more on the characteristics of individual movements or gestures. One set of studies has compared performance of transitive and intransitive gestures. Transitive gestures involve use of objects, whereas intransitive gestures are typically used to communicate a message such as a wave or a salute and, so, do not incorporate objects. Considerable research has shown that apractic patients make more errors performing transitive gestures (Haaland & Flaherty, 1984; Haaland & Yeo, 1989; Roy et al., 1991). The poorer performance of these gestures has been thought to be a reflection of their greater complexity. One interpretation is that transitive gestures require the integration of egocentric (body-centered) and allocentric space (Haaland & Flaherty, 1984). Another is that transitive gestures often involve a component, repetitive action (e.g., flexion–extension movements in hammering), not usually seen in intransitive gestures.

A second dimension that may contribute to the complexity of individual gestures is whether hand movements are directed toward or away from the body. Research involving both children and adults with apraxia reveals that gestures incorporating movements toward (e.g., salute) or on the body (e.g., brush teeth) are performed more poorly. Kinematic analyses comparing these two types of gesture reveal that gestures made toward the body involve lower peak velocities and more time spent in *deceleration* as the subject approaches the target location for performing the gesture (Roy, Brown, & Winchester, 1992). This pattern has been found to reflect more precise movements (e.g., Marteniuk, MacKenzie, Jeannerod, Athenes, & Dugas, 1987), suggesting that these egocentric gestures may demand greater movement precision.

Jason (1986) has done one of the only studies to examine systematically the effect of complexity on the performance of single-hand gestures. Four groups of patients with left- or right-hemisphere damage restricted to either the frontal or temporal lobes and a group of age-matched normal adults participated in this study. The subjects performed 18 gestures, six involving the arm only, six involving the hand only, and six involving both hand and arm movements. Performance was scored using a detailed criterion incorporating finger and elbow positions. Analyses revealed that gestures requiring both hand and arm components were performed more poorly than the other gesture types that were not different. Although all of the brain-damaged patients performed more poorly than the normal control subjects, there were no differences between the frontal and temporal patients nor between the left- and right-hemisphere-damaged patients. Complexity, then, affects performance but to an equal degree in all the brain-damaged groups.

These findings concur with those by De Renzi et al. (1980) and Kimura (1982) to the extent that the left-hemisphere-damaged patients were impaired on these single gestures. The observation that the right-hemisphere-damaged patients were equally impaired is not consistent with this earlier work. The implication of this discrepancy is that if one examines performance in enough detail, deficits not apparent using less detailed analyses may be revealed. In a subsequent part of this study Jason (1986) examined performance of a sequence of these single gestures. As in his previous work (Jason, 1983), the subjects imitated the sequence performed by the examiner by successively copying each gesture as it was demonstrated. The time interval between each gesture was controlled by a metronome, such that the intervals became successfully shorter over a series of trials. Performance was reflected as the shortest interresponse interval before the patient made an error copying a gesture. The interresponse interval for the patients with damage to the frontal area was significantly longer than that for those with temporal lobe damage. The frontal patients, then, were more impaired, suggesting that the frontal lobe is particularly important for controlling the sequencing of hand gestures, as others (e.g., Kimura, 1982) had observed. This impairment with frontal damage was apparent for both right- and left-hemisphere-damaged patients, however, in contrast to a number of other studies reporting greater impairments in sequencing with left-hemisphere damage (e.g., Kimura, 1982).

This inconsistency likely reflects the differences in performance conditions alluded to in our discussion of the effects of memory demands on movement sequencing. The majority of the other studies that found greater impairment with left-hemisphere damage in performing complex, sequential movements required the patients to perform the sequence from memory. In this study (Jason, 1986) performance placed no demands on memory. The impact of movement complexity as reflected in the number of movements in a sequence, then, depends on whether the sequence must be generated from memory. Increasing the number of movements in the sequence affects performance in both left- and right-hemisphere-damaged patients, particularly those with frontal and parietal damage. The selective impairment observed with left-hemisphere damage only appears to arise when these sequences must be generated from memory (but see Harrington & Haaland, 1991, 1992).

Given these two dimensions of complexity pertaining to single gestures and gestural sequences, to what extent are they independent. Is performance of single gestures affected when they are embedded in a sequence? Work on coarticulation effects in speech motor control indicates that the articulatory control of a particular phoneme is influenced by the other phonemes with which is embedded. Inter- and intraarticular coarticulation in speech demonstrates the influence of context reflected in the vowel-to-consonant and consonant-to-vowel transitions. Intraarticular context effects indicate that the observed movement of an articulator is affected by the extent and direction of the preceding (carry-over effects) and subsequent (anticipatory effects) movements of that articulator. These effects are expressed both in spatial and temporal measures. Several studies of the spatial effects reveal that tongue movements in the horizontal plane during an intervocalic stop consonant closure tend to be in the direction of the tongue position for the subsequent vowel (e.g., Perkell, 1969). Work focusing on the temporal effects has shown that during the contact period for a velar stop, the tongue dorsum will begin to move sooner if the following vowel is open than if it is closed (e.g., Parush, Ostry, & Munhall, 1983). This type of effect was also observed in our recent work on gestural sequencing. For the left-hemisphere-damaged patients, performance of the individual gestures became distorted when these were embedded in a sequence (Roy, Square-Storer, & Adams, 1992, see below for details). These context effects in the control of movement suggest that these two dimensions of movement complexity may not be independent. Careful analyses of the nature of their interaction will contribute to a more complete understanding of movement complexity.

C. Disruptions to Movement Sequencing

Disruptions to the sequencing of movement is frequently seen in apraxia, particularly ideational apraxia (e.g., De Renzi & Luchelli, 1988; Poeck, 1986). Several issues have been raised in this work. One issue that has been considered in a previous section is concerned with the role of memory in movement sequencing disorders. Basically, the findings suggest that patients with left-hemisphere damage are much less impaired in performing a sequence of movements when imitating the examiner's movements than when generating the sequence from memory.

A second issue concerns the nature of the deficit in movement sequencing and its relationship to lesion localization. Impairments in the performance of movement sequences have been observed most frequently in patients with left-hemisphere damage (Harrington & Haaland, 1991; Jason, 1983, 1985, 1986; Kimura, 1982; Roy, 1981). One of the characteristic errors is a perseveration in which the patient repeats a movement element in the sequence. Kimura (1979) argued that the predominance of preservative errors suggested that left-hemisphere damage does not lead to a problem in sequencing per se but rather in making transitions between elements in the sequence.

Work by Roy (1981) looked more closely at the nature of the sequencing errors. Sequencing errors were broken down into their order and position components and the relative combination of these components were examined in the left- and right-hemisphere-damaged patients. These sequencing errors were categorized into simple or complex errors. The simple sequencing errors were ones with two position errors and one order error, whereas the complex sequencing errors involved higher combinations of these components. Roy (1981) found a higher incidence of simple sequencing errors for the right-hemisphere-damaged patients but a higher frequency of complex sequencing errors for those with left-hemisphere damage. Thus, although there were no differences between the left- and right-hemisphere-damaged patients in the total incidence of sequencing errors, there was a difference in the complexity of these errors, with the left-hemisphere-damaged patients making complex sequencing errors more frequently.

Although these findings suggest that left-hemisphere damage leads to deficits in sequencing, Roy, Square-Storer, & Adams (1992) have shown that left-hemisphere damage may impair the performance of the individual movements in the sequence as evidenced in the distortions to these movements. Distortions are aberrations in the performance of the individual movements (e.g., wrong hand orientation or posture) which are otherwise correct. Although Roy and Square (1992) found that distortions of individual movements performed in isolation do not appear only with left-hemisphere damage, as the right-hemisphere-damaged patients also exhibited such distortions, it was only in the left-hemisphere-damaged patients that the incidence of these distortions increased in the context of the sequence. These findings suggest that damage to either hemisphere may lead to some impairment in the control of the individual movements in the sequence. With left-hemisphere damage, however, this impairment increases when demands for movement sequencing are added. This increased incidence of distortions may reflect a greater effect of movement context on the performance of the individual movements with left-hemisphere damage and may provide a key to understanding another basis for the sequencing problem in these patients. These context effects were also reported by Harrington and Haaland (1992).

Considerable work in motor control in recent years has focused on the effect of context on the planning and control of movement. In reaching, for example, analyses of the velocity profile of the reaching movement (i.e., trajectory of the wrist movement) have shown that the time after peak velocity increases as target size decreases, suggesting that the time in deceleration increases with the demands for spatial precision (Soechting, 1984). These effects of context have also been observed in a two-element sequence. The time in deceleration in picking up a small disk (the first movement) was greater if the subsequent movement required the subject to place the disk into a small receptacle as opposed to throwing it into a box (Marteniuk et al., 1987). The precision demands of the second movement, then, affected the planning and control of the first.

Given this work on context, the distortions of any individual movement in the sequences may reflect the influence of the other movements on the planning and control of this movement. The deficits in sequencing observed in this study (Roy, Square-Storer, & Adams, 1992), then, may arise to some extent from these context effects as defined by the task demands of each movement. In the limb sequence, for example, the hand posture and orientation (grasp vs. index finger pointing), the direction of the movement (slide across vs. pull down) and the type of action (point vs. turn vs. slide vs. pull) for a particular movement in the sequence may all serve to influence the planning and control of previous and subsequent movements. This effect of context in sequencing might be best reflected in the strong tendency for these left-hemisphere-damaged patients to perseverate. In this case some dimension of the previous movement is carried over into the performance of the subsequent movement resulting in a repetition of either the entire response or one or more dimensions of it.

In this study a closer examination of the distortions on the limb sequencing task in several of the left-hemisphere-damaged patients provided some support for this point. Many of the distortions of the otherwise correct movements involved repeating either the posture or the action from the previous movement. For example, one movement in the sequence involved grasping a knob on the sequencing board and sliding it horizontally across a short groove. The previous movement may have been one where the patient pointed at the top of the previous knob with the extended index finger or grasped and turned the knob. In many of the patients the slide movement was made correctly but it was distorted either in terms of the posture used (an extended index finger instead of a grasp) or the action (a turning movement occurred simultaneously with the slide). These findings indicate the importance of movement context on sequencing performance and suggest that we must look more closely at these effects to understand the nature of the movement sequencing deficit associated with left-hemisphere damage.

D. Coordination of Movement Components

A number of studies using instrumental analyses of the performance of verbal apractic speakers suggest that the impairment may involve disruptions in the temporal coordination of speech movements or speech subsystems (e.g., articulation with resonance). Analyses of the coordination of voice onset times with supralaryngeal articulation have suggested that many of the voicing errors perceived in apractic speech may result from disruptions in the temporal coordination of laryngeal movements with articulation. For example, work by Itoh, Sasanuma, Hirose, Yosioka, and Ushijima (1980) examining movements of the articulators using X-ray microbeam analyses revealed a dyscoordination among several articulators (lower lip and incisor, tongue dorsum and lower surface of the velum) in their apractic subject. Analyses using electromyography provided support for this finding of poor temporal coordination among the articulators (e.g.,

Keller, 1984). Finally, acoustic analyses have revealed disruptions of anticipatory coarticulation in apractic speech (Scholten & Square-Storer, 1994;
Zeigler & von Cramon, 1986).

Few studies have examined the temporal coordination of movements in
limb apraxia in the detail used in the analyses of apraxia of speech. Disruptions in the coordination of movement components has been suggested by
Charlton, Roy, Marteniuk, MacKenzie, and Square-Storer (1988) to appear
in limb apraxia. In demonstrating a salute gesture the apractic patient made
the appropriate axial and proximal postures but assumed an incorrect hand
posture, a clenched fist. Charlton et al. (1988) argued that the patient was
unable to coordinate the distal (hand) segment of the gesture with the
proximal (arm) and axial (body) components. This proposition was more
formally tested by observing the same patient performing a reach-and-grasp
task using a three-dimensional movement analysis system. This prehension
task involved the coordination of a distal, grasp component involving the
hand with a proximal transport component involving movement of the
arm. Although the patient moved more slowly, the velocity profile for
the transport component was found to be much like that of a normal age-
matched person examined at the same time. However, the coordination
between the transport and grasp components and the grasp component
itself were considerably different. Initial opening of the grasp and maximum grasp aperture occurred much earlier in time and the hand was opened
more widely. These findings are similar to those using fiber-optic and X-ray
microbeam analyses, which demonstrated impairments in the spatiotemporal coordination of movement in verbal apraxia (Itoh et al., 1980).

Work by Poizner (Poizner & Kegl, 1992; Poizner, Mack, Verfaellie, Roth,
& Heilman, 1990) and Roy (Roy, Brown, & Winchester, 1992; Roy, Brown,
& Hardie, 1993) have examined movement coordination in limb gestures
typically used in assessing apraxia. Poizner found three types of disruption
in movement coordination: impaired spatial orientation of movement, spatiotemporal decoupling, and disturbed joint use. In a transitive gesture, for
example, pantomiming carving a turkey, the control subjects oriented their
movements in the sagittal plane, whereas the apractics' movements were
predominantly oriented in the transverse plane. Spatiotemporal decoupling
was evidenced in the breakdown in the relationship between velocity and
the degree of curvature in the repetitive movements associated with carving.
Typically, as the hand approaches a change in direction in such movements
the velocity of movement reaches a low point. In the apractics this relationship broke down, giving their movements a rather jerky, awkward appearance. The third characteristic, disturbed joint use, was evident through
analyzing the ratio of displacements of the hand that involve movements at
the elbow and shoulder to displacements of the elbow that reflect primarily
movement at the shoulder. The larger this ratio the greater is the contribu-

tion of movement at the elbow, the more distal joint. Generally, these analyses revealed much larger ratios for the control subjects, suggesting that their movements were generated distally from the elbow, whereas the apractics generated movements proximally at the shoulder.

In their work, Roy et al. (1993) emphasized the importance of examining individual differences in the control of gestural movements. Movement control is exerted in both hand space, as revealed in the trajectory of the hand, and in arm and joint space, reflected in the angular displacements at each joint involved in the movement (e.g., Roy et al., 1993). In a salute gesture, analyses of displacement and spatial variability of the hand in the three movement planes (i.e., hand space) revealed two subjects who employed quite different means of controlling their movements in joint space. In one subject (EK) displacement and spatial variability of the hand was greatest in the sagittal plane. In the other subject (LZ) these measures were greatest in the coronal plane.

Analyses of movements in joint space revealed that EK's movements were controlled primarily at the elbow with relatively little movement at the shoulder. In her case then the salute primarily involved keeping the elbow at the side and raising the hand to the head by moving from the elbow. For LZ, however, movements were controlled at both the shoulder and the elbow such that the movement was much more complex. Abduction at the shoulder bringing the elbow away from the body was followed by flexion at the elbow bringing the hand in contact with the forehead. The differing complexity of these two salute gestures was evident in the overall spatial variability of movement in the three movement planes and impacted on the movement kinematics. For LZ, who generated the more complex movement pattern overall, spatial variability was much greater, peak velocity was much smaller, and the time spent in deceleration after peak velocity was much longer.

These findings point to the importance of developing detailed kinematic analyses of limb movements in order to understand the nature of disruptions to movement coordination in limb apraxia. Similar analyses of speech motor control have proven invaluable in understanding coordination problems in verbal apraxia. Central to these studies, however, will be investigations of the nature and extent of variability in the control of movement in the normal population.

E. Common Expressions of Apraxia across Movement Systems

One of the key indicators that apraxia may reflect a disruption to a central production system is that gestures controlled by different movement systems are all affected. With this in mind Kimura (e.g., Kimura, 1979, 1982; Kimura & Archibald, 1974) and others (e.g., Roy et al., 1991) have shown that deficits in gesturing were seen across different movements systems such that their left-hemisphere-damaged patients, many of whom were aphasic, were equally impaired in oral verbal, oral nonverbal, and limb gestures. These observations led Kimura (1982) to argue that the co-occurrence of aphasia and apraxia arose from a common underlying motor control deficit. Gesturing, whether expressed verbally, orally, or manually, was equally impaired.

This hypothesis would predict that there might be a marked co-occurrence of apractic deficits across the movements systems. We recently completed a study (Hogg, Square-Storer, & Roy, 1994) that supported this prediction. We examined the co-incidence of limb, oral, and verbal apraxia in groups of right- or left-hemisphere-damaged patients, all but three of whom were aphasic. The incidence of apraxia was very low in the right-hemisphere-damaged patients, with 10% (1/10) showing limb and verbal apraxia and 30% (3/10) showing oral apraxia. The incidence of apraxia in the left-hemisphere-damaged patients was significantly higher. Limb apraxia was observed in 85% (22/26), oral apraxia in 81% (21/26), and verbal apraxia in 77% (20/26) of the cases. Analyses of the co-incidence revealed that 73% (19/26) of the cases demonstrated all three types. In two of the cases (8%) two types of apraxia were observed, with one showing limb and oral apraxia and the other oral and verbal apraxia. A further two cases showed only one type, limb apraxia. The remaining three cases did not exhibit any of the apraxias. These findings are consistent with a large number of investigations (see Roy & Square-Storer, 1990; Square-Storer & Roy, 1989), which reveal a co-incidence among these apraxias and suggest that spatial disorders, impairments in sequencing and movement coordination, and increased movement time are all common to apractic disorders seen across movement systems.

A number of studies have examined the relationship between impairments in the performance of nonrepresentational oral and limb gestures outside of the context of apraxia per se. Kolb and Milner (1981) examined patients with frontal, temporal, or parietal lesions to the left or right hemisphere, comparing the performance of single and sequenced limb and oral gestures. They found that single oral gestures were most impaired in the frontal patients, whereas single limb gestures were most impaired in the parietal patients. Sequencing of oral gestures was impaired in patients with frontal damage regardless of laterality and in patients with left parietal damage. Sequencing of limb gestures was impaired only in patients with left-hemisphere damage. Both frontal and parietal damage was associated with an impairment, although parietal damage led to more severe deficits.

More recent work by Kimura (1982) also examined performance of limb and oral gestures and found that left frontal damage was associated with impairments in the performance of oral gestures both in isolation and in a sequence. Left parietal damage involved impairments in the performance of single manual gestures and sequences of oral and manual gestures.

Another facet of this question as to the pervasiveness of apractic deficits concerns whether the disorder is apparent in gestures involving axial or whole body movements. Geschwind (1965) had argued that apraxia only affects movements controlled through the pyramidal system, that is, primarily upper limb and buccofacial movements. Work by Poeck, Lehmkuhl, and Willmes (1982) and more recently by Roy et al. (1991) and Alexander et al. (1992), however, has shown that axial movements are affected by apraxia.

Taken together this evidence suggests that apraxia may be seen across several movement systems. The association among the apraxias may reflect some common disorder in motor control in that similar types of errors and performance deficits seem to be exhibited in all the apraxias. The characteristics of this common disorder are by no means clear, however. Some clue to the nature of this disorder may come from carefully studying disruptions to praxis as they relate to the location of brain damage and the *task demands* (e.g., Alexander et al., 1992). The analyses here should focus on the processes involved in the preparation and execution of movement using measures that will afford a detailed description of the temporal and spatial dimensions of performance. Such studies may provide a clearer view of commonalities in the control of gestural movements across the movement systems (see Roy & Square-Storer, 1990, for further discussion).

IV. APRAXIA AND THE COGNITIVE-MOTOR INTERFACE

The notion that apraxia may involve disruptions to sensory-perceptual, conceptual, and production systems points to the complex nature of this disorder, which reflects the interface among perceptual, cognitive, and motor processes. These disorders may arise from disruptions at various stages in the evolving gesture or sequence. Early stages associated with analyzing visual gestural information and identifying key features of tools and objects to be used, somewhat later stages involving response selection or image generation, and still later stages associated with movement sequencing and coordination may be affected to varying degrees. Identifying which of these stages are affected will require careful task manipulation so as to place demands on particular stages (cf. Roy et al., 1991). One manipulation of task demands that we have considered involves how the patient is asked to perform the gesture, that is, to pantomime or imitate the gesture.

A. A Model of Gesture Production

A model developed by Roy and Hall (1992) depicts the stages involved in performing single gestures under different task conditions involving either pantomime or imitation. In the pantomime condition, the context for the gesture (e.g., the tools and objects) is not present and must in a sense be created mentally. The various movement components must also be selected and organized internally, as there is no information in the environment on which to rely. In this situation the patient must create the context based on past experience. Information pertaining to the location of the hand in space, the hand posture, and the arm–hand action must be accessed in order to perform the gesture correctly. Roy and Hall (1992) have argued that this information may be stored as motor images. Indeed, it is just these types of processes (selection, organization, context creation) in which the imagery system is thought to play an important role (see Paivio, 1986, chap. 4). According to this model impairments in pantomiming gestures in apraxia may arise from a deficit in generating these images.

Work by Farah (Farah, 1989) suggests that the posterior left hemisphere is important for the process of visual image generation. Using Kosslyn's (Kosslyn, Holtzman, Farah, & Gazzaniga, 1985) componential model of visual imagery, Farah inferred through a process of elimination which particular components of mental imagery ability were impaired with lateralized brain damage. The patients with the clearest deficit in the image generation component were those with damage in the posterior left quadrant of the brain. Although considerable controversy exists as to the potential role of the left hemisphere in image generation (see Sergent, 1990), work by Goldenberg provides some support for the importance of the left hemisphere in image generation. In studies of normal adults using the regional cerebral blood flow technique (e.g., Goldenberg, Steiner, Podreka, & Deecke, 1992), Goldenberg found that image generation was associated with increased blood flow to the left inferior occipital region. Studies of patients with lateralized cerebral brain damage (Goldenberg, 1989) revealed that patients with left-hemisphere damage had greater deficits in image generation than those with right-hemisphere damage. Given that imagery processes can play a role in movement (Hall, Buckolz, & Fishburne, 1992) and that visual image generation may be impaired by left-hemisphere damage, Roy and Hall (1992) reasoned that the a loss of the image generation process might contribute to the impairment in pantomiming gestures associated with left-hemisphere damage.

Rothi and Heilman (1985) alluded to the role of imagery in apraxia arguing that visuokinesthetic engrams are embodied in the region of the supramarginal gyrus of the left hemisphere. Evidence for the integrity of these engrams, they suggest, comes from studies of gesture recognition (Heilman et al., 1982; Rothi et al., 1985, 1986). They attributed one form of ideomotor apraxia to a destruction of these visuokinesthetic engrams, as the affected patients exhibited an impairment in gesture recognition (Heilman et al., 1982). From Heilman's account it would seem that these representations are involved in either the selection or the control or both of the movements used in pantomiming the gesture. More recently, Goldenberg (1992) also pointed to the potential importance of impairments to image generation as one basis for the impairment in pantomiming gestures in apraxia.

In the model, performance to pantomime is contrasted with imitation of a gesture performed by the examiner. In pantomime performance the patient must generate the gesture from memory. One of the first stages in this process must involve response selection. Once selected an image of the response must be generated and retained in working memory. Kosslyn (Kosslyn et al., 1985) has identified a number of components involved in visual image generation (i.e., picture, put and find components). Although it is not possible to identify the components of image generation involved in gesture production in much detail at this point in time, it is likely several components are involved. One would be associated with the tools (e.g., hammer) and objects (e.g., that which tools act upon, a nail; see Rothi et al., 1991) used in the gesture, where the others are associated with the movements that compose the gesture.

The tool–object components are likely static. Because tools and objects have both intrinsic (e.g., size and shape) and extrinsic (e.g., location and orientation) properties (e.g., Arbib, 1990), it is likely that these properties are incorporated into the image generated. The movement components may have both static and dynamic aspects. The static aspect may relate to the hand posture involved in grasping the tool. The dynamic component may involve the visual and kinesthetic information associated with the movements that compose the gesture. This information may play a role in the organization and control of the gesture. This image may to some extent play a role in establishing the internal (i.e., body centered) context for the gesture. The kinesthetic component may be involved in the initial stages of response preparation by establishing the postural context for the gesture through a type of pretuning mechanism (e.g., Frank & Earl, 1990). Upon movement initiation, both the visual and kinesthetic components may afford information as to the expected sensory consequences.

In contrast, when the patient is asked to imitate a gesture, access to memory and the associated response selection and image generation processes are not required. Rather, the visual and kinesthetic modalities are seen to provide the primary sources of information. The patient must be able to analyze the visual and kinesthetic information in order to detect the critical features for imitating accurately what he has seen or felt. When visual information about the examiner's demonstration is present continuously throughout the patient's imitative performance, the patient may visually monitor his own performance to determine how well it conforms to that present in the model. This is the case for gestures performed in allocentric space (i.e., away from the body), such as hammering a nail. For gestures performed in body space, such as brushing one's teeth, which are not easily monitored visually, the patient may have to carry out a visuokinesthetic transformation and monitor the felt position of his hand movements. In either situation little reliance is placed on memory.

When the visual information from the examiner's demonstration is not available during the patient's imitative performance, he must retain an image of the gesture and subsequently use this to control his movement. In this case, image encoding and retention are involved. Performance in this situation shares the image retention stage with that involved when the patient must perform the gesture from memory. When performing from memory the image retained in working memory is generated from secondary memory, whereas the image retained in this imitation condition is formed based on information available in the environment.

The final stage in response production in the model is concerned with mechanisms involved in initiating, organizing, and controlling movement during gestural performance.

Using this model, Roy et al. (in press) envisage that impairments in pantomiming a single gesture can arise from disruptions at a number of stages in gesture production. One stage involves the memory structures from which images are generated. Roy (1983a, 1983b; Roy & Square, 1985; Roy & Square-Storer, 1990) has described several aspects of knowledge relevant to objects (e.g., knowledge of objects, knowledge of object functions) and actions (knowledge of action), which may form important components of these memory structures. As we have seen, work by Roy (1983a, 1983b), Heilman (Ochipa et al., 1992; Rothi et al., 1986), and others (e.g., Wang & Goodglass, 1992) revealed that impairments to these structures may underlie the difficulty these patients have in pantomime production.

Disruptions to image generation may also underlie deficits in pantomime production. Given the potential number of components alluded to above in the image used to generate the gesture, impairments in pantomime production may arise from disruptions in generating any number of these components. Two components alluded to above involve the intrinsic (e.g., shape) and extrinsic (e.g., location) properties of objects. Arbib's (1990) coordinated control program model of motor performance suggests that these components pertaining to object properties are linked with programs controlling different movement components. For example, the grasp component associated with movements of the hand in reaching appears to be particularly sensitive to the intrinsic properties of objects, whereas the transport component (movement of the arm) is more closely attuned to the extrinsic properties.

A number of studies suggest that these perceptual-motor components may have different neural substrates such that damage to a particular brain region selectively impairs one of these components. Farah (1989) argues that generating and inspecting images of these components is affected by damage in particular brain areas, with damage to posterior parietal and inferior temporal areas disrupting imagery processes associated with extrinsic and intrinsic properties, respectively. Jeannerod (1986, 1988) has shown that the movement components sensitive to each of these object properties are also disrupted with damage in particular brain regions. Damage to the sensorimotor area, for example, selectively impairs the grasp component. Based on this evidence it would seem that image generation, for each of these components may be selectively disrupted by brain damage, thus impairing pantomime production in different ways, depending on which component has been affected (c.f. Decety & Ingvar, 1990).

Recent work by Brown, Roy, and Hall (1993) has compared reaching for real or imaged objects in order to examine this image generation process. Using kinematic analyses they found that the control of movement when pantomiming a reach is comparable to that when reaching for a real object. The time to complete the movement, the time spent in deceleration, the size of the grasp aperture at the end of the movement and the time to achieve this aperture are all comparable in the two movement conditions. To some extent the ability to generate these movements in the pantomime condition depends on the subject's ability to generate an image of the objects and the movements used to interact with them. Variations of this paradigm will be used to examine gestural pantomime in apractic patients.

Disruptions in initiating, organizing, and controlling the gestural response may also underlie impairments in pantomiming gestures. Apractic patients are frequently able to perform gestures in the appropriate environmental context, their inability to do so in a clinical assessment devoid of this context cannot be attributed to some basic deficit in the control of movement, such as would be seen in hemiparetic movements (partially paralyzed limb due to stroke). Rather, disruptions at this stage likely involve some higher level problem in organizing and controlling movement. In the case of pantomime, this problem may be expressed as an inability to use the representation in working memory to organize and control the gestural movement. Borrowing from Farah and Kosslyn's work on visual imagery the patient may be unable to effectively inspect the image in order to identify the particular values of movement parameters (e.g., arm action, hand posture) necessary to program the appropriate movement. Alternately, the patient may have difficulty with movement programming such that he or she is unable to use these parameter values to provide the appropriate constraints on movements.

B. Patterns of Performance Predicted from the Model

One approach to examining this model involves comparing performance in the pantomime and imitation conditions. Impairments in the conceptual system, particularly the knowledge of action component, should have their greatest effect in this condition as these knowledge components form an integral part of the memory system from which gestures are generated. In the imitation condition, no demands are placed on secondary memory. Rather, the patient analyzes and attempts to reproduce the spatiotemporal pattern of movement in the examiner's demonstration. Patients with disruptions to the knowledge components in the conceptual system but no impairments to the production system should demonstrate a marked improvement in gestural performance when imitating a gesture. Gestural imitation, then, is a reflection of the integrity of the production system.

As we have seen, performance in these two conditions is not routinely compared by all investigators. Some limit apraxia assessments to imitation (e.g., De Renzi et al., 1980). Others view pantomime and imitation on a continuum of difficulty and so do not directly compare performance between these two conditions. Still others do compare these performance conditions but use the relative level of performance as a basis for classifying the apraxia as either ideational (improvement when imitating) or ideomotor (no improvement when imitating). We argue that within the context of our model of apraxia it is crucial to be able to compare these two conditions as a basis for determining what the underlying basis for the apraxia might be. Along with an assessment of the integrity of the knowledge components in the conceptual system these comparisons may provide even clearer insight into which system is affected. Such an analysis may lead to a more theory-based classification of apraxia much like what has been developed in other disorders, such as the dyslexias and the aphasias.

Three patterns of performance are plausible indicators of an apractic deficit: (1) pantomime impaired–imitation intact (P−/I+), (2) pantomime impaired–imitation impaired (P−/I−) and (3) pantomime intact–imitation impaired (P+/I−). When examined in conjunction with an assessment of gesture recognition (knowledge of action component) and tool knowledge (knowledge of object function) our model proposes that each pattern reflects a disruption at a particular stage in gesture production.

Disruptions to the sensory-perceptual system should give rise to patterns of performance that reflect poor analysis of visual gestural and tool–object information. The hallmark of these disorders should be poor gesture recognition and poor imitation of gestures but a preserved ability to pantomime gestures (P+/I−). Although patients exhibiting this pattern can generate gestures accurately from memory, suggesting that they are able to express through movement what they know about gestures, they are unable to imitate gestures shown to them. Their inability to analyze the spatiotemporal characteristics of movement, then, affects not only gesture recognition but also the organization and control of movement.

Disruptions may also affect communication between the sensory-perceptual system and the production system, leading to a variety of disconnection syndromes originally described by Geschwind (1975). If communication with auditory and verbal processing is affected, patients may not be able to pantomime gestures when the commands to do so involve auditory and verbal information. Pantomime should be intact when the patient is shown the tool visually or allowed to feel it in his hand without vision prior to pantomiming the gesture (i.e., when visual or tactual-kinesthetic information is used to elicit the gesture), depending on what neuroanatomical structures are affected in the disconnection.

This type of disconnection, has been examined in patients with damage to the corpus callosum (e.g., Geschwind, 1975), which results in the disconnection of the two hemispheres. Movements made with the left hand controlled by the right hemisphere are no longer affected by processes subserved by the left hemisphere. Given that auditory and verbal comprehension is subserved by the left hemisphere, the effect of this disconnection should be seen only in performing with the left hand. That is, when auditory and verbal information is used the patient should be unable to pantomime with the left hand (the P−/I+ pattern). One might also expect poor intermanual transfer of tactual-kinesthetic information about the tool. That is, pantomime should be poor when the patient feels the tool with one hand but performs with the other. Pantomime elicited by visual information about the tool, however, should be unimpaired with either hand. Performance to imitation and gesture recognition and tool knowledge should also be unimpaired.

Another possible auditory and verbal disconnection is one arising from damage to fiber tracts within the left hemisphere communicating between areas subserving auditory and verbal comprehension and those involved with movement organization and control (e.g., Heilman et al., 1982). In this case the patient should be impaired when pantomiming with either hand. Pantomime performance elicited by visual or tactual and kinesthetic information as well as imitation, gesture recognition, and tool knowledge should be intact.

Comparable disconnections may exist between visual and tactual-kinesthetic processes and the production system. Pilgrim and Humphreys (1991) has stressed the importance of a direct route to the production system from visual tool information. Several patients with disruptions to this route were found to be impaired in pantomiming the use of a tool when it was presented visually but not when given the tool's name. De Renzi et al. (1983) have also described such modality-specific apractic disorders. In some cases pantomime was impaired when the tool was presented visually, whereas in others the impairment arose when the tool was presented tactually (i.e., the patient felt the tool in his hand prior to pantomiming).

Disruptions to the conceptual system should result in poor performance on cognitive tasks assessing the integrity of the knowledge structures. Gesture recognition and tool knowledge tasks, then, should be performed poorly. Performance to pantomime should also be impaired. Imitation of the gesture should be intact, however (i.e., the P−/I+ pattern). Patients with a disruption to the conceptual system may exhibit meaningless hand gestures that bear little resemblance to the target gesture ("neologistic jargon" movements), a reflection of the profound disorder to the conceptual system. At the same time they may be very sensitive to visual gestural information and, so, be prone to echopraxia, a tendency to repeat movements made by the examiner even when they are not asked to do so. As such this disorder seems conceptually similar to transcortical sensory aphasia.

Our prediction that imitation will not be affected by disruptions to the conceptual system is at variance with a proposal set forth by Heilman et al. (1982). He argues that damage to his visuokinesthetic engrams, which seem comparable to the knowledge of action component in our model, should impair performance to imitation. Since visual gestural information is provided in the examiner's demonstration, however, we argue that the patient should not need to access these knowledge structures when imitating the gesture and, hence, imitation should be unaffected.

A disruption in the early stages of gesture production reflecting response selection and image generation should also be seen in the P−/I+ pattern. In this case, however, gesture recognition and tool knowledge will be intact. These patients know what the gesture should look like and what the tool is used for but have difficulty in translating what they know into action.

Disruptions to the later stages of the production system will be seen in two patterns (P+/I− and P−/I−). In contrast to the P+/I− pattern indicative of a disruption in the sensory-perceptual system, a disruption in the production system producing this pattern should not result in poor gesture recognition or tool knowledge. Patients with an impairment at this stage, then, should be capable of analyzing visual gestural and tool information. Their poor performance on imitation indicates more an inability to use this information to organize and control movement, a stage in the production system involving communication with the sensory-perceptual system. As such this disconnection disorder seems remarkably similar to conduction aphasia.

A disruption at the latest stage in the production system will be seen in the P−/I− pattern without impairments to gesture recognition or tool knowledge. Patients with a disruption at this stage know what the gesture should look like, although they are unable to produce it even when the movement patterns are demonstrated for them by the examiner. This disorder might be considered a pure production disorder involving the latest stages in the production system associated with the organization and control of movement. This disorder seems similar to Broca's aphasia.

Disruptions to both the conceptual and production systems will also give rise to the P−/I− pattern. In this case, however, the gesture recognition and tool knowledge will be impaired. Not only do patients with these disruptions not know what the gesture should look like, but they are also unable to produce it even when this information is provided. Thus, these patients might be considered to have the most severe apraxia. As such, one might liken this disorder to a global aphasia.

Using this paradigm involving manipulating task demands, we will be testing these predictions. These studies in conjunction with detailed analyses of lesion localization will provide clearer insights into the neurobehavioural bases of these disorders.

Acknowledgment

Preparation of this manuscript and the research reported were supported through grants from the Natural Sciences and Engineering Research Council of Canada, Health and Welfare, Canada, and the Ontario Mental Health Foundation.

References

Alexander, M. P., Baker, F., Naeser, M., Kaplan, E., & Palumbo, C. (1992). Neuropsychological and neuroanatomical dimensions of ideomotor apraxia. *Brain, 115,* 87–108.

Arbib, M. A. (1990). Programs, schemas and neural networks for control of hand movements: Beyond the RS framework. In M. Jeannerod (Ed.), *Attention and performance XIII: Motor representation and control* (pp. 111–138) Hillsdale, NJ: Erlbaum.

Brown, L., Roy, E. A., & Hall, C. (1993). Image generation in movement control. Implications for understanding apraxia. *Journal of Clinical and Experimental Neuropsychology, 19,* 64.

Charlton, J., Roy, E. A., Marteniuk, R. G., & MacKenzie, C. L. (1988). Disruptions to reaching in apraxia. *Society for Neuroscience Abstracts, 14,* 1234.

Decety, J., & Ingvar, D. N. (1990). Brain structures participating in mental simulation of motor behavior: A neuropsychological interpretation. *Acta Psychologica, 73,* 13–34.

De Renzi, E. (1985). Methods of limb apraxia examination and their bearing on the interpretation of the disorder. In E. A. Roy (Ed.), *Advances in psychology: Vol. 23. Neuropsychological studies of apraxia and related disorders* (pp. 45–64). Amsterdam: North-Holland Publ.

De Renzi, E., Faglioni, P., Lodesani, M., & Vecchi, A. (1983). Performance of left brain-damaged patients on imitation of single movements and motor sequences: Frontal and parietal-injured patients compared. *Cortex, 19,* 333–343.

De Renzi, E., & Luchelli, F. (1988). Ideational apraxia. *Brain, 111,* 1173–1185.

De Renzi, E., Motti, F., & Nichelli, P. (1980). Imitating gestures: A quantitative approach to ideomotor apraxia. *Archives of Neurology (Chicago), 37,* 6–10.

Duffy, R. J., & Duffy, J. R. (1990). The relationship between pantomime expression and recognition in aphasia: The search for causes. In G. E. Hammond (Ed.), *Cerebral control of speech and limb movements* (pp. 417–449). Amsterdam: Elsevier.

Farah, M. J. (1989). The neural basis of mental imagery. *Trends in Neuroscience, 12,* 354–359.

Frank, J. S., & Earl, M. (1990). Coordination of posture and movement. *Physical Therapy, 70,* 885–863.

Gainotti, G. (1980). Nonverbal cognitive disturbances in aphasia. In H. Whitaker (Ed.), *Contemporary reviews in neuropsychology* (pp. 129–158). New York: Springer-Verlag.

Gainotti, G., & Lemmo, M. A. (1976). Comprehension of symbolic gestures in aphasia. *Brain and Language, 3,* 451–460.

Geschwind, N. (1965). Disconnection syndromes in animals and man. *Brain, 88,* 237–294, 585–644.

Geschwind, N. (1975). The apraxias: Neural mechanisms of disordered learned movement. *American Scientist, 63,* 188–195.

Goldenberg, G. (1989). The ability of patients with brain damage to generate mental visual images. *Brain, 112,* 305–325.

Goldenberg, G. (1992, September). *The riddle of apraxia.* Paper presented at the International Workshop on Imagery and Motor Processes, Leicester.

Goldenberg, G., Steiner, M., Podreka, I., & Deecke, L. (1992). Regional cerebral blood flow patterns related to verification of low- and high-imagery sentences. *Neuropsychologia, 30,* 581–586.

Goodglass, H., & Kaplan, E. (1963). Disturbances of gesture and pantomime in aphasia. *Brain, 86,* 703–720.

Haaland, K. Y., & Flaherty, D. (1984). The different types of limb apraxia errors made by patients with left or right hemisphere damage. *Brain and Cognition, 3,* 370–384.

Haaland, K. Y., Porch, B. E., & Delaney, H. D. (1980). Limb apraxia and motor performance. *Brain and Language, 9,* 315–323.

Haaland, K. Y., & Yeo, R. A. (1989). Neuropsychological and neuroanatomic aspects of complex motor control. In E. D. Bigler, R. A. Yeo, & E. Turkheimer (Eds.), *Neuropsychological function and brain imaging* (pp. 219–244). New York: Plenum.

Hall, C., Buckolz, E., & Fishburne, G. (1992). Imagery and the acquisition of motor skills. *Canadian Journal of Sport Sciences, 17,* 19–27.

Harrington, D. L., & Haaland, K. Y. (1991). Hemispheric specialization for movement sequencing: Abnormalities in levels of programming. *Neuropsychologia, 29,* 147–163.

Harrington, D. L., & Haaland, K. Y. (1992). Motor sequencing with left hemisphere damage. *Brain, 115,* 857–874.

Heilman, K. M. (1975). A tapping test in apraxia. *Cortex, 11,* 259–263.

Heilman, K. M., Rothi, L. J., & Valenstein, E. (1982). Two forms of ideomotor apraxia. *Neurology, 32,* 342–346.

Hogg, S., Square-Storer, P. A., & Roy, E. A. (1994, in preparation) Disruptions to limb, oral and verbal praxis and their dissociation from aphasia.

Itoh, M., Sasanuma, S., Hirose, H., Yosioka, H., & Ushijima, T. (1980). Abnormal articulatory dynamics in a patient with apraxia of speech. *Brain and Language, 11,* 66–75.

Jason, G. (1983). Hemispheric asymmetries in motor function: I. Left hemisphere specialization for memory but not performance. *Neuropsychologia, 21,* 35–46.

Jason, G. (1985). Manual sequence learning after focal cortical lesions. *Neuropsychologia, 23,* 35–46.

Jason, G. (1986). Performance of manual copying tasks after focal cortical lesions. *Neuropsychologia, 23,* 41–78.

Jeannerod, M. (1986). Mechanisms of visuomotor coordination: A study in normal and brain-damaged subjects. *Neuropsychologia, 24,* 41–78.

Jeannerod, M. (1988). *The neural and behavioral organization of goal-directed movements.* Oxford: Clarendon Press.

Keller, E. (1984). Simplification and gesture reduction in apraxia and aphasia. In J. C. Rosenbek, M. McNeil, & A. Aronson (Eds.), *Apraxia of speech: Physiology, acoustics, linguistics and management* (pp. 221–256). San Diego: College Hill Press.

Kertesz, A., & Hooper, P. (1982). Praxis and language. The extent and variety of apraxia in aphasia. *Neuropsychologia, 20,* 275–286.

Kertesz, A., Ferro, J. M., & Shewan, C. (1984). Apraxia and aphasia: the functional anatomical basis for the dissociation. *Neurology, 30,* 40–47.

Kimura, D. (1979). Neuromotor mechanisms in the evolution of human communication. In H. D. Steklis & M. J. Raleigh (Eds.), *Neurobiology of social communication in primates* (pp. 197–219). New York: Academic Press.

Kimura, D. (1982). Left-hemisphere control of oral and brachial movements and their relationship to communication. *Philosophical Transactions of the Royal Society of London, Series B, 298,* 135–149.

Kimura, D., & Archibald, Y. (1974). Motor functions of the left hemisphere. *Brain, 97,* 337–350.

Kolb, B., & Milner, B. (1981). Performance of complex arm and facial movements after focal brain lesions. *Neuropsychologia, 14,* 491–503.

Kosslyn, S. M., Holtzman, J. D., Farah, M. J., & Gazzaniga, M. S. (1985). A computational analysis of mental image generation: Evidence from functional dissociations in split-brain patients. *Journal of Experimental Psychology: General, 114,* 311–341.

Lehmkuhl, G., Poeck, K., & Willmes, K. (1983). Ideomotor apraxia and aphasia. An examination of types and manifestations of apraxic syndromes. *Neuropsychologia, 21,* 199–212.

Liepmann, H. K. (1913). Motor aphasia, anarthria, and apraxia. *Transactions of the 17th International Congress of Medicine,* Sect. XI, Part II, pp. 97–106.

Marteniuk, R. G., MacKenzie, C. L., Jeannerod, M., Athenes, S., & Dugas, C. (1987). Constraints on human arm movement trajectories. *Canadian Journal of Psychology, 41,* 365–378.

Ochipa, C., Rothi, L. J. G., & Heilman, K. (1990). Conduction apraxia. *Journal of Clinical and Experimental Neuropsychology, 12,* 89.

Ochipa, C., Rothi, L. J., & Heilman, K. M. (1992). Conceptual apraxia in Alzheimer's disease. *Brain, 115,* 1061–1071.

Paivio, A. (1986). *Mental Representations: A Dual Coding Approach.* New York: Oxford.

Parush, A., Ostry, D. J., & Munhall, K. G. (1983). A kinematic study of lingual coarticulation in VCV sequences. *Journal of the Acoustical Society of America, 74,* 1115–1125.

Perkell, J. S. (1969). *Physiology of speech production: Results and implications of a quantitative cineradiographic study.* (Research Monograph No. 53). Cambridge, MA: MIT Press.

Peters, M. (1980). Why the preferred hand taps more quickly than the nonpreferred hand: Three experiments on handedness. *Canadian Journal of Psychology, 34,* 62–71.

Pilgrim, E,. & Humphreys, G. W. (1991). Impairment of action to visual objects in a case of ideomotor apraxia. *Cognitive Neuropsychology, 8,* 459–473.

Poeck, K. (1983). Ideational apraxia. *Journal of Neurology, 230,* 1–5.

Poeck, K. (1986). The clinical examination for motor apraxia. *Neuropsychologia, 24,* 129–134.

Poeck, K., Lehmkuhl, G., & Willmes, K. (1982). Axial movements in ideomotor apraxia. *Journal of Neurology, Neurosurgery and Psychiatry, 45,* 1125–1129.

Poizner, H., & Kegl, J. (1992). Neural basis of language and motor behaviour: perspectives from American Sign Language. *Aphasiology, 6,* 219–256.

Poizner, H., Mack, L., Verfaellie, M., Rothi, L. J. G., & Heilman, M. (1990). Three-dimensional computergraphic analysis of apraxia: Neural representations of learned movement. *Brain, 113,* 85–101.

Rothi, L. J. G., & Heilman, K. (1985). Apraxia. In K. Heilman & E. Valenstein (Eds.), *Clinical neuropsychology* (pp. 131–150). New York: Oxford University Press.

Rothi, L. J. G., Heilman, K. M., & Watson, R. T. (1985). Pantomime comprehension and ideomotor apraxia. *Journal of Neurology, Neurosurgery and Psychiatry, 48,* 207–210.

Rothi, L. J. G., Mack, L., & Heilman, K. M. (1986). Pantomime agnosia. *Journal of Neurology, Neurosurgery and Psychiatry, 49,* 451–454.

Rothi, L. J. G., Ochipa, C., & Heilman, K. M. (1991). A cognitive neuropsychological model of limb praxis. *Cognitive Neuropsychology, 8,* 443–458.

Roy, E. A. (1978). Apraxia: A new look at an old syndrome. *Journal of Human Movement Studies, 4,* 191–210.

Roy, E. A. (1981). Action sequencing and lateralized cerebral damage: Evidence for asymmetries in control. In J. Long & A. Baddeley (Eds.), *Attention and performance IX* (pp. 487–498). Hillsdale, NJ: Erlbaum.

Roy, E. A. (1982). Action and performance. In A. Ellis (Ed.), *Normality and pathology in cognitive function* (pp. 265–298). New York: Academic Press.

Roy, E. A. (1983a). Current perspectives on disruptions to limb praxis. *Journal of American Physical Therapy Association, 63,* 1998–2003.

Roy, E. A. (1983b). Neuropsychological perspectives on apraxia and related action sequencing disorders. In R. Magill (Ed.), *Advances in psychology: Vol. 12. Memory and control of action* (pp. 293–322). Amsterdam: North-Holland Publ.

Roy, E. A. (Ed.) (1985). *Advances in psychology: Vol. 23. Neuropsychological studies of apraxia and related disorders.* Amsterdam: North-Holland Publ.

Roy, E. A., Brown, L., & Hardie, M. (1993). Movement variability in limb gesturing. In K. Newell & D. Corcos (Eds.), *Variability in motor performance* (pp. 449–474). Champaign, IL: Human Kinetics Publishers.

Roy, E. A., Brown, L., & Winchester, T. (1992). Kinematic analyses of limb gesturing. *Journal of Clinical and Experimental Neuropsychology, 14,* 62.

Roy, E. A., Brown, L., Winchester, T., Square, P., Hall, C., & Black, S. (1993). Memory processes and gestural performance in apraxia. *Adapted Physical Activity Quarterly, 4,* 293–311.

Roy, E. A., Clark, P., Aigbogun, S,. & Square-Storer, P. A. (1992). Ipsilesional disruptions to reciprocal finger tapping. *Archives of Clinical Neuropsychology, 7,* 213–219.

Roy, E. A., Clark, P., & Square-Storer, P. A. (1989). *Manual and hemispheric asymmetries in fine motor control.* Canadian Psychomotor Learning and Sport Psychology Society, Vancouver.

Roy, E. A., & Hall, C. (1992). Limb apraxia: A process approach. In L. Proteau & D. Elliott (Eds.), *Vision and motor control* (pp. 261–282). Amsterdam: Elsevier.

Roy, E. A., & Square, P. A. (1985). Common considerations in the study of limb, verbal and oral apraxia. In E. A. Roy (Ed.), *Advances in psychology: Vol. 23. Neuropsychological studies of apraxia and related disorders* (pp. 111–159). Amsterdam: North-Holland Publ.

Roy, E. A., & Square-Storer, P. A. (1990). Commonalities and dissociations among the apraxias. In G. R. Hammond (Ed.) *Cerebral Control of speech and Limb Movements* (pp. 451–476). Amsterdam: North Holland Co.

Roy, E. A., Square-Storer, P. A., & Adams, S. (1992). Impairments to limb and oral sequencing: The effects of memory demands and sequence length. *Journal of Clinical and Experimental Neuropsychology, 14,* 62.

Roy, E. A., Square, P. A., Adams, S., & Friesen, H. (1985). Error/movement notation systems in apraxia. *Recherches Semiotiques/Semiotics Inquiry, 5,* 402–412.

Roy, E. A., Square-Storer, P. A., Adams, S., & Friesen, H. (1989). Disruptions to central programming of sequences. *Canadian Psychology, 30,* 423.

Roy, E. A., Square-Storer, P. A., Hogg, S., & Adams, S. (1991). Analysis of task demands in apraxia. *International Journal of Neuroscience, 56,* 177–186.

Scholten, L., & Square-Storer, P. A. (1994). Coarticulation within CV syllables in apractic patients (in preparation).

Sergent, J. (1990). The neuropsychology of visual image generation: Data, method and theory. *Brain and Cognition, 13,* 98–129.

Soechting, J. F. (1984). Effect of target size on spatial and temporal characteristics of a pointing movement in man. *Experimental Brain Research, 54,* 121–132.

Square-Storer, P. A., & Roy, E. A. (1989). The apraxias: Commonalities and distinctions. In P. A. Square-Storer (Ed.), *Acquired apraxia of speech in aphasic adults: Theoretical and clinical issues* (pp. 20–63). London: Taylor & Francis.

Square-Storer, P. A., Roy, E. A., & Hogg, S. (1990). Aphasia and apraxia. In G. R. Hammond (Ed.), *Cerebral control of speech and limb movements* (pp. 477–502). Amsterdam: North-Holland Publ.

Todor, J., & Smiley, A. (1985). Performance differences between the hands: Implications for studying disruption to limb praxis. In E. A. Roy (Ed.), *Advances in psychology: Vol. 23. Neuropsychological studies of apraxia and related disorders* (pp. 309–344). Amsterdam: North-Holland Publ.

Vaughan, H. S., & Costa, L. D. (1962). Performance of patients with lateralized cerebral lesions. II. Sensory and motor tests. *Journal of Nervous and Mental Disorders, 134,* 237–243.

Wang, L., & Goodglass, H. (1992). Pantomime, praxis and aphasia. *Brain and Language, 42,* 402–418.

Wyke, M. (1968). The effect of brain lesions in the performance of an arm-hand movement. *Neurology, 17,* 1113–1120.

Zaidel, D., & Sperry, R. W. (1977). Some long-term motor effects of cerebral commissuro-tomy in man. *Neuropsychologia, 15,* 193–204.

Ziegler, W., & von Cramon, D. (1986). Disturbed coarticulation in apraxia of speech: Acoustic evidence. *Brain and Language, 29,* 34–47.

CHAPTER 10

Developmental Aspects of Neuropsychology

Childhood

Maureen Dennis
Marcia Barnes

Developmental neuropsychology is concerned with specifying age-related changes in cognition as a function of both normal and aberrant changes in the brain. Twenty years ago, both the problems posed in neuropsychological studies of children and the methods used to study these problems were quite different. Then, the reference point was adult cognitive function, so the issues addressed in empirical studies (critical periods, plasticity, and the like) concerned the adult end points of cognition; now, a more genuinely developmental neuropsychology has emerged, with a greater focus on cognitive and brain development, and on how the timing of experience affects the development of both brain and behavior (Turkewitz & Devenny, 1993). Twenty years ago, neuroimaging of brain damage characterized mainly adult cortical damage; now, newer neuroimaging procedures can identify many of the white matter disorders and diseases characteristic of childhood brain damage. In short, advances have been made in neuroimaging, in cognitive modeling, and in the analysis of behavioral change over time and development. The combination of an explicitly developmental perspective, improved neuroimaging, and advances in the modeling of cognitive function has changed the manner in which developmental neuropsychology is

Neuropsychology

conducted, increased the number of clinical or special populations studied, and has broadened its conceptual mandate.

As brain, cognitive function, and the nature of developmental change become more fully understood, a sense of the mutual interdependence between cognitive-developmental psychology and developmental neuropsychology is gradually emerging. We believe that models of acquisition are important for understanding mature cognition, that is, understanding the end state of a cognitive skill is enhanced by knowing how that skill was acquired. We also argue that developmental pathologies of the brain are important preparations for studying the normal acquisition of cognitive skills. We consider, further, that the theories and methods of cognitive development provide both the formal language and the tools with which to assess brain–behavior relationships; and also that, in a reciprocal manner, analyses of how the brain shapes the course of cognitive development speak to theories of normal development. For example, a study of reading comprehension in two groups of children with different but clearly specified forms of brain injury might provide descriptive information about reading in these populations; such a study might also generate theoretically interesting data about the nature of the relationship between decoding speed and comprehension, or between inferencing and comprehension. Information of the latter type would bear on hypotheses about reading comprehension, as well as on hypotheses linking brain and cognitive function, such as the idea that different forms of brain injury affect different aspects of comprehension. Developmental neuropsychological studies designed to select among theories of cognitive function, then, may provide data relevant, not only to particular systemic diseases or brain disorders, but also to our views of cognitive and brain development.

Within this perspective, the specific goals of developmental neuropsychology are, first, to use models of cognitive development to explore those features of brain development important for cognition; and, second, to use models of brain development to address broader theories about cognitive development and age-related cognitive change. The developmental neuropsychological perspective emerging from current studies does not simply show that children are less than adultlike in their skills, nor does it simply chart age-related changes in behavior. Rather, it analyzes how cognitive competencies are acquired, and how that acquisition might be related to demonstrable changes in brain function and organization. Although these questions are not yet answered, an analysis of current research is instructive in showing how they are currently being shaped. In this chapter, we discuss the core problem of developmental neuropsychology—accounting for age-related changes in brain and cognition—and then provide an overview of five current research paradigms.

I. MAPPING COGNITIVE AND BRAIN CHANGES: THE CORE PROBLEM IN DEVELOPMENTAL NEUROPSYCHOLOGY

A. Age as a Marker of Change

The relation between age at time of brain insult and later cognitive function has long been an important topic in developmental neuropsychology. For many years, the protective function of a young age was stressed, so it was believed that young children could sustain brain damage with relative impunity (Lenneberg, 1967). However, neuronal plasticity has proved to be a feature of mature as well as immature brains (e.g., Finger & Stein, 1982). Further, as a fuller range of behavioral observations was made, it has become apparent, not that children are deficit-free after brain injury, but that different types and patterns of cognitive deficit are evident at different points in the life span.

To predict how brain damage affects cognitive function in children, it is necessary to understand the time course of normal cognitive development. More than half a century ago, Kennard's (1940, 1942) studies of the effects of brain lesions on the motor system in infant monkeys were referenced against normal motor development. She found that lesions normally producing motor deficits in adult animals had no immediate effect on motor function in infants, a finding superficially congruent with the idea of greater plasticity in the infant. As the infant monkeys matured, however, significant motor deficits emerged, a finding quite inconsistent with the infant plasticity viewpoint. Kennard concluded that behavioral impairments occurring immediately after brain insult in the immature brain are different from those that appear immediately after lesions in the mature brain; that the difference between the behavioral effects of immature and mature brain lesions varies with the type of behavior being considered; and that certain functional or behavioral impairments are not apparent immediately after early brain damage, but emerge only later in development, at a time when the relevant behavior would normally appear. Later research (Goldman, 1972) has confirmed and extended Kennard's important idea that many effects of brain damage or dysfunction in the immature organism have their greatest impact on cognitive function at a point in development far removed from the insult.

What this means is that the behavioral effects of early brain lesions may emerge at various points throughout development. Therefore, the age of the child is neither a form of recovery mechanism (Fletcher, Miner, & Ewing-Cobbs, 1987), nor a variable with direct explanatory significance for the development of cognition (Fletcher, Levin, & Landry, 1984; Fletcher & Satz, 1983). Age is best considered as an independent variable that marks the temporal course of development, demarcates periods of developmental change, and delineates different developmental phases (Siegel, Bisanz, & Bisanz, 1983; Wohlwill, 1973). It is with this understanding that we consider age effects.

B. Studying Age Effects

How may the neuropsychological effects of age on cognitive function be studied? One approach involves assessing children at a single point in their development and comparing brain and behavior with older children or adults. Another approach is to analyze brain and behavior variables in age groups stratified cross-sectionally. For example, Dennis, Hendrick, Hoffman, and Humphreys (1987) studied language function in a large sample of children; all were diagnosed with hydrocephalus in the first year of life and were stratified into five age groups (6, 8, 10, 12, and 14 yr olds) at the time of neuropsychological testing. An important methodology is the study of longitudinal neuropsychological change. For example, linguistic milestones in early development have been inferred from babble and first words studied longitudinally in infants with focal brain lesions (Marchman, Miller, & Bates, 1991; Thal et al., 1991). Language recovery after focal brain lesions in middle childhood has been monitored from intervals of 6 mo (Dennis, 1980c), 2 yr (Martins & Ferro, 1992), and 10 yr (Chevrie-Muller & Le Normand, 1987). One important longitudinal method involves the study of adults who have sustained childhood brain injury. For example, Kohn (1980) studied understanding of syntax in adults, all with right-hemisphere brain representation of speech and all with epileptogenic damage to the left hemisphere at various times during childhood. Grattan and Eslinger (1989) assessed the effects on adult neuropsychological and psychosocial function of frontal lobe lesions sustained in childhood.

An enduring problem in developmental neuropsychology is how best to characterize the cognitive developmental changes that are obliquely marked by chronological age. Even for normal skill acquisition, it is often difficult to ascertain the whole developmental trajectory of a skill (although, especially for any skill that is still undergoing development, multiple age points provide a better perspective than does a single age point). Nevertheless, the expected sequence of normal developmental changes for a skill must be understood reasonably well before that skill can be studied in brain-injured children. Otherwise, there exists no baseline against which to evaluate how brain damage or disease might alter the course of cognitive development.

C. Developmental Heuristics and Individual Change Models

One approach to specifying age-related changes in cognitive development has been to develop heuristics to show how brain damage early in development affects the time course of cognitive skill acquisition. Dennis (1988) has proposed a behavioral heuristic for describing the effects of brain disorder early in development (Figure 1), that is, how brain damage at various points in the acquisition of a behavioral skill influences the extent to which, and the manner in which, that skill will develop.

The heuristic distinguishes three degrees of skill maturation: emerging, developing, and established. An *emerging skill* is one that is not yet functional or in the preliminary stages of acquisition. A *developing skill* has been partially acquired and it is incompletely functional. An *established skill* is one that has been fully acquired. The heuristic distinguishes six aspects of function for any skill: onset, order, rate, strategy, mastery, control, and upkeep. The *onset* of a skill is that developmental point when it would normally be evident. The onset of a skill may be normal or delayed, the latter involving a deferral in its expected onset. The *order* in which a skill is acquired refers to its emergence in time relative to other skills. Skill order may be normal or garbled, the latter referring to a missequencing in the expected order of skill emergence. The *rate* of skill acquisition is the speed of its developmental course, the slope relating chronological age and skill. Skill rate may be normal or lagging, the latter referring to a slowed progression of the projected developmental course. The tactics for effecting a skill define skill *strategy*. The strategic mode may be normal or detoured, the latter involving an atypical, circuitous, or time-consuming tactic. Skill *mastery* refers to the level of final competence. Skill mastery may be normal or involve a shortfall, where the final level of a skill is truncated. The *control* of a skill refers to how well it can be deployed in the short term. The control of a skill may be normal or symptomatic, a symptom being the short-term loss of the ability to effect the skill. The *upkeep* of a skill refers to its long-term maintenance.

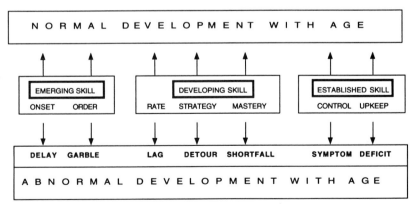

FIGURE 1   Heuristic for studying how brain damage at various points in the acquisition of a behavioral skill influences how that skill will develop.

Skill upkeep may be normal or defective, a deficit involving a long-term loss of skill maintenance.

Age heuristics are loose frameworks that require content in the form of cross-sectional or longitudinal information from neuropsychological studies. The longitudinal analysis of adult neuropsychological function in individuals with childhood brain lesions provides one important source of data. Following a frontal lobe lesion sustained in childhood, for example, Eslinger, Grattan, Damasio, and Damasio (1992) have identified a sequence of delayed onset of certain skills followed by a window of cognitive progression that ends in a developmental arrest of those skills in adolescence.

The goal of any account of age and cognitive function is to describe what is known and to project what has not been directly observed. Recent individual change models have formalized the idea of developmental change into series of procedures that serve to plot the entire developmental trajectories of different cognitive functions for an individual over time (Burchinal & Appelbaum, 1991; Fletcher et al., 1991). An important idea here for developmental neuropsychology is that brain damage rarely arrests ongoing development, but rather alters its course or trajectory. Change within individuals measured at several time points, and as particular cognitive skills unfold, allows evaluation of the effects of different medical and environmental variables on the rate and level of development. From such information, intra- and interindividual differences in the rate or level of the development of particular skills may be projected.

Individual change models add both to the practice and to the theory of development. By plotting the behavioral trajectory in the absence of systemic disease or brain disorder, they permit evaluation of those alterations in the trajectory of development imposed by disease or disorder. Thus, the method is a potentially powerful one for evaluating disease progression, and recovery from brain injury in children (Francis, Fletcher, Stuebing, Davidson, & Thompson, 1991). More broadly, individual change models provide age-sensitive indices of the child's developing cognitive skills that might be tied to measurable changes in brain structure and function. Such an application of individual change models would produce data useful in evaluating theories about the nature of developing brain–behavior relations.

II. CURRENT RESEARCH PARADIGMS

Developmental neuropsychology is broadly concerned with gathering information about developing brain–behavior relationships, and a variety of paradigms guide current research. We have identified five paradigms— cognitive dysfunction paradigms; systemic disease paradigms; brain disorder paradigms; brain development paradigms; and cognitive development paradigms. The paradigms may be contrasted in terms of their core topics, which, in turn, have dictated the choice of particular populations and research methodologies. Within each paradigm, individual research investigations have addressed a variety of issues, ranging from those concerned with gross outcome to theory-driven questions about the nature of brain development and the acquisition of cognitive competences.

III. COGNITIVE DYSFUNCTION PARADIGM

This paradigm begins from the existence of cognitive dysfunction. The target populations include children who cannot read, who cannot sustain attention, who are hyperactive, and who have difficulty acquiring or using language. Children are selected for study within this paradigm because of anomalous behavior or cognition. The behavioral typologies are inferred or demonstrated to be symptomatic of disordered neuropsychological function.

A. Behavior–Behavior Relations

These studies select individuals because of anomalous behavior, and what is studied is a related type of behavior. Establishing behavior–behavior relations actually has a long history in developmental neuropsychology (see Benton, 1962). For example, Rourke and Fisk (1988) studied the neuropsychological test profile of learning-disabled children and related different patterns of academic underachievement in reading, spelling, and arithmetic to different patterns of intact and deficient neuropsychological test performance. From such observations, it was inferred that different brain pathologies might underlie the behavioral typologies, and an attempt was made to propose a central nervous system basis for different forms of learning disability (H. G. Taylor, 1988).

One particular proposal from behavior–behavior paradigms concerns nonverbal learning disabilities (Rourke, 1989), for which Rourke, Del Dotto, Rourke, and Casey (1990) have listed the signature assets (auditory perception; simple motor skill; rote material; auditory and verbal attention and memory; phonology; verbal reception, repetition, storage, associations, and output; late graphomotor skill; word decoding; and spelling) and deficits (tactile and visual perception, attention, and memory; complex psychomotor skills; oral-motor skill, speech prosody; language semantics and pragmatics; early graphomotor skill; reading comprehension; computational mathematics; science; novel, exploratory, or conceptual processing and problem solving; social competence; emotional stability; and activity level). The syndrome is argued to cause both academic and psychosocial problems. Although the proposal includes a hypothesis about white matter dysfunction in the brain (Casey, Rourke, & Picard, 1991), the brain bases are not central to the framework, at least in the sense that study of individuals identified as having nonverbal learning disability requires only the neuropsychological profile (described above) that defines the condition.

B. Behavior–Underlying Process Relations

In these investigations, an anomalous behavioral marker is assumed to derive from a deficient process. The putative deficient process is deemed validated when its indices can be shown to covary with the presence of the behavioral marker for the typology. For example, the inability to produce and perceive rapidly changing auditory stimuli characterizes young children with developmental language impairment, suggesting a core processing deficit in auditory temporal analysis that causes developmental language impairment, the brain bases of which may then be investigated (Tallal, Galaburda, Llinas, & von Euler, 1992). In particular, left-hemisphere dysfunction has been proposed to cause disorders of auditory temporal analysis that result in developmental language impairment (Tallal, 1991); and left-hemisphere dysfunction and impaired interhemispheric communication have been suggested as the basis of the poor temporal resolution, not specific to linguistic material, deemed to be the core cognitive deficit (Wolff, Michel, Ovrut, & Drake, 1990).

C. Brain Dysfunction Inferred from Analogies with Adult Brain Lesions

The effects of adult brain damage are sometimes used as a reference point for defining abnormal cognitive function in children without demonstrable brain lesions. Here, similar neuropsychological profiles in children and adults are assumed to entail similar brain damage. For example, hypotheses about frontal lobe deficits in children with attention deficit hyperactivity disorder have been explored by comparing their neuropsychological test performance to that of normally developing children or to adults with frontal lobe lesions (Barkley, Grodzinsky, & DuPaul, 1992). Hypotheses about brain dysfunction in individuals with nonverbal learning disabilities have been tested by comparing their test performance to that of adults with right-hemisphere lesions (Semrud-Clikeman & Hynd, 1990). Some studies have charted the normal developmental course of skills thought to be subserved by different brain regions; within this focus, cognitive skills of neurologically impaired adults are compared with those of normally developing children of different ages (Welsh, Pennington, & Groisser, 1991).

D. Explicit Brain–Behavior Relations

The relation between anomalous behavioral development and brain dysfunction has also been studied more directly. Several studies have tested the intactness of the central nervous system (CNS) in individuals with behaviorally defined conditions. For example, neuroimaging, electrophysiological, and autopsy studies of dyslexia have revealed alterations in brain asymmetry, as well as anomalies of the cerebral cortex and lateral geniculate nucleus (Galaburda, 1993; Hynd & Semrud-Clikeman, 1989).

IV. SYSTEMIC DISEASE PARADIGMS

The focus of these paradigms is the consequence of particular diseases for neuropsychological function, so subjects are accrued on the basis of a medical diagnosis. In some studies, psychological information serves as a method of diagnostic assessment, and psychological status or cognitive function is viewed as an aspect of outcome, or as a medical marker of morbidity. In others, the age of the child at disease onset or treatment is the focus. Information from these paradigms is important for understanding how neuropsychological function is affected by various medical conditions. Many studies of systemic disease do not provide information about cognitive processing, nor do their data constrain developmental theories in any obvious manner. In some recent studies, however, neuropsychological function in children with systemic diseases, such as congenital hypothyroidism or acute lymphoblastic leukemia, is proving pertinent to understanding the developmental timing of cognitive skills.

A. Systemic Disease and Outcome

Pediatric systemic disease is often associated with impaired neuropsychological function, either because of direct effects of the disease and its treatment, or because of indirect effects (frequent absences from school, prolonged hospitalization, and change in family status; Brown & Madan-Swain, 1993). For example, children with diabetes melitus who have experienced hypoglycemia in childhood have later difficulties with attention and academic skills (S. B. Johnson, 1980). CNS radiation and intrathecal chemotherapy impair neuropsychological function in survivors of childhood cancers such as acute lymphoblastic leukemia (Brown & Madan-Swain, 1993; Fletcher & Copeland, 1988; Maria, Dennis, & Obonsawin, 1993).

B. Age, Systemic Disease, and Outcome

The age of the child at disease onset is an important determinant of cognitive outcome, and a younger age at onset has often proved to involve more cognitive impairment than has an older age. For example, in children treated for acute lymphoblastic leukemia, younger children are overall more vulnerable to neuropsychological dysfunction than are older children (Mulhern, Kovnar et al., 1992; Mulhern, Ochs, & Fairclough, 1992). In evaluating cognitive morbidity, not just total scores but score profiles are important, and such profiles have been related to age at treatment for children with acute lymphoblastic leukemia (Waber, Bernstein, Kammerer, Tarbell, & Sallan, 1992).

C. Developmental Timing

One recent focus in developmental neuropsychology has been an attempt to specify time windows during which particular cognitive skills are normally acquired. Empirical evidence for such time windows has emerged from studies of the optimal timing of treatment for pediatric systemic diseases. In these studies, the developmental timing of the disease and its treatment may be used to explore the time window within which particular cognitive skills develop. For example, newborn screening and treatment of congenital hypothyroidism now prevents mental retardation, and early-screened children are being evaluated throughout childhood to identify the factors that increase or moderate the risk of cognitive impairment (Rovet, 1990). Different cognitive skills appear to be correlated with specific factors that index the timing of thyroid deficiency (Rovet, Ehrlich, & Sorbara, 1992). Such data suggest that the acquisition of particular skills depends on the timing of hormonal influences on the brain. In children with acute lymphoblastic leukemia, younger treated children are less phonologically accurate spellers than are older treated children (Kleinman & Waber, 1992), which suggests a developmental window for the acquisition of phonemic awareness and phonemic analysis skills.

V. BRAIN DISORDER PARADIGMS

These paradigms focus explicitly on the consequence of particular brain disorders for neuropsychological function. Typically, subjects are accrued on the basis of a medical diagnosis of congenital brain malformation or acquired brain pathology from brain tumor, head injury, and the like. In an earlier era of limited neuroimaging techniques, many childhood brain lesions were either not identified or were underspecified, or else their unique character was not perceived. For example, it was not known until recently that the study of children with congenital hydrocephalus might reveal some of the cognitive consequences of cerebral white matter dysfunction (Dennis, 1994).

Research investigations now attempt systematically to relate differences in children's brains to their cognitive function. In some studies, cognitive function is viewed as an aspect of outcome in relation to the presence or absence of the brain disorder, or as a medical marker of morbidity. Studies with larger samples have stratified brain-injured children into age groups and analyzed whether and how cognitive functioning varies with the age of the child at brain injury or at treatment, or have analyzed the symptoms, signs, pathology, and neuroanatomical substrates of the brain disorder.

A. Brain Disorder and Outcome

Many conditions of childhood brain disorder are associated with impaired cognitive development. Studies here range from global overviews of outcome to studies of specific cognitive skill constituents. Outcome has most commonly been studied in relation to variables that index the type, severity, and extent of the brain injury, or the type and form of treatment.

1. Early-Onset Hydrocephalus

Hydrocephalus is a dynamic pathological condition that involves a progressive increase in volume of the cerebral ventricles. Hydrocephalus alters brain structure and function, both directly and as an indirect result of ventricular enlargement: the lining of the ventricles suffers focal destruction; cerebral blood vessels become distorted or dysfunctional; axons and myelin in the periventricular white matter are damaged; neurons may be injured; and the concentration of cerebral water, extracellular spaces, and neurotransmitters is altered.

Hydrocephalus is the common factor in a group of conditions that affect early brain development. Children with hydrocephalus were once at risk for mental retardation, and earlier studies monitored cognitive outcome as a function of whether or not hydrocephalus had been treated. Better and more widely available treatment has reduced the incidence of mental retardation after early-onset hydrocephalus; however, treatment may restore the cortical mantle (Del Bigio, 1993), but it need not prevent some degree of cognitive dysfunction (Prigatano, Zeiner, Pollay, & Kaplan, 1983). Recent neuropsychological studies of early-onset hydrocephalus have attempted to describe the specific cognitive impairments that limit school attainments and achievement.

Hydrocephalus stems from diverse etiologies and it has a range of physical symptoms and manifestations, some of which are associated with poorer performance on nonverbal intelligence or perceptual–motor tasks involving time constraints. For example, Dennis, Fitz et al., (1981) found hydrocephalic children to have generally lower Performance IQ than Verbal IQ scores.

Recent research investigations have suggested that the cognitive deficits of early-onset hydrocephalus are relatively specific in nature, that is, hydrocephalus affects the development of only certain skills within a cognitive domain and the development of these skills is independent of general intellectual level. For example, some oral language skills develop to age-appropriate levels in children with hydrocephalus, but others do not (Dennis & Barnes, 1993; Dennis et al., 1987). In reading, children with hydrocephalus develop age-appropriate word recognition skills that do not translate into proficient comprehension of written text (Barnes & Dennis, 1992b). These specific effects hold even for children with normal or better intelligence (Barnes & Dennis, 1992b; Dennis & Barnes, 1993). Such findings contribute to better descriptions of cognitive outcome after early-onset hydrocephalus, but they also address broader questions. For example, comparisons of the origins of comprehension failure in children with hydrocephalus (Barnes & Dennis, 1992a) and in poor comprehenders without demonstrable brain damage (Barnes & Savard, 1993) are relevant to theories of reading comprehension, and to hypotheses about the neural substrates that support particular components of comprehension.

The analysis of language in children with early-onset hydrocephalus has also been used to address more general cognitive questions, such as those concerning pragmatic communication. Traditionally, the pragmatic principles of language are based on social factors (Grice, 1975), but a second class of principles is independent of social conventions and follows some general constraints of language processing (Prideaux, 1991). More particularly, Leech (1983) has distinguished between *interpersonal rhetoric* (which includes social principles like cooperation and turn-taking), and *textual rhetoric,* which is oriented towards the production and interpretation of texts, oral or written, and involves constraints related to whether the text is clear, economic, easy to process, and meaningful.

Interpersonal rhetoric seems largely preserved in children with hydrocephalus, who are polite and friendly (E. M. Taylor, 1961, described them as very sociable), cooperative, and highly interested in talking (Hadenius, Hagberg, Hyttnas-Bensch, & Sjögren, 1962, noted their love of chatter). In conversations, they initiate as many (Murdoch et al., 1990) or more (Swisher & Pinsker, 1971) turns and exchanges as controls, and the appropriateness of their turn-taking in narratives seems relatively unimpaired (Murdoch, Ozanne, & Smyth, 1990). Children with hydrocephalus deploy a vocabulary to express mental states, and they produce the same number of direct speech acts as peers, an index of turn-taking (Dennis, Jacennik, & Barnes, 1994). In contrast, their textual rhetoric is unclear, uneconomic, difficult to process, and deficient in content (Dennis et al., 1994). These data not only help interpret the clinical observation of fluent but empty speech in this condition (E. M. Taylor, 1961), but also provide data pertinent to hypotheses about different forms of cognitive-pragmatic knowledge.

2. Head Injury

Cognitive deficit often follows closed head injury in children and adolescents (e.g., Chadwick, Rutter, Shaffer, & Shrout, 1981; Dennis & Barnes,

1990; Ewing-Cobbs, Fletcher, Landry, & Levin, 1985; Fletcher et al., 1987; Levin & Eisenberg, 1979; Winogron, Knights, & Bawden, 1984). Cognitive outcome varies with age at injury and recovery time, which has implications for how cognitive deficits might be ameliorated (e.g., D. A. Johnson, Uttley, & Wyke, 1989; Lehr, 1990).

Specific cognitive skills have also been studied in childhood head injury populations. For example, head-injured children and adolescents perform poorly on memory tests involving selective reminding (Ewing-Cobbs & Fletcher, 1987; Lehr, 1990; Levin, Benton, & Grossman, 1982; Levin & Eisenberg, 1979). Recent studies have attempted to identify which medical features make one head-injured child more vulnerable than another to poor memory (Ewing-Cobbs, Levin, Fletcher, Miner, & Eisenberg, 1989). Disorders of attention that persist into the chronic stage of recovery are also common after childhood head injury (Chadwick et al., 1981; D. A. Johnson & Roethig-Johnson, 1989; Murray, Shum, & McFarland, 1992). Attention deficits after childhood head injury are imperfectly understood, although recent studies suggest that, just as do head-injured adults (Trexler & Zappala, 1988), head-injured children have particular difficulty with selective attention, that is, in maintaining vigilance in the presence of distracting visual information (Dennis, Koski, Wilkinson, & Humphreys, 1993).

3. Brain Tumors

Neuropsychological studies of pediatric brain tumors (reviewed recently in Ris & Noll, 1994) have used outcome indices ranging from measures of length of survival and quality of life (e.g., Choux, 1982; Mandigers et al., 1990) to measures of intelligence and academic achievement scores (e.g., Chin and Maruyama, 1984; Danoff, Cowchuk, Marquette, Mulgrew, & Kramer, 1982; Duffner, Cohen, & Thomas, 1983; Ellenberg, McComb, Siegel, & Stowe, 1987; Kun, Mulhern, & Crisco, 1983; Spunberg, Chang, Goldman, Auricchio, & Bell, 1981). These studies have shown that many children with brain tumors have persisting cognitive dysfunction that affects learning, academic performance, and social adaptation (Lannering, Marky, Lundberg, & Olsson, 1990). More recently, investigations have identified impairments in specific neuropsychological functions such as memory (e.g., Brookshire, Copeland, Moore, & Ater, 1990; Hoffman et al., 1992; Kun & Mulhern, 1983; Packer et al., 1989; Winston, Cavazzuti, & Arkins, 1979).

B. Age, Brain Disorder, and Outcome

Cognitive function is not spared more in younger than in older children, as was once believed under the older view of a negative linear relationship between age at brain injury and amount of functional plasticity. Nevertheless, the relation between cognitive status and age at brain disorder onset or treatment is a complex one. Studies in which children with the same brain pathology are compared at different ages (of disease onset, or of treatment) now provide a clearer perspective on age effects than did older studies comparing recovery in children and adults with different underlying brain pathologies (e.g., Lenneberg, 1967).

For disorders with a characteristic diffuse or *multifocal* effect on the brain, a younger age is often associated with greater vulnerability to cognitive deficit. For example, age at radiation for brain tumor affects general cognitive function, and intellectual impairment is more likely in younger-radiated than in older-radiated children (e.g., Danoff et al., 1982; Mulhern, Hancock, Fairclough, & Kun, 1992; Spunberg et al., 1981). Even preschoolers show cognitive problems following closed head injury (Ewing-Cobbs, Miner, Fletcher, & Levin, 1989), and memory impairment seems more severe in head-injured children than in head-injured adolescents (Fletcher et al., 1987).

For *focal* vascular lesions, in contrast to tumors and head injury, age is related to distinct patterns of deficit within a cognitive domain. Early vascular malformations of the left hemisphere produce problems in fairly discrete language functions (e.g., Dennis, 1980a; Dennis & Kohn, 1975); later cerebrovascular accidents produce a variety of language impairments (Dennis, 1980b).

C. Cognitive Outcome in Relation to Indices of Brain Disorder

Studies here overlap with other indices of outcome, but differ in their focus, which is to analyze cognitive outcome in relation to particular types of brain pathology and to indices of explicit brain dysfunction.

1. Early-Onset Hydrocephalus

Language function is related to the pathology of early-onset hydrocephalus. For example, on semantic naming tasks, intraventricular but not extraventricular hydrocephalus pathology is associated with finding fewer target words, whereas a spinal dysraphism pathology impairs controlled verbal fluency (Dennis et al., 1987).

Recent neuroimaging studies of the brains of children with hydrocephalus have revealed changes in cerebral white matter tracts, problems in myelination, and atrophic states of midline commissural structures like the corpus callosum (Fletcher et al., 1992; Gilbert, Jones, Rorke, Chernoff, & James, 1986). These developmental anomalies have been related to standardized measures of general cognitive function, and current research involves the charting of more specific brain–behavior relationships using this methodology.

2. Head Injury

Some types of cognitive outcomes, although not others, can be related to features of pediatric head injury. Deficits in memory and attention are common after head injury, although these impairments are not well predicted by indices of postinjury clinical status. In adults, the Glascow Coma Scale (GCS) does not always accurately predict neuropsychological outcome after severe head injury (Lieh-Lai et al., 1992), and typical head injury severity indices do not correlate with the severity or the type of disorders of attention (Trexler & Zappala, 1988).

Neuroimaging provides a better delineation of brain damage after head injury, but the correlation between neuroimaging and cognitive function is yet to be fully established. In children, magnetic resonance imaging (MRI) delineates areas of focal brain contusion (Levin et al., 1989; Luerssen, Hesselink, Ruff, Healy, & Grote, 1987). Some of the abnormalities identified on MRI can be related to neuropsychological function (Levin et al., 1993). Future studies will continue to evaluate the relation between cognitive outcome and short- and long-term brain changes as visualized by neuroimaging techniques.

3. Brain Tumors

Although brain tumors are commonly associated with cognitive impairment (e.g., Chin & Maruyama, 1984; Kun et al., 1983), not all children are equally at risk for disordered cognition. The neuroanatomical features of the brain tumor are one determinant of cognitive outcome. For example, working memory is most disrupted by tumors that invade the pineal–habenular region and the anterior and medial thalamic nuclei (e.g., Dennis et al., 1991). Treatment variables such as radiation that are known to disturb brain structure and function also influence the cognitive outcome for children with brain tumors (e.g., Dennis et al., 1992; Ellenberg et al., 1987). In future studies, the consequences of childhood brain tumors for cognitive function will need to be considered with respect to variables that include maturational rate, hormone status, radiation history, and tumor location.

VI. BRAIN DEVELOPMENT PARADIGMS

The focus of these paradigms is how developmental data from young nonhuman primates and human children bear on theories about the time course of brain development. Research studies within this paradigm have drawn from a variety of animal and clinical material, as well as from some of the clinical conditions discussed earlier. In all of them, the topic of interest is the mapping of developmental brain–behavior relationships.

A. Developmental Timing of Brain Events

Which events in the brain are necessary for mature cognitive function to emerge? Although this question has not been answered in full, knowledge of the normal sequence and mechanisms of neural maturation is emerging from the research literature (Goldman-Rakic, 1987). Evidence for the developmental timing of events in the brain has been drawn from the normal and abnormal behavioral development of animals and children, as well as from neuroanatomical developmental data. Many recent studies within developmental neuropsychology have explicitly attempted to link specific advances in behavior with features of brain development.

What are some events that happen during maturation of the brain? One proposal (Thatcher, 1991a) is that the brain matures in "traveling waves" beginning near conception and extending through the life span. To the extent that the mechanics of the wave processes reflect tension between competing and cooperative neuronal networks, the waves represent dynamic competition for the growth of dendritic synaptic contacts. These traveling waves are suggested to have consequences for cognitive function. For example, in older children, growth spurts occur in each frontal lobe throughout childhood and adolescence (evidenced from analyses of EEG phase and coherence), and these spurts appear to correspond to Piagetian cognitive-developmental stages (Thatcher, 1991b).

One important feature of cerebral maturation appears to free the young organism from reliance on the immediate environment. Freedom and flexibility of responding is available when a remembered goal rather than an immediate stimulus is used to guide behavior. The dorsolateral prefrontal cortex underlies the maintenance of this skill in adult nonhuman primates, and maturation of this brain region enables the acquisition of the same skill in human infants (Diamond & Goldman-Rakic, 1989; Diamond, 1990, 1991). Development of the dorsolateral prefrontal cortex appears to facilitate the emergence of an important, time-binding feature of primate behavior.

The timing of early experience itself influences how the brain develops. Individual differences in early language exposure as a result of congenital deafness have been used to explore the sensitivity of different brain regions to the timing of experience early in development (Neville, 1991).

B. Regressive and Inhibitory Changes in the Brain and Cognitive Development

As an organism grows, its brain develops, and there are many indices of brain changes over the course of development. These changes may be accretions, that is, the *addition* of new connections or pathways, or regressions, that is, the *loss* of connections or pathways. Regressive events in brain development may be important for the normal acquisition of cognitive skills.

Neurons die early in development (Hamburger & Oppenheim, 1982) and the connections of surviving neurons are pruned (Stanfield, 1984). These early regressive changes in the nervous system are important mechanisms in the normal ontogeny and regulation of behavior (Cowan, Fawcett, O'Leary, & Stanfield, 1984; Purves & Lichtman, 1980). Regressive changes have also been implicated in anomalies of development. Animal models of developmental dyslexia (Galaburda, 1993) showing early pathogenesis related to the immune system have suggested defective neural pruning as a precursor of the cognitive anomaly. It has even been argued that the constituents of aberrant personality are shaped by interference with early regressive CNS events (Carlson, Earls, & Todd, 1988).

Like regressive processes, inhibitory mechanisms occur throughout the course of cognitive development. Some important features of language development depend on inhibition. For example, the ability to speak occurs only after the child deletes that subset of phonemes produced early in development but that are not part of the mother tongue (Werker, 1986). Many frameworks now being developed in cognitive psychology assign a central role to inhibition. For example, Gernsbacher and Faust (1991) have proposed that we access semantic information by a temporal sequence of events that involves activation of a pool of relevant semantic information and selection of the contextually relevant information from that pool, followed by suppression of the irrelevant information. According to such frameworks, the inability to suppress irrelevant information leads to difficulties in understanding linguistic and nonlinguistic material. Recently, there has been interest in identifying the neural underpinnings of the inhibitory mechanisms in cognitive processing that affect attention, memory, and language (Dagenbach & Carr, 1994).

An important question for developmental neuropsychology, the answer to which is not clear at present, is whether the developmental timing of regressive events in the brain is actually what enables the emergence of inhibitory cognitive changes. One oblique approach to this issue has been to study conditions of anomalous brain development in which disinhibited behavior appears to persist throughout development. The logic of these studies is that an expected developmental advance in function that requires functional inhibition will not occur if particular, time-tagged, features of the brain were to develop in an anomalous manner. For example, the development of inhibition within the sensorimotor system with age permits the acquisition of increasingly fine-grained sensation and movement, such that normal seven-yr-old children can make discrete finger movements within one hand while inhibiting overflow movements in the hand contralateral to the intended movement. High-functioning individuals with congenital absence of the corpus callosum but with no other major brain anomalies continue to show overflow movements through adolescence and into adulthood, demonstrating a failure of inhibitory sensorimotor development (Dennis, 1976). This suggests that the acquisition of a sensorimotor inhibitory mechanism in middle childhood is facilitated by normal development of the corpus callosum in the first 4 mo of gestation.

VII. COGNITIVE DEVELOPMENT PARADIGMS

Recent developments in cognitive science have produced a tighter and better conceptualization of cognitive function. For example, memory is now viewed, not as a quantitative bin, but as a skill where constituent processes can be formally dissociated (Jacoby, 1991), which has contributed to establishing a common language within which theoretical disputes about memory can be entertained. Research questions can be framed to decide among theoretical positions, not just to gather descriptive data. Adult cognitive neuropsychology tests models originally developed within cognitive psychology, using special populations as preparations either to study cognitive processes (here, the goal is to use the behavioral manifestations of amnesia to test cognitive models of memory), or to infer the neural substrates of particular processing systems (e.g., the study of memory in diseases such as Parkinson's and Korsakoff's syndrome that affect contrasting brain regions has yielded information about the separability of different memory processes in the brain).

Cognitive models and models of cognitive development are now being explored within developmental neuropsychology in much the same way as cognitive development has been used to inform the study of mature cognition. The interest lies in what we can learn about cognition itself from studies of the development of cognitive function, anomalies of brain development, and the time course of normal brain development. As an example, we will consider some of the ways in which the issue of the modularity of syntax may be evaluated within developmental neuropsychology.

A. Modularity of Syntax

The modularity hypothesis for syntax argues that human syntactic ability derives from an encapsulated module, that is, a mechanism functionally distinct from modules governing other aspects of language (Fodor, 1983). In adult neuropsychology, various lines of evidence, some weaker and some stronger, have been adduced for and against the hypothesis of syntactic modularity. In developmental neuropsychology, one approach to syntactic modularity has analyzed single cases or described dissociations of language skills within and between groups. Here, syntactic modularity has been approached in terms of construct representation, a form of validation that decomposes the mechanisms of task performance (Embretson, 1983). A stronger form of evidence relevant to syntactic modularity has taken a nomothetic span approach (Embretson, 1983), that is, one that emphasizes the degree to which the pattern and structure of individual difference data can be used to reveal a theoretical construct.

One hypothesized feature of a syntactic module is that it should develop independent of the level of general intellectual function. The language abilities of children with mental retardation are relevant to this feature (as Umilta, 1991, points out, if a particular cognitive function remains intact despite general intellectual loss it can be maintained that lack of general knowledge has no effect on it, i.e., that it is informationally encapsulated). Children with a particular form of genetically based mental retardation, Williams syndrome, acquire syntax, inflectional morphology, vocabulary, and affective prosody to a higher level than do children with other forms of genetically based mental retardation (e.g., Down syndrome, Reilly, Klima, & Bellugi, 1990; see also Yamada, 1990).

Under the hypothesis of syntactic modularity, syntax should also be dissociable from other aspects of language as a consequence of brain damage, even in individuals with normal levels of cognition. Children with brain damage but with overall normal intellectual development are relevant to this issue. The question is whether a particular form of brain damage disrupts syntactic development but spares the development of other language functions. This seems to be the case. In school-aged children with massive early lateralized lesions and hemidecortication, in whom language is acquired with only half the normal cortical mass (the typical half, the left hemisphere, or the atypical half, the right hemisphere), the isolated right hemisphere develops syntactic skills slowly (Dennis & Whitaker, 1976), poorly (Dennis & Kohn, 1975), and with aberrant strategies (Dennis, 1980a). The isolated right hemisphere is relatively insensitive to higher order grammatical structures and syntax-signaling functors (Dennis, 1980a, 1980b); is unable to exploit fully the higher order syntactic structures that carry meaning in a written text (Dennis, Lovett, & Wiegel-Crump, 1981); is strategically less efficient in understanding syntactically diverse sentences; and is less likely to use thematic information about subject and topic when such information is conveyed by variations in syntactic structure (Dennis, 1980b). Syntactic impairments in the isolated right hemisphere are independent of verbal intelligence (Dennis & Kohn, 1975; Kohn, 1980) and also of a wide variety of phonological and lexical semantic functions (Dennis, 1980b; Dennis & Kohn, 1975; Dennis & Whitaker, 1976).

Another line of evidence for syntactic modularity concerns the effects of early experience on language constituents. Deprivation of language experience early in life affects syntactic development more than other language domains. Severe deprivation of language experience in the first decade of life severely limits the ability to acquire language, and the language that is eventually acquired is stronger in lexical-semantic features than in grammar, which remains primitive (Fromkin, Krashen, Curtiss, Rigler, & Rigler, 1974). Compared to hearing adults, congenitally deaf adults produce a different pattern of evoked response potentials to syntactic but not to semantic information (Neville, 1991).

The pattern and structure of individual difference data from young brain-damaged individuals, a nomothetic span approach, has also been used to approach the question of syntactic modularity. Dennis (1987) has proposed a set of criteria for deciding whether, and how strongly, a given constituent of language (e.g., syntax) might be said to be selectively affected by brain damage. A data base of language measures was obtained from a large group of brain-damaged children, adolescents, and young adults, each of whom had sustained brain damage *in utero,* at birth, in infancy, or during childhood. The language evaluation included phonology, morphology and syntax, lexical-semantics, and pragmatic use and understanding; then, the language data were analyzed by means of factor analyses to reduce them to a smaller set of language "factors." Three levels of syntactic modularity were operationalized (Dennis, 1987). Syntax was considered *discrete* when it remained separate from other language functions; that is, if it did not rise and fall within a group of brain-damaged individuals in the same manner as did other language functions. Discrete syntax factors would thus emerge as separate in factor analyses. Syntax was deemed *distinct* when it could be shown to have a characteristic pattern of brain damage that disrupted or moderated it. The strongest criterion (Dennis, 1987) concerned autonomy. Syntax was considered *autonomous* to the extent that it maintained its boundaries in the face of brain damage, that is, when brain damage-induced changes in its level were not accompanied by compensatory changes in the levels of other functions. Decisions about functional autonomy are complex, because they would require a set of procedures for specifying the structure of factor interrelationships (Joreskog & Sorbom, 1979).

Although the question of autonomy was not studied, the factor analyses showed syntax to be both discrete and distinct. Among a broader group of language factors, a constellation of three syntax factors emerged: (1) production of surface structure syntax, (2) speed, and (3) accuracy of comprehension of grammatical forms. Different, albeit somewhat overlapping, features of brain damage were predictive of each. Knowing how well a young brain-damaged individual uses and understands formally specifiable aspects of language was not sufficient for predicting other language abilities, such as those that symbolize and categorize experience or those that match linguistic form and content with truth values and real-world considerations.

Within the syntactic domain, the rules mapping surface structure on to phonetic representation could be separated from the rules that map surface structure on to logical form. The evidence from this individual difference perspective, then, suggests that syntax (aspects of language that involve form rather than content, and that concern constructed representations rather than reference to the real world) has both external and internal autonomy (Chomsky, 1982), where the first sense of autonomy means that syntax is separate from other aspects of language and the second sense means that the subcomponents of syntax are autonomous with respect to one another.

The above discussion, although far from exhaustive, serves to show how developmental neuropsychological data may be used to explore cognitive models such as the modularity of syntax. As newer techniques for the on-line analyses of syntactic processing are applied to populations in developmental neuropsychology, the question of syntactic modularity will undoubtedly be refocused and extended.

VIII. CONCLUSION

As we come to understand the nature of cognitive development, we will have a better grasp of the significance of key events in brain development for the emergence of cognitive milestones. Equally, as a clearer picture of the details of brain development emerges, the opportunity opens to evaluate hypotheses about the core constituents of cognitive development. In this manner, information derived from the study of developing brain–behavior relationships becomes part of the data base that forms and informs models of both normal and abnormal cognitive development.

Acknowledgment

The authors' research described in this paper was supported by project grants to the first author from the Physicians Services Incorporated Foundation and to both authors from The Ontario Mental Health Foundation, The Ontario Ministry of Community and Social Services, and the Ontario Ministry of Health.

References

Barkley, R. A., Grodzinsky, G., & DuPaul, G. J. (1992). Frontal lobe functions in attention deficit disorders with and without hyperactivity: A review and research report. *Journal of Abnormal Child Psychology, 20,* 163–188.

Barnes, M. A., & Dennis, M. (1992a). Inferencing and reading comprehension in children with hydrocephalus and their age peers. *Canadian Psychology, 33,* 434. (Abstract)

Barnes, M. A., & Dennis, M. (1992b). Reading in children and adolescents after early onset hydrocephalus and in normally developing age peers: Phonological analysis, word recognition, word comprehension, and passage comprehension skills. *Journal of Pediatric Psychology, 17,* 445–465.

Barnes, M. A., & Savard, A. (1993). *Coherence and elaborative inferencing from a controlled knowledge base in poor and average comprehenders.* Abstracts of the 60th Anniversary meeting of the Society for Research in Child Development.

Benton, A. L. (1962). Behavioral indices of brain injury in school children. *Child Development, 33,* 199–208.

Brookshire, B., Copeland, D. R., Moore, B. D., & Ater, J. (1990). Pretreatment, neuropsychological status and associated factors in children with primary brain tumors. *Neurosurgery, 27,* 887–891.

Brown, R. T., & Madan-Swain, A. (1993). Cognitive, neuropsychological and academic sequelae in children with leukemia. *Journal of Learning Disabilities, 26,* 74–90.

Burchinal, M., & Appelbaum, M. I. (1991). Estimating individual developmental functions: Methods and their assumptions. *Child Development, 62,* 23–43.

Carlson, M., Earls, F., & Todd, R. D. (1988). The importance of regressive changes in the development of the nervous system: Towards a neurobiological theory of child development. *Psychiatric Developments, 1,* 1–22.

Casey, J. E., Rourke, B. P., & Picard, E. M. (1991). Syndrome of nonverbal learning disabilities: Age differences in neuropsychological, academic, and socioemotional functioning. *Development and Psychopathology, 3,* 329–345.

Chadwick, O., Rutter, M., Shaffer, D., & Shrout, P. E. (1981). A prospective study of children with head injuries: IV. Specific cognitive deficits. *Journal of Clinical Neuropsychology, 3,* 101–120.

Chevrie-Muller, C., & Le Normand, M. T. (1987). Neuropsychological pattern in a child with a severe language-acquisition disorder: A ten-year follow-up case study. *Aphasiology, 1,* 347–359.

Chin, H. W., & Maruyama, Y. (1984). Age at treatment and long-term performance results in medulloblastoma. *Cancer (Philadelphia), 53,* 1952–1958.

Chomsky, N. (1982). *The generative enterprise.* Dordrecht: Foris.

Choux, M. (1982). Medulloblastomas in children. *Child's Brain, 9,* 280–283.

Cowan, W. M., Fawcett, J. W., O'Leary, D. D. M., & Stanfield, B. B. (1984). Regressive events in neurogenesis. *Science, 225,* 1258–1265.

Dagenbach, D. & Carr, T. H. (1994). *Inhibitory processes in attention, memory, and language.* New York: Academic Press.

Danoff, B. F., Cowchock, F. S., Marquette, C., Mulgrew, L., & Kramer, S. (1982). Assessment of the long-term effects of primary radiation therapy for brain tumors in children. *Cancer (Philadelphia), 49,* 1580–1586.

Del Bigio, M. (1993). Neuropathological changes caused by hydrocephalus. *Acta Neuropathologica, 85,* 573–585.

Dennis, M. (1976). Impaired sensory and motor differentiation with corpus callosum agenesis: A lack of callosal inhibition during ontogeny? *Neuropsychologia, 14,* 455–469.

Dennis, M. (1980a). Capacity and strategy for syntactic comprehension after left or right hemidecortication. *Brain and Language, 10,* 287–317.

Dennis, M. (1980b). Language acquisition in a single hemisphere: Semantic organization. In D. Caplan (Ed.), *Biological studies of mental processes* (pp. 159–185). Cambridge, MA: MIT Press.

Dennis, M. (1980c). Strokes in childhood: I. Communicative intent, expression, and comprehension after left hemisphere arteriopathy in a right-handed nine-year-old. In R. Rieber (Ed.), *Language development and aphasia in children* (pp. 45–67). New York: Academic Press.

Dennis, M. (1987). Using language to parse the young damaged brain. *Journal of Clinical and Experimental Neuropsychology, 9,* 723–753.

Dennis, M. (1988). Language and the young damaged brain. In T. Boll & B. K. Bryant (Eds.), *The master lecture series: Clinical neuropsychology and brain function: Research measurement and practice* (pp. 89–123). Washington, DC: American Psychological Association.

Dennis, M. (1994). Hydrocephalus. In J. G. Beaumont & J. Sergent (Eds.), *The Blackwell dictionary of neuropsychology.* Oxford: Blackwell.

Dennis, M., & Barnes, M. A. (1990). Knowing the meaning, getting the point, bridging the gap, and carrying the message: Aspects of discourse following closed head injury in childhood and adolescence. *Brain and Language, 39,* 428–446.

Dennis, M., & Barnes, M. A. (1993). Oral discourse after early-onset hydrocephalus: Linguistic ambiguity, figurative language, speech acts, and script-based inferences. *Journal of Pediatric Psychology, 18,* 639–652.

Dennis, M., Fitz, C. R., Netley, C. T., Sugar, J., Harwood-Nash, D. C. F., Hendrick, E. B., Hoffman, H. J., & Humphreys, R. P. (1981). The intelligence of hydrocephalic children. *Archives of Neurology (Chicago), 38,* 607–615.

Dennis, M., Hendrick, E. B., Hoffman, H. J., & Humphreys, R. P. (1987). Language of hydrocephalic children and adolescents. *Journal of Clinical and Experimental Neuropsychology, 9,* 593–621.

Dennis, M., Jacennik, B., & Barnes, M. A. (1994). The content of narrative discourse in children and adolescents after early-onset hydrocephalus and in normally-developing age peers. *Brain and Language, 46,* 129–165.

Dennis, M., & Kohn, K. B. (1975). Comprehension of syntax in infantile hemiplegias after cerebral hemidecortication: Left hemisphere superiority. *Brain and Language, 2,* 472–482.

Dennis, M., Koski, L., Wilkinson, M., & Humphreys, R. P. (1993). Sustained attention, selective attention, and impulsivity after childhood head injury. *Clinical Neuropsychologist, 7,* 326.

Dennis, M., Lovett, M., & Wiegel-Crump, C. A. (1981). Written language acquisition after left or right hemidecortication in infancy. *Brain and Language, 12,* 54–91.

Dennis, M., Spiegler, B. J., Fitz, C. R., Hoffman, H. J., Hendrick, E. B., Humphreys, R. P., & Chuang, S. (1991). Brain tumors in children and adolescents. II. The neuroanatomy of deficits in working, associative and serial-order memory. *Neuropsychologia, 29,* 829–847.

Dennis, M., Spiegler, B. J., Obonsawin, M. C., Maria, B. L., Cowell, C., Hoffman, H. J., Hendrick, E. B., Humphreys, R. P., Bailey, J. D., & Ehrlich, R. M. (1992). Brain tumors in children and adolescents. III. Effects of radiation and hormone status on intelligence and on working, associative and serial-order memory. *Neuropsychologia, 30,* 257–275.

Dennis, M., & Whitaker, H. A. (1976). Language acquisition following hemidecortication: Linguistic superiority of the left over the right hemisphere. *Brain and Language, 3,* 404–433.

Diamond, A. (1990). The development and neural bases of memory functions as indexed by the AB and delayed response tasks in human infants and infant monkeys. *Annals of the New York Academy of Sciences, 608,* 267–317.

Diamond, A. (1991). Frontal lobe involvement in cognitive changes during the first year of life. In K. R. Gibson & A. C. Petersen (Eds.), *Brain maturation and cognitive development: Comparative and cross-cultural perspectives* (pp. 127–180). New York: de Gruyter.

Diamond, A., & Goldman-Rakic, P. S. (1989). Comparison of human infants and rhesus monkeys on Piaget's AB task: Evidence for dependence on dorsolateral prefrontal cortex. *Experimental Brain Research, 74,* 24–40.

Duffner, P. K., Cohen, M. E., & Thomas, P. (1983). Late effects of treatment on the intelligence of children with posterior fossa tumors. *Cancer (Philadelphia), 51,* 233–237.

Ellenberg, L., McComb, J. G., Siegel, S. E., & Stowe, S. (1987). Factors affecting intellectual outcome in pediatric brain tumor patients. *Neurosurgery, 21,* 638–644.

Embretson, S. (1983). Construct validity: Construct representation versus nomothetic span. *Psychological Bulletin, 93,* 179–197.

Eslinger, P. J., Grattan, L. M., Damasio, H., & Damasio, A. R. (1992). Developmental consequences of childhood frontal lobe damage. *Archives of Neurology (Chicago), 49,* 764–769.

Ewing-Cobbs, L., & Fletcher, J. M. (1987). Neuropsychological assessment of head injury in children. *Journal of Learning Disabilities, 20,* 526–535.

Ewing-Cobbs, L., Fletcher, J. M., Landry, S. H., & Levin, H. S. (1985). Language disorders after pediatric head injury. In J. Darby (Ed.), *Speech and language evaluation in neurology: Children and adolescents* (pp. 71–89). San Diego: Grune & Stratton.

Ewing-Cobbs, L., Levin, H. S., Fletcher, J. M., Miner, M. E., & Eisenberg, H. M. (1989). Posttraumatic amnesia in children: Assessment and outcome. *Journal of Clinical and Experimental Neuropsychology, 11,* 58.

Ewing-Cobbs, L., Miner, M. E., Fletcher, J. M., & Levin, H. S. (1989). Intellectual, motor, and language sequelae following closed head injury in infants and preschoolers. *Journal of Pediatric Psychology, 14,* 531–547.

Finger, S., & Stein, D. G. (Eds.). (1982). *Brain damage and recovery: Research and clinical perspectives.* New York: Academic Press.

Fletcher, J. M., Bohan, T. P., Brandt, M. E., Brookshire, B. L., Beaver, S. R., Francis, D. J., Davidson, K. C., Thompson, N. M., & Miner, M. E. (1992). Cerebral white matter and cognition in hydrocephalic children. *Archives of Neurology (Chicago), 49,* 818–824.

Fletcher, J. M., & Copeland, D. R. (1988). Neurobehavioral effects of central nervous system prophylactic treatment of cancer in children. *Journal of Clinical and Experimental Neuropsychology, 10,* 495–538.

Fletcher, J. M., Francis, D. J., Pequegnat, W., Raudenbush, S. W., Bornstein, M. H., Schmitt, F., Brouwers, P., & Stover, E. (1991). Neurobehavioral outcomes in diseases of childhood. Individual change models for pediatric human immunodeficiency viruses. *American Psychologist, 46,* 1267–1277.

Fletcher, J. M., Levin, H. S., & Landry, S. H. (1984). Behavioral consequences of cerebral insult in infancy. In C. R. Almi & S. Finger (Eds.), *Early brain damage: Research orientations and clinical observations* (pp. 189–213). New York: Academic Press.

Fletcher, J. M., Miner, M. E., & Ewing-Cobbs, L. (1987). Developmental issues and recovery from head injury in children. In H. S. Levin, J. Grafman, & H. M. Eisenberg (Eds.), *Neurobehavioral recovery after head injury* (pp. 279–291). New York: Oxford University Press.

Fletcher, J. M., & Satz, P. (1983). Age, plasticity, and equipotentiality: A reply to Smith. *Journal of Consulting and Clinical Psychology, 51,* 763–767.

Fodor, J. A. (1983). *The modularity of mind.* Cambridge, MA: MIT Press.

Francis, D. J., Fletcher, J. M., Stuebing, K. K., Davidson, K. C., & Thompson, N. M. (1991). Analysis of change: Modeling individual growth. *Journal of Consulting and Clinical Psychology, 59,* 27–37.

Fromkin, V. A., Krashen, S., Curtiss, S., Rigler, D., & Rigler, M. (1974). The development of language in Genie: A case of language acquisition beyond the critical period. *Brain and Language, 1,* 81–107.

Galaburda, A. M. (1993). Neuroanatomic basis of developmental dyslexia. *Neurologic Clinics, 11,* 161–173.

Gernsbacher, M. A., & Faust, M. E. (1991). The mechanism of suppression: A component of general comprehension skill. *Journal of Experimental Psychology: Learning, Memory, & Cognition, 17,* 245–262.

Gilbert, J. N., Jones, K. L., Rorke, L. B., Chernoff, G. F., & James, H. E. (1986). Central nervous system anomalies associated with meningomyelocele, hydrocephalus and the

Arnold-Chiari malformation: Reappraisal of theories regarding the pathogenesis of posterior neural tube closure defects. *Neurosurgery, 18,* 559–564.

Goldman, P. S. (1972). Developmental determinants of cortical plasticity. *Acta Neurobiologiae Experimentalis, 32,* 495–511.

Goldman-Rakic, P. S. (1987). Development of cortical circuitry and cognitive function. *Child Development, 58,* 601–622.

Grattan, L. M., & Eslinger, P. J. (1989). Higher cognition and social behavior: Changes in cognitive flexibility and empathy after cerebral lesions. *Neuropsychology, 3,* 175–185.

Grice, H. P. (1975). Logic and conversation. In P. Cole & J. L. Morgan (Eds.), *Syntax and semantics: Vol. 3. Speech acts* (pp. 41–58). New York: Academic Press.

Hadenius, A.-M., Hagberg, B., Hyttnas-Bensch, K., & Sjögren, I. (1962). The natural prognosis of infantile hydrocephalus. *Acta Paediatrica Scandinavica, 51,* 117–118.

Hamburger, V., & Oppenheim, R. W. (1982). Naturally occurring neuronal death in vertebrates. *Neuroscience Commentary, 1,* 39–55.

Hoffman, H. J., De Silva, M., Humphreys, R. P., Drake, J. M., Smith, M. L., & Blaser, S. (1992). 1. Aggressive surgical management of craniopharyngiomas in children. *Journal of Neurosurgery, 76,* 47–52.

Hynd, G. W., & Semrud-Clikeman, M. (1989). Dyslexia and brain morphology. *Psychological Bulletin, 106,* 447–482.

Jacoby, L. L. (1991). A process dissociation framework: Separating automatic from intentional uses of memory. *Journal of Memory and Language, 30,* 513–541.

Johnson, D. A., & Roethig-Johnson, K. (1989). Life in the slow lane: Attentional factors after head injury. In D. A. Johnson, D. Uttley, & M. Wyke (Eds.), *Children's head injuries: Who cares?* (pp. 96–110). New York: Taylor & Francis.

Johnson, D. A., Uttley, K. D., & Wyke, M. (Eds.). (1989). *Children's head injuries: Who cares?* New York: Taylor & Francis.

Johnson, S. B. (1980). Psychosocial factors in juvenile diabetes: A review. *Journal of Behavioral Medicine, 3,* 95–116.

Joreskog, K. G., & Sorbom, D. (1979). *Advances in factor analysis and structural equation models.* Cambridge, MA: Abt Books.

Kennard, M. A. (1940). Relation of age to motor impairment in man and in subhuman primates. *Archives of Neurology and Psychiatry, 44,* 377–397.

Kennard, M. A. (1942). Cortical reorganization of motor function: Studies on series of monkeys of various ages from infancy to maturity. *Archives of Neurology and Psychiatry, 47,* 227–240.

Kleinman, S. N., & Waber, D. P. (1992). Neurodevelopmental bases of spelling acquisition in children treated for acute lymphoblastic leukaemia. *Cognitive Neuropsychology, 9,* 403–425.

Kohn, B. (1980). Right hemisphere speech representation and comprehension of syntax after left cerebral injury. *Brain and Language, 9,* 350–361.

Kun, L. E., & Mulhern, R. K. (1983). Neuropsychological function in children with brain tumors: II. Serial studies of intellect and time after treatment. *American Journal of Clinical Oncology, 6,* 651–656.

Kun, L. E., Mulhern, R. K., & Crisco, J. J. (1983). Quality of life in children treated for brain tumors. Intellectual, emotional, and academic functioning. *Journal of Neurosurgery, 58,* 1–6.

Lannering, B., Marky, I., Lundberg, A., & Olsson, E. (1990). Long-term sequelae after pediatric brain tumors: Their effect on disability and quality of life. *Medical and Pediatric Oncology, 18,* 304–310.

Leech, G. N. (1983). *Principles of pragmatics.* New York: Longmans.

Lehr, E. (1990). *Psychological management of traumatic brain injuries in children and adolescents.* Rockville, MD: Aspen.

Lenneberg, E. H. (1967). *Biological foundations of language.* New York: Wiley.

Levin, H. S., Amparo, E. G., Eisenberg, H. M., Miner, M. E., High, W. N., Ewing-Cobbs, L., Fletcher, J. M., & Guinto, F. C. (1989). Magnetic resonance imaging after closed head injury in children. *Neurosurgery, 24,* 223–227.

Levin, H. S., Culhane, K. A., Mendelsohn, D., Lilly, M. A., Bruce, D., Fletcher, J. M., Chapman, S. B., Harward, H., & Eisenberg, H. M. (1993). Cognition in relation to magnetic resonance imaging in head-injured children and adolescents. *Archives of Neurology, 50,* 897–905.

Levin, H. S., Benton, A. L., & Grossman, R. G. (1982). *Neurobehavioral consequences of closed head injury.* New York: Oxford University Press.

Levin, H. S., & Eisenberg, H. M. (1979). Neuropsychological outcome of closed head injury in children and adolescents. *Child's Brain, 5,* 281–292.

Lieh-Lai, M. W., Theodorou, A. A., Sarniak, A. P., Meert, K. L., Moylan, P. M., & Canady, A. I. (1992). Limitations of the Glascow coma scale in predicting outcome in children with traumatic head injury. *Journal of Pediatrics, 120,* 195–199.

Luerssen, T. G., Hesselink, J. R., Ruff, R. M., Healy, M. E., & Grote, C. A. (1987). Magnetic resonance imaging of craniocerebral injury. In A. E. Marlin (Ed.), *Concepts in pediatric neurosurgery* (pp. 190–208). Basel: Karger.

Mandigers, C. M. P., Lippens, R.J.J., Hoogenhout, J., Meijer, E., van Wieringen, P. M. V., & Theeuwes, A. G. M. (1990). Astrocytoma in childhood: Survival and performance. *Pediatric Hematology and Oncology, 7,* 121–128.

Marchman, V. A., Miller, R., & Bates, E. A. (1991). Babble and first words in children with focal brain injury. *Applied Psycholinguistics, 12,* 1–22.

Maria, B. L., Dennis, M., & Obonsawin, M. (1993). Severe permanent encephalopathy in acute lymphoblastic leukemia. *The Canadian Journal of Neurological Sciences, 20,* 199–205.

Martins, I. P., & Ferro, J. M. (1992). Recovery of acquired aphasia in children. *Aphasiology, 6,* 431–438.

Mulhern, R. K., Hancock, J., Fairclough, D., & Kun, L. (1992). Neuropsychological status of children treated for brain tumors: A critical review and integrative analysis. *Medical and Pediatric Oncology, 20,* 181–191.

Mulhern, R. K., Kovnar, E., Langston, J., Carter, M., Fairclough, D., Leigh, L., & Kun, L. E. (1992). Long-term survivors of leukemia treated in infancy: Factors associated with neuropsychologic status. *Journal of Clinical Oncology, 10,* 1095–1102.

Mulhern, R. K., Ochs, J., & Fairclough, D. (1992). Deterioration of intellect among children surviving leukemia: IQ test changes modify estimates of treatment toxicity. *Journal of Consulting and Clinical Psychology, 60,* 477–480.

Murdoch, B. E., Ozanne, A. E., & Smyth, V. (1990). Communicative impairments in neural tube disorders. In B. E. Murdoch (Ed.), *Acquired neurological speech/language disorders in childhood* (pp. 216–244). London: Taylor & Francis.

Murray, R., Shum, D., & McFarland, K. (1992). Attentional deficits in head-injured children: An information processing analysis. *Brain and Cognition, 18,* 99–115.

Neville, N. J. (1991). Neurobiology of cognitive and language processing: Effects of early experience. In K. R. Gibson & A. E. Petersen (Eds.), *Brain maturation and cognitive development: Comparative and cross-cultural perspectives* (pp. 355–380). New York: de Gruyter.

Packer, J. R., Sutton, L. N., Atkins, T. E., Radcliffe, J., Bunin, G. R., D'Angio, G., Siegel, K. R., & Schut, L. (1989). A prospective study of cognitive function in children receiving whole-brain radiotherapy and chemotherapy: 2-year results. *Journal of Neurosurgery, 70,* 707–713.

Prideaux, G. D. (1991). Syntactic form and textual rhetoric: The cognitive basis for certain pragmatic principles. *Journal of Pragmatics, 16,* 113–129.

Prigatano, G. P., Zeiner, H. K., Pollay, M., & Kaplan, R. J. (1983). Neuropsychological functioning in children with shunted uncomplicated hydrocephalus. *Child's Brain, 10,* 112–120.

Purves, D., & Lichtman, J. W. (1980). Elimination of synapses in the developing nervous system. *Science, 210,* 153–157.

Reilly, J., Klima, E. S., & Bellugi, U. (1990). Once more with feeling: Affect and language in atypical populations. *Development and Psychopathology, 2,* 367–391.

Ris, M. D., & Noll, R. B. (1994). Long-term neurobehavioral outcome in pediatric brain-tumor patients: Review and methodological critique. *Journal of Clinical and Experimental Neuropsychology, 16,* 21–42.

Rourke, B. P. (1989). *Nonverbal learning disabilities: The syndrome and the model.* New York: Guilford Press.

Rourke, B. P., Del Dotto, J. E., Rourke, S. B., & Casey, J. E. (1990). Nonverbal learning disabilities: The syndrome and a case study. *Journal of School Psychology, 28,* 361–385.

Rourke, B. P., & Fisk, J. L. (1988). Subtypes of learning-disabled children: Implications for a neurodevelopmental model of differential hemispheric processing. In D. L. Molfese & S. J. Segalowitz (Eds.), *Brain lateralization in children* (pp. 547–565). New York: Guilford Press.

Rovet, J. F. (1990). Congenital hypothyroidism: Intellectual and neuropsychological functioning. In C. S. Holmes (Eds.), *Psychoneuroendocrinology, brain, behavior, and hormonal interactions* (pp. 273–322). New York: Springer-Verlag.

Rovet, J. F., Ehrlich, R. M., & Sorbara, D. L. (1992). Neurodevelopment in infants and preschool children with congenital hypothyroidism: Etiological and treatment factors affecting outcome. *Journal of Pediatric Psychology, 17,* 187–213.

Semrud-Clikeman, M., & Hynd, G. W. (1990). Right hemispheric dysfunction in nonverbal learning disabilities: Social, academic, and adaptive functioning in adults and children. *Psychological Bulletin, 107,* 196–209.

Siegel, A. W., Bisanz, J., & Bisanz, G. L. (1983). Developmental analysis: A strategy for the study of psychological change. *Contributions to Human Development, 8,* 53–80.

Spunberg, J. J., Chang, C. H., Goldman, M., Auricchio, E., & Bell, J. J. (1981). Quality of long-term survival following irradiation for intracranial tumors in children under the age of two. *International Journal of Radiation Oncology, 7,* 727–736.

Stanfield, B. B. (1984). Postnatal reorganization of cortical projections: The role of collateral elimination. *Trends in NeuroSciences, 7,* 37–41.

Swisher, L. P., & Pinsker, E. J. (1971). The language characteristics of hyperverbal, hydrocephalic children. *Developmental Medicine and Child Neurology, 13,* 746–755.

Tallal, P. (1991). Neuropsychological foundations of specific developmental disorders of speech and language: Implications for theories of hemispheric specialization. In R. Michaels, A. Cooper, S. Guze, L. Judd, G. Kleman, A. Solnit, & A. Stankard (Eds.), *Psychiatry.* Philadelphia: Lippincott.

Tallal, P., Galaburda, A. M., Llinas, R., & von Euler, C. (Eds.). (1992). *Temporal information processing in the central nervous system.* New York: New York Academy of Sciences.

Taylor, E. M. (1961). *Psychological appraisal of children with cerebral defects.* Cambridge, MA: Harvard University Press.

Taylor, H. G. (1988). Neuropsychological testing: Relevance for assessing children's learning disabilities. *Journal of Consulting and Clinical Psychology, 56,* 795–800.

Thal, D. J., Marchman, V., Stiles, J., Aram, D., Trauner, D., Nass, R., & Bates, E. (1991). Early lexical development in children with focal brain injury. *Brain and Language, 40,* 491–527.

Thatcher, R. W. (1991a). Are rhythms of human cerebral development "travelling waves"? *Behavioral and Brain Sciences, 14,* 575.

Thatcher, R. W. (1991b). Maturation of the human frontal lobes: Physiological evidence for staging. *Developmental Neuropsychology, 7,* 397–419.

Trexler, L. E., & Zappala, G. (1988). Re-examining the determinants of recovery and rehabilitation of memory defects following traumatic brain injury. *Brain Injury, 2,* 187–203.

Turkewitz, G., & Devenny, D. A. (1993). Timing and the shape of development. In G. Turkewitz & D. A. Devenny (Eds.), *Developmental time and timing* (pp. 1–11). Hillsdale, NJ: Erlbaum.

Umilta, C. (1991). More on modularity. *Behavioral and Brain Sciences, 14,* 455.

Waber, D. P., Bernstein, J. H., Kammerer, B. L., Tarbell, N. J., & Sallan, S. E. (1992). Neuropsychological diagnostic profiles of children who received CNS treatment for acute lymphoblastic leukemia: The systemic approach to assessment. *Developmental Neuropsychology, 8,* 1–28.

Welsh, M. C., Pennington, B. F., & Groisser, D. B. (1991). A normative-developmental study of execution function: A window on prefrontal function in children. *Developmental Neuropsychology, 7,* 131–150.

Werker, J. F. (1986). The effect of multilingualism on phonetic perceptual flexibility. *Applied Psycholinguistics, 7,* 141–156.

Winogron, H. W., Knights, R. M., & Bawden, H. N. (1984). Neuropsychological deficits following head injury in children. *Journal of Clinical Neuropsychology, 6,* 269–286.

Winston, K. R., Cavazzuti, V., & Arkins, T. (1979). Absence of neurological and behavioral abnormalities after anterior transcallosal operation for third ventricular lesions. *Neurosurgery, 4,* 386–393.

Wohlwill, J. (1973). *The study of behavioral change.* New York: Academic Press.

Wolff, P. H., Michel, G. F., Ovrut, M., & Drake, C. (1990). Rate and timing precision of motor coordination in developmental dyslexia. *Developmental Psychology, 26,* 349–359.

Yamada, J. E. (1990). *Laura: A case for the modularity of language.* Cambridge, MA: MIT Press.

CHAPTER 11

Neuropsychology of Aging and Dementia

Elisabeth Koss

In this chapter I will review findings of cognitive changes in healthy and pathological aging. I will put these findings in the context of current views of aging, and attempt to address the importance of societal values on research concepts.

I. HEALTHY AGING

A. Definition of Aging

One of the many difficulties in aging research is a lack of agreement on the best definition of what old age is and what defines aging (Bourliere, 1970; Costa & McCrae, 1980). The conventional delimiter of old age is 65 yr of age. The practice of designating 65 yr as the lower limit of old age started in Germany in the late nineteenth century as a conventional qualification of professional retirement. However, scientists have come to the realization that chronological age is not the best indicator of the age state of an organism. On the one hand, not all organ systems age at the same rate within an individual. On the other hand, even genetically and environmentally similar organisms have been shown not to age at the same rate. Other definitions have been proposed to supplant the use of chronological age, such as biological or functional age. However, the same problem of lack of satisfactory indices applies to such delimiters (Bourliere, 1970). Therefore, 65 yr of age remains, by default, the arbitrary beginning of old age until a more objective scientific rationale is developed.

1. Sensory and Perceptual Changes in Normal Aging

From a neuropsychological perspective, the *aging process* encompasses changes in the peripheral and central nervous system (CNS), sensorimotor changes, cognitive changes, and changes in motivation and self-perception. Probably the two most reliable and significant changes occurring with advancing age are a general slowing in the processing of information for sensory and perceptual mechanisms, and slowing in reaction time (Fozard, 1985). Because so many daily activities depend on accurate sensory and perceptual integration, it is important to understand the extent of possible peripheral deficits faced by an older person to avoid erroneously attributing sensory impairment to cognitive deficits. Also, it should be kept in mind that these changes do not occur independently of each other. The dissociation of these different elements is, in fact, the hardest aspect of aging research. For the purpose of clarity, however, age-associated changes in perception and cognition will be discussed separately.

a. Visual Changes

There are many physiological and anatomical changes in the visual system in later adulthood, which become increasingly marked with advancing age. The crystalline lens of the eye becomes denser and more opaque. The retina undergoes macular changes (mottling), the pupil is smaller at low light intensity (senile miosis). The increasing disability of the older lens to accommodate resulting in presbyopia, or difficulty to focus at short distances. Most older adults require corrective lenses for near vision. Older adults also have difficulties with dark adaptation, as they show elevated thresholds for both rods and cones (Owsley, Sekuler, & Siemsen, 1981).

The primary visual cortex is relatively preserved compared to secondary association cortex. Some reports suggest, nevertheless, neural changes in later life, such as decrease in optic nerve fibers, cell loss in the visual cortex, and shrinkage of dendritic spines (Scheibel & Scheibel, 1975; Wisniewski & Terry, 1976). These changes are indeed present but are much less severe than in other areas of the cortex, such as the prefrontal and superior temporal areas (Kemper, 1984; Pearson, Esiri, Hiorns, Wilcock, & Powell, 1985).

Interestingly, not all aspects of visual functions are impaired equally with age. For example, there appears to be little change in stereoacuity before age 40 (Bell, Wolf, & Bernholtz, 1972; Jani, 1966). Also, older adults do not differ from younger adults in terms of the stability of eye fixation, or saccade accuracy, although they show definite increased latency of saccadic onset, and have a progressive symmetric limitation of upward gaze (Chamberlain, 1971).

These peripheral and neural changes lead to decreased visual acuity at lower light levels (Pitts, 1982), loss of sensitivity at higher spatial frequencies (Gilmore, Andrist, & Royer, 1991; Owsley, Sekuler, & Siemsen, 1983), longer latency for locating a target, and loss of color discrimination, particularly in the yellow–blue range (Knoblauch et al., 1987). Also, older adults require about twice the contrast to discriminate faces than younger adults (Owsley et al., 1981), even when controlling for visual acuity or cognition. They show also many errors in a task measuring perception of verticality and horizontality (Tobis, Nayak, & Hoehler, 1981). These visual difficulties account in part for the increased propensity of older persons to fall. Older adults also tend to have decreased sensitivity for detecting the direction of two closely related moving targets (i.e., motion detection, Sekuler, Hutman, & Owsley, 1980). These visual difficulties may affect driving capacities of older adults, who, as an age group, have disproportionately more accidents and cited traffic violations. Nighttime driving may be particularly difficult for older adults. The mechanisms underlying these difficulties are not well understood, and have been ascribed to undetected ocular pathologic neural and degenerative metabolic factors (Owsley et al., 1983; Pitts, 1982; Weale, 1982, 1987).

In summary, many, but not all, aspects of visual function decline in later adulthood. The visual cortex seems relatively spared with aging and different visual channels respond differently to age. Nevertheless, older persons appear impaired on laboratory-type visual tasks, as well as on tasks related to daily activities. Finally, there seems to be wide individual variability as to the extent of these changes that cannot be explained by physiological factors.

b. Auditory Changes

As with vision, the rate of change in hearing accelerates positively between the ages of 50 and 90 yr. Clear age-related changes in the characteristics of most auditory structures result in loss of absolute sensitivity. Age-related changes in hearing are summarized by the term *presbycusis,* characterized by impairment in four areas: pure-tone thresholds, particularly at high frequency; frequency discrimination; temporal discrimination and sound localization ability; ability to understand distorted speech, and to recall long sentences (Fozard, 1990).

There appear to be two types of changes in hearing thresholds with age. One is a continuous age-related increase for high-frequency stimuli, and the other is a discontinuous change for low to medium frequencies (Brant & Fozard, 1990). However, the exact relationship between these resulting losses in absolute sensitivity and loss of abilities is not well established

(Werner, Harkins, & Lenhardt, 1985). To exemplify this complex interrelationship, I will concentrate on the practical issue of the often reported speech recognition in older persons. Gelfant, Piper, and Silman (1985) proposed that decline in speech recognition with aging is primarily due to decrease of intelligibility of consonants. By increasing the energy of consonants like *p, t, k, b, d, g,* they demonstrated an enhancement in the recognition of these consonants presented in noise. However, these findings do not account for the fact that older persons typically recognize fewer words in a sentence than younger adults, and become increasingly more sensitive to contextual changes, temporal characteristic of the sounds, as well as to stimulus familiarity. Increasing processing time and clarifying the context of sentences significantly improves speech understanding in older persons (Stine & Wingfield, 1987; Wingfield, Poon, Lombardi, & Lowe, 1985). Thus, decline in speech understanding may be ascribed in part to memory loss, high-frequency hearing loss, and temporal processing. The plasticity of performance in older persons suggests also the role of nonneural factors, such as response bias or poorer application of linguistic rules.

c. Chemosensory Changes

The ability to smell and taste declines steadily with increasing age. On average, persons over the age of 50 yr have increasing difficulty in all aspects of olfaction: detection threshold, odor identification and recognition, and odor memory (Murphy, 1985; Schiffman, 1983). Decrease occurs at an earlier age in men than in women, and the gender difference becomes more marked with age (Doty et al., 1984).

Substantial individual variability is observed, which may have a physiological basis but may be ascribed also to the contribution of environmental factors such as smoking habits and exposure to pollutants. Medical problems such as the effects of cumulative viral infections, head trauma, and neurological diseases are also known to affect olfactory abilities (Doty, 1989). Although fairly prominent, dulling olfaction rarely reaches consciousness. By contrast, the resulting decline in taste sensitivity is readily noticed by most persons. Changes in olfaction and taste in older persons may have some implication in the aging process in terms of the diminished pleasure derived from eating (and thus greater likelihood of malnutrition) and subtle but definite decline in environmental sensory stimulation. The contribution of this sensory deprivation to cognition and general well-being is not well known at this point. Olfactory structures are very closely related to the limbic system. Interestingly, parts of this system, namely the hippocampus and the temporal lobe, are affected very early and to a considerable extent in Alzheimer's disease (AD) (Pearson et al., 1985). The suggestion that olfactory deficits may be an early sign of dementia (Roberts, 1986) has merit, but may depend on the type of olfactory deficit observed (Koss, Weiffenbach, Haxby,

& Friedland, 1988) and may only be pathognomonic of neurological insult in general.

B. Cognitive Changes in Aging

It is commonly accepted that intellectual decline is an integral part of the normal aging process. The *classic aging pattern* refers to the often described age-related decline in visuospatial performance and the preservation of verbal abilities. Interestingly, this pattern does not mention memory changes, which are probably most often cited as cognitive impairments associated with aging. The reason is that the classic aging pattern was derived from cross-studies of performance on the Wechsler Adult Intelligence Test (WAIS and WAIS-R) (Wechsler, 1955, 1981), which does not include memory tests. The complex interaction of study design, chosen tests, and findings is discussed in Section II, Issues in Aging Research. It is, however, extensively documented that performance subtests decline earlier and more than verbal subtests. Verbal IQ peaks between the ages of 24–35, and remains stable until the early seventies, whereas unadjusted performance subtests peak in the twenties and decline sharply to reach the borderline retarded range by early 70 (Schaie, 1983).

One obvious difference between the verbal and performance subtests of the WAIS is that performance tests are timed, and therefore they are particularly sensitive to age-related psychomotor slowing. The other difference concerns the nature of the tasks. Verbal tasks typically involve knowledge acquired over the lifetime, whereas performance tasks require manipulation of new and unfamiliar material, which would further put the older person at a disadvantage.

1. Memory

Of all the complaints of old age, decline in memory is the one most commonly mentioned (Baddeley, 1986; Chiarello & Hoyer, 1988; Craik, 1977; Hultsch, Hertzog, Dixon, & Davidson, 1988; Schacter, 1987) and the most studied. Poon (1985) has summarized no less than 18 reviews between 1977 and 1982. Memory has been conceptualized in various terms. A distinction in terms of sensory, primary, or secondary memory refers to the time lapse between stimulation and response, and covers generally intervals of a few milliseconds, 30 s and greater than 1 hr. The distinction between encoding, storage, and retrieval concentrates on the mechanisms underlying learning. In contrast, the distinction between semantic and episodic memory focuses on the nature of the task to be learned. Recently, interest in the awareness and intention to remember and conscious recollection has led to a distinction between implicit and explicit memory (Schacter, 1987). Baddeley (1986) convincingly argues that the notion of working memory, which demands simultaneous storage of recently learned memory and processing of additional information, can be distinguished as a critical memory system.

Many reviews have summarized the age-associated changes in different types of memory, across different information-processing stages. The oldest and best known distinction between primary and secondary memory indicates most pronounced deficits in secondary memory with preservation of primary memory (Craik, 1977). Earlier work suggested that episodic tasks typically showed age-related decline, in contrast to preserved semantic tasks. However, recent work disproved this position (Light & Burke, 1988). Explicit and implicit memory tasks appear to show different patterns of age-related decline, with impairment on performance of explicit memory tasks and little or no decline for implicit memory tasks (Chiarello & Hoyer, 1988; Howard, 1988). Research on working memory suggests that older persons' deficits are apparent in the processing component and not in the storage component of working memory.

Recent research on cognitive aging indicates the importance of experience and practice in skill maintenance for a particular activity (Salthouse, 1987). Perhaps not surprisingly, such expertise is relatively domain-specific, and does not extend to other tasks (Hoyer, 1985).

Memory changes of normal aging overlap with those observed in dementing disorders. In diseased states, memory disorders are more severe and generalized than in normal aging, but in the very early state, the distinction between "normal" and "pathological" changes may be quite difficult.

2. Attention

All aspects of attention (divided, switching, sustained, and selective) seem to be affected by advancing age for all but the simplest tasks (McDowd & Birren, 1990). As an exception, attention switching appears to be modality dependent. It is preserved in the visual mode for older adults, but impaired in the auditory mode (Braun & Wickens, 1985; Hartley, 1981). Older adults are particularly susceptible to distracting or irrelevant stimuli (Madden, 1986; Rabbitt, 1965). Plude and Hoyer (1985) have postulated, in their spatial localization hypothesis, that age decline in selective attention is due to a decrease in the capacity to locate task-relevant information in the visual field. Stankov (1988) has done a factor analysis on measures of attention, intelligence, and speed of search. The attentional factors explained age-related changes in fluid intelligence, opening the door to multilevel explanation of behavior.

3. Language

In general, language abilities are believed to be maintained with age (phonologic and semantic abilities and syntactic knowledge are well preserved).

Increased word-finding difficulties are reported anecdotally (Bayles & Kaszniak, 1987). Although syntactic knowledge appears also to be well preserved, on-line processing of syntactically complex material may be hindered when a high memory load is involved. The types of errors made by
older adults on naming tasks increase with age. These include circumlo-
cution, nominalization, perceptual errors, and semantic association errors
(M. L. Albert, Heller, & Millberg, 1988; Bowles, Obler, & Albert, 1987).

Aging does not seem to substantially alter word-finding abilities, as
measured by the Boston Naming test (LaBarge, Edward, & Knesevich,
1986), or ability to provide word definition as in the vocabulary test of the
WAIS. In contrast, verbal fluency tests do show age-related decline. These
tests reflect word-finding ability, but also capacity of sustained attention,
speed of cognitive processing and speech production, and ability to suppress
the dominant responses (Perret, 1974). The difference in performance also
may be ascribed to the amount of effortful lexical semantic processing.
Analysis of written language (Obler, 1980) indicates that older adults tend
to use fewer sentences with more words than younger adults, suggesting
that older adults' discourse was syntactically and thematically more elaborate. These suggest that automatic language is preserved whereas effortful
deliberate processing decline with age. This remains to be supported.

4. Executive Functions

Lezak (1983) defines *executive functions* as those capacities that enable a person to engage in independent, purposive, self-serving behavior successfully
(p. 507). This broad set of abilities is taken by some authors to include also
initiating and terminating activities, attentional shifts, planning and imple-
menting behavior, emotional self-control, and maintenance of socially appropriate behavior.

A significant portion of older persons shows increased difficulty with
laboratory tests requiring logical problem solving. Older persons seem to
have sizable difficulties in the formation of concept, and in making inferences (Arenberg, 1982). They are more repetitious, making redundant in-
quiries, and tend to use more concrete responses with increasing age. They
seem, however, to benefit from practice and training.

Cross-sectional studies (Arenberg, 1982) show monotonic decline with
age, whereas age-related changes are less noticeable in longitudinal studies.
LaRue (1992) discusses several important modifying variables, such as education, health, performance anxiety, familiarity with the stimuli, and training and practice. In general, there appears to be changes in attentional
flexibility. Such changes may influence performance on WAIS—where novelty and speed are important factors to success. The significance of these
findings in everyday function is less clear. A mild decrease in observed
flexibility changes has minimal impact on daily proficiency and the extrapo-

lation of these findings to everyday activities involving judgment and practical problem solving is not strong.

C. Models of Aging

These findings have been interpreted variously to develop models to explain the aging process. Three main models are reviewed here.

1. The Cattell/Horn Model

The most influential model of the effects of "normal" aging on basic intellectual abilities is the fluid or crystallized conceptualization proposed by Cattell (1963) and expanded by Horn (1982). This model divides human intellectual abilities into two categories: (1) the accumulation of formal and informal knowledge resulting in crystallized abilities; and (2) the abilities reflecting maturational growth and decline in neural structures (or fluid intelligence). In "normal" aging, crystallized abilities are expected to improve or remain stable, whereas fluid abilities are predicted to decline, because of decline in the CNS and peripheral nervous system. Although this model may be supported in part by performance on well-known tests (i.e., WAIS), the concept has been criticized as being artifactual, and depending on factors such as reduced sensory acuity, differential familiarity with testing, and difference in motor speed. Proponents of the model point out, however, that removing time constraints, improving size of stimuli, or providing training improved performance of older subjects somewhat, but without raising their performance to the level of younger individuals (Erber, Botwinnick, & Storandt, 1981; Storandt, 1977).

2. The Right-Hemisphere Hypothesis

Similarities in performance between older persons and patients with right-hemisphere damage, and the observation that language processes resist aging relatively well, are at the origin of the hypothesis that the right hemisphere ages faster than the left hemisphere. This interpretation of aging is not well supported by hard data, because this hypothesis is based on tests such as the Halstead-Reitan Neuropsychological Test Battery (Reitan & Holfson, 1985) and the WAIS, which do not evaluate memory and learning. Also, comparison of performance on the Verbal IQ and Performance IQ scales of the WAIS presents difficulties, because the two scales are not equated for difficulty. When these variables are controlled, there is no evidence to suggest differential aging of the right hemisphere (Hoyer & Rysbach, 1992).

A similar hypothesis suggesting similarities in cognitive changes found in aging and chronic alcoholism led to similar ideas of vulnerability of the right hemisphere in both conditions and is subject to the same criticisms delineated above.

A related issue is the oft presented suggestion that lateralization increases with age. This hypothesis, introduced by Brown and Jaffe (1975) was based on the authors' observation that the type of language disturbance occurring as a result of brain injury differed across the life span, suggesting that brain organization for language does not remain constant throughout adulthood, and that the relative role of the left hemisphere in language increases with age. However, the majority of studies does not support the notion of increased degree of lateralization with age.

Thus, the hypothesis of differential rates of aging for the two hemispheres is derived from methodologically weak studies, and does not take into consideration task characteristics and familiarity with the test material.

Do gender differences in performance and presumably in hemispheric lateralization observed in childhood and adulthood persist and increase in later years? It is true that the superior verbal ability reported in girls and women (see Chapter 13 by Weekes, this volume) on tests of verbal ability is maintained with aging, as is the superior male performance in spatial abilities (Willis & Schaie, 1988). However, the difference is small and subject to training. Women have been found to respond more positively than males to training on visual tasks (Schaie & Willis, 1986), suggesting that the observed gender differences are an extension of previous training and responses to societal expectations, rather than the expression of physiological evidence that brains of men and women age differently. Nevertheless, such conclusions may need to be revisited, as a study by Gur et al. (1991) has shown the presence of gender selective brain atrophy, measured by magnetic resonance imaging (MRI). The authors, therefore, concluded that women may be less vulnerable to age-related changes in mental abilities, whereas men may be more susceptible to changes occurring in the left hemisphere. These data await confirmation from further studies.

Finally, it is not known whether the selective hemispheric impairment in glucose metabolism observed in many persons with Alzheimer's disease is an extension of premorbid predispositions or a chance feature of the disease (Koss, Friedland, Ober, & Jagust, 1985).

3. The Frontal Deficit Hypothesis

Researchers have observed also that performance of older persons resembles that of patients with frontal lobe lesions (M. S. Albert & Kaplan, 1980). This hypothesis is supported partly by findings of frontal hypometabolism in older persons' glucose utilization, by observations of poor performance on tests measuring cognitive flexibility, and the presence of errors similar to those seen in frontal lesions patients. However, the evidence is not very compelling, as the literature is mixed concerning biological loss limited to the frontal lobe in aging and also because other hallmark behaviors of frontal deficits (i.e., emotional lability, social inappropriateness) are not observed in healthy older persons.

II. ISSUES IN AGING RESEARCH

None of these models fully account for age-related decline. One reason may be that they do not take into consideration individual differences.

We talk and think about the *elderly* as if older persons were homogeneous and the elderly represented some unitary construct. Yet we know intellectually that the elderly are heterogeneous on nearly all attributes, such as age itself, health status, educational background, past achievement, motivation, self-perception, psychological function, as well as societal values.

A. Age

It is simplistic to combine under a single heading individuals varying by as much as 30 yr. To account for the increased life span, new categorizations have been introduced such as the concept of *young old* and *old* to refer to persons aged 65–75 yr and 75–85 yr (Neugarten, 1974), respectively. More recently, the *oldest old* describes primarily persons over the age of 85 yr. Unfortunately, normative data for these age categories are sparse or nonexistent.

B. Health Status

The study of age-associated cognitive changes in aging has focused for the most part on average, statistically "normal" decrements. Considering that the average older person is plagued with one or more age-related physical ailments, one must wonder to what extent does disease contribute to the aging process. Many health-related conditions are known to affect cognition, such as neoplasm, diabetes, emphysema, and renal function (Nolan & Blass, 1992).

Rowe and Kahn (1987) have argued convincingly that overlooking the potentially modifying factors of diet, exercise, and personality has led to exaggeration of the effects of aging. They distinguish between usual aging and successful aging. In usual aging, extrinsic factors heighten the effect of aging, whereas successful aging is characterized by preserved health. Indeed, chronological age accounts for only 20% of the variance of the full-scale IQ scores (Botwinnick, 1977).

The importance of health status is illustrated by the phenomenon of terminal drop (Siegler, 1975). Several longitudinal studies suggest that persons who show decline across successive testing may be closer to death than others. Thus, a drop in cognitive performance may be a signal of failing health, (either subclinical cerebral dysfunctions, or medical conditions). However, the link between cognitive decline and death does not hold for very old people (White & Cunningham, 1988) suggesting that some of the losses attributed to "normal aging" may in fact reflect cognitive loss due to secondary effects of illness (Jarvik, 1988).

C. Motivation, Expectation and Societal Values

Variability in motivation, societal demands, and self-perception may have considerable, albeit hard to measure, influence on daily activities of older persons. Although subjective reports of memory loss are not correlated with objective memory decline, a negative self-perception may become a self-fulfilling prophecy and limit the social adaptation of older persons (Perlmutter et al., 1987). This is particularly true for women and cultural and ethnic minorities.

Another issue that deserves more than passing emphasis is the interrelationship of societal values and research findings. The vast majority of studies on aging has concentrated on age-associated decline. In a society where youth and unblemished physical appearance are valued, there are definite negative undertones associated with aging, both arising from the society but also as negative self-perception of what an older person can and cannot do. Robert Butler (1989) is credited to have coined the term *ageism* to describe this societal pattern of attitudes and stereotypes that devalue aging and old people. Such societal values may be reflected in the topics chosen to be investigated. The vast majority of studies on aging focus on the decline and decrements associated with age. There is little research on age-related development and the positive aspects of aging. Tests to evaluate potential age-related growth or the positive effect of age on cognition are not available.

D. Designs for Studies of Aging

Additionally, the studies design themselves, whether cross-sectional or longitudinal, introduce their own biases estimating aging. The most commonly used design, the cross-sectional design, evaluates performance of a group of individual matched for age, education, and other relevant variables. This design has the advantage of having no attrition component and being quick to complete, but may confound age and cohort effects. Also, the cross-sectional design relies on chronological age, which has already been discussed as being an artificial, unreliable, and probably invalid index of aging. In contrast, a longitudinal design allows to follow individual subjects over several years, and is not marred by a cohort effect. This design introduces a different type of confounding, as the less able individuals tend to drop out of the study because of death or disease. Thus, longitudinal studies are sensitive to selective attrition and tend to underestimate age-associated cognitive decline. Also, it is a very time-consuming and expensive endeavor.

The best theoretical design is a cross-sequential design, (proposed by Schaie, 1980) which follows subjects from different groups longitudinally and also compares them cross-sectionally. It measures both the effects of age, cohort, and the interaction between these variables, but has the disadvantage of being expensive and quite time-consuming. For the sake of expediency and economy, most studies use a cross-sectional design. Findings from longitudinal studies point to a decline in memory and learning, problem solving, and intelligence similar to the pattern of normal aging observed in cross-sectional studies. Although group means show definite decline, there are marked individual variations. It is unknown how much undiagnosed age-associated diseases may influence downward declines in performance. Also, changes in cognitive status are likely to be influenced by race, education, and socioeconomic background (Manton, Siegler, & Woodbury, 1986).

III. DEMENTIAS

A. Definition of Dementia

The generic term of dementia collectively includes abnormal and persistent age-related cognitive declines of sufficient severity to interfere with everyday activities (Friedland, 1992). This mental deterioration is now recognized to be pathological and arising from many causes.

Age-related dementias are extremely rare before the age of 65 yr (less than 1%), with the rate of occurrence doubling for each 5-yr interval. Forty percent of persons over the age of 90 yr are believed to be suffering from this disease (Jorm, Korten, & Henderson, 1987). The costs of the disease (both economic, loss of productivity of the caregivers, and emotional) are staggering (Katzman, 1986). With the extension of life expectancy and the graying of the baby boomers, it is expected that dementia will reach epidemic proportion by year 2020.

The criteria of primary degenerative dementia set by the American Psychiatric Association in the *Diagnostic and Statistical Manual of Mental Disorders (DSM-III-R)* (1987) include an impairment in short- and long-term memory and at least one of the following: impairment of abstract thinking, impaired judgment, disturbances of higher cortical functions (aphasia, apraxia, agnosia, or constructional difficulties), and personality changes.

It is important to underscore that the term *dementia* refers to a decline in previously adequate intellectual functions, and that it is a nonspecific term rather than a final diagnosis. The term, therefore, does not include mental retardation.

Dementia may be caused by a variety of events (e.g., stroke, head injury, drug toxicity, depression), which may or may not be reversible. It should be distinguished from delirium, which is a confusional state, usually of acute onset, characterized also by memory disturbances but usually accompanied by reduced level of consciousness, abnormal movements, hallucinations, delusions, and change in affect.

There is an ongoing debate as to whether dementing disorders represent accelerated aging or whether there are qualitative differences between the decline observed in both conditions. The argument in favor of quantitative differences is based on neuropathological findings that the pathological diagnosis of dementia (neurofibrillary plaques and tangles) is primarily quantitative, and very much influenced by chronological age. Thus, the brain of an 85-year-old mentally alert person may resemble (in terms of pathological findings of plaques and tangles) that of a 65-year-old person with AD.

The extrapolation of these neuropathological findings to cognitive performance is more tenuous. Decline in cognition, proficiency in activities of daily living, and emotional well-being do not lend themselves to measurements on a single-dimensional linear scale. Performance decline in pathological aging is superimposed on the normal age-related changes, but should not be confused with them. Also, it is only for heuristic convenience that we conceive of cognition as composed of independent functions. For example, adequacy of memory is directly related to linguistic capabilities, to attentional proficiency, and relatively intact sensory functions. Compromise in one area will most certainly impinge on other functions and create a snowball effect, both because of the lack of refinement of available testing instruments, and because of the complex and continuous interrelationship of the different categories of mental functions.

B. Types of Dementia

1. Alzheimer's Disease

AD is the most common form of dementia in older adults. Although the term is relatively recent, the disease in itself is not a new phenomenon, and it used to be called hardening of the arteries, senility, or senile dementia of the Alzheimer type (or SDAT). It accounts for 50 to 60% of all the cases (M. S. Albert & Moss, 1988), although figures as high as 80% have been proposed (Evans et al., 1989). Thus, conservatively AD affects over 2.5 million people in the United States, and this number is expected to double by year 2040 (Evans et al., 1989). AD may occur relatively early in life (before age 65) and is called presenile dementia, or at a more advanced age (over age 65) at which point it is referred to as senile dementia. There is continuing debate as to whether the presenile and the senile forms of AD are the same disease or represent two distinct entities. In both forms, AD is marked by a disproportionate number of neurofibrillary tangles and amyloid plaques in the association cortex of the brain, and principally in the temporoparietal cortices. Additionally, Hirano bodies and granulovacuolar degeneration of neurons are observed. Recently, research has focused on the structure of the protein accumulating in the center of the classic Alzheimer plaques. This protein accumulates to form a β amyloid. The role of this amyloid in the development of both plaque and tangles, and the protein precursor of this amyloid, called the amyloid precursor protein (APP), have attracted much research interest. Advances in immunocytochemistry have provided new understanding into the mechanisms leading to the formation of such amyloid (see Blass, K., & Wisniewski, 1991, for an excellent review).

AD is characterized typically by a gradual and insidious onset of memory impairment, together with compromise in at least two other cognitive or behavioral domains.

In the current absence of specific biological markers, the diagnostic process in AD is primarily that of exclusion. Neurological examination will determine the integrity of the CNS and peripheral nervous system. Psychiatric evaluation will eliminate the possibility of previous major mental disorders. Laboratory tests will rule out evidence of active or occult infections, toxic exposure, or various metabolic deficiencies. Brain imaging will document the absence of tumors, space-occupying lesions, and diffuse deep lesions of the white matter. The absence of encephalopathies may have to be demonstrated with EEG. It is only after elimination of all these other possible causes of dementia that the diagnosis of AD is made.

The NINCDS-ADRDA task force has established standardized research definitions of AD (McKhann et al., 1984). A diagnosis of *probable* AD is used when there is no evidence of other illness that could account for the impairment, and in the presence of dementia with a typically progressive course. *Possible* AD is used when there are variations in the course, onset, or clinical features of the disease, or when another disease coexists with AD that could account for the dementia, although it is not usually considered to be the primary cause. A diagnosis of *definite* AD can only be made at autopsy, or through biopsy (this procedure is strongly discouraged in the United States, due to the relative futility of such an invasive and potentially dangerous procedure). It should be emphasized that the terms *probable* and *possible* AD refer to the statistical probability of the presence of AD, and not to the severity of the disease. Currently the diagnostic accuracy of AD is between 78 and 90% (Katzman, Lasker, & Bernstein, 1988; Morris, McKeel, Fulling, Torack, & Berg, 1988).

The reader is referred to specialized texts for in-depth understanding of age-related dementias. Excellent reviews of the medical aspects of AD can be found in Katzman (1986), Katzman et al. (1988), Chui (1989), and Friedland (1992). The neuropsychology of AD is superbly presented in M. S. Albert and Moss (1988), Kaszniak (1986), and Nebes (1992).

2. Vascular Dementia

The next most common form of dementia (in Western countries) is vascular dementia. Previously referred to as multi-infarct dementia (MID), it occurs in 15–20% of cases, although recent figures are much higher in persons over 85 yr. This dementing disease includes the presence of focal neurological signs (i.e., gait abnormality or weakness of an extremity). As suggested by its name, this form of dementia results from multiple cerebral vascular accidents, hence its focal distribution of cerebral dysfunction. This syndrome includes the basic dementia criteria in the presence of abrupt onset of cognitive symptoms, stepwise disease progression and "patchy" distribution of deficits, a history of stroke, combined with focal neurological signs and symptoms. The summation of these features comprises the Hachinsky scale (Hachinski et al., 1975), which is useful to estimate the likelihood of ischemic events, and thus the presence of dementia due to vascular disease.

3. Parkinson's Disease

The symptoms typical of PD include tremor, rigidity, difficulty in initiating movement (hypokinesia), slowness of movement (bradykinesia), stooped posture, poor balance, and gait disturbance. Medical causes may include encephalitis, toxic exposure, and neuroleptic medications. PD also is a common age-related disease. Although primarily a movement disorder, patients with PD experience some form of dementia in about 40% of the cases.

4. Other Forms of Dementia and Pseudodementia

Huntington's disease is an autosomal dominant progressive disease, characterized by choreic motor disturbances, cognitive decline (including impaired recent and remote memory), and psychiatric problems (Brandt, Folstein, & Folstein, 1988).

Several other forms of dementia deserve mention, although they are extremely rare. Pick's disease occurs earlier than AD, between the ages of 40 to 60 yr, and is more common in women than men. It is characterized by a marked frontal lobe atrophy, Pick bodies within the neurons, relatively sparing of the posterior part of the brain, in contrast to the diffuse deterioration pattern seen in AD.

Frontal lobe dementia has been identified fairly recently (Brun, 1987; Neary, Snowden, Mann, Northern, & Golding, 1988) as a distinct disease entity. It may possibly represent a form of Pick's disease, of which it shares many characteristics, except for the typical Pick inclusions.

Other rare dementias include Creutzfeldt-Jacob disease, an uncommon viral degenerative disorder, and Korsakoff's disease, resulting from chronic alcohol abuse. Creutzfeldt-Jacob disease has a very rapid course (patients usually die within 2 yr of diagnosis) and is characterized by various widespread neurological disturbances, including seizures, apraxia, and agnosia. The disease is thought to be caused by a slow virus contracted early on but with prolonged latency. It may be transmitted from human to human via corneal transplants, use of contaminated EEG electrodes, or administration of human pituitary growth hormone. It can be transmitted also via uncooked sheep's brain.

Depression is very common in older persons and can induce cognitive impairment. Pseudodementia refers to patients with depression who have reversible cognitive impairments (Wells, 1979). Indeed, it is not easy to differentiate depression from dementia, especially in the early stages of dementia, because persons with early dementia may rightfully feel very sad or even be intermittently clinically depressed.

Clinical features of pseudodementia that differ from irreversible dementias include a rapid onset of cognitive impairment with prominent depressed mood, subjective complaints about cognitive dysfunction, and fluctuation of cognitive performance over time.

C. Neuropsychological Features of Dementias

Neuropsychological tests are useful to distinguish dementia from "normal" aging changes, but should not be used to identify a particular type of dementia, because of the considerable overlap between the cognitive deficits. The differentiation between the types of dementias is done by relying on a combination of information derived from the patient's history, clinical presentation, and patterns of neuropsychological deficits, rather than outstanding features on individual tests.

1. Neuropsychological Features of Alzheimer's Disease

The first and foremost deficit is observed in secondary memory. Other likely areas of impairments eventually include word finding, attentional deficits, and visuoconstructive deficits. Clearly the extent of the deficit(s) is related to the severity and progression of the disease. However, AD is marked by unpredictable heterogeneity in its behavioral manifestations and its speed of progression (Friedland, 1988). Because by definition at least two areas of cognition are impaired, secondary memory is universally compromised in AD, in addition to another feature. There is some variability as to the first presenting symptom in individual cases. Very early detection of

AD represents a challenge for the diagnostician and the researcher. The differential diagnosis between AD and benign aging decline, whereas depression, PD, or other dementias in the very early cases remain primarily based on the family history, exclusionary criteria, and the classic constellation of symptoms. Any unusual presentation will delay diagnosis until the pattern of symptoms worsens and becomes clearer. This "wait and see approach" is prudent since at present there is no cure for AD. The issue of early detection will become more important with the discovery of treatment to prevent or slow down disease progression.

2. Neuropsychological Features of Vascular Dementia

The distinction between AD and vascular dementia is primarily based on clinical signs and a high Hachinsky score. Neuropsychological tests alone are not sufficient to distinguish between the two syndromes, although they are helpful in estimating the severity of the cognitive compromise. The multifocal nature of vascular dementia compromise is reflected in *pronounced* interested variability, and with deficits consistent with those observed in areas of cerebral infarction. The presence of motor speech deficits is more frequent in vascular dementia than AD (Powell, Cummings, Hill, & Benson, 1988). However, patchiness of deficits has not been operationalized, and may not be specific to vascular dementia. AD and vascular dementia may coexist in 15% of the cases (Tomlinson, 1977), blurring further the neuropsychological distinction of deficits specific to each syndrome.

3. Neuropsychological Features of Parkinson's Disease

Neuropsychological deficits in early PD are generally confined to three areas: (1) psychomotor slowing, (2) loss of cognitive flexibility, and (3) mildly reduced learning and recall, as well as other symptoms of frontal lobe dysfunctions (i.e., loss of spontaneity; lack of initiative) (see review in LaRue, 1992).

One third of PD patients show dementing symptoms. Principal features of PD include depression, bradyphrenia (Mayeux, Stern, Rosen, & Leventhal, 1981), visuospatial disturbances (Boller et al., 1984), and deficits in executive functioning (Cummings & Duchen, 1981). Recall is impaired also, although other aspects of memory are relatively spared (Stern & Mayeux, 1987). PD patients show disturbances in frontal and executive functions early in the disease process. They also have more prominent speech deficits (in terms of slowness) and writing abnormalities than AD patients, although language per se is relatively preserved.

4. Neuropsychological Features of Other Dementias and Pseudodementia

Cognitive and psychiatric disturbances are early manifestations of patients with Huntington's chorea (Mayeux, Stern, Herman, Greenbaum, & Fahn,

1986) who also manifest problems in language organization and naming problems, and equal impairment in recent and remote memory (M. S. Albert, Butters, & Brandt, 1981).

Neuropsychological features of Pick's disease follow the brain degeneration: expressive language and socially appropriate behavior are compromised early, whereas memory and visuospatial abilities are proportionally better preserved until fairly advanced stages of the disease (Friedland, Koss, & Lerner, 1993). Patients eventually show generalized signs of dementia and become mute at later disease stages (Cummings & Duchen, 1981).

Depressed patients show considerable deficits on tests requiring effortful cognitive processing (Weingartner, Cohen, Murphy, Martello, & Gerdt, 1981). In contrast, cognitive disorders in dementia are insidious, slowly progressive, more constant, and not as evident on casual inspection. As a rule of thumb, depressed patients appear more demented than they are, whereas the reverse is true for patients with AD.

IV. CONCLUSION

Studies on aging mitigate popular belief that intellectual decline is part of the normal aging process. Areas showing greatest impairment include fluid intellectual abilities, complex attentional processes, secondary memory, accessing working knowledge, visuospatial abilities, abstract reasoning, and problem solving. Although widespread and statistically significant, the changes observed with increasing age are small until very advanced age. Most of the research has focused on the characterization of decline with aging. However, recent developments have emphasized the plasticity of older adults and the value of training and cuing. Cognitive psychologists are increasingly viewing cognitive performance as the product of complex interaction among the characteristics of the task and the individual performing it. The marked individual variations in decline suggest the possibility that secondary aging effects due to diseased states may be confused for primary age-related changes. Also, optimal health and higher education have been found to be protective against the observed age-related changes (Friedland, 1993; Koss et al., 1991).

Intellectual changes observed as part of the natural process of aging are trivial compared to that observed in persons with dementia. All the age-related dementias have in common memory loss as the most pronounced behavioral abnormality. They all also have to various degrees disturbances in awareness, orientation, insight, general behavior, general information, language function, praxis, visuospatial function, topographical orientation, problem-solving ability, judgment, calculation, and affect.

Clearly, these dysfunctions are very unspecific, as they cover all the realms of the cognitive domain and are present in aging as well. The issue here is intensity of dysfunction, qualitative differences with "normal" aging, the specific symptom constellation and the progressive nature and presentation of the deficits.

The twentieth century has experienced a population explosion unprecedented in history, together with a rapid extension of human life span due to biomedical advances and improvements in socioeconomic conditions. The graying of America in particular has expanded the scope of aging research and has brought to consciousness the urgent need for information on what constitutes normal and abnormal aging.

References

Albert, M. L., Heller, H. S., & Milberg, W. (1988). Changes in naming ability with age. *Psychology and Aging, 3,* 173–178.

Albert, M. S., Butters, N., & Brandt, J. (1981). Patterns of remote memory in amnesic and demented patients. *Archives of Neurology (Chicago), 38,* 495–500.

Albert, M. S., & Kaplan, E. (1980). Organic implications of neuropsychological deficits in the elderly. In L. W. Poon, J. L. Fozard, & L. S. Cermak (Eds.), *New directions in memory and Aging* (pp. 403–432). Hillsdale, NJ: Erlbaum.

Albert, M. S., & Moss, M. B. (Eds.). (1988). *Geriatric neuropsychology.* New York: Guilford Press.

American Psychiatric Association. (1987). *Diagnostic and statistical manual of mental disorders* (3rd rev. ed.). Washington, DC: Author.

Arenberg, D. (1982). Changes with age in problem solving. In F. I. M. Craik & S. Trehub (Eds.), *Aging and cognitive processes* (pp. 221–236). New York: Plenum.

Baddeley, A. (1986). *Working memory.* Oxford: Clarendon University Press.

Bayles, K. A., & Kaszniak, A. W. (1987). *Communication and cognition in normal aging and dementia.* Austin, TX: PRO-ED.

Bell, M. D., Wolf, E., & Bernholtz, C. D. (1972). Depth perception as a function of age. *Aging and Human Development, 3,* 77–81.

Blass, J. P., Ko, L.-W., & Wisniewski, H. M. (1991). Pathology of Alzheimer's disease. *Alzheimer's Disease. Psychiatric Clinics of North America, 14,* 397–420.

Boller, F., Passafiume, D., Keefe, N. C., Rogers, K., Morrow, L., & Kim, Y. (1984). Visuospatial impairment in Parkinson's disease. *Archives of Neurology (Chicago), 41,* 485–490.

Botwinnick, J. (1977). Intellectual abilities. In J. E. Birren & K. W. Schaie (Eds.), *Handbook of the psychology of aging* (pp. 580–605). New York: Van Nostrand-Reinhold.

Bourliere, F. (1970). *The assessment of biological age in man* (No. 37, pp. 1–67). Geneva: World Health Organization.

Bowles, N. L., Obler, L., & Albert, M. L. (1987). Naming errors in healthy aging and dementia of the Alzheimer type. *Cortex, 23,* 519–524.

Brandt, J., Folstein, S. E., & Folstein, M. F. (1988). Differential cognitive impairment in Alzheimer's disease and Huntington's disease. *Annals of Neurology, 23,* 555–561.

Brant, L. J., & Fozard, J. L. (1990). Age changes in pure tone thresholds in a longitudinal study of normal aging. *Journal of the Acoustical Society of America, 88,* 813–820.

Braun, R., & Wickens, C. D. (1985). The functional age profile: An objective decision criterion for the assessment of pilot performance capacities and capabilities. *Human Factors, 27,* 681–693.

Brown, J., & Jaffe, J. (1975). Hypothesis on cerebral dominance. *Neuropsychologia, 13,* 107–110.

Brun, A. (1987). Frontal lobe degeneration of non-Alzheimer type: Neuropathology. *Archives of Gerontology and Geriatrics, 6,* 193–208.

Butler, R. N. (1989). Dispelling ageism: The cross-cutting intervention. *Annals of the American Academy of Political and Social Science, 503,* 139–147.

Cattell, R. B. (1963). Theory of fluid and crystallized intelligence, a critical experiment. *Journal of Educational Psychology, 54,* 1–22.

Chamberlain, W. (1971). Restriction in upward gaze with advancing age. *American Journal of Ophthalmology, 71,* 341–346.

Chiarello, C., & Hoyer, W. J. (1988). Adult age differences in implicit and explicit memory: Time course and encoding effects. *Psychology and Aging, 3,* 358–366.

Chui, H. C. (1989). Dementia: A review emphasizing clinicopathologic correlation and brain-behavior relationships. *Archives of Neurology (Chicago), 46,* 806–814.

Costa, P. T., Jr., & McCrae, R. R. (1980). Functional age: A conceptual and empirical critique. In S. G. Haynes & M. Feinleb (Eds.), *Epidemiology of aging,* NIH Publ. No. 80–969, pp. 23–46). Washington, DC: U.S. Government Printing Office.

Craik, F. I. M. (1977). Age differences of human memory. In J. E. Birren & K. W. Schaie (Eds.), *Handbook of the psychology of aging* (pp. 384–420). New York: Van Nostrand-Reinhold.

Cummings, J. L., & Duchen, L. W. (1981). Kluver-Bucy syndrome in Pick's disease. Clinical and pathologic correlations. *Neurology, 31,* 1415–1422.

Doty, R. L. (1989). The influence of age and age-related diseases on olfactory function. *Annals of the New York Academy of Sciences, 561,* 76–86.

Doty, R. L., Shaman, P., Applebaum, S. L., Giberson, R., Sikorski L., & Rosenberg, L. (1984). Smell identification ability: Changes with age. *Science, 226,* 1441–1443.

Erber, J. T., Botwinnick, J., & Storandt, M. (1981). The impact of memory on age differences in Digit Symbol performance. *Journal of Gerontology, 36,* 586–590.

Evans, D. A., Funkenstein, H. H., Albert, M. S. Scherr, P. Q., Cook, N. R. Chown, M. J., Hebert, L. E., Hennekens, C. H., Taylor, J. O. (1989). Prevalence of Alzheimer's disease in a community population of older persons: Higher than previously reported. *JAMA, Journal of the American Medical Association, 262,* 2551–2556.

Fozard, J. L. (1985). Psychology of aging: Normal and pathological ages differences in memory. In J. C. Brocklehurst (Ed.), *Textbook of geriatric medicine and gerontology* (3rd ed., pp. 122–142). London: Churchill-Livingstone.

Fozard, J. L. (1990). Vision and hearing in aging. J. E. Birren & K. W. Schaie (Eds.), *Handbook of the psychology of aging* (3rd ed., pp. 150–170). San Diego: Academic Press.

Friedland, R. P. (1988). Alzheimer's disease, clinical and biological heterogeneity. *Annals of Internal Medicine, 109,* 298–311.

Friedland, R. P. (1992). Dementia. In J. G. Evans & T. F. Williams (Eds.), *Oxford textbook of geriatric medicine* (pp. 483–489). Oxford: Oxford University Press.

Friedland, R. P. (1993). Epidemiology, education, and the ecology of Alzheimer's disease. *Neurology, 43,* 246–249.

Friedland, R. P., Koss, E., & Lerner, A. L. (1993). Functional imaging, the frontal lobes, and dementia. *Dementia, 4,* 192–203.

Gelfant, S. A., Piper, N., & Silman, S. (1985). Consonant recognition in quiet as a function of aging among normal hearing subjects. *Journal of the Acoustical Society of America, 78,* 1198–1206.

Gilmore, G. C. Andrist. C. W., & Royer, F. L. (1991). Comparison of two methods of contrast sensitivity assessment with young and elderly adults. *Optometry and Vision Science, 68,* 104–109.

Gur, R. C., Mozley, P. D., Resnick, S. M., Gottlieb, G. L., Kohn, M., Zimmerman, R., Herman, G., Atlas, S., Grossman, R., Beretta, D., Erwin, R., & Gur, R. E. (1991). Gender differences in age effect on brain atrophy measured by magnetic resonance imaging. *Proceedings of the National Academy of Sciences of the U.S.A., 88,* 2845–2849.

Hachinski, V. C., Iliff, L. D., Zihla, E., Barclay, G. H., McAllister, V. L., Marshall, J., Russell, R. W., & Symon, L. (1975). Cerebral blood flow in dementia. *Archives of Neurology (Chicago), 32,* 632–637.

Hartley, A. A. (1981). Adult age differences in deductive reasoning processes. *Journal of Gerontology, 36,* 700–706.

Horn, J. L. (1982). The aging of human abilities. In B. B. Wolman (Ed.), *Handbook of developmental psychology* (pp. 847–870). New York: Prentice-Hall.

Howard, D. V. (1988). Implicit and explicit assessment of cognitive aging. In M. L. Howe & J. C. Brainerd (Eds.), *Cognitive development in adulthood: Progress in cognitive developmental research* (pp. 3–37). New York: Springer-Verlag.

Hoyer, W. J. (1985). Aging and the development of expert cognition. In T. M. Schlecter & M. P. Toglia (Eds.), *New directions in cognitive science* (pp. 69–87). Norwood, NJ: Ablex.

Hoyer, W. J., & Rysbach, J. M. (1992). Age and individual field differences in computing visual-spatial relations. *Psychology and Aging, 7,* 339–342.

Hultsch, D. F., Hertzog, C., Dixon, R. A., & Davidson, H. A. (1988). Memory self-knowledge and self-efficacy in the aged. In M. L. Howe & J. C. Brainerd (Eds.), *Cognitive development in adulthood: Progress in cognitive development research* (pp. 65–92). New York: Springer-Verlag.

Jani, S. N. (1966). The age factor in stereopsis screening. *American Journal of Optometry, 43,* 653–657.

Jarvik, L. F. (1988). Aging of the brain: How can we prevent it? *Gerontologist, 28,* 739–747.

Jorm, A. F., Korten, A. E., & Henderson, A. S. (1987). The prevalence of dementia, A quantitative integration of the literature. *Acta Psychiatrica Scandinavica, 76,* 465–479.

Kaszniak, A. W. (1986). The neuropsychology of dementia. In I. Grant & K. M. Adams (Eds.), *Neuropsychological assessment of neuropsychiatric disorders* (pp. 172–229). New York: Oxford University Press.

Katzman, R. (1986). Alzheimer's disease. *New England Journal of Medicine, 314,* 964–973.

Katzman, R., Lasker, B., & Bernstein, N. (1988). Advances in the diagnosis of dementia accuracy of diagnosis and consequences of misdiagnosis of disorders causing dementia. In R. D. Terry (Ed.), *Terry and the brain* (pp. 17–62). New York: Raven Press.

Kemper, T. (1984). Neuroanatomical and neuropathological changes in normal aging and dementia. In M. L. Albert (Ed.), *Clinical neurology of aging* (pp. 9–52). London: Oxford University Press.

Knoblauch, K., Saunders, F., Kusuda, M., Hynes, R., Podgor, M., Higgins, K. E., & deMonasterio, F. M. (1987). Age and illuminance effects in the Farnsworth-Munsell 100-hue test. *Applied Optics, 26,* 1441–1448.

Koss, E. Friedland, R. P., Ober, B. A., & Jagust, W. J. (1985). Differences in lateral hemispheric asymmetries of glucose utilization between early- and late-onset Alzheimer-type dementia. *Journal of Psychiatry, 142,* 594–610.

Koss, E., Haxby, J. V., DeCarli, C., Shapiro, M. B., Friedland, R. P., & Rapaport, S. I. (1991). Patterns of performance preservation and loss in healthy aging. *Developmental Neuropsychology, 7,* 99–113.

Koss, E., Weiffenbach, M., Haxby, J. V., & Friedland, R. P. (1988). Olfactory detection and identification performance are dissociated in early Alzheimer's disease. *Neurology, 38,* 1228–1232.

LaBarge, E., Edwards, D., & Knesevich, J. W. (1986). Performance of normal elderly on the Boston Naming Test. *Brain and Language, 27,* 380–384.

LaRue, A. (1992). *Aging and neuropsychological assessment.* New York: Plenum.

Lezak, M. D. (1983). *Neuropsychological assessment* (2nd ed.). New York: Oxford University Press.

Light, L. L., & Burke, D. M. (1988). Patterns of language and memory in old age. In L. L. Light & D. M. Burke (Eds.), *Language, memory and aging* (pp. 244–271). New York: Cambridge University Press.

Madden, D. J. (1986). Adult age differences in the attentional capacity demands of visual search. *Cognitive Development, 1,* 335–363.

Manton, K. G., Siegler, I. C., & Woodbury, M. A. (1986). Patterns of intellectual development in later life. *Journal of Gerontology, 41,* 486–499.

Mayeux, R., Stern, Y., Herman, A., Greenbaum, L., & Fahn, S. (1986). Correlates of early disabilities in Huntington's disease. *Annals of Neurology, 20,* 727–731.

Mayeux, R., Stern, Y., Rosen, J., & Leventhal, J. (1981). Depression, intellectual impairment, and Parkinson's disease. *Neurological Clinics, 2,* 527–540.

McDowd, J. M., & Birren, J. E. (1990). Aging and attentional processes. In J. E. Birren & K. W. Schaie (Eds.), *Handbook of the psychology of aging* (3rd ed., pp. 222–233). San Diego: Academic Press.

McKhann, G., Drachman, D., Folstein, J., Katzman, R., Price, D., Stadlan, E. M. (1984). Clinical diagnosis of Alzheimer's disease, report of the NINCDS-ADRDA Work Group under the auspices of Department of Health and Human Services Task Force on Alzheimer's Disease. *Neurology, 9,* 939–944.

Morris, J. C., McKeel, D. W., Jr., Fulling, K. Torack, R. M., & Berg, L. (1988). Validation of clinical diagnostic criteria for Alzheimer's disease. *Annals of Neurology, 24,* 17–22.

Murphy, C. (1985). Cognitive and chemosensory influences on age-related changes in the ability to identify blended foods. *Journal of Gerontology, 40,* 47–52.

Neary, B., Snowden, J. S., Mann, D. M. A., Northern, B., & Golding, P. (1988). Dementia of the frontal lobe type. *Journal of Neurology, Neurosurgery and Psychiatry, 51,* 353–361.

Nebes, R. D. (1992). Cognitive dysfunction in Alzheimer's disease. In F. I. M. Craik & T. A. Salthouse (Eds.), *The handbook of aging and cognition* (pp. 373–446). New York: Erlbaum.

Neugarten, B. L. (1974). Age groups in American Society and the rise of the young-old. *Annals of the American Academy of Political and Social Science, 415,* 187–198.

Nolan, K. A., & Blass, J. P. (1992). Preventing cognitive decline. *Clinics in Geriatric Medicine, 8,* 19–34.

Obler, L. K. (1980). Narrative discourse style in the elderly. In L. K. Obler & M. L. Albert (Eds.), *Language and communication in the elderly* (pp. 75–90). Lexington, MA: Heath.

Owsley, C., Sekuler, R., & Siemsen, D. (1981). Aging and low-contrast vision: Face perception. *Investigative Ophthalmological Visual Sciences, 21,* 362–364.

Owsley, C., Sekuler, R., & Siemsen, D. F. (1983). Contrast sensitivity throughout adulthood. *Vision Research, 23,* 689–699.

Pearson, R. C. A., Esiri, M. M., Hiorns, R. W., Wilcock, G. K., & Powell, T. P. S. (1985). Anatomical correlates of the distribution of the pathological changes in the neocortex in Alzheimer's disease. *Proceedings of the National Academy of Science of the U.S.A., 82,* 4531–4534.

Perlmutter, M., Adams, C., Berry, J., Kaplan, M., Person, D., & Verdonick, F. (1987). Aging and memory. *Annual Review of Gerontology and Geriatrics.* 57–92.

Perret, E. (1974). The left frontal lobe of man and the suppression of habitual responses in verbal categorical behavior. *Neuropsychologia, 13,* 167–173.

Pitts, D. G. (1982). The effects of aging on selected visual functions, dark adaptation, visual acuity, stereopsis, and brightness contrast. In R. Sekuler, D. Kline, & K. Dismukes (Eds.), *Aging and human visual functions* (pp. 131–159). New York: Liss.

Plude, D. J., & Hoyer, W. J. (1985). Attention and performance: Identifying and localizing age deficits. In N. Charness (Ed.), *Aging and performance* (pp. 47–99). New York: Wiley.

Poon, L. W. (1985). Differences in human memory with aging: Nature, causes, and clinical implications. In J. E. Birren & K. W. Schaie (Eds.), *Handbook of the psychology and aging* (2nd ed., pp. 427–462). New York: Van Nostrand.

Powell, A. L., Cummings, J. L., Hill, M. A., & Benson, D. F. (1988). Speech and language alterations in multi-infarct dementia. *Neurology, 38,* 717–719.

Rabbitt, P. (1965). An age-decrement in the ability to ignore irrelevant information. *Journal of Gerontology, 20,* 233–238.

Reitan, R. M., & Wolfson, D. (1985). *The Halstead-Reitan neuropsychological test battery.* Tempe, AZ: Neuropsychology Press.

Roberts, E. (1986). Alzheimer's disease may begin in the nose and may be caused by aluminosilicates. *Neurobiology of Aging, 7,* 561–567.

Rowe, J. W., & Kahn, R. L. (1987). Human aging, usual and successful. *Science, 237,* 143–149.

Salthouse, T. A. (1987). The role of experience in aging. *Annual Review of Gerontology and Geriatrics, 7,* 135–158.

Schacter, D. L. (1987). Implicit memory: History and current status. *Journal of Experimental Psychology: Learning, Memory, and Cognition, 13,* 501–518.

Schaie, K. W. (1980). Intelligence and problem solving. In J. E. Birren & K. W. Schaie (Eds.), *Handbook of the psychology of aging* (pp. 39–58). New York: Van Nostrand-Reinhold.

Schaie, K. W. (1983). The Seattle Longitudinal Study: A 21 year exploration of psychometric intelligence in adulthood. In K. W. Schaie (Ed.), *Longitudinal studies of adult psychological development* (pp. 64–135). New York: Guilford Press.

Schaie, K. W., & Willis, S. L. (1986). Can intellectual decline in the elderly be reversed? *Developmental Psychology, 22,* 223–232.

Scheibel, M. E., & Scheibel, A. B. (1975). Structural changes in the aging brain. In H. Brody, D. Harmon, & J. M. Ordy (Eds.), *Aging* (pp. 11–37). New York: Raven Press.

Schiffman, S. (1983). Taste and smell in disease. *New England Journal of Medicine, 308,* 1275–1279, 1337–1343.

Sekuler, R., Hutman, L. P., & Owsley, C. (1980). Human aging and spatial vision. *Science, 209,* 1255–1256.

Siegler, I. C. (1975). The terminal drop hypothesis: Fact or artifact? *Experimental Aging Research, 1,* 169–185.

Stankov, L. (1988). Aging, attention and intelligence. *Psychology and Aging, 3,* 59–74.

Stern, Y., & Mayeux, R. (1987). Intellectual impairment in Parkinson's disease. *Advances in Neurology, 45,* 405–408.

Stine, E. L., & Wingfield, A. (1987). Process and strategy in memory for speech among younger and older adults. *Psychology and Aging, 2,* 272–279.

Storandt, M. (1977). Age, ability level and method of administering and scoring the WAIS. *Journal of Gerontology, 32,* 175–178.

Tobis, J. S., Nayak, L., & Hoehler, F. (1981). Visual perception of vertical and horizontal among elderly fallers. *Archives of Medical Rehabilitation, 62,* 619–622.

Tomlinson, B. E. (1977). The pathology of dementia. In C. E. Wells (Ed.), *Dementia* (pp. 57–621). Philadelphia: Davis.

Weale, R. A. (1982). Senile ocular changes, cell death, and vision. In R. Sekuler, D. Kline, & K. Dismukes (Eds.), *Aging and human visual function* (pp. 161–171). New York: Liss.

Weale, R. A. (1987). Senescent vision: Is it all the fault of the lens? *Eye, 1,* 217–221.

Wechsler, D. (1955). *Wechsler Adult Intelligence Scale.* New York: Psychological Corporation.

Wechsler, D. (1981). *Wechsler Adult Intelligence Scale (revised).* New York: Psychological Corporation.

Weingartner, H., Cohen, R. M., Murphy, D. L., Martello, J., & Gerdt, C. (1981). Cognitive processes in depression. *Archives of General Psychiatry, 38,* 42–47.

Wells, C. E. (1979). Pseudodementia. *American Journal of Psychiatry, 136,* 895–900.

Werner, L., Harkins, S. W., & Lenhardt, M. L. (1985). Aging and the auditory system. In J. E. Birren & K. W. Schaie (Eds.), *Handbook of the psychology of aging* (2nd ed., pp. 332–377). New York: Van Nostrand-Reinhold.

White, N., & Cunningham, W. R. (1988). Is terminal drop pervasive or specific? *Journal of Gerontology: Psychological Sciences, 43,* P141–P144.

Willis, S. L., & Schaie, K. W. (1988). Gender differences in spatial ability in old age: Longitudinal and intervention findings. *Sex Roles, 18,* 189–203.

Wingfield, A., Poon, L. W., Lombardi, L., and & Lowe, D. (1985). Speed of processing in normal aging: Effects of speech rate, linguistic structure, and processing time. *Journal of Gerontology, 40,* 579–585.

Wisniewski, H. M., & Terry, R. D. (1976). Neuropathology of aging brain. In R. D. Terry & S. Gershon (Eds.), *Neurobiology of aging* (pp. 265–280). New York: Raven Press.

CHAPTER 12

Cognitive and Emotional Organization of the Brain: Influences on the Creation and Perception of Art

Wendy Heller

I. INTRODUCTION

The making of art is commonly viewed as one of the most sublime manifestations of the unique human capacity to represent information and depict meaning in symbolic form. As such, it is the singular product of the unparalleled human cortex, the functional capacities of which are far more complex and elaborate than those of any other form of animal life. Neuropsychologists, who study brain–behavior relationships, have been intrigued by the manner in which the distinctive structures and functions that characterize the cortex are involved in the creation and appreciation of art.

One of the most fundamental principles of cortical organization is its division into two hemispheres, each of which oversees distinct classes of cognitive operations. The left hemisphere, which controls the motor functions of the right side of the body, is also specialized to process linguistic information and produce speech. The right hemisphere, which controls the motor functions of the left side of the body, is specialized to process nonverbal, visuospatial information (see Levy, 1988, for review). These findings have stimulated the appearance of claims in the popular press that the right hemisphere is more "creative," and artistic people have been referred to as more "right-brained." In fact, the reality is far more complex.

Neuropsychology
Copyright © 1994 by Academic Press, Inc. All rights of reproduction in any form reserved.

II. ART CREATION

Many skills go into the making of a work of art. As demonstrated by the work of artists and other individuals with damage to the brain, these special skills call upon the cognitive talents of the left as well as the right hemisphere. For example, the left hemisphere specializes in the execution of fine motor movements required to produce a work of art, whereas the right hemisphere specializes in understanding complex spatial relationships. As many case examples graphically illustrate, damage to either hemisphere often interferes with the ability of the artist to create artwork that lives up to his or her intention or vision. Furthermore, most studies that investigate spontaneous or freehand drawing in individuals with damage to one or the other hemisphere find that any type of brain damage interferes with their performance. However, patients show different kinds of deficits, depending on the side that is damaged.

A. Effects of Right-Brain Damage on Drawing

Damage to the right hemisphere of the brain interferes dramatically with the ability to represent spatial relationships accurately, but these patients are often able to reconstruct the details (Kirk & Kertesz, 1989; Lezak, 1983; McFie & Zangwill, 1960). According to Lezak (1983), their drawings are often overdetailed and repetitive in content. Right-brain damage also compromises the ability to distribute attention evenly and consistently across both sides of space, and these individuals tend to ignore information on the left side of the page (see Kinsbourne, Chapter 5, this Volume, on hemineglect). Often, the left side of the page is left blank in their drawings, or objects are depicted with blurred, distorted, or missing features on the left (Kirk & Kertesz, 1989). This tendency is particularly obvious in freehand drawings (Frederiks, 1963; Kirk & Kertesz, 1989), but can also be seen when patients are asked to copy or reproduce a picture, even a very simple one like a flower or a clock (Borod, Goodglass, & Kaplan, 1980). Drawings of right-brain-damaged patients have also been reported to be larger than those of left-brain-damaged patients (Larrabee, Kane, Morrow, & Goldstein, 1982), and more fragmented (Belleza, Rappaport, Hopkins, & Hall, 1979; McFie & Zangwill, 1960).

The specific region of the right hemisphere that is damaged also seems to influence the nature of the drawing deficit (Grossman, 1988). Patients with damage to the parietal regions of the right hemisphere were most impaired at expressing shape attributes in their drawings, whereas patients with damage to temporal regions had special difficulty with color. Patients with damage to the anterior region of the right hemisphere were the most impaired overall, in that they had difficulty with relative size, as well as with shape and color.

FIGURE 1 This drawing was produced by Reynold Brown, a well-known American artist, shortly after suffering a stroke to the right hemisphere. It shows the tendency to ignore the left side of the space.

One of the more intriguing findings reported by Grossman (1988) suggests that the cognitive contribution of the right hemisphere involves more than the ability to process complex spatial relationships. He noted that right-brain-damaged patients often attributed specific features of a category, like vegetables, in an indiscriminate or inappropriate manner, resulting in an anomalous picture, such as a "potato bush". These findings are remarkably similar to those of Gardner and colleagues (Gardner, Brownell, Wapner, & Michelow, 1983), in which they describe the tendency of right-brain-damaged patients to violate the overall reality of a verbal narrative in favor of irrelevant or nonsensical details. They suggest that the intact right hemisphere plays a special role in judging the likelihood that a particular event is appropriate with reference to a particular context; in other words, an ability to assess "plausibility." Grossman's (1988) results suggest that the right hemisphere is similarly specialized to assess the plausibility of stimulus configurations. These findings are compatible with the results of studies examining hemispheric memory for incongruous scenes (D. Zaidel, 1988) and the role of the right versus the left hemisphere in the comprehension of certain metaphors (e.g., Brownell, Simpson, Bihrle, Potter, & Gardner, 1990). In sum, not only does the right hemisphere play an important role in accurately representing the spatial interrelationships of features within a configuration, it also locates the specific configuration within a larger context.

B. Effects of Left-Brain Damage on Drawing

In contrast, damage to the left hemisphere of the brain interferes with the representation of details, but the fidelity of the spatial relationships is more often maintained than in damage to the right hemisphere. Difficulty drawing has most often been attributed to a deficit in the ability to plan and carry out complex motor sequences (McFie & Zangwill, 1960; Piercy, Hecaen, & Ajuriacuerra, 1960; Warrington, James, & Kinsbourne, 1966). Indeed, Kimura and Faust (1987) reported that compared to right-brain-damaged patients, left-brain-damaged patients' drawings were less recognizable, had fewer lines, and were smaller. The largest proportion of poor drawings came from patients with apraxia (difficulty in executing planned, coordinated motor sequences). These patients were impaired in almost every aspect of drawing.

Kirk and Kertesz (1989) also found left-brain-damaged patients to be more impaired, overall, than right-brain-damaged patients. They suggested that low-level execution errors due to weakness or paralysis of the dominant hand may be just as important as a planning disorder in explaining the drawing disabilities in left-brain-damaged patients. In addition, they found that the quality of drawings by these patients correlated significantly with comprehension deficits as measured by the Western Aphasia Battery, implying that difficulty with concept formation could also contribute to their tendency to simplify and leave out details.

In sum, the left hemisphere also contributes significantly to the ability to draw in more ways than one. In addition to skilled use of the dominant hand, and the ability to plan and carry out fine motor movements, left-hemisphere abilities in the areas of concept formation and comprehension may contribute significantly to the making of art.

C. Effects of Brain Damage on Creation in Artists

Most of what we know about the effects of brain damage on artists comes from individual case reports. To some extent, these reports seem to belie the predictions that might be made on the basis of the observations described above of nonartist patients with brain damage (see Levy, 1988; Winner, 1982). In many of the individual case reports of artists, neither right- nor left-hemisphere damage proved devastating to the artist's capacity to continue to produce works of merit. The most common sequela appears to be a change in style. There have also been frequent reports of hemineglect after right-hemisphere damage (an attentional deficit in which people ignore or fail to perceive the left side of space or the left side of the body), and a switch to left-handedness after left-hemisphere damage. For example, Lovis Corinth was a German expressionist painter who experienced a massive stroke to the right hemisphere. Despite severe neglect of the left side of the page, he continued in his career with great success. However, his style of painting changed, and became bolder, more expressive, and less representational. A more recent example is that of Reynold Brown, whose work was represented at an art exhibit associated with a symposium in Chicago called "Art and the Brain." Reynold Brown experienced a similar stroke to the right hemisphere, and like Corinth, showed severe hemineglect. Marked changes could be seen in his style as well, with a greater emphasis on bold strokes and a decreased emphasis on exact detail.

Similarly, there are at least two reports of artists with left-hemisphere damage who continued to paint with success; one of these is reported also to have shown a change in style (Winner, 1982). These observations led both Winner (1982) and Levy (1988) to suggest that cognitive functions in artists are not impaired after brain damage in the same way as they are in nonartists. Winner (1982) suggests further that the results of case studies imply that the right hemisphere is more crucial than the left. In contrast, Levy (1988) argued that neither hemisphere is more crucial; rather, she suggested that cognitive functions are more bilaterally represented in the artist, such that after brain damage, each hemisphere is capable of carrying out activities that are normally restricted to the other side of the brain.

An alternative hypothesis is possible, however. Little is actually known

FIGURE 2   An example of the work of American artist Reynold Brown *before* suffering a right-hemisphere stroke.

FIGURE 3   An example of the work of American artist Reynold Brown *after* suffering a right-hemisphere stroke.

about the processes and experiences that accompany the artistic endeavors of successful artists who have experienced brain damage. On the basis of an interview with a brain-damaged artist (Heller, 1991), I believe that artists with brain damage do in fact experience deficits similar to those seen in nonartists with brain damage. From this perspective, it is not the case that the nondamaged hemisphere is inherently capable of the activities of the damaged hemisphere, as suggested by Levy (1988). Rather, I would argue that the change of style seen in these artists is a compensation for a loss of skill or specialized activity previously sustained by the damaged hemisphere.

These conclusions were engendered by an interview that I had the good fortune to conduct with an artist who had experienced severe damage to the right hemisphere several years before (Heller, 1991). My discussions with Loring Hughes made it very clear that she had experienced all the losses in function that one might have expected after right brain damage. In the interview, she described poignantly the many ways in which her skills and abilities had changed. She spoke of continuing difficulties with a tendency to neglect the left half of space, and of having to change the media she worked with because of motor coordination problems. Perhaps not the least of her problems were the warnings by medical personnel that she would never succeed as an artist. Yet she persevered in her drawing endeavors, and like the other artists with brain damage we have heard about, changed her style to compensate. The following is an illustrative account of her experience (Heller, 1991):

> Perhaps one of the greatest challenges had to do with her spatial difficulties. When Loring began again to paint, she found that she simply could not appreciate the spatial relationships between the lines she was producing. At

first, she was not even aware of the degree to which the lines and shapes they represented were distorted. Gradually, she came to sense that something was wrong, but still needed someone to point it out to her. At first, she struggled mightily to make her images look "real," like the things they were meant to represent, a style that had previously been her trademark. Now, however, she found she could not get the perspective right, and the products of her efforts appeared to her imperfect and lacking. For over two years, she fought to accept the fact that the work she was producing would not be the same as it was before, and to learn not to compare. Over time, she came to be grateful simply that she could draw, and she learned to stop asking whether it was "correct" or not. . . . Now, her work often surprises her, and sometimes she finds herself dismayed—but as she has come to see the images as an expression of her inner reality, she grows more and more to like them. . . .

After the damage to her brain . . . two things contributed to a newfound freedom from inhibition. First, her difficulties with spatial relationships made it impossible for her to replicate the world on paper, and this forced her to accept and explore the world of her own emotions. As she describes it, she gave up trying to reproduce things and turned, instead, to her imagination. . . .

Two years ago, Loring was too ashamed to show her work. A year ago, she found herself getting comfortable with her new style. To her surprise, when she did start showing, the feedback from the artistic community was much more encouraging than before. Her paintings "deliver an emotional wallop" according to art critic Eileen Watkins (p. 18).

FIGURE 4   An example of the work of Loring Hughes *before* experiencing damage to the right hemisphere.

FIGURE 5   An example of the work of Loring Hughes *after* experiencing damage to the right hemisphere.

Loring Hughes's willingness to speak frankly of her experience as a brain-damaged artist continuing to paint provides us with unique and valuable information about the underlying processes that may be involved in the changes in style that have been observed in other artists who have suffered trauma to the brain. Her story suggests that these artists do indeed experience deficits of the same ilk as reported by nonartists with brain damage—however, when they persevere in their work, they are likely to find ways to compensate for their difficulties. One wonders how many of the artists described in the case reports as successful and talented also found themselves "dismayed" at times by the changes in their abilities.

These considerations suggest that the true measure of an artist is not dependent on the perceptual and motor skills that are localized to each hemisphere. These skills may indeed be the tools of the artist's trade—but the creative vision and drive may rely, at least in part, on some other region of the brain. For example, there is evidence that the frontal lobes play an important role in creative thought processes, as well as in planning and motivation (Kolb and Whishaw, 1990). Furthermore, the fact that these artists continued to paint highlights a critical difference between them and their nonartistic, brain-damaged counterparts. Their commitment to an artistic identity mandated that they persevere. As can be seen in the case of Loring Hughes, her ongoing attempts to keep working provided the conditions for learning to develop successful compensatory strategies.

D. Art Creation and Brain Functions in Emotion

Loring Hughes's story raises another issue that is potentially important to our understanding of the neuropsychological mechanisms that mediate the creation of art. Theorists have described the primary impact of art as emotional. A work of art is considered to be meaningful when it evokes and gives form and sense to an affective state (see Arnheim, 1974, and Schweiger, 1985). The capacity of the artist to arouse an emotional response in the viewer is thus a fundamental measure of the artist's skill. This capacity will depend not only upon the artist's cognitive and motor skills, as described above, but also upon her ability to exercise control over the emotional impact of the work.

A passage from my interview with Loring Hughes illustrates the importance of the role of emotion in the artistic endeavor:

> Looking back, she perceives herself as rigid and restrictive in her emotional expression, preferring not to share her feelings at all. After the damage to her brain, however, two things contributed to a newfound freedom from inhibition. First, her difficulties with spatial relationships made it impossible for her to replicate the world on paper, and this forced her to accept and explore the world of her own emotions. . . . Secondly, her brush with death gave her the impetus to come out of her shell; "like truth knocking on the door," she felt she had to expose herself. (Heller, 1991, p. 18).

The artist's ability to express emotion in an effective way is likely to involve at least two processes that have been shown to be dependent on particular brain regions: one having to do with the experience of emotion (emotional state), and one having to do with the cognitive processing of emotional information. *The experience of emotion,* particularly with regard to valence (the positive–negative continuum of feelings) seems to be associated with the *frontal lobes of the brain.* In contrast, the ability to understand emotional information seems to depend primarily upon posterior regions of the right hemisphere (Heller, 1990; Heller & Levy, 1981). Thus, it may be possible to lose certain cognitive or motor functions that contribute to drawing (such as fine motor control of the right hand, which is mediated by a particular region of the left hemisphere), without losing the capacity to experience feelings and the ability to understand and express those feelings. This phenomenon may help to explain why, when a group of neuropsychologists, neurologists, and art critics was reviewing artwork by brain-damaged artists for an art exhibit associated with a symposium "Art and the Brain," we all differed significantly in our assessment of the works. The neurologists and neuropsychologists, and often the artist, focused on the deterioration in technical skill after brain trauma, and pointed to the loss of spatial relationships or precision in motoric execution. In contrast, the art critics and art therapists were struck by the moving quality of many of the posttraumatic works, and found their emotional impact far more salient.

Another way in which brain functions for emotion may affect the production and perception of art has to do with the fact that activity in different parts of the brain influences our attentional responses to the environment. In particular, asymmetric activation of the hemispheres is known to produce biases of movement and attention towards the side of space opposite the more active hemisphere (Heilman, 1979; Kinsbourne, 1974). For instance, when one hemisphere is more active than the other, the person tends to move the eyes more frequently toward the opposite side of space.

A variety of studies using different methodologies have found that hemispheric activity over the frontal lobes is asymmetric during different moods. In particular, when a person is sad or depressed, frontal regions of the right hemisphere are more active than the same parts of the left hemisphere, but when a person is cheerful or happy, frontal regions of the left hemisphere are more active than the same parts of the right hemisphere (Davidson, 1984, 1992). For example, one way to measure brain activity is to record electroencephalographic (EEG) patterns over different parts of the brain. The activity level of that region is then reflected in a particular type of brain wave. Studies that have measured EEG in clinically depressed subjects have found increased activity in *right relative to left frontal regions* (Davidson, 1984, 1992; Schaffer, Davidson, & Saron, 1983). Using another approach, Tucker, Stenslie, Roth, and Shearer (1981) used hypnosis to induce depression in normal subjects. These subjects also showed an increase in the activity level of the right hemisphere compared to the left. The same results were found in a similar paradigm where normal subjects watched depressing scenes from television shows (Davidson, Schwartz, Saron, Bennett, & Goleman, 1979).

It seems possible, therefore, that manifestations of asymmetric attention and movement would occur during different mood states as a result of a concomitant asymmetry in activation of the cerebral hemispheres. There is some evidence to support this notion. In one study, clinically depressed subjects showed more leftward eye movements in response to neutral questions (Myslobodsky & Horesh, 1978). Similarly, nondepressed subjects in another study directed more eye movements to the left in response to emotionally negative questions and more eye movements to the right in response to emotionally positive questions (Ahern & Schwartz, 1979). These findings are consistent with the idea that when a person is happy, the *left* frontal region is more active, and she or he is likely to move the eyes more often toward the *right* side of space. When a person is sad, the *right* frontal region is more active, and he or she is likely to move the eyes more often toward the *left* side of space.

I hypothesized that these patterns of brain activity for different moods would affect the way people organize the space on the page when they are creating a picture or drawing (see Heller, 1990). In particular, I predicted that the emotional content in sad pictures would be displaced towards the left side of the page, due to asymmetrically higher right-hemisphere activation. In contrast, I predicted that the emotional content in happy pictures would be displaced towards the right side of the page, due to asymmetrically higher left-hemisphere activation. To test these predictions, children were asked to draw pictures of something that made them feel either happy or sad. Note that they were not asked to draw "happy" or "sad" pictures; it was of particular concern that they become emotionally involved in the drawings and that they express a personal emotional experience. As a control condition, all children were asked to draw a picture of anything they wished, before drawing either of the emotional pictures. Since a review of the literature on children's drawings suggested that human figures tend to be the emotional focus, it was decided to compare the placement of the figure or figures in the different drawings.

About two hundred children in kindergarten through sixth grade were asked to draw a picture of something that made them feel happy, and a picture of something that made them feel sad (Heller, 1986, 1987), and the location of the figures in each picture was measured. Since the question of interest concerned placement of emotional content, figures were distinguished according to whether or not they were expressing an emotion or representative of one. Two judges independently scored the location of the figures in the pictures.

As predicted, the figures in the sad pictures were significantly displaced

FIGURE 6 An example of a sad picture drawn by a child with the emotional content depicted to the left of center.

FIGURE 7   An example of a happy picture drawn by a child with the emotional content depicted close to the center of the page and slightly to the right.

toward the left, compared to the figures in the happy pictures. The results were especially strong for the figures that were actually expressing emotion.

These findings suggest that different activity levels of the two sides of the brain during different emotions affected the use of space on the page. Sad emotional states caused the right hemisphere to become more active than the left, and biased the child's attention toward the left side of space, where they then placed the important emotional content. Happy emotional states had the opposite effect.

One might argue that children are different from adults when they create a work of art; that they are more emotional and less affected by considerations of form or style. To test this possibility, the same instructions were given to a group of art therapy students who had had anywhere from 2 to 45 years of formal training in art. Since these individuals were all studying to become art therapists, they were not only accustomed but had been encouraged to view their artwork as a medium for emotional expression; therefore, the task they were given was extraordinarily compatible with their training and values. In fact, for this group, the effect was even stronger than for the children's drawings.

Although more research is clearly needed on this topic, the results from these studies suggest that the organization of space during the composition of a work of art may be influenced by the brain activity of the artist, which in turn is likely to depend, at least in part, on the artist's mood at the moment of creation.

In summary, the foregoing discussion has elucidated some of the neuropsychological influences on the creation of art, ranging from cognitive and motor to emotional mechanisms. To date, research has identified several

FIGURE 8   An example of a sad picture drawn by one of the participants in the art therapy class.

distinct aspects of cortical organization that play a role in art creation. These include the specializations of the right hemisphere for spatial and emotional information processing, and the specializations of the left hemisphere for fine motor coordination, planning, and aspects of comprehension. In addition, the activity of the frontal regions, which are involved in emotional experience, may also influence art creation. These influences may include the emotional "spark" (i.e., the feeling state) that motivates creation as well as potential attentional effects on composition. These attentional effects may

FIGURE 9   An example of a happy picture drawn by one of the participants in the art therapy class.

be mediated by differential left versus right hemisphere activity during different emotional states; specifically, left frontal regions are relatively more active in positive (i.e., happy) emotional states, whereas right frontal regions are more active in negative (i.e., sad) emotional states.

III. ART PERCEPTION

Neuropsychologists have also been interested in the way in which the organization of the brain influences the way people process the information contained in a work of art and the effect that has on the experience of art.

A. Right- versus Left-Hemisphere Memory for Artwork

One approach examined memory for works of art depending on whether the picture has been presented to the left or the right hemisphere (D. Zaidel & Kasher, 1989). These researchers used two types of pictures: surrealistic, defined as portraying impossible representations of objects in the known world, and realistic, defined as portraying the known world correctly. They found that compared to the right hemisphere, the left hemisphere remembered surrealistic paintings especially well. Although there were no statistically significant differences between the hemispheres in their performance on the realistic paintings, the right hemisphere was biased to select realistic paintings among decoys. Furthermore, when the pictures were assigned metaphoric or literal titles, the surrealistic-metaphoric pairs were better remembered when presented to the left than the right hemisphere. These results are compatible with a previous study (D. Zaidel, 1988), in which the left hemisphere was faster (although not more accurate) at recognizing otherwise regular scenes that had incongruous elements in them. D. Zaidel and Kasher (1989) interpreted their findings to indicate that the left hemisphere is superior to the right in transcending the constraints of concrete reality, thus demonstrating less "rigid" and more flexible patterns of thought. From this perspective, their results seem inconsistent with a number of other findings, including those reviewed above in which the right hemisphere has often been found to be important in the interpretation of metaphor and narrative. They also seem to contradict the findings of Warrington and Taylor (1973) who found that right-brain-damaged patients were selectively impaired in the ability to recognize noncanonical views of everyday objects. These studies would have led us to predict the opposite pattern (i.e., that the right hemisphere would be better at processing surrealistic paintings and incongruous scenes).

I would like to argue that the cognitive demands imposed by the memory task for surrealistic paintings and incongruous pictures are not comparable to the cognitive demands associated with the processing of cultural metaphor, narrative, or even the ability to comprehend noncanonical views of objects. Current views of metaphor emphasize several aspects of their structure and function that are consistent with a special role for the right hemisphere—and that are not consistent with the structure and function of surrealistic paintings.

In general, many metaphors are viewed as a means to represent and communicate knowledge about things, particularly concepts that might otherwise be hard to describe verbally (e.g., emotions, time) (Glucksberg & Keysar, 1990; Lakoff, 1987; Lakoff & Johnson, 1980). These types of metaphors are thought to be much more than indirect comparisons or implicit similes (Glucksberg & Keysar, 1990). Rather, they are viewed as class-inclusion statements that promote understanding of a topic or a concept. In other words, when a person says "my job is a jail," the intended meaning is that their job belongs to category that is referred to as a jail. As Glucksberg and Keysar (1990) point out, a jail, like any other thing in the world, can be classified in any number of ways on the basis of similarities to other things. Thus, the use of a particular metaphor functions to highlight or specify more precisely the attributes that facilitate the intended meaning of a speaker communicating about a topic (Glucksberg & Keysar, 1990; Lakoff, 1987; Lakoff & Johnson, 1980).

In Western culture, there are many metaphors which are highly familiar to members of the same social group. The particular attributes that are highlighted will depend on the context of the utterance. Included in context are such things as shared knowledge and assumptions about the attributes of categories, interactional variables such as goals of the interchange or utterance, and sensitivity to conversational rules. These contextual elements are part of what Lakoff (1987) and Lakoff and Johnson (1980) refer to as an *experiential gestalt,* which is an array of dimensions (perceptual, motor activity, part/whole, functional, etc.) that together constitute each of our categories representing objects, activities, events, and experiences.

If, as stated by Lakoff and Johnson (1980), an experiential gestalt typically serves as background for understanding something we experience as an aspect of that gestalt, the ability to make sense of categories, or to understand things in terms of categories, depends on a capacity to comprehend the relations among and between the elements and attributes that make up the experiential gestalt that informs the category. Simply on the basis of its relative superiority at comprehending relational information, the evidence suggests that the right hemisphere is likely to play a significant role in this type of information processing.

It is also of interest that Lakoff (1987; Lakoff & Johnson, 1980) emphasizes the role of real-life sensory and motor experience in the representation of categories and the organization of cultural metaphors. Lakoff and Johnson (1980) argue that the dimensions of categories arise out of our physical interactions with the world, and that the properties of those dimensions are therefore defined in terms of our interactions with them, as opposed to being something inherent to the objects themselves. A number of authors have hypothesized a special role for the right hemisphere in the perception and integration of multimodal sensory information, that is, information obtained from a variety of sensory channels (e.g., Goldberg & Costa, 1981). Such a mechanism has been proposed to account for a right-hemisphere superiority in processing cause-and-effect relationships, novel information, and information characterized by increased complexity (e.g., Rourke, 1989). From this perspective, the right hemisphere might thus be hypothesized to play a key role in processing the sensory information that informs the construction of the experiential gestalts that make up representations of categories.

In summary, the comprehension of metaphor seems to depend upon a capacity to comprehend the relationships between objects, concepts, and experiences as they are shaped by individual experience and social convention. Viewed in this way, the issue is not one of rigid or conventional thinking; rather, it is about the capacity to construct a network of representations that are interrelated in systematic ways on the basis of certain understandings about real life. Thus, the ability to remember a surrealistic painting might actually be hindered by a bias to pay attention to characteristics that represent real-life relationships, a tendency that appears to characterize the right hemisphere.

In addition, cultural metaphors do not constitute a case where category membership is violated, such as is the case in surrealistic paintings. In contrast, comprehension of this type of metaphor seems to require a sophisticated and inclusive understanding of the limits and boundaries of a category. Indeed, D. Zaidel and Kasher's (1989) findings that the left hemisphere remembers surrealistic paintings better than the right, and Grossman's findings of category violations in right-brain-damaged people suggest that the left hemisphere is relatively insensitive to the boundaries and properties of categories. This conclusion is supported by an earlier study by D. Zaidel (1988). Zaidel tested the sensitivity to the boundary of categories and found absence of sensitivity to typicality effects in the left hemisphere. In contrast, the right hemisphere was sensitive to these effects.

It is also worth considering the constraints of the memory task used by D. Zaidel and Kasher, which relied on rapid presentation of the information and a measure of accuracy and speed of identification. In contrast, if the task had involved appreciation of the painting, or a judgment regarding its cleverness or skill, the capacity of the right hemisphere to assess categorical and contextual relationships might have given it an advantage.

B. Left and Right in Pictures

One aspect of picture perception that has intrigued researchers is the fact that the appearance of a picture is changed when it is mirror-imaged. Thus, the lateral orientation of a composition changes the way it is perceived, in spite of the fact that the stimulus configuration is exactly the same.

Levy (1976) was the first to examine this phenomenon from a neuropsychological perspective. She found that when people view asymmetric photographs of scenery, they have a tendency to prefer the picture in which the more important content (as judged by raters) is on the right side of space (Levy, 1976; also Banich, Heller, & Levy, 1989). Right-handers judged whether they preferred a picture in its normal or mirror orientation. The location of the important content in the pictures had been previously determined by the judgments of another group of subjects. Regardless of the orientation of the picture, right-handers found slides with right-biased content more aesthetically pleasing. Left-handers, in contrast, were not biased. Similar results were obtained for right-handers by Banich et al. (1989) using vacation scenes, by Beaumont (1985) using simple compositions of drawings, and by McLaughlin, Dean, and Stanley (1983) in one experiment using works of art.

Two theoretical accounts have been proposed for these findings. Levy (1976) suggested that the right hemisphere is differentially activated by the picture-viewing behavior (because the right hemisphere is specialized for processing visuospatial information). Other research indicates that asymmetric activity of one or the other hemisphere is accompanied by a bias of attention to the opposite side of space (see Levy, 1976). Thus a bias of attention to the left side of space during picture viewing might cause that part of the picture to appear more prominent or to be mentally highlighted in some way. Levy suggested that when the right-biased content is more important, it serves to balance the neuropsychologically induced highlighting of the left side of the picture. The picture is then perceived as more appealing by virtue of being more balanced.

Beaumont (1985) suggested a different hypothesis. He argued that the presence of more important content on the right causes the viewer to move their eyes toward that side of the painting. The effect of moving the eyes in that particular direction causes more of the picture to fall into the left visual field, which stimulates the right hemisphere more directly. Since the right hemisphere is specialized for processing visuospatial information, the picture is seen as more appealing because there is a better match between the information and the hemisphere that is best suited for the task.

Beaumont's (1985) hypothesis seems to account for the fact that another stimulus characteristic of pictures, apparent motion from left to right, is found to be more appealing than apparent motion from right to left (Freimuth & Wapner, 1979; Mead & McLaughlin, 1992; but see Banich et al., who found the opposite pattern for vacation slides). If the eyes are encouraged to move from left to right, it is reasonable to assume that more information is being projected to the left visual field and hence to the right hemisphere. Supporting evidence that people actually do move their eyes from left to right while viewing pictures that have apparent left-to-right motion has been obtained by A. M. Mead and J. P. McLaughlin (unpublished manuscript). However, neither of these hypotheses has been disconfirmed.

Another explanation for some of these effects has to do with the emotional organization of the brain, which may affect the *perception* of pictures as well as the creation of art. Recall that increased activity of the right frontal region relative to the left is associated with a more negative, sad, and pessimistic view of the world, whereas increased activity of the left frontal region relative to the right is associated with a more positive, cheerful, and optimistic view of the world. In studies that have presented the identical picture or scene to both hemispheres (mainly using a special instrument called a tachistoscope that allows one to direct information, initially, to only one hemisphere), the person thinks the picture is more negative when presented to the right hemisphere than to the left, regardless of the emotion the picture is actually expressing (see Heller, 1990). This tendency has been found in both adults (see Davidson, 1984) and children (Heller, 1988). These results may be explained by the fact that when information is presented to one hemisphere or the other, that hemisphere becomes more active, in order to process the input. In this way, the balance of hemispheric activity can be manipulated. When the left hemisphere is stimulated, the internal feeling state of a person is biased towards the positive pole of experience, and the information presented is judged in a more favorable light. In contrast, when the right hemisphere is stimulated, the internal feeling state is biased towards the more negative pole of experience, and the information presented is then judged in a more negative light.

Thus, another possible explanation of the finding that certain kinds of pictures are preferred when the important content is on the right is that when the placement of information draws the attention of the viewer toward the right half of space, the left hemisphere becomes activated, causing the picture to be perceived as more pleasing.

Although the right-biased content effect has been found quite consistently for vacation slides and advertisements, it has not held as well for recognized works of art. Studies similar to the ones described above but using famous paintings have not found them to be perceived as more pleasing when the asymmetric content is on the right (Freimuth & Wapner, 1979; McLaughlin et al., 1983). In fact, Swartz and Hewitt (1970) found that right-handed subjects show a small but significant preference for famous paintings in their original orientation over the mirror image, and Mead and McLaughlin (1992) found a preference for paintings in which the greatest weight was on the left side of the composition. Furthermore, artists do not appear to show a tendency to place important or emotional content more towards the right than the left in famous paintings (W. Heller, unpublished data). In this study, there were no differences in the relative location of the important or emotional content in positive, negative, or neutral paintings, nor were there consistent patterns in either across the three groups of paintings.

The first two hypotheses described are not particularly helpful in explaining why the effect should be less apparent for famous paintings than for other kinds of compositions. One would expect that a balancing of the stimulus salience, or a matching of material and hemisphere, would be desirable regardless of the nature of the composition. The third hypothesis may be slightly more promising. Possibly, famous paintings are preferred in their original orientation, and are not judged as asymmetric in location of important or emotional content, because the aesthetic impact of a good painting is not dependent upon a simple appeal to a more positive emotional state, one that is perhaps associated with a more active left hemisphere. A truly talented artist may have little desire to produce an optimistic, cheerful experience; rather, the artist's skill may lie in his or her ability to arouse surprise, shock, wonder, or fear. Such an artist would thus have little desire to differentially stimulate the left hemisphere of the viewer. He or she would be interested in provoking a more complex blend of emotions.

IV. SUMMARY

This chapter has reviewed the evidence that various aspects of brain organization play a role in both the creation of art and the appreciation of art. This is, of course, not surprising. The brain is not a photographic plate that registers the world "as it is": perceptual experience is constructed by an active process that involves sensory information, memories of past experiences, and motivations and goals in the present (Levy, 1988). Since each hemisphere of the brain has unique ways of processing sensory information, of representing that information in memory, and of evaluating that information with regard to current goals and situations, it seems completely predictable that each would participate in art creation and appreciation in different ways.

We have reviewed the ways that each hemisphere is involved in particular aspects of the creative process, and seen that damage to the brain can influence artistic creation in many ways. The right hemisphere seems to be involved in understanding visuospatial relationships, in attending to the left side of space, and in understanding the way objects are related to each other in a real-world context. This side of the brain is also important in the comprehension and expression of emotional information. In contrast, the left hemisphere seems to be involved in manual control of the right hand, in programming motor activities, and possibly in aspects of conceptual understanding that are relevant to art creation. We have also seen, however, that meaningful artistic creation is not dependent on either hemisphere, and that artists can continue to be productive despite damage to one or the other side of the brain that causes them to lose specific skills.

We have also seen that the composition of a work of art may be influenced by asymmetric brain activity, and that people respond differently to pictures depending on where the information is located. The possibility was raised that the emotional state of the artist might influence the way he or she composes a work of art. At the same time, the location of the content in the work of art may affect the brain activity of the viewer in ways that are still matters of speculation. In all likelihood, there is a complex interaction of neuropsychological factors that are involved in both the creation and the perception of a work of art. As suggested, the artists' emotional state may influence the way he or she conceptualizes the spatial representation of the subject matter; the way this representation is depicted will in turn be guided by the artist's personal experience of the work as it unfolds, always with an eye to the communicative impact of the developing work. Thus, the neuropsychology of the producer (the artist) will interact with the neuropsychology of the perceiver to generate, through the skillful and intentional manipulation of form, space, structure, and movement, a unique and complex emotional and aesthetic experience.

Acknowledgments

The research described herein would not have been possible without the assistance of Marie Ifollo, art teacher for the Park Forest School District; the librarians, teachers, and children at the University of Chicago Laboratory School; Don Seiden, professor at The School of the Art Institute of Chicago. I am indebted to Marie T. Banich and Jerre Levy for their collaboration and invaluable input, to Connie Boronat and Linde Brocato for helpful discussions, to Andrea Gellin Shindler for organizing the "Art and the Brain" symposium at the Art Institute of Chicago, and to Dahlia Zaidel for her editorial support.

References

Ahern, G. L., & Schwartz, G. E. (1979). Differential lateralization for positive versus negative emotion. *Neuropsychologia, 17,* 693–698.
Arnheim, R. (1974). *Art and visual perception.* Berkeley: University of California Press.
Banich, M. T., Heller, W., & Levy, J. (1989). Aesthetic preference and picture asymmetries. *Cortex, 25,* 187–196.
Beaumont, J. G. (1985). Lateral organization and aesthetic preference: The importance of peripheral visual asymmetries. *Neuropsychologia, 23,* 103–113.

Belleza, T., Rappaport, M., Hopkins, H. K., & Hall, K. (1979). Visual scanning and matching dysfunction in brain-damaged patients with drawing impairment. *Cortex, 15,* 19–36.

Borod, J., Goodglass, H., & Kaplan, E. (1980). Normative data on the Boston Diagnostic Aphasia Examination Parietal Lobe Battery, and the Boston Naming Test. *Journal of Clinical Neuropsychology, 2,* 209–216.

Brownell, H. H., Simpson, T. L., Bihrle, A. M., Potter, H. H., & Gardner, H. (1990). Appreciation of metaphoric alternative word meanings by left and right brain-damaged patients. *Neuropsychologia, 28,* 375–383.

Davidson, R. J. (1984). Affect, cognition, and hemispheric specialization. In C. E. Izard, J. Kagan, & R. Zajonc (Eds.), (pp. 320–365). *Emotion, cognition, and behavior.* New York: Cambridge University Press.

Davidson, R. J. (1992). Anterior cerebral asymmetry and the nature of emotion. *Brain and Cognition, 20,* 125–151.

Davidson, R. J., Schwartz, G. E., Saron, C., Bennett, J., & Goleman, D. J. (1979). Frontal versus parietal EEG asymmetry during positive and negative affect. *Psychophysiology, 16,* 202–203.

Frederiks, J. A. M. (1963). Constructional apraxia and cerebral dominance. *Psychiatria, Neurologia, Neurochirurgia, 66,* 522–530.

Freimuth, M. & Wapner, S. (1979). The influence of lateral organization in the evaluation of paintings. *British Journal of Psychology, 70,* 211–218.

Gardner, H., Brownell, H. H., Wapner, W., & Michelow, D. (1983). Missing the point: The role of the right hemisphere in the processing of complex linguistic materials. In E. Perecman (Ed.), *Cognitive processing in the right hemisphere* (pp. 169–191). New York: Academic Press.

Glucksberg, S., & Keysar, B. (1990). Understanding metaphorical comparisons: Beyond similarity. *Psychological Review, 97,* 3–18.

Goldberg, E., & Costa, L. D. (1981). Hemispheric differences in the acquisition and use of descriptive systems. *Brain and Language, 14,* 144–173.

Grossman, M. (1988). Drawing deficits in brain-damaged patients' freehand pictures. *Brain and Cognition, 8,* 192–213.

Heilman, K. M., Watson, R. T., & Valenstein, E. (1985). Neglect and related disorders. In K. M. Heilman & E. Valenstein (Eds.), (pp. 243–293). *Clinical neuropsychology,* 2nd Edition. New York: Oxford University Press.

Heller, W. (1986). *Cerebral organization of emotional function in children.* Doctoral dissertation, University of Chicago.

Heller, W. (1987). Lateralization of emotional content in children's drawings. *Scientific Proceedings of the Annual Meeting of the American Academy of Child and Adolescent Psychiatry, 3,* 63.

Heller, W. (1988). Asymmetry of emotional judgements in children. *Journal of Clinical and Experimental Neuropsychology, 10,* 36.

Heller, W. (1990). The neuropsychology of emotion: Developmental patterns and implications for psychopathology. In N. Stein, B. L. Leventhal, & T. Trabasso (Eds.), *Psychological and biological approaches to emotion* (pp. 167–211). Hillsdale, NJ: Erlbaum.

Heller, W. (1991). New territory: Creativity and brain injury. *Creative Woman, 11,* 16–18.

Heller, W., & Levy, J. (1981). Perception and expression of emotion in right-handers and left-handers. *Neuropsychologia, 19,* 263–272.

Kimura, D., & Faust, R. (1987). Spontaneous drawing in an unselected sample of patients with unilateral brain damage. In D. Ottoson (Ed.), *Duality and unity of the brain: Unified functioning and specialisation of the hemispheres* (pp. 114–146). New York: Plenum.

Kinsbourne, M. (1974). Direction of gaze and distribution of cerebral thought processes. *Neuropsychologia, 12,* 279–282.

Kirk, A., & Kertesz, A. (1989). Hemispheric contributions to drawing. *Neuropsychologia, 27,* 881–886.

Kolb, B., & Whishaw, I. Q. (1990). *Fundamentals of Human Neuropsychology* (Third ed.). New York: W. H. Freeman and Company.

Lakoff, G. (1987). *Women, fire, and dangerous things: What categories reveal about the mind* (pp. 296, 380–415). Chicago: University of Chicago Press.

Lakoff, G., & Johnson, M. (1980). *Metaphors we live by.* Chicago: University of Chicago Press.

Larrabee, G. J., Kane, R. L., Morrow, L., & Goldstein, G. (1982). *Differential drawing size associated with unilateral brain damage.* Paper presented at the 10th annual meeting of the International Neuropsychological Society, Pittsburgh.

Levy, J. (1976). Lateral dominance and aesthetic preference. *Neuropsychologia, 14,* 431–445.

Levy, J. (1988). Cerebral asymmetry and aesthetic experience. In I. Rentschler, B. Herzberger, & D. Epstein (Eds.), *Beauty and the brain* (pp. 219–242). Basel: Birkhaeuser.

Lezak, M. D. (1983). *Neuropsychological assessment* (2nd ed.). New York: Oxford University Press.

McFie, J., & Zangwill, O. L. (1960). Visual constructive disabilities associated with lesions of the left cerebral hemisphere. *Brain, 83,* 242–260.

McLaughlin, J. P., Dean, P., & Stanley, P. (1983). Aesthetic preference in dextrals and sinistrals. *Neuropsychologia, 21,* 147–153.

Mead, A. M., & McLaughlin, J. P. (1992). The roles of handedness and stimulus asymmetry in aesthetic preference. *Brain and Cognition, 20,* 300–307.

Myslobodsky, M. S., & Horesh, N. (1978). Bilateral electrodermal activity in depressive patients. *Biological Psychiatry, 6,* 111–120.

Piercy, M., Hécaen, H., & Ajuriacuerra, J. (1960). Constructional apraxia associated with unilateral cerebral lesions. Left and right sides cases compared. *Brain, 83,* 225–242.

Rourke, B. P. (1989). The syndrome of nonverbal learning disabilities: Developmental manifestations in neurological disease, disorder, and dysfunction. *Clinical Neuropsychologist, 2,* 293–330.

Schaffer, C. E., Davidson, R. J., & Saron, C. (1983). Frontal and parietal EEG asymmetry in depressed and non-depressed subjects. *Biological Psychiatry, 18,* 753–762.

Schweiger, A. (1985). Harmony of the spheres and the hemispheres: The arts and hemispheric specialization. In D. F. Benson & E. Zaidel (Eds.), *The dual brain: Hemispheric specialization in humans* (pp. 359–373). New York: Guilford Press.

Swartz, P., & Hewitt, D. (1970). Lateral organization in pictures and aesthetic preference. *Perceptual and Motor Skills, 30,* 991–1007.

Tucker, D. M., Stenslie, C. E., Roth, R. S., & Shearer, S. L. (1981). Right frontal lobe activation and right hemisphere performance: Decrement during a depressed mood. *Archives of General Psychiatry, 38,* 169–174.

Warrington, E. K., James, M., & Kinsbourne, M. (1966). Drawing disability in relation to laterality of cerebral lesion. *Brain, 89,* 53–82.

Warrington, E. K., & Taylor, A. M. (1973). The contribution of the right parietal lobe to object recognition. *Cortex, 9,* 152–164.

Winner, E. (1982). *Invented worlds: The psychology of the arts.* Cambridge, MA: Harvard University Press.

Zaidel, D. W. (1988). Hemi-field asymmetries in memory for incongruous scenes. *Cortex, 24,* 231–244.

Zaidel, D. W., & Kasher, A. (1989). Hemispheric memory for surrealistic versus realistic paintings. *Cortex, 25,* 617–641.

CHAPTER 13

Sex Differences in the Brain

Nicole Yvette Weekes

I. INTRODUCTION

A. Introduction to Chapter and Theories

In the last several decades, many theories have supported sex differences in both cognition and neuropsychological functioning. Three of the best supported of these deal with sex differences in cognitive competence, hemispheric specialization, and interhemispheric relations. Respectively, they include (1) male superiority for visuospatial and mathematical tasks and female superiority for verbal fluency, perceptual speed, and manual dexterity (Harshmann, Hampson, & Berenbaum, 1983; Maccoby & Jacklin, 1974); (2) greater hemispheric specialization primarily for language and secondarily for other cognitive functions in males (Bryden, 1989; Harshmann, 1991; McGlone, 1980); and (3) greater functional connectivity between the two hemispheres in females (Bryden, 1989; E. Zaidel, Aboitiz, Clarke, Kaiser, and Matteson, in press; Potter and Graves, 1988, but see Burton, Pepperrell, & Stredwick, 1991).

Although each of these theories is based on converging evidence from the fields of cognition, neuropsychology, and neuroanatomy, there is still reason for conservatism in our interpretation of the supporting evidence. In particular, causal connections between anatomical and behavioral sex differences are often posited by researchers when evidence for only one of these two types of sex differences is directly supported by their data or any related research. An early lesson in empiricism is that *coexistence does not causation make,* that is, the coexistence of two phenomena is not sufficient to prove causality.

One of the goals of this chapter, then, is to explore both the implied and empirically supported relationship between anatomical and behavioral sex differences. It is for this reason that a major portion is dedicated to a review of specific evidence supporting sex differences in cognition and hemispheric functioning, exploring in particular what is known about the etiology of these differences. Let us begin with a review of the way in which the mammalian organism becomes sexually differentiated, considering the development of the gonads and brain separately. The remainder of the chapter will focus on behavioral and anatomical sex differences as well as alternate theories and classifications of individual differences in neuropsychological research.

B. Sexual Differentiation in Mammals

1. Gonadal Development

In the sexual differentiation of humans, there are two important types of premordial (or preformed) tissue. Some tissue is bipotential, and therefore has the ability to form either set of sex-specific anatomical structures. Conversely, other tissue is unipotential and can only form the specific structures of one of the two sexes. In sexual development, these two types of premordial tissues give rise to three specific types of anatomical structures: (1) the gonads, (2) the internal genitalia, or (3) the external genitalia. Although the development of these structures involves some rather complex activities, a review of the crucial developmental landmarks will suffice for the current purposes.

Males and females differ in the constitution of their sex chromosomes. In males, these are X and Y, whereas in females, they are X and X. The first steps in sexual differentiation are initiated by the Y chromosome. The absence of such a chromosome results in the development of the female phenotype or external physical characteristics. As we will see, however, the presence of the Y chromosome by no means guarantees normal male development. On the Y chromosome there is a gene referred to as the testis determining factor. The presence of this gene determines whether testes, the male gonads, will develop. The absence of testis determining factor, on the other hand, allows the bipotential gonad to become an ovary.

If testes develop, they produce two hormones: (1) testosterone and (2) Mullerian regressing factor. In its undifferentiated state, the fetus has two sets of ducts that connect the gonads to the external genitalia, the Mullerian and Wolffian ducts. Mullerian regressing factor causes regression of the Mullerian ducts. Testosterone, on the other hand, causes development of the Wolffian ducts. The absence of Mullerian regressing factor and testosterone, the environment in the normally developing female, results in the opposite pattern of duct development—causing development of the Mullerian ducts and regression of the Wolffian ducts. Wolffian duct development gives rise to the epididymis, vas deferens, and seminal vesicles in males. The penis and scrotum result from testosterone's effect on the genital skin. Mullerian duct development gives rise to the fallopian tubes, uterus, and inner vagina in females. The genital skin develops into the clitoris, outer vagina, and the labia when testosterone is absent (Wilson, George, & Griffin, 1981).

While the developmental landmarks discussed above represent the normal sexual differentiation, many factors can alter this course of development and these may occur at different stages of sexual differentiation. Consider first genetic mutations. Turner's syndrome results when an organism receives only one chromosome, and is genetically labeled XO to denote this chromosomal absence. Instances of YO have not been described and are thought to lead to fetal miscarriage or embryonic fatality. The XO individual is phenotypically female, although ovarian development is often abnormal. Turner's syndrome is also characterized by mental retardation.

Klinefelter's syndrome, on the other hand, results when an organism receives multiple copies of one of the two chromosomes. The chromosomes of an individual with this syndrome can either be XXY or XYY. In either case, the Klinefelter's individual manifests a masculine phenotype with fairly normal testicular development but also with sterility. As is the case with Turner's syndrome, Klinefelter's syndrome can lead to mental retardation although it is far less common. Another chromosome-related mutation occurs with an X-dependent dysfunction of the androgen receptor. A genetic male (XY) results, but the individual is insensitive to androgen in a syndrome aptly named androgen insensitivity. Because testis-determining factor and Mullerian regressing factor are unaffected, testes develop and the Mullerian ducts begin to regress, but the insensitivity of the receptors to the testosterone secreted by the testes generates female forms of the internal and external genitalia. Mental processes are not necessarily disturbed in this disorder.

Congenital adrenal hyperplasia or pseudohermaphroditism results from the absence of an enzyme that converts androstenedione to cortisol in the adrenal cortex. Without the cortisol necessary for an important negative feedback mechanism, the adrenal gland enlarges (known as hyperplasia) and enhancement of androgen secretion ensues. Again, without the negative feedback mechanism that cortisol would regularly help supply, aberrant androgen secretion continues until treated. In females, the external genitalia will enlarge and may begin to resemble masculine genitalia. Not only is mental ability typically unimpaired, but IQ scores in congenital adrenal hyperplasia are actually higher on average than in the general population (Money & Lewis, 1966).

To this point in our discussion of sexual differentiation, we have primarily reviewed the role of genetics and hormonal availability and receptivity on the development of the gonads and genitalia. Let us consider next the role of hormones on the development of both the animal and human brain.

2. Cerebral Development

Prior to discussing the specific empirical evidence supporting sex differences in the brain structure, let us review the general effects of hormones on the mammalian organism. Hormones have two sets of effects on their target tissues, organizational and activational. The clearest examples of organizational effects are those in which the perinatal environment results in permanent, structural changes that are often different in the two sexes due to differences in the activity and availability of specific hormones. On a cellular level, these organizational effects may result from the action of a particular hormone or set of hormones on (1) proliferation, (2) axonal growth and (3) survival of regional neurons. There are several lines of evidence that support the hypothesis that organizational effects underlie both sex differences in neuroanatomy and in sexual behavior (see Hines & Gorski, 1985, for a review).

Hormones also have another group of effects on the tissues of the organism. These are known as activational effects, and refer to transient changes (usually demonstrated in adulthood) that diminish or disappear if the hormone underlying the effect is not readily available. These will be discussed later in this chapter.

The strongest support for the role of hormones on the organization of the brain came with the discovery of the sexually dimorphic region in the preoptic area of the hypothalamus of the rat (Gorski, Gordon, Shryne, & Southam, 1978). Gorski and his colleagues demonstrated that this region is larger in males than in females and its size is under hormonal control. A female treated perinatally with testosterone will demonstrate an increase in the size of the sexually dimorphic region comparable to that seen in the normal males. Behaviorally, the female will begin to demonstrate an increase in mounting, a typically masculine sexual behavior. The testosterone-treated female will also demonstrate a decrease in lordosis, a typically feminine sexual posture that allows the animal to be receptive to mounting. In the same way, a castrated (testosterone-depleted) male will demonstrate both an anatomical decrease in the size of the sexually dimorphic nucleus and a behavioral decrease in typical mounting behavior given that the rats are sexually naive. While these behavioral effects on sexual behavior were originally thought to result from changes in hormone availability, more recent studies have directly implicated the sexually dimorphic nucleus in these effects. (De Jonge, Louwerse, Ooms, Evers, & van de Poll, 1989).

Another anatomical sex difference involving hormones in animals for which corresponding behavioral concomitants have been established involves the neurological song apparatus in canaries and zebra finch (Nottebohm & Arnold, 1976). Because song represents the mating call specifically of the male of the species, females rarely sing and the nuclei that control song are severely diminished or absent. Like the sexually dimorphic nucleus in male rats, the size of these "song nuclei" in songbirds is hormone dependent. Further, if the male songbird is denied access to the necessary hormones, not only do the nuclei diminish in size, but song becomes fragmented or disappears. These findings remain two of only a few examples in the literature where a strong connection between anatomy and behavior is directly supported by the data.

Several sexually dimorphic regions in the brain have been discovered for which behavioral concomitants are either unclear or appear contradictory. The spinal nucleus of the bulbocavernosus, which aids in motoric control of the penis, is one of these (Breedlove & Arnold, 1983). Although this nucleus is also present in the human, its sexual differentiation is both more obvious and more easily manipulated in the rat. Although the cells of this sexually dimorphic nucleus are present in the female, and innervate the anal sphincter, they are more abundant and larger in the male of the species. Studies of this nucleus have been useful in helping researchers to identify the cellular mechanisms responsible for the organizational effect of hormones on anatomical dimorphisms. Through these studies, for example, researchers have been able to establish the role of testosterone in preventing cell death.

An example of sex differences in anatomy for which behavioral evidence is contradictory is the sex difference in cortical hemispheric asymmetry reported by Diamond, Johnson, and Ehlert (1979). Through their research, a greater right–hemisphere thickness in male rats was discovered along with the absence of just such an asymmetry in females (see Section II.B., Cerebral Development and the Role of Hormones). This finding led to an exploration of the extent to which anatomical sex differences are under hormonal control. By removing the testes of male rats at birth, Diamond was able to restrict testosterone availability and demonstrate a loss of this anatomical asymmetry in the experimental group. Similar studies in females ovariectomized at birth, involving a loss of estrogen availability, led to an anatomical pattern similar to that of the control males. However, the extent to which this finding is related to any specific behavior is unclear. Indeed, much of the behavioral data available from Diamond's control rats demonstrate greater behavioral asymmetries in females with regard to both paw and circling preferences (Hines & Gorski, 1985) than males.

In recent years corresponding dimorphic regions in both the hypothalamus and cortical regions with similar dependence on hormonal environment have also been located in humans (Forger & Breedlove, 1986; Swaab & Fliers, 1985). However, methodological issues have restricted the extent of experimentation into etiological matters of interest.

II. SEX DIFFERENCES IN COGNITION, HEMISPHERIC SPECIALIZATION, AND INTERHEMISPHERIC INTERACTIONS: A PROGRESSIVE ETIOLOGICAL MODEL

For many, it is impossible to discuss sex differences in cognitive capability without concurrently exploring sex differences in hemispheric specialization. This connection arises from a long-held belief that the latter somehow gives rise to the former. Further, in a related fashion, the causal relationship between specialization and cognitive capability is usually tied to the notion that functional hemispheric specialization is somehow neuroanatomically determined. Let us explore these assumptions systematically. In terms of sex differences, the connection between the assumptions (that specialization gives rise to cognitive aptitudes and results from neuroanatomy) may assume the following: (1) that a different genetic and/or hormonal environment begets different hemispheric development; (2) that different neuroanatomy (i.e., hemispheric development) begets different hemispheric specialization; and (3) that this different hemispheric specialization begets different cognitive aptitudes. This developmental progression is a subtle but pervasive assumption in neuropsychology, even as it requires a bit more "beget"-ing than we can empirically support. The causal connection between cognition, hemispheric specialization, and perinatal environment has limited support thus far and deserves further exploration.

A. Cerebral Development and the Role of Hormones

In a discussion of the role of hormones in cerebral development, organizational effects of hormones become crucial. In particular, perinatal hormones are proposed to affect the anatomical organization of the cerebral cortex. Let us begin by exploring the evidence for specialized, anatomical development of the cerebral hemispheres and related sex differences. An examination of the evidence for the role of different hormonal environments in this organizational development will follow.

Although Lenneberg (1966) believed the cerebral hemispheres to be equipotential based on young children's early recovery from hemispheric infarct, most recent research supports the notion that some form of hemispheric specialization is present from the first months of life (see Levine, 1983, and Witelson and Pallie, 1973, for reviews). One of the most important issues in this reevaluation of equipotentiality is the recognition that recovery of function may indicate enhanced plasticity (or ability to reorganize) without necessarily supporting a developmental absence of specialization (Bullock, Liederman, & Todorovic, 1987). Although long ago Broca (1865) argued for a left-to-right gradient in development, there is also evidence for the reverse pattern of development. Probably the strongest piece of evidence for the right-to-left gradient is that right-hemisphere fissures (or envelopings in the brain) develop 1 to 2 wk earlier than the corresponding left-hemisphere structures. Evidence for the right-left gradient (along with other developmental gradients) is also well supported in the behavioral data (Best, Hoffman, & Glanville, 1982; Witelson, 1989). Still other reports, including that from an EEG study (Thatcher, Walker, & Guidace, 1987), argue against a strict hemisphere-to-hemisphere gradient in either direction. Instead, the results support a left-to-right gradient for frontal-occipital and frontal-temporal development, and a right-to-left gradient for the development of the frontal pole.

The strongest piece of evidence that hormonal environment affects the development of the cerebral hemispheres comes from Diamond's work on rats (1979; Diamond, Dowling, & Johnson, 1981; Diamond, 1991) with sex differences in cortical densities. However, although the finding is usually taken as support for larger right than left hemispheres in male rats and the opposite pattern in females (both of which have been shown to be reversible with proper perinatal hormonal environment), the original result is both more specific and more limited. The greater right-hemisphere density in male rats actually results from an increased thickness in posterior cortical regions of 17, 18a, and 39, as identified by Krieg (1946) and has recently been demonstrated to result from inhibited growth of the left hemisphere rather than enhanced growth of the right (Stewart and Kolb, 1988). No other regions of the right hemisphere exceeded those of the left in density in either sex. Furthermore, the increased left-hemisphere density usually attributed to the female rats in Diamond's study does not reach significance.

Although compelling, the findings of Diamond et al. (1981) must be interpreted with caution. It is misleading to say that males have a greater right hemisphere than females without proper qualification. What does seem reasonable to conclude from the results of Diamond et al. (1979) and Diamond et al. (1981) is that although hormones do appear to affect hemispheric development, the effect (1) is specific to the posterior cortical regions, (2) has not been demonstrated to correlate with any specific behavioral effect, and (3) remains to be shown in humans.

B. Hemispheric Specialization and the Role of Cerebral Development

Consider next the evidence for sex differences in hemispheric specialization and the possibility that these differences result from different cerebral development. Two general types of lateralized tasks have been used extensively for these purposes. The strongest evidence comes from dichotic listening tests in which men manifest a greater right ear advantage for verbal stimuli and tend towards a greater left ear advantage for nonverbal stimuli, including music and emotional expression (Bryden, 1989; Harshmann, 1991; Lake and Bryden, 1976). Some lateralized visual tasks have also shown reliable sex differences, but they are far more difficult to obtain. Again, when such differences do exist they tend to demonstrate a greater laterality effect in males than in females, especially for verbal material.

There are many theories to account for these sex differences in hemispheric specialization. Grey and Buffery (1971) posited that females were more specialized for nonverbal functions because of earlier establishment of left-hemisphere language. This hypothesis, however, has received little support from data from either normal or brain-damaged populations (see Galaburda, Rosen, & Sherman, 1990). However, a rather contradictory theory, that females are generally less specialized than males, has been well received and extensively supported by empirical studies. Both Levy (1969, 1976) and McGlone (1980), for instance, have argued that females possess both more nonverbal skills in the left hemisphere and more verbal skills in the right hemisphere than the average male. There are also those who believe that males are more specialized for some skills and females are more specialized for others. This *complementary specialization* view is espoused by Hines and Gorski (1985) among others (Zaidel et al., in press) who note that although behavioral studies tend to demonstrate greater laterality in males, evidence from other measures, such as handedness and cerebral blood flow, supports greater laterality in females.

As we will discuss later, although the theory of decreased specialization in females has become widely accepted, there remain many who believe that hemispheric specialization is generally constant across sex. One proponent of this view is Kimura (1983, 1987) who posits that the two sexes differ in intrahemispheric, rather than interhemispheric, organization of both language and motor programming skills. Others (Hiscock, Hiscock, & Inch, 1991) believe that no reliable differences have been established either inter- or intrahemispherically. We will review some of the data from brain-damaged populations that support these varying views in the next section.

In terms of the connection between cerebral (hemispheric) development and hemispheric specialization, Geschwind and Levitsky (1968) have demonstrated that the planum temporale, which lies along the Sylvian fissure in the temporal lobe and is assumed to be important in language, is larger on the left side in 65% of brains tested with the left side planum temporale, on average, being 33% larger. Further, Wada, Clarke, and Hamm (1975) have reported that females in their adult series were more likely to demonstrate a reversed asymmetry, relative both to adult males and to infant brains of either sex (see also Galaburada, Corsiglia, Rosen, & Sherman, 1987). However, although the planum temporale is thought to be important for verbal processing, the incidence of a larger left planum temporale (65%) does not parallel the incidence of left-hemispheric specialization for language predicted by the Wada sodium amytal test, results of which indicate left-hemisphere specialization in close to 97% in right-handers.

C. Cognition and the Role of Hemispheric Specialization

Of all the instances of sex differences that have been reported in the literature, most researchers today believe only a few of them to be well supported by empirical data. Harshmann et al. (1983), for instance, report only four reliable differences between the two sexes, three of which involve cognitive performance. They are (1) superior visuospatial skill in males, (2) superior mathematic skill in males, and (3) superior verbal fluency in females. Furthermore, Ferguson and Maccoby (1966) have argued that the male superiority in visuospatial skill is far more reliable than the female superiority in verbal skill. In terms of hemispheric specialization, most reviews of the literature conclude that males appear to be, somewhat, more specialized for language and possibly other cognitive skills than females, although the data is less convincing than that reported from cognitive task performance. What has remained a puzzle is what the connection is between these sex differences and hemispheric specialization.

In order to elucidate this role, Geschwind and Galaburda (1985) have proposed a relatively new theory, namely, that the natural progression of hemispheric development coupled with differences in the availability of and receptivity to hormones in the two sexes accounts for individual differences in both cognition and hemispheric specialization. Specifically, this differential development is proposed to give rise to left hemispheric specialization for language and handedness (right-handedness). When the "usual" progression of development is altered, given increased levels of testosterone, an increase in right-hemisphere functioning results. This enhanced right-hemisphere ability promotes superior visuospatial skill while also increasing the incidence of left-handedness.

Like Geschwind and Galaburda (1985), both Kinsbourne (1970) and Levy (1969, 1976) have suggested that language specialization is related to spatial and verbal abilities. Levy proposes that both types of cognitive tasks are maximized when there is dramatic left-hemisphere specialization of verbal skills and right-hemisphere specialization of nonverbal skills. In the case of females, some language ability is proposed to be aberrantly represented in the right hemisphere, leading to a condition known as *crowding* or *invasion,* which in this case optimizes language skills at the expense of spatial skills. Although compelling, this theory does not account for the interrelationship between specific sex differences demonstrated in cognition and specific sex differences in hemispheric specialization. Moreover, the incidence of aphasia following right-hemisphere damage is not greater in females than in males (Kimura, 1987).

Theoretically, the connection between hemispheric specialization and cognition can be most clearly understood from brain-damaged populations where clear distinctions between clinical outcomes in the two sexes are often demonstrated. The classic interpretation of these findings is that the behavioral result of cerebral damage (whether the product of lobectomy or vascular infarct, damage to the blood supply of the brain) depends more on the side of damage in males than in females. In males, for instance, left-hemisphere damage more often leads to language or language-related deficits, whereas right-hemisphere damage results in visuospatial or nonverbal deficits. In females, on the other hand, the resulting deficits tend to be less severe and less dependent on location (i.e., side or hemisphere of damage). This has been taken as evidence that females have a more diffuse (or bilateral) representation of cognitive functions than males (see Lansdell & Uberach, 1965; McGlone, 1978).

In McGlone's studies (1978), this sex difference is demonstrated by differences in Wecshler Adult Intelligence Scale (WAIS) Verbal and Performance mean IQ scores after damage. In this study, men with left-sided infarct had a significantly lower verbal IQ than did the other three groups (i.e., males with right-sided infarct, females with left-sided infarct, and females with right-sided infarct). Females with left-sided infarct, on the other hand, performed "well within the average range" on the same measure. Performance IQ scores did not differ by classification of sex or side of lesion. Likewise, in Lansdell and Uberach's (1965) work with unilateral temporal lobectomy patients, males with left-sided surgery were the only group to manifest significant deficits on a proverb comprehension task.

Together, the findings from diverse brain-damaged populations have been taken as evidence that males have a more lateralized representation of verbal and other cognitive capabilities than females. However, Inglis and Lawson (1982) undertook an extensive metanalysis, and concluded that although males and females are differently lateralized, this sex difference after brain damage results primarily from a decline in *both* language (WAIS—Verbal IQ) and spatial (WAIS—Performance IQ) skill following left-hemisphere damage in females. Only verbal IQ was reported to decline following similar damage in males. The deficit in performance IQ following left-hemisphere infarct is proposed to result from the use of verbal strategies in spatial processing or from bilateral representation of spatial processing, so that damage to one hemisphere is sufficient to impair performance. Although right-hemisphere damage resulted in a significant decline in Performance IQ in males, females showed no such deficit in either scale (Verbal and Performance) subtest following right-hemisphere damage. The results from both sets of studies support the existence of sex differences in hemispheric specialization. What differentiates the studies is the profile of localization of specific functions in the two sexes.

In the time since Lansdell and McGlone's classic studies, awareness of the importance of determining the specific *site* of infarct within a hemisphere has increased. The importance of such a determination is demonstrated by Kimura (1987), who argues that sex differences in behavioral deficits following cerebral infarct are the result of *intra*-hemispheric rather than *inter* hemispheric differences in organization. A reanalysis of McGlone (1986, 1992) also supports this view.

The brain-damage research highlights another issue regarding the relationship between sex differences in cognition and laterality. Consider the fact that performance on visuospatial tasks, the most prevalent sex difference function in cognitive processing, has been shown in more recent studies (McGlone, 1986; Kimura, 1987) *not* to demonstrate reliable sex differences following unilateral cerebral infarcts. This places limits on the extent to which cognitive sex differences can be explained through sex differences in anatomy. Even without the controversies in the brain-damage studies, evidence of different optimal specialization patterns for verbal and visuospatial tasks are needed in order to explain the finding that females are less lateralized and excel at verbal tasks, whereas males are more lateralized and excel at visuospatial tasks.

D. Hemispheric Specialization and Cognition and the Role of Interhemispheric Interactions

The human corpus callosum, the principal band of fibers connecting the left and right hemispheres, is thought to play many roles, including but not limited to the following: (1) sensory transfer, (2) reciprocal hemispheric inhibition, (3) governing development of hemispheric organization, and (4) "attentional and regulatory functions involved in sensory processing, motoric action, emotion and cognition" of the hemispheres (Levy, 1983, p. 4). Morphologically, the corpus callosum is divided into five regions, anterior to posterior: (1) the rostrum, (2) the genu, (3) the body, (4) the isthmus, and (5) the splenium, and is thought to transfer different types of sensory information through these different regions.

Consider next what is known about the corpus callosum with respect to anatomical sex differences and how they help to elucidate behavioral sex differences in hemispheric specialization. Similar to the assumption that sex differences in hemispheric specialization give rise to sex differences in cognition is the assertion that sex differences in callosal interactions give rise to sex differences in hemispheric specialization. This would amend the second

progression discussed above, that hemispheric development begets specialization, to include the possibility that the corpus callosum is involved either
in the anatomical organization of hemispheric specialization or in functionally contributing to differential laterality patterns most often attributed
to hemispheric specialization.

Although a role for steroid hormones in the development of the corpus
callosum is supported by a number of animal studies (Denenberg et al.,
1991; Fitch, Crowell, Schrott, and Denenberg, 1991), very little is known
about the direct effect of these hormones on callosal development in humans. It is however, accepted that there are no reliable sex differences in
the absolute size of the callosum at any time during development, from fetal
life to maturity (Witelson & Kigar, 1988). What researchers have found,
however, are both anatomical sex differences in specific regions of the corpus callosum and differences in the correlation between specific callosal
regions and the sizes of specific cortical regions. In one of the first definitive
studies of sex differences in the corpus callosum, de Lacoste-Utamsing and
Holloway (1982) found females to have a more bulbous splenium than males
(see also Holloway & de Lacoste, 1986). Similarly, based on postmortem
studies, Witelson (1989), for instance, has demonstrated that the size of the
isthmus (relative to both total callosal area and overall cerebral weight) is
larger in females than in consistently right-handed males. Others have
found a similar relationship between minimal callosal body width and sex
(Byne, Bleier, & Houston, 1988; Clarke, 1990). In a related study, Aboitiz,
Scheibel, Fisher, and Zaidel (1992) report a significant negative correlation
between Sylvian fissure asymmetries and total numbers of fibers in the
isthmus of males, and in the anterior splenium in females.

Clarke (1990), for the first time, has reported that although the size of the
isthmus is negatively correlated with behavioral laterality in males (as measured by a primed lexical decision task), females show the opposite effect
(i.e., greater isthmus size being positively correlated with the same behavioral measure). Still, the meaning of these correlations remains unclear.

Although the existence of sex differences is supported at every stage of
the progressive model outlined earlier, the notion that the specific hormonal
sex differences discussed cause the specific hemispheric, callosal, and cognitive sex differences discussed remains less well supported. As we have
stated, hypotheses of causal connections between anatomical and behavioral
sex differences suffer from numerous downfalls. Paramount among these
problems are the following: (1) one of the strongest anatomical sex differences (increased right-hemisphere density in male rats) only correlates with
contradictory behavioral effects, (2) the strongest evidence for sex differences in human cognition (visuospatial skill) shows weak effects in terms of
differences in hemispheric specialization (based on brain-damaged popula-

tions); and (3) the degree and incidence of behavioral hemispheric specialization for language is not well predicted by anatomical measures.

III. ALTERNATIVE EXPLANATIONS OF SEX DIFFERENCES

Although theories of differential hemispheric specialization and interhemispheric interactions are most often used to explain sex differences in neuropsychological functioning, other explanations remain plausible. We will briefly discuss three of these: (1) Waber's Growth Rate Hypothesis, (2) individual differences in cognitive strategy or field dependence, and (3) individual differences in arousal.

A. Waber's Growth Rate Hypothesis

The Waber Growth Rate Hypothesis (Waber, 1977) posits that individual differences in neuropsychological functioning that have routinely been attributed to sex alone may be better explained by an inter relationship between sex and maturational rate (see also Vrbanic & Bryden, 1989). In terms of cognition, Waber notes that late-maturating people perform better than earlier-maturing people on spatial tasks, regardless of sex. Although this spatial superiority is most often attributed to males, this research indicates that the decisive factor may be the increased likelihood of males to mature at a slower rate than females of the same age. In terms of hemispheric specialization, late-maturing adolescents demonstrate an increase in hemispheric specialization as indexed by a phoneme identification dichotic listening task, the processing of which is known to be specialized in the left hemisphere (Kimura, 1961; Studdert-Kennedy & Shankweiler, 1970; Zaidel, 1976). This theory is related to the Geschwind and Galaburda model in that different rates of hemispheric development are proposed to account for individual differences in both cognition and hemispheric specialization.

B. Field Dependence and Strategies

Another mediating factor in the discussion of sex differences in the literature may be individual differences in cognitive strategy. Witkin and colleagues (Witkin, Goodenough, & Karp, 1967) have differentiated individuals into two groups: field independent and field dependent, based on performance on a rod-and-frame task that requires individuals to ignore background distractors in order to identify specific characteristics of a visual display. They claim that field dependence is a better predictor of laterality patterns than is sex. This prediction is borne out in greater laterality effects in field-independent individuals than in field-dependent ones (Pizzamiglio & Zoccolotti, 1981). Matteson (1991) further investigated this role of individual differences in strategy in producing sex differences in both cognition and laterality, and based on a similar measure of field dependence found partial support for earlier findings. Although, in the case of her experiments, the specific interaction of laterality and field dependence was task specific.

C. Arousal Measures

The possibility that there are individual differences in arousal of the hemispheres is supported by both animal and human research. In rats, for instance, asymmetries in dopamine distribution are connected to head- and body-turning biases, both of which differ in the population but which are constant within individuals (Glick, Jerussi, & Zimmerberg, 1977). Similarly, both cerebral blood flow and electroencephalography (EEG) studies in humans show reliable individual differences in hemispheric arousal in response to cognitive tasks, where increased left-hemisphere arousal optimizes verbal skills and right-hemisphere arousal has a similar effect on spatial skills (Dabbs & Choo, 1980; Gur & Reivich, 1980). Based on these and their own behavioral data, Levy and her colleagues (1983) have proposed that many of the perceptual asymmetries reported in the literature as supporting individual differences in hemispheric specialization for a particular task are actually demonstrations of individual differences in hemispheric arousal. Although compelling, the arousal paradigm cannot easily account for sex differences in perceptual asymmetries because reliable sex differences in arousal have not been found (Kim, Levine, & Kertesz, 1990). Nevertheless, sex differences in hemispheric specialization may be best explained by an intricate interaction between sex, hormones, strategies, and arousal.

IV. ALTERNATIVE CATEGORIZATIONS OF SEX AND SEXUAL ATTRIBUTIONS

In conjunction with the development of alternative explanations of sex differences, researchers have recently extended the study of sex differences in humans through the use of sexual attribution factors. Although these factors were created to differentiate individuals or groups of individuals from others in the same sex group, they are now also used to categorize the state an individual is in at the time of testing. Although both between- and within-subject factors can be established using any of several different methods, the two most popular means are hormonal assays and the analysis of psychological variables.

A. Between-Subject Classifications

As mentioned earlier, the between-subject classifications of interest in the present discussion involve stable characteristics that distinguish a particular individual or group of individuals from other members of the same or opposite sex. One of the most compelling debates in the sex difference literature involves different accounts of the relationship between just such a measure of individual "masculinity" and cognitive performance. The most obvious of these explanations will be referred to as the Linear Relationship Model. This model predicts that the more "masculine" an individual of either sex, the more likely s(he) is to demonstrate the prototypically masculine pattern of performance on any given task. This model is supported by Christiansen and Knussman (1987), for instance, who demonstrate a positive correlation between masculinity (measured by secondary sex characteristics) and (typically male superior) spatial ability in both sexes (see also Tan, 1990).

Alternatively, the Optimal Level Model predicts that the individuals who are most likely to demonstrate the typically masculine pattern are high-masculine females and low-masculine males. These groups may also be referred to as androgynous. Masculine pattern results from an optimal "masculinity" level slightly *above* that of the average female and *below* that of the average male. This model is supported by demonstrations of spatial ability negatively correlated to testosterone levels in men and positively correlated to the same measure in women (Broverman, Klaiber, Kobayashi, & Vogel, 1968; Gouchie & Kimura, 1991; Shute, Pelligrino, Hubert, & Reynolds, 1983). The Optimal Level Model is also supported in cases where peer or self-ratings of masculinity based on personality or physical characteristics instead of testosterone level were examined (Broverman et al., 1968; Ferguson & Maccoby, 1966; McKeever, 1986). In both the Linear and Optimal Models, it is predicted that verbal performance will be negatively correlated with spatial skill and is often borne out in the empirical data (Broverman et al., 1968; Petersen, 1976).

Evidence for the role of hormones in cognitive aptitudes and hemispheric specialization is also found in anomalies of genetic makeup and perinatal hormonal environment. Individuals with Turner's syndrome, for instance, tend to manifest a selective deficit in visuospatial scores (Dellantonio, 1984; Money & Lewis, 1966) and a decrease in hemispheric specialization (Lewandowski, Costender, & Richman, 1985). The cognitive effects are demonstrated in a selective decline in nonverbal performance in the Wecshler Intelligence Scale for Children (WISC) and on the Spatial score of the Diagnostic Aptitude Test. The decline in hemispheric specialization is demonstrated by a decreased ear advantage on a verbal dichotic listening task. Individuals with congenital adrenal hyperplasia, a genetic anomaly, also demonstrate possibly hormone-dependent cognitive performance patterns. Females with congenital adrenal hyperplasia have been reported to perform better on visuospatial skills, including mental rotation, than their unaffected relatives. Males with congenital adrenal hyperplasia, on the other hand, do not differ in their performance from controls (Resnick, Berenbaum, & Gottesman, 1986).

Individuals whose mothers were given the synthetic estrogen diethylstilbestrol (DES) during pregnancy to prevent miscarriage also demonstrate different patterns on cognitive and hemispheric tasks than would be expected given their sex alone. But although Hines and Shipley (1984) have reported increased hemispheric specialization on a verbal dichotic listening in DES-exposed women relative to their unaffected sisters, the researchers found no difference in performance on either verbal or visuospatial tasks. DES-exposed males, on the other hand, have been reported to demonstrate lower visuospatial performance than their unaffected brothers. Together, the results from anomaly studies can be taken as partial evidence for the Optimal Level Model.

The role of sexual attribution characteristics in predicting different patterns of hemispheric specialization has also been tested by the current author and her colleagues (Weekes, Zaidel, & Zaidel, in press). They found that individuals of both sex, but more so males, demonstrated a positive correlation between male-typical patterns of laterality and masculinity scores on the Bem Sex Role Inventory (Bem, 1974). Although this research accentuates the importance of categorizing individuals not only by discrete, but also by continuous measures of sex, it also lends support for the Linear Relationship Model (see also Casey & Brabeck, 1990).

Another between-subject classification involves sexual orientation. McCormick and Witelson (1991) have reported that homosexual males perform more poorly on visuospatial tasks, such as the Spatial Relations subtest of the Primary Mental Abilities and the Piagetian Water level test, and better on verbal tasks, such as the Animal Naming test, than do heterosexual men. Indeed, the general pattern demonstrated by the homosexual males was similar, although not identical, to that shown by heterosexual females. In a related fashion, the researchers also found an increased incidence of left-handedness in homosexual men (although, having tested for HIV as well as handedness, Marchant, McManus and Wilson [1991] report no increased incidence of left-handedness in HIV-negative homosexuals). This increased incidence may seem counterintuitive with respect to the Geschwind and Galaburda (1985) model of increased testosterone and left-handedness. However, the finding is congruent with an Optimal Level Hypothesis of hormone level and typical masculine behavior, in that the model predicts lower than average testosterone levels in males to be positively correlated with typically masculine characteristics, of which an increased incidence of left-handedness is one. However, these connections are speculative, as the issue of different hormone levels in homosexual and heterosexual males has not yet been resolved (Newmark, 1979; Schiavi & White, 1976).

B. Within-Subject Classifications

Probably the best piece of evidence that the relationship between sex and cognitive ability has a biological component and is not merely the result of differences in the socialization of the two sexes comes from studies of within-subject variations in performance patterns. By using the natural fluctuations of both estrogen and progesterone in spontaneously menstruating females, Hampson and Kimura (1988) have investigated the extent to which "state" (or transient) effects within an individual can mimic "trait" (or stable) effects across individuals. Let us consider how such a comparison is possible.

As discussed, through the progressive etiological model, sex differences in hormone level may explain sex differences in cognitive aptitude. Let us discuss male superiority for visuopatial skill in this context. How might we expect performance on this and other skills to change with endogenous changes in the levels of particular hormones? Between subjects, we have discussed two possible predictions: (1) a positive relationship between hormone (in this case, testosterone level) and skill (in this case, visuospatial ability) in both sexes, as predicted by the Linear Relationship Model, or (2) a negative relationship between these two factors in males and a positive relationship between the same two factors in females, as predicted by the Optimal Level Model. There is evidence to support both of these possibilities. Theoretically, within a single subject, we can make similar predictions. Both the Linear Relationship Model and the Optimal Level Model, however, predict the same general performance patterns for females. In either instance, high-testosterone females (females in a high-testosterone state) are predicted to perform best on visuospatial tasks and less well on verbal tasks. The opposite pattern is predicted in low-testosterone females or females in a low-testosterone state.

Although testosterone remains relatively constant across the menstrual cycle (other than a slight midcycle peak), the relationship between estrogen and testosterone does not. During menses, estrogen and progesterone are low, whereas during both midfollicular and midluteal stages of the menstrual cycle estrogen peaks. Progesterone peaks only during the midluteal stage. We consider testosterone's influence greatest relative to estrogen during menses. In this way, we will discuss low-estrogen phases of the menstrual cycle as also being indicative of higher testosterone phases.

During menses, both models would predict an increase in visuospatial skill and a decrease in verbal skill. During high-estrogen phases (midfollicular and midluteal), the opposite predictions are made. By giving females a battery of both verbal and spatial tasks (along with other measures), Hampson and Kimura (1988; Hampson, 1990) have been able to demonstrate this general pattern (see also Ho, Gilger, & Brink, 1986), with the highest performance on visuospatial tasks and the lowest performance on verbal fluency occurring at menses, and the opposite pattern occurring at both midfollicular and midluteal phases (however, see Gordon, Corbin, & Lee, 1986). The effect of within-subject hormone fluctuations on hemispheric specialization has also been investigated by these and other authors (Chiarello, McMahon, & Schaefer, 1989; Hampson & Kimura, 1988) with promising results. In general, the results support the assertion that the degree of functional laterality fluctuates with hormone level, dependent on task. Together, these results strongly emphasize the role of hormones and other biological factors primarily in cognition, and have implications to hemispheric specialization and interhemispheric interactions.

V. CONCLUSIONS

Based on the available literature, some general conclusions can be drawn about sex differences in the brain. First, although the evidence does seem to support the assertion that the sexes differ in cognition, hemispheric specialization, and callosal activity, the etiology of such differences remains unclear. Second, both alternative explanations or mediating factors and alternative categorizations of sex have emphasized an important trend in sex-difference research. The classic dichotomy of male and female, alone, may prove less useful in understanding individual differences than the categorizations that emphasize the benefits of viewing sex as a continuous, rather than discrete, factor.

Acknowledgments

The author would like to thank the following individuals for critical readings of earlier drafts of this manuscript: Michael Bloch, Jacqueline Liederman, and Minne Kendrick. She would also like to extend a special thanks to Sarah Copeland for tireless editing comments. Most especially she would like to thank her family and David Earl Mitchell, for all the ordinary reasons and for some rather extraordinary ones, as well.

References

Aboitiz, F., Scheibel, A. B., Fisher, R. S., & Zaidel, E. (1992). Individual differences in brain asymmetries and fiber composition in the human corpus callosum. *Brain Research, 598,* 154–161.

Bem, S. L. (1974). The measurement of psychological androgyny. *Journal of Counseling and Clinical Psychology, 42,* 155–62.

Best, C. T., Hoffman, H., & Glanville, B. B. (1982). Development of infant ear asymmetries for speech and music. *Perception and Psychophysics, 31,* 75–85.

Breedlove, S. M., & Arnold, A. P. (1983). Hormonal control of a developing neuromuscular system. I. Complete demasculinization of the spinal nucleus of the bulbocavernosus in male rats using the anti-androgen flutamide. *Journal of Neuroscience, 3,* 417–423.

Broca, P. (1865). Du siège de la faculté du langage article. *Bulletins et Memoires de la Societe d'Anthropologie (Paris), 6,* 377–393.

Broverman, D. M., Klaiber, E. L., Kobayashi, Y., & Vogel, W. (1968). Roles of activation and inhibition in sex differences in cognitive ability. *Psychological Review, 75,* 23–50.

Bryden, M. P. (1989). *Sex differences in cerebral organization: Real or imagined.* Presented at the 10th annual conference of the New York Neuropsychology Group, New York Academy of Sciences.

Bullock, D., Liederman, J., & Todorovic, D. (1987). Reconciling stable asymmetry with recovery of function: An adaptive systems perspective on functional plasticity. *Child Development, 58,* 689–697.

Burton, A., Pepperrell, S. & Stredwick, J. (1991). Interhemispheric transfer in males and females. *Cortex, 27,* 425–429.

Byne, W., Bleier, R., & Houston, L. (1988). Variations in human corpus callosum do not predict gender: A study using magnetic resonance imaging. *Behavioral Neuroscience, 229,* 665–668.

Casey, M. B., & Brabeck, M. M. (1990). Women who excel on spatial tasks: Proposed genetic and environmental factors. *Brain and Cognition, 12,* 73–84.

Chiarello, C., McMahon, M. A., & Schaefer, K. (1989). Visual cerebral lateralization over phases of the menstrual cycle: A preliminary investigation. *Brain and Cognition, 11,* 18–36.

Christiansen, K., & Knussman, R. (1987). Sex hormones and cognitive functioning in men. *Neuropsychology, 18,* 27–36.

Clarke, J. M. (1990). *Interhemispheric functions in humans: Relationships between anatomical measures of the corpus callosum. Behavioral laterality effects and cognitive profiles.* Doctoral dissertation, University of California, Los Angeles, Department of Psychology.

Dabbs, J. M., Jr. and Choo, G. (1980). Left–right carotid blood flow predicts specialized mental ability. *Neuropsychologia, 18,* 711–713.

De Jonge, F. H., Louwerse, A. L., Ooms, M. P., Evers, P., & van de Poll, N. E. (1989). Lesions of the SDN-POA inhibit sexual behavior of male Wistar rats. *Brain Research Bulletin, 23,* 483–492.

de Lacoste-Utamsing, C., & Holloway, R. L. (1982). Sexual dimorphism in the human corpus callosum. *Science, 216,* 1431–1432.

Dellantonio, A. (1984). Spatial performance and hemispheric specialization in the Turner syndrome. *Acta Medica Auxologica, 16,* 193–203.

Denenberg, V. H., Fitch, R. H., Schrott, L. M., Crowell, P. E., et al. (1991). Corpus callosum: Interactive effects of infantile handling and testosterone in the rat brain. *Behavioral Neuroscience, 105,* 562–566.

Diamond, M. C. (1991). Hormonal effects on the development of cerebral lateralization. *Psychoneuroendocrinology, 16,* 121–129.

Diamond, M. C., Dowling, G. A., & Johnson, R. E. (1981). Morphologic cerebral cortical asymmetry in male and female rats. *Experimental Neurology, 71,* 261–268.

Diamond, M. C., Johnson, R. E., and Ehlert, J. (1979). A comparison of cortical thickness in male and female rats—normal and gonadectomized, young and adult. *Behavioral and Neural Biology, 26,* 485–491.

Ferguson, L. R., & Maccoby, E. E. (1966). Interpersonal correlates of differential abilities. *Child Development, 37,* 549–571.

Fitch, R. H., Crowell, P. E., Schrott, L. M., and Denenberg, V. H. (1991). Corpus callosum: Ovarian hormones and feminization. *Brain Research, 542,* 313–317.

Forger, N. G., & Breedlove, S. M. (1986). Sexual dimorphism in human and canine spinal cord: Role of early androgen. *Proceedings of the National Academy of Sciences of the U.S.A., 83*, 7527–7531.

Galaburada, A. M., Corsiglia, J., Rosen, G. D. and Sherman, G. F. (1987). Planum temporale asymmetry, reappraisal since Geschwind and Levitsky. *Neuropsychologia, 25*, 853–868.

Galaburda, A. L., Rosen, G. D., & Sherman, G. F. (1990). Individual variability in cortical organization: Its relationship to brain laterality and implications to function. *Neuropsychologia, 28*, 529–546.

Geshwind, N., & Galaburda, A. M. (1985). *Cerebral lateralization: Biological mechanisms, associations, and pathology.* Cambridge, MA: MIT Press.

Geshwind, N., & Levitsky, W. (1968). Human brain: Left-right asymmetries in temporale speech region. *Science, 161*, 186–187.

Glick, S. D., Jerussi, T. P., & Zimmerberg, B. (1977). Behavioral and neuropharmacological correlates of nigrostriatal asymmetry in rats. In S. Harnad, R. W. Doty, L. Goldstein, J. Jaynes, & G. Krauthamer (Eds.), *Lateralization in the nervous system.* (pp. 213–249). New York: Academic Press.

Gordon, H. W., Corbin, E. D., & Lee, P. A. (1986). Changes in specialized cognitive function following changes in hormone levels. *Cortex, 22*, 399–415.

Gorski, R. A., Gordon, J. H., Shryne, J. E., & Southam, A. M. (1978). Evidence for a morphological sex difference within the medial preoptic area of the rat brain. *Brain Research, 143*, 333–346.

Gouchie, C., & Kimura, D. (1991). The relationship between testosterone levels and cognitive ability patterns. *Psychoneuroendocrinology, 16*, 323–334.

Gray, J. A., & Buffery, A. W. (1971). Sex differences in emotional and cognitive behavior in mammals including man: Adaptive and neural bases. *Acta Psychologica (Amsterdam), 35*, 89–111.

Gur, R. C., & Reivich, M. (1980). Cognitive task effects on hemispheric blood flow in humans: Evidence for individual differences in hemispheric activation. *Brain and Language, 9*, 78–92.

Hampson, E. (1990). Variations in sex-related cognitive abilities across the menstrual cycle. *Brain and Cognition, 14*, 26–43.

Hampson, E., & Kimura, D. (1988). Reciprocal effects of hormonal fluctuations on human motor and perceptual-spatial skills. *Behavioral Neuroscience, 102*, 456–459.

Harshmann, R. A. (1991). Dichotic listening assessment of group and individual differences: Methodological and practical issues. In K. Hugdahl (Ed.) *Handbook of Dichotic Listening: Theory, Methods and Research.* Chichester: Wiley and Sons.

Harshmann, R. A., Hampson, E., & Berenbaum, S. A. (1983). Individual differences in cognitive abilities and brain organization. Part I. Sex and handedness differences in ability. *Canadian Journal of Psychology, 37*, 144–192.

Hines, M., & Gorski, R. A. (1985). Hormonal influences of the development of neural asymmetries. In D. F. Benson & E. Zaidel (Eds.), *The dual brain: Hemispheric specialization in humans.* (pp. 75–96) New York: Guilford Press.

Hines, M. & Shipley, C. (1984). Prenatal exposure to diethylstilbestrol (DES) and the development of sexually dimorphic cognitive abilities and cerebral lateralization. *Developmental Psychology, 20*, 81–94.

Hiscock, M., Hiscock, C. K., & Inch, R. (1991). Is there a sex difference in visual laterality? *Journal of Clinical and Experimental Neuropsychology, 13*, 37 (Abstract)

Ho, H.-Z., Gilger, J. W., & Brink, T. M. (1986). Effects of menstrual cycle on spatial information-processes. *Perceptual and Motor Skills, 63*, 743–751.

Holloway, R. L. and de Lacoste, M. C. (1986). Sexual dimorphism in the human corpus callosum: An extension and replication study. *Human Neurobiology, 5*, 87–91.

Inglis, J., & Lawson, J. S. (1982). A meta-analysis of sex differences in the effects of unilateral brain damage on intelligence test results. *Canadian Journal of Psychology, 36*(4), 670–683.

Juraska, J. (1991). Sex differences in "cognitive" regions of the rat brain. *Psychoneuroendocrinology, 16,* 105–119.

Kim, H., Levine, S. C., and Kertesz, S. (1990). Are variations among subjects in lateral asymmetry real individual differences or random error in measurement: Putting variability in its place. *Brain and Cognition, 14,* 220–242.

Kimura, D. (1961). Cerebral dominance and the perception of verbal stimuli. *Canadian Journal of Psychology, 15,* 166–171.

Kimura, D. (1983). Sex differences in cerebral organization for speech and praxic functions. *Canadian Journal of Psychology, 37,* 19–35.

Kimura, D. (1987). Are men's and women's brains really different? *Canadian Journal of Psychology, 37,* 19–35.

Kinsbourne, M. (1970). The cerebral basis of lateral asymmetries in attention. *Acta Psychologica, 33,* 193–201.

Krieg (1946). Connections of the cerebral cortex. *Journal of Comparative Neurology, 84,* 221–275.

Lake, D. A. and Bryden, M. P. (1976). Handedness and sex differences in hemispheric asymmetry. *Brain and Language, 3,* 226–282.

Lansdell, H., & Uberach, N. (1965). Sex differences in personality measures related to size and side of temporale lobe ablation. *Proceedings of the American Psychology Association. American Psychologist, 21,* 1119–1172.

Lenneberg, E. (1966). *Biological foundations of language.* New York: Wiley.

Levine, S. (1983). Hemispheric specialization and functional plasticity during development. *Journal of Children in Contemporary Society, 16,* 77–89.

Levy, J. (1969). Possible basis for the evolution of lateral specialization in the human brain. *Nature (London), 224,* 614–615.

Levy, J. (1976). Cerebral lateralization and spatial ability. *Behavioral Genetics, 6,* 171–188.

Levy, J. (1983). Interhemispheric Collaboration: Single-mindedness in the asymmetric brain. In C. T. Best (Ed.) Developmental Neuropsychology and Education: Hemispheric Specialization and Integration. New York: Academic Press.

Levy, J., Heller, W., Banich, M. T., & Burton, L. A. (1983). Are variations among right-handed individuals in perceptual assymmetries caused by characteristic arousal differences between the hemispheres? *Journal of Experimental Psychology: Human Perception and Performance, 9,* 329–59.

Lewandowski, L. J., Costenbader, V., & Richman, R. (1985). Neuropsychological aspects of Turner's syndrome. *International Journal of Clinical Neuropsychology, 7,* 144–147.

Maccoby, E. E., & Jacklin, C. N. (1974). *The psychology of sex differences.* Stanford, CA: Stanford University Press.

Marchant, H., McManus, I. C., & Wilson, G. D. (1991). Left-handedness, homosexuality, HIV infection and AIDS. *Cortex, 27,* 49–56.

Matteson, R. L. (1991). *Individual differences in interhemispheric relations.* Unpublished doctoral dissertation, University of California, Los Angeles, Department of Psychology.

McCormick, C. M., & Witelson, S. F. (1991). A cognitive profile of homosexual men compared to heterosexual men and women. *Psychoneuroendocrinology, 16,* 459–473.

McGlone, J. (1978). Sex differences in functional brain asymmetry. *Cortex, 14,* 122–128.

McGlone, J. (1980). Sex differences in functional brain asymmetry: A critical survey. *Behavioral and Brain Sciences, 3,* 215–263.

McGlone, J. (1986). The neuropsychology of sex differences in human brain organization. In G. Goldstein & R. Tarter (Eds.), *Advances in clinical neuropsychology* (Vol. 3, pp. 1–30). New York: Plenum.

McGlone, J. (1992). *Sex differences in the WAIS-R VIQ minus PIQ after temporal lobectomy.* Poster presentation at the International Neuropsychological Society.

McKeever, W. F. (1986). The influences of handedness, sex, familial sinistrality and androgyny on language laterality, verbal ability, and spatial ability. *Cortex, 22,* 521–537.

Money, J., & Lewis, V. (1966). I.Q., genetics, and accelerated growth: Adrenogenital syndrome. *Bulletin of the Johns Hopkins Hospital, 118,* 365–373.

Newmark, S. R. (1979). Gonadotropin, estradiol, and testosterone profiles in homosexual men. *American Journal of Psychiatry, 136,* 767–771.

Nottebohm, F., & Arnold, A. (1976). Sexual dimorphism in vocal control areas of the songbird brain. *Science, 194,* 211–213.

Petersen, A. C. (1976). Physical androgyny and cognitive functioning in adolescence. *Developmental Psychology, 12,* 87–90.

Pizzamiglio, L. and Zoccolotti, F. (1981). Sex and cognitive influence on visual hemifield superiority for shape and letter recognition. *Cortex, 17,* 215–226.

Potter, S. M. & Graves, R. E. (1988). Is interhemispheric transfer related to handedness and gender? *Neuropsychologia, 26,* 319–225.

Resnick, S. M., Berenbaum, S. A., & Gottesman, I. I. (1986). Early hormonal influences on cognitive functioning in congenital adrenal hyperplasia. *Developmental Psychology, 22,* 191–198.

Schiavi, R. C., & White, D. (1976). Androgens and male sexual function: A review of human studies. *Journal of Sex and Marital Therapy, 2,* 214–228.

Shute, V. J., Pelligrino, J. W., Hubert, L., & Reynolds, R. W. (1983). The relationship between androgen levels and human spatial abilities. *Bulletin of the Psychonomic Society, 21,* 465–68.

Stewart, J. and Kolb, B. (1988). The effects of neonatal gonadectomy and prenatal stress on cortical thickness and asymmetry in rats. *Behavioral Neural Biology, 49,* 344–360.

Studdert-Kennedy, M., & Shankweiler, D. (1970). Hemispheric specialization for speech perception. *Journal of the Acoustic Society of America, 48,* 579–594.

Swaab, D. F., & Fliers, E. (1985). A sexually dimorphic nucleus in the human brain. *Science, 228,* 1112–1115.

Tan, U. (1990). Testosterone and nonverbal intelligence in right-handed men and women. *International Journal of Neuroscience, 54,* 277–282.

Thatcher, R. W., Walker, R. A., & Guidace, S. (1987). Human cerebral hemispheres develop at different rates and ages. *Science, 236,* 1110–1113.

Vrbanic, M. I. & Bryden, M. P. (1989). Rate of maturation, cognitive ability, handedness, and cerebral asymmetry. *Canadian Psychologist, 30,* 455.

Waber, D. P. (1977). Sex differences in mental abilities, hemispheric lateralization, and rate of physical growth at adolescence. *Developmental Psychology, 13*(1), 29–38.

Wada, J. A., Clarke, R., & Hamm, A. (1975). Cerebral hemispheric asymmetry in humans. *Archives of Neurology (Chicago), 32,* 239–246.

Weekes, N. Y., Zaidel, D. W., & Zaidel, E. (In press). The effects of sex and sex role attribution on the ear advantage in dichotic listening. *Neuropsychology.*

Wilson, J. D., George, F. W., & Griffin, J. E. (1981). The hormonal control of sexual development. *Science, 211,* 1278–1284.

Witelson, S. F. (1989). Handedness and sex differences in the isthmus and genu of the corpus callosum in humans. *Brain, 112,* 799–835.

Witelson, S. and Kigar, D. L. (1988). Asymmetry in brain function follows asymmetry in anatomical form: Gross, microscopic, postmortem and imaging studies. In F. Boller and J. Grafman (Eds.) *Handbook of Neuropsychology* (pp. 111–142). Amsterdam: Elsevier.

Witelson, S. and Pallie, W. (1973). Left hemisphere specialization for language in the newborn. *Brain, 96,* 641–646.

Witkin, H. A., Goodenough, D. R., & Karp, S. A. (1967). Stability of cognitive style from childhood to young adulthood. *Journal of Personality and Social Psychology, 7,* 291–300.

Zaidel, E. (1976). Language, dichotic listening, and the disconnected hemispheres. In D. O. Walter, L. Rogers, & J. M. Finzi-Fried (Eds.), *Conference on human brain function* (pp. 103–110). Brain Information Service, BRI Publications Office. Los Angeles: UCLA.

Zaidel, E., Aboitiz, F., Clarke, J. Kaiser, D., & Matteson, R. (in press). Sex differences in interhemispheric language relations. To Appear in F. Kitterle (Ed.), Hemispheric Interaction: The Toledo Symposium.

CHAPTER 14

Neuropsychological Rehabilitation

Robert Hanlon

I. INTRODUCTION

Neuropsychological rehabilitation is an emerging area of specialization that has seen rapid expansion in the last 20 yr in response to the increased emphasis on neurorehabilitation following traumatic brain injury, stroke, and other neurological disorders. In light of the fact that approximately 500,000 people require hospitalization for head injury per year in the United States alone (Goldstein, 1990) and the American Heart Association (1992) estimates that another 500,000 new victims of stroke are treated each year in the United States, it is no surprise that the demand for neuropsychological or cognitive rehabilitation services is at an all-time high. The combination of these incidence rates with steadily declining mortality rates, the resultant effect of advances in medical technology and emergency medical care, has created the current reality: more patients with severe cognitive and behavioral impairments survive, requiring intensive and protracted cognitive rehabilitation.

This subspecialization within neuropsychology was, in part, the result of the merging of elements of cognitive neuropsychology (i.e., brain–behavior relationships, experimental paradigms to examine cognitive processes), clinical neuropsychology (assessment of cognitive, intellectual, and emotional status with objective, standardized instruments), and rehabilitation psychology (i.e., rehabilitation process, psychological adjustment to disability). The need for cognitively oriented rehabilitation services developed in response to increased awareness and understanding of the long-term cognitive and behavioral impairments resulting from brain injury, and the impact of these impairments on functional independence, vocational potential, socioeconomic status, and quality of li.

The primary objective of neuropsychological rehabilitation is to improve the quality of life of individuals who have sustained neurological insult, which may involve cognitive, behavioral, emotional, and social factors. Any and all of these factors may affect interpersonal, marital, vocational, educational, and recreational domains, in addition to functional independence in activities of daily living. Numerous outcome studies have reported positive results in defending the efficacy of neuropsychological rehabilitation programs, with regard to psychosocial status (e.g., Christensen, Pinner, Moller Pedersen, Teasdale, & Trexler, 1992), neuropsychological functions (e.g., Prigatano et al., 1984; Ruff et al., 1989; Scherzer, 1986), vocational outcome (e.g., Ben-Yishay, Silver, Piasetsky, & Rattok, 1987), and functional performance in activities of daily living (e.g., Mills, Nesbeda, Katz, & Alexander, 1992). However, controlled studies that examine the effect of a rehabilitation program are uncommon (e.g., Prigatano et al., 1984) and studies incorporating a randomized design with a control group are rare (Ruff et al., 1989).

To date, it is clear that the potential of cognitive rehabilitation looms much larger than its realized capacity, as demonstrated by the effect of current approaches in cognitive remediation and psychosocial intervention following brain damage. Presently, neuropsychological rehabilitation holds great promise in its primary objective, but remains only partially tested and largely unproven (Levin, 1990). As a result, there is an increasing demand for efficacy studies that unequivocally demonstrate the effect of a specific cognitive intervention, psychosocial therapy, or rehabilitation program on functional performance.

II. THEORETICAL MODELS OF NEUROPSYCHOLOGICAL REHABILITATION

A. Overview

Theoretical models of cognitive processing and neuropsychological function have attempted to explain brain–behavior relationships and provide a basis for understanding cognitive dysfunction and neurobehavioral disorders. However, the application and integration of such models in the development of therapeutic interventions has been limited (e.g., Ben-Yishay,

1980; Luria, 1963; Sohlberg & Mateer, 1989a). Wood (1990) has noted that although cognitive rehabilitation is considered to be an important component of brain injury rehabilitation, it suffers from the lack of a theoretical foundation from which treatment methods are derived and cognitive interventions assessed, with ▆▆▆▆ to their efficacy in meeting treatment objectives.

Numerous models are currently utilized in the development and application of therapeutic approaches aimed at the remediation and amelioration of cognitive deficits resulting from brain injury. Some treatment models are theory-based and have emerged from research in clinical neuropsychology, cognitive psychology, behavioral psychology, and rehabilitation. With regard to the latter, the disciplines of speech–language pathology and occupational therapy have been intricately and actively involved in the delivery of cognitive rehabilitation services, and primarily responsible for the implementation of such therapy in many programs, since the beginning of the cognitive rehabilitation movement.

B. Program Models

Currently, two programmatic models of service delivery characterize the majority of outpatient cognitive rehabilitation programs. First, structured treatment procedures, involving a wide range of individual and group activities, aimed at the remediation and restoration of cognitive deficits, are provided by interdisciplinary treatment team members, which commonly include neuropsychologists, speech pathologists, occupational therapists, physical therapists, recreational therapists, vocational rehabilitation specialists, and in some programs, clinical psychologists and physicians. Therapeutic interventions and treatment goals are individualized and tailored to meet the specific needs of a given patient, regardless of the severity of impairment. Second, patients are treated within a therapeutic milieu with a strong group focus, which emphasizes cognitive, emotional, and psychosocial issues from a psychotherapeutic orientation, in which patients who are roughly equivalent with regard to neuropsychological impairment are engaged in a systematic sequence of treatment procedures (e.g., Ben-Yishay & Prigatano, 1990). Such programs are generally more selective, in terms of severity and type of neuropsychological impairment (e.g., patients with severe behavioral disorders, severe motoric impairments, and dense aphasia are generally not treated in such programs). The uniformity of treatment procedures, the structured course of therapeutic progression, and the time-limited nature of this approach lends itself to ongoing research on the efficacy of rehabilitation.

C. Approaches to Cognitive Intervention

Following Zangwill (1947), Prigatano (1986) differentiated three basic approaches to cognitive retraining, which essentially represent the fundamental models of cognitive rehabilitation: compensation, substitution, and direct retraining. *Compensatory approaches* involve the implementation of strategies and devices that enable the patient to functionally bypass or circumvent an impairment. *Substitution* consists of the incorporation of alternative sensory and cognitive systems to perform tasks normally mediated by the damaged cognitive system. Finally, direct retraining is an approach of questionable efficacy, requiring insight, introspection, and self-awareness, which holds that repeated engagement in therapeutic exercises and tasks that stress disrupted cognitive systems will eventually enhance or restore the dysfunctional component.

Gross and Schutz (1986) differentiated five treatment models commonly employed in neuropsychological rehabilitation: (1) environmental control; (2) stimulus–response conditioning; (3) skill training; (4) strategy substitution; (5) the cognitive cycle model. Environmental control is a behavioral approach that focuses on restructuring the patient's environment in attempt to elicit or eliminate specific behaviors. The stimulus–response model consists of *behavioral modification* techniques, involving reinforcement schedules and their effect on target behaviors. Skills training is an instructional and educational model that holds that deliberate and persistent training on the skills needed to perform a given task will eventually improve task performance. The strategy substitution model is based on the notion of substitution, described above. This approach holds that a given task may be performed in more than one way and alternative strategies may effectively be substituted when the cognitive strategy that is normally involved is disrupted following a lesion. The cognitive cycle model involves training in the implementation of a structured organizational sequence that may be repeated and modified as needed to complete tasks requiring complex problem solving. Gross and Schutz (1986) propose that these models correspond to a functional hierarchy, based on capacity for learning. Environmental control is employed with patients who cannot learn, while stimulus–response conditioning is appropriate for patients who can learn, but cannot generalize. Skill training is used with patients who can learn and generalize the effects of training, whereas strategy substitution requires the capacity for self-monitoring. Only patients with the capacity for generalization, self-monitoring, and the formulation of realistic goals may benefit from the cognitive cycle approach.

Sohlberg and Mateer (1989a) proposed a process-specific model of cognitive rehabilitation, which is a structured but flexible approach incorporating elements of compensation, substitution, and direct retraining. They consider the process-specific approach to be a restorative model which focuses on the treatment of specific cognitive processes through repeated engagement in hierarchically structured therapy tasks, followed by treatment generalization probes. Sohlberg and Mateer stress the importance of a well-defined theoretical foundation for cognitive intervention, based on existing research and the current literature in experimental cognition, learning, neuropsychology, and behavioral psychology. They differentiated this approach from two other models of cognitive remediation commonly used in neurorehabilitation programs in North America, namely the *general stimulation approach* and the *functional adaptation approach*. The process-specific approach appears to be growing in popularity, as a result of its structure, applicability, and conceptual foundation.

D. Four Primary Models of Treatment

Four primary approaches to cognitive rehabilitation are currently practiced: (1) the general stimulation or direct retraining approach, (2) the substitution-transfer approach, (3) functional compensation and adaptation, and (4) behavioral approaches, based on operant conditioning and behavior modification. As previously described, the general stimulation approach involves routine engagement in repetitive drills and exercises (i.e., list learning, conditioning reaction time, cognitive rehabilitation workbooks, and most commercially available computer programs marketed for cognitive retraining). Although the most widely used approach in cognitive rehabilitation (Wilson, 1989), there is essentially no evidence that practice alone, regardless of the intensity or frequency, results in real functional gains or generalization beyond the sterile confines of the clinic. Techniques based on this model generally lack a defined theoretical orientation and merely attempt to stimulate cognitive processing in a gross manner.

The substitution–transfer model is truly a neuropsychological approach, in which interventions to a variable degree are based on research findings in neuropsychology, behavioral neurology, and speech pathology. This approach involves training in the substitution of an intact or comparatively intact cognitive system for an impaired cognitive function. Techniques based on this model include the use of visual imagery to facilitate verbal retention, verbal mediation and elaboration to compensate for visual memory dysfunction, and Melodic Intonation Therapy (Sparks, Helm, & Albert, 1974) with nonfluent aphasics. Although these approaches may be effective with specific patients, they lack global applicability and are cognitively demanding techniques that often exceed the learning capacity of many patients.

Luria (1963) provided the most elaborate and detailed model of strategic cognitive intervention, based on the notion of system substitution and derived from a unified theory of neuropsychological function. Founded on the theory of dynamic localization of psychological functions (Luria, 1966), he developed an integrated model of cognitive intervention, based on the reorganization of functional systems. He differentiated two types of reorganization of functional systems: (1) basic intrasystematic reorganization occurs when a relatively well-preserved system compensates for a dysfunctional system; conceptual intrasystematic reorganization requires intensive therapeutic training to enable the patient to restructure and process information using alternative methods and processes; (2) intersystematic reorganization requires the incorporation of a separate sensory or cognitive system to facilitate functional performance.

The functional compensation model is clearly the most applicable and one of the most effective approaches in rehabilitation. Functional adaptation involves the use of any and all strategies, techniques, devices, and adaptive equipment available to increase functional performance and enable the patient to perform tasks that can no longer be performed in the conventional manner. Based on the principles of functional compensation, patients are trained in the use of external devices (e.g., memory notebooks, checklists, tape recorders, computers) and alternative strategies (e.g., visual communication systems, structured systematic approaches to problem solving) to compensate for deficits in memory, attention, communication, perception, motor integration, and executive function.

Behavioral approaches to neuropsychological rehabilitation are founded on the principles of learning theory and behavioral modification, and have been employed with considerable success, particularly with patients manifesting behavioral disorders, executive dysfunction, and severe intellectual impairment. Approaches include environmental control and restructuring (Gross & Schutz, 1986), various reinforcement schedules and shaping (Wood, 1987), response cost (Alderman & Ward, 1991), and training of incompatible behaviors (Hanlon, Clontz, & Thomas, 1993). It has only been recently that neuropsychologists, trained in brain–behavior relations and the assessment of neurocognitive function, have begun to seriously consider and utilize learning principles and behavior modification techniques in cognitive rehabilitation.

III. REHABILITATION OF SPECIFIC COGNITIVE FUNCTIONS

The following review will focus on specific neuropsychological functions and cognitive systems, and approaches that have been employed in an attempt to remediate cognitive deficits following brain injury. Due to space constraints, the description of approaches and interventions within each of the following cognitive domains will be limited to selected examples of interventions that have been proven to be effective or have been influential within the field of neuropsychological rehabilitation.

A. Attention

Difficulties in attention and concentration are one of the most common disturbances and functional changes reported by patients following head injury. Attentional deficits are among the most frequent symptoms following concussive injury (Binder, 1986). Although a variable degree of recovery of attentional capacity typically occurs during the first 3 mo following minor head injury, patients who have suffered severe neurotrauma often manifest notable attentional problems 2 yr postonset (Gronwall, 1987). Despite the prevalence of attentional dysfunction, therapeutic approaches with demonstrable effects on functional performance are limited.

Ben-Yishay and his colleagues at New York University (NYU) have reported considerable success in the remediation of basic attentional dysfunction following traumatic brain injury (Ben-Yishay, Piasetsky, & Rattok, 1987; Ben-Yishay et al., 1980). As one of the core treatment modules of the head trauma rehabilitation program at NYU, the orientation remedial module (ORM) is a hierarchically organized clinical strategy consisting of five separate treatment components addressing interdependent elements of arousal and attention or concentration. Treatment procedures involve computerized psychomotor tasks of increasing difficulty. These tasks in hierarchic order include visual reaction time, maintenance of focused visual attention, sustained and selective visual attention, time estimation, and rhythmic response sequencing. Significant task-specific effects with some evidence of generalization to related tasks have been reported (Ben-Yishay et al., 1987; Rattok et al., 1982), suggesting that the ORM module is an effective approach to remediating basic attentional deficits with selective brain-injured patients.

Sohlberg and Mateer (1987) used a multiple-baselines-across-behaviors design to assess the effectiveness of a hierarchic attention retraining procedure with four brain-injured patients undergoing cognitive rehabilitation. A multiple-baseline design, which involves the assessment of several different functions over time, enabled them to assess the effect of treatment on a specific function (i.e., attention), independent of other cognitive functions (Barlow & Hersen, 1984). The therapeutic procedure was composed of tasks representing five levels of attention (i.e., focused attention, sustained attention, selective attention, alternating attention, divided attention). They used the Paced Auditory Serial Addition Task (PASAT) (Gronwall, 1977), a measure of rate of information processing, requiring the rapid addition of consecutive single-digit numbers, as the dependent variable. Based on PASAT performance, they reported considerable gains in attentional capacity, resulting from the process-specific approach. For additional reports of the effects of structured treatment procedures on basic attentional functions, see Gray and Robertson (1989), Scherzer (1986), and Wood (1986). Although unilateral spatial inattention is a form of attentional dysfunction, treatment approaches aimed at the remediation of hemi-inattention and the neglect syndrome will be discussed in the section on visuospatial processing and perception (see Chapter 5, this volume, for additional discussion of attention).

B. Memory

It is generally accepted that impairments of memory are among the most common residual deficits following even relatively mild head injury. In cases of moderate to severe head injury, up to 90% of patients experience persistent functional memory problems (Brooks, 1983; Rimel, Giordani, Barth, & Jane, 1982) one year postinjury. Given the integral role of memory and learning in nearly all aspects of everyday functioning, memory impairment, particularly when combined with attentional dysfunction, represents one of the most debilitating manifestations of brain injury. Furthermore, given the inherent role of learning in most therapeutic interventions and the rehabilitation process, in general, memory and learning difficulties further limit the potential for significant gains in other functional domains.

There is essentially no evidence that direct retraining approaches, involving repetitive drills, memory "exercises," and rote practice, may result in functional memory improvement (Glisky & Schacter, 1986; Schacter & Glisky, 1986). These approaches, which are based on a restoration of function model derived from physical rehabilitation techniques, approximate the remediation of memory impairments to mental muscle building. Despite this lack of efficacy, these techniques are among the most widely used in cognitive rehabilitation (Wilson, 1989) and are the basis of nearly all commercial computer programs intended for memory retraining.

Approaches based on the substitution or indirect retraining model, including mnemonics such as visual imagery, verbal elaboration, face–name association, peg words, and rehearsal, are also popular techniques, but suffer from a lack of efficacy studies demonstrating incontrovertible effects on functional memory capacity outside the walls of the clinic. Several studies have reported significant gains in recall of task-specific information resulting from visual imagery training (e.g., Gasparrini & Satz, 1979; Kovner, Mattis, & Goldmeier, 1983), verbal elaboration (e.g., Gianutsos & Gianutsos, 1979), face–name associations (Glasgow, Zeiss, Barrera, & Lewinsohn, 1977; Lewinsohn, Danaher, & Kikel, 1977; Wilson, 1981), peg systems (e.g., Patten, 1972), and retrieval practice (Schacter, Rich, & Stampp, 1985). However, reports of maintenance and generalization of these effects are infrequent (e.g., Stern & Stern, 1989), which is understandable given the excessive cognitive demands that the acquisition and application of such techniques requires of an already dysfunctional memory system (Cermak, 1980; Richardson, 1992). One organizational strategy, the PQRST technique (i.e., Preview, Question, Read, State, Test) does appear to have considerable utility with some generalization to naturalistic settings (Glasgow et al., 1977; Grafman, 1984).

Compensatory techniques, based on the functional adaptation model, are generally considered to be the most applicable and effective approaches to the remediation of memory. Training in the use of external memory aids (Harris, 1978, 1984), including notebooks, checklists, computers, calendars, alarm watches, diaries, calculators, labels, and posted reminders, are practical and may be efficiently generalized to different situations. Of course, the effective use of such external devices by patients with memory impairments necessitates extensive and detailed instruction and practice. Sohlberg and Mateer (1989b) described a structured and systematic training sequence for implementation of a memory notebook, progressing through stages of acquisition, application, and adaptation. In addition to the acquisition and utilization of a compensatory memory notebook, they reported effective carry-over to activities of daily living (ADL) and work in a patient with severe memory impairment. Finally, two functionally oriented approaches that have considerable potential for memory rehabilitation, based on findings from experimental work with amnesic patients, include the acquisition of domain-specific knowledge (Schacter & Glisky, 1986) and prospective memory training (Sohlberg, White, Evans, & Mateer, 1992). Focusing on the preserved memory and learning processes of amnesic patients, specifically priming and procedural learning, Glisky and Schacter and their colleagues (e.g., Glisky & Schacter, 1989; Glisky, Schacter, & Tulving, 1986; Schacter & Graf, 1986) have demonstrated that even severely amnesic patients can acquire and retain domain-specific knowledge (i.e., commands, vocabulary, and procedures necessary for computer operation) that is directly applicable to tasks of everyday life.

C. Language

Approaches aimed at increasing the communicative capacity of aphasic patients through the implementation of basic language interventions and supplementary communication strategies have traditionally been the focus of speech and language pathologists. However, there is increasing emphasis on the incorporation of recent findings from research on language processing in cognitive neuropsychology and neurolinguistics, in the development and assessment of techniques for aphasia rehabilitation. As in the therapeutic approaches to memory impairment, the major approaches in aphasia rehabilitation include direct stimulation, substitution, and functional compensation. The direct stimulation model is based on the assumptions that aphasia represents a dissolution of language with a reduced capacity to access language knowledge, and that language can be restored through repetition and drills involving systematic cuing and stimulus manipulation. This approach has generated considerable controversy because of the lack of controlled studies definitively demonstrating the efficacy of such techniques (Basso, 1989). Miller (1984) has noted that there is little evidence that attempts to stimulate language through repetitive verbal exercises results in functional gains in communicative capacity beyond those expected from spontaneous recovery.

Aside from the direct stimulation model, other models include the functional substitution approach of Luria (1963), psycholinguistic approaches (Basso, 1987), and operant conditioning (Holland, 1967). Based on the theory of dynamic organization of functional systems, Luria proposed detailed systematic strategies for speech and language therapy, founded on the concept of functional substitution and compensation. The 1969 paper by Luria, Naydin, Tsvetkova, Vinarskaya presents a series of classic examples of Luria's approach to language therapy. Goodglass (1987) has also provided a concise analysis of the Lurian approach to aphasia rehabilitation.

Numerous techniques have evolved from work in psycholinguistics. Glass, Gazzaniga, and Premack (1973) demonstrated that global aphasics could learn a symbol system for communicative purposes, and Gardner, Zurif, Berry, and Baker (1976) found that global aphasics could effectively use a visual communication system. Additional approaches include Melodic Intonation Therapy (Sparks et al., 1974), Blissymbols (Johannsen-Horbach, Cegla, Mager, Schempp, & Wellesch, 1985), and deblocking language production via gestural expression (Weigl, 1981). Hanlon, Brown, and Gerstman (1990) demonstrated that pointing gestures using the hemiparetic limb significantly increased oral naming in a series of nonfluent aphasics. This technique was based on a microgenetic model of cognitive processing (see Brown, 1988; Hanlon, 1991).

Compensatory approaches have focused on various aspects of nonverbal communication and other pragmatics. Signal systems such as Amerind (Skelly, Schinsky, Smith, Donaldson, & Griffin, 1975), pantomime therapy (Schlanger & Freimann, 1979), and gestural communication systems (Helm-Estabrooks, Fitzpatrick, & Barresi, 1982) have been applied with some success, particularly with severe nonfluent and global aphasics. PACE (promoting aphasics' communicative effectiveness) therapy, developed by Davis and Wilcox (1981, 1985), focuses on various pragmatic elements of communication in the context of face-to-face conversation. Other commonly used compensatory communication devices include communication boards, picture charts, and electrical scanning units.

D. Visuospatial Processing and Perception

Impairments of visual processing and visuoperceptual function are common following head injury, cerebrovascular accidents, neoplastic disease, and other neurological disorders. Disturbances of basic visual processing include decreased acuity, oculomotor dysfunction, binocular integration deficits, visual field cuts, particularly hemianopsia, form and color discrimination deficits, and cortical blindness. Lesions that disrupt integrated visuoperceptual systems and visuospatial processing may result in deficits of object recognition or agnosias, defective discrimination of spatial relations, unilateral spatial inattention, and spatial integration deficits. The impact of visuoperceptual deficits on functional performance is pervasive, affecting the entire range of human activities from self-care to most vocational tasks, from reading to driving.

Efforts to remediate basic visual processing following brain injury have been limited and the direct retraining or stimulation approach has generally been employed. Through repeated engagement in computerized tasks involving visual scanning and reaction time, Gianutsos and Matheson (1987) noted improvement in the visual discrimination of patients with visual field defects. Zihl and von Cramon (1979) also reported significant restoration of visual fields through perimetric stimulation.

Luria (1963) experimented with techniques to improve visuospatial processing, founded on the system substitution approach. One example, based on the principle of intrasystematic reorganization of functional systems, consisted of an intervention for simultanagnosia, characterized by difficulty in perceiving more than one visual stimulus simultaneously. Luria proposed that the perceptual field may essentially be widened by restructuring visual elements, such as geometric forms, into semantically based groups, which may be perceived as words. Luria's theoretical views and principles for therapeutic intervention have been extremely influential (e.g., Abreu & Toglia, 1987; Ben-Yishay & Prigatano, 1990).

Based on the process-specific approach, Sohlberg and Mateer (1989a) demonstrated notable improvement in the visual discrimination of form and spatial relations, using multiple-baseline-across-behaviors designs with single cases. Their approach utilized hierarchically organized tasks that were purportedly consistent with the hierarchic levels of the visual-processing system.

Unilateral spatial inattention is a common component of the unilateral neglect syndrome, characterized by failure to respond or attend to stimuli in the hemispace contralateral to a cerebral lesion (Heilman, Watson, & Valenstein, 1985). Unilateral neglect is more common following right-hemisphere lesions (Weintraub & Mesulam, 1987) and is a primary focus in stroke rehabilitation, due to the disruptive impact of this impairment on functional performance (Denes, Semenza, Stoppa, & Lis, 1982).

The original work by Weinberg and Diller (Weinberg et al., 1977; Diller & Weinberg, 1977), and their colleagues at NYU on training right-hemisphere-lesioned patients to compensate for left visual inattention through systematic and functionally oriented treatment procedures remains the most effective and influential approach to the remediation of left hemi-inattention. In a controlled group study, they effectively trained patients to actively scan left hemispace through the implementation of a left visual field anchor (i.e., a salient stimulus such as a bright red vertical line in the periphery of left hemispace to serve as an anchoring point), response pacing (i.e., requiring patients to name or number visual stimuli during scanning in order to decrease the rate of scanning), low-density visual stimuli (i.e., increased horizontal and vertical spacing between visual stimuli), and immediate feedback regarding performance. Significant improvement was demonstrated regardless of the severity of hemi-inattention, with maintenance of the effect at 1 yr posttraining. Significant effects were also achieved following training on somatosensory awareness and spatial organization (Weinberg et al., 1979). These findings were replicated in a sequentially administered remediation program (Gordon et al., 1985).

Using a multiple-baselines-across-behaviors design, Hanlon, Dobkin, Hadler, Ramirez, and Cheska (1992) demonstrated a significant increase in attention to left hemispace when treatment was initiated 7 mo following a right-hemisphere stroke. A multisensory cuing strategy (i.e., visual, auditory, proprioceptive, and tactile) involving explicit left-sided cuing was employed with therapeutic tasks and procedures similar to those used by Weinberg et al. (1977). Visual tasks included the following: copying sentences and paragraphs of increasing horizontal length using a left visual field anchor; reading newspaper and magazine articles of increasing horizontal length using a left visual field anchor; the use of a mirror for visual feedback during gait training; environmental visual search tasks, involving counting and identification of various indoor and outdoor stimuli, including money, people, automobiles, trees, windows, buildings, and so forth. Auditory cuing included verbal commands to scan left hemispace and auditory-nonverbal stimuli to direct and orient the subject to left hemispace. Auditory tasks included the spatial localization of auditory stimuli. Proprioceptive and tactile cues included the positioning, placement, and touching of his left-hemiparetic arm, initially by the therapist and subsequently by the patient himself, with progressive use of the left arm for stabilization during paper-and-pencil tasks and self-care. Interventions were progressively refined according to the *saturation cuing technique* (Diller & Gordon, 1981), which involves the systematic reduction in cues necessary for successful task completion. Despite ongoing thalamocortical hypometabolism, established by positron emission tomography (PET), the patient was effectively trained to compensate for left hemi-inattention with carry-over to functional tasks, including mobility and self-care. Also see Diller et al. (1980), Carter, Howard, and O'Neil (1983), and Pizzamiglio et al. (1992) for additional techniques and approaches for treating hemispatial inattention (see Chapter 4, this volume, for additional discussion).

E. Executive Function

Executive dysfunction, involving deficits of goal formulation, planning, organization, sequencing, and self-regulation, is common following head injury, primarily due to the vulnerability of the frontal region to damage from impact forces. It is well known that frontal lobe systems are integrally involved in the mediation of executive functions (Damasio, 1985; Luria, 1966). The frontal region is the most common site of focal lesions following mild to moderate closed head injury (Levin, Goldstein, Williams, & Eisenberg, 1991) and cerebral contusions, secondary to head injury, are usually more severe in the frontal and temporal lobes, regardless of the site of impact (Jennett & Teasdale, 1981). Although deficits in planning, self-regulation, and problem solving are often not as obvious to the patient or significant others as primary deficits of memory and attention, executive deficits and disturbances of problem solving are notoriously debilitating. Furthermore, the governing role of executive functions on the selection and prioritization of information, as well as behavioral control, has an indirect but significant impact on memory function and attention, in particular. Despite the prevalence of executive deficits in traumatically brain-damaged individuals, therapeutic interventions with demonstrable effects on functional performance are limited.

Approaches based on environmental control and behavioral modification are the most widely used techniques to manage self-regulation deficits (Benedict, 1989). Wood (1987), among others, has reported success with traditional behavior modification techniques, such as time-out and positive reinforcement, in the management of aggression, sexual disinhibition, and other socially inappropriate behaviors following brain damage. Response cost, a behavioral technique based on the principle of negative punishment, has been proven to be effective in the management of verbal outbursts, repetitive speech, and aggression, with maintenance of treatment gains demonstrated following treatment withdrawal (Alderman & Burgess, 1990; Alderman & Ward, 1991). Hanlon et al. (1993) demonstrated significant improvement in self-regulation following training of an incompatible response with a patient manifesting severe behavioral dyscontrol, characterized by involuntary oral exhalations, vocalizations, and oral-facial dyskinesia. Maintenance of treatment gains following discharge and limited generalization were also evident.

Cognitive-behavioral therapy approaches that attempt to modify cognition as well as overt behavior are being utilized increasingly in the treatment of self-regulation deficits. Self-instructional training (Meichenbaum, 1977) has been successfully employed in the remediation of executive deficits. Cicerone and Wood (1987) used a self-instructional training procedure to teach a patient with frontal lobe damage to verbalize a plan of behavior before and during execution of a therapeutic task requiring planning and problem solving (i.e., modified version of the Tower of London). As a result of overt verbalization of the plan and self-monitoring, combined with progressive internalization of speech, his performance improved and off-task behaviors decreased, with some evidence of generalization to novel situations. More recently, Cicerone and Giacino (1992) reported similar results with this verbal regulation strategy, following the self-instructional training of six frontal patients in a multiple-baselines-across-subjects design.

A problem-solving training approach, based on a technique aimed at enabling patients with frontal lesions to break down complex multistep problems into more manageable components, resulted in significant effects on psychometric measures of planning and problem solving in a group study using a pre- and posttreatment design (von Cramon & Matthes-von Cramon, 1990). The problem-solving training program consisted of four modules: (1) generating goal-directed ideas or alternatives to a given problem; (2) careful analysis and comparison of the information provided; (3) multiple sources of information that required simultaneous processing (e.g., timetables, schedules); (4) tasks requiring inferential reasoning. Sohlberg and Mateer (1989a) have also developed a therapeutic program for the treatment of executive deficits composed of three major components: selection and execution of cognitive plans, time management, and self-regulation. However, the results of efficacy studies using this program have yet to be reported. Also, see Ylvisaker, Szekeres, Henry, Sullivan, and Wheeler (1987) for a detailed description of practical compensatory approaches to the management of executive deficits, particularly organizational problems.

IV. PHARMACOLOGIC INTERVENTIONS

Pharmacotherapy is a crucial component of the medical management of brain-damaged patients, particularly during the acute stage following traumatic brain injury. However, like the task- and process-oriented approaches to cognitive remediation, pharmacologic rehabilitation suffers from a lack of efficacy studies that unequivocally demonstrate effects of drug therapy on neuropsychological status and functional performance (Cope, 1987). Controlled group studies are nearly nonexistent and well-designed double-blind, placebo-controlled trials are underrepresented, given the widespread use of psychotropic medications with brain-injured patients. The majority of work on neuropharmacologic intervention with brain-injured patients has focused on the management of behavioral disorders, particularly agitation and aggression. In keeping with the cognitive focus of the previous section, a brief review of the effects of pharmacologic agents on cognition in clinical trials with brain-injured patients will follow (see also McLean, Cardenas, Haselkorn, & Peters, 1993). Drug therapy for neurobehavioral disorders will not be discussed (see Gualtieri, 1988; O'Shanick & Parmelee, 1989).

The use of cholinergic drugs in the treatment of patients with Alzheimer's disease has been studied extensively with mixed results. Diminished levels of acetylcholine, secondary to the loss of choline acetyltransferase in selective cortical regions of Alzheimer's patients has prompted this work, but the results are inconclusive. *Physostigmine,* an inhibitor of acetylcholinesterase that results in an increased concentration of acetylcholine, has been demonstrated to possess some clinical utility in the treatment of memory impairment following brain injury. In a double-blind study Peters and Levin (1977) demonstrated notable gains in verbal learning on the Selective Reminding Test in response to physostigmine treatment with a patient with anterograde amnesia, secondary to herpes encephalitis. Goldberg et al. (1982) also reported significant increases on the Wechsler Memory Scale and the Selective Reminding Test, in response to physostigmine treatment of a patient with posttraumatic anterograde amnesia. Using a double-blind A-B-A design, McLean, Stanton, Cardenas, and Bergerud (1987) examined the effect of a memory retraining strategy (i.e., PQRST study method) combined with the administration of physostigmine in two patients with memory impairment, secondary to anoxic brain damage. They demonstrated that this combined memory retraining and physostigmine treatment approach resulted in significant improvement on both standardized and nonstandardized measures of memory function, but were unable to determine the relative effectiveness of drug therapy vs. memory retraining.

The clinical utility of psychostimulants, such as methylphenidate, in the treatment of attention deficit disorder (ADD) in both children and adults, is well established. However, the therapeutic efficacy of psychostimulants is limited with regard to traumatically brain-injured patients (e.g., Evans & Gualtieri, 1987; Evans, Gualtieri, & Patterson, 1987). In response to evidence that tricyclic antidepressants, specifically imipramine and desipramine, may effectively be used to treat ADD in patients who fail to respond to psychostimulants, clinical trials of desipramine with brain-injured patients have been undertaken with limited but encouraging results (Mysiw, Corrigan, & Gribble, 1986).

In contrast to psychostimulants, dopamine agonists, such as bromocriptine have received increasing attention in response to reports of positive effects on cognitive function with brain-injured patients. In an open label study using a test-retest design, Albert, Bachman, Morgan, and Helm-Estabrooks (1988) reported a notable increase in fluency, naming and speech initiation following administration of bromocriptine in a patient with chronic transcortical motor aphasia, secondary to a left frontal intracerebral hemorrhage. These findings were replicated in another open-label study with two patients with chronic nonfluent aphasia (Gupta & Mlcoch, 1992). However, the fact that open trials were used restricts any conclusion, with regard to the efficacy of bromocriptine in the treatment of aphasia. Bromocriptine has also been demonstrated to significantly increase performance on psychometric measures of hemi-inattention with three right-hemisphere-lesioned patients in two studies using reversal designs (ABA) (Fleet, Valenstein, Watson, & Heilman, 1987; McNeny & Zasler, 1991).

More recently, with a double-blind, alternating repeated measures design, Dobkin and Hanlon (1993) examined the effect of several pharmacological agents on functional memory capacity and verbal learning in a patient with chronic anterograde amnesia, secondary to surgical lesioning of the rectus gyrus, cingulate cortex, and lower genu of the corpus callosum. Using the alternate forms of the Selective Reminding Test and the Rivermead Behavioural Memory Test, the patient was assessed repeatedly over a period of 18 mo, during alternating medication trials, which included bromocriptine, physostigmine, amphetamine, pergolide, and a placebo. Only bromocriptine significantly and consistently improved verbal learning and functional memory performance.

It is clear from this brief review of selective studies on drug therapy that neuropharmacological research with brain-injured patients is in need of well-designed controlled studies that may conclusively demonstrate therapeutic efficacy. The well-designed studies that have demonstrated notable effects of pharmacological intervention on cognitive function in brain-injured patients are encouraging. Hopefully, these trials will serve as the springboard for further investigations. The potential of psychopharmacological treatment in neuropsychological rehabilitation is immense and the need is obvious.

V. CONCLUDING REMARKS

The efficacy of neuropsychological rehabilitation remains a controversial issue. Results of ongoing research, consisting of studies designed to examine the effect of a specific cognitive intervention or rehabilitation program, are highly encouraging. Despite the inherent confounds that impede research on the clinical utility and efficacy of therapeutic approaches with brain-injured patients (i.e., spontaneous recovery, heterogeneity of subjects, and ethical considerations regarding the withdrawal of an intervention or withholding a treatment), advances are being made. Therapeutic procedures developed for the remediation of disturbances in attention, memory, language, visual perception, and executive functions, secondary to brain injury, are now more than ever required to incontrovertibly demonstrate effects through adherence to conceptually based and theory-driven experimental and quasi-experimental designs. It is surprising that the field of neuropsychology, founded on scientific examination and the use of experimental paradigms in the assessment of brain–behavior relations, has been so slow to adopt these same standards for therapeutic intervention. Given the confounds described above and the resultant limitations on controlled group studies, the use of single-case experimental designs has enabled researchers to conduct efficacy studies that could not otherwise have been completed.

However, despite the demonstrated effects of specific cognitive interventions and rehabilitation programs in a number of studies, as described in this review, relatively few studies have proven that cognitive rehabilitation therapy has a significant impact on the quality of living of brain-injured individuals. Herein lies the challenge of neuropsychological rehabilitation. Future work examining the effect of structured cognitive interventions must demonstrate that these therapeutic procedures and programs directly influence functional performance and have a notable impact on the quality of life of brain-damaged patients.

References

Abreu, B. C., & Toglia, J. P. (1987). Cognitive rehabilitation: A model for occupational therapy. *American Journal of Occupational Therapy, 41,* 439–448.

Albert, M. L., Bachman, D. L., Morgan, A., & Helm-Estabrooks, N. (1988). Pharmacotherapy for aphasia. *Neurology, 38,* 877–879.

Alderman, N., & Burgess, P. W. (1990). Integrating cognition and behavior: A pragmatic approach to brain injury. In R. L. Wood & I. Fussey (Eds.), *Cognitive rehabilitation in perspective* (pp. 204–228). London: Taylor & Francis.

Alderman, N., & Ward, A. (1991). Behavioural treatment of the dysexecutive syndrome: Reduction of repetitive speech using response cost and cognitive overlearning. *Neuropsychological Rehabilitation, 1,* 65–80.

American Heart Association. (1992). *Heart and stroke facts.* New York: Author.

Barlow, D. H., & Hersen, M. (1984). *Single case experimental designs: Strategies for studying behavior change.* New York: Pergamon.

Basso, A. (1987). Approaches to neuropsychological rehabilitation: Language disorders. In M. Meier, A. Benton, & L. Diller (Eds.), *Neuropsychological rehabilitation* (pp. 294–314). New York: Guilford Press.

Basso, A. (1989). Spontaneous recovery and language rehabilitation. In X. Seron & G. Deoche (Eds.), *Cognitive approaches in neuropsychological rehabilitation* (pp. 17–37). Hillsdale, NJ: Erlbaum.

Benedict, R. H. (1989). The effectiveness of cognitive remediation strategies for victims of traumatic head-injury: A review of the literature. *Clinical Psychology Review, 9,* 605–626.

Ben-Yishay, Y. (Ed.). (1980). *Working approaches to remediation of cognitive deficits in brain damaged persons* (Rehabilitation Monograph No. 61). New York: New York University Medical Center.

Ben-Yishay, Y., Piasetsky, E., & Rattok, J. (1987). A systematic method for ameliorating disorders in basic attention. In M. J. Meier, A. L. Benton, & L. Diller (Eds.), *Neuropsychological rehabilitation* (pp. 165–181). New York: Guilford Press.

Ben-Yishay, Y., & Prigatano, G. (1990). Cognitive remediation. In M. Rosenthal, E. R. Griffith, M. Bond, & J. D. Miller (Eds.), *Rehabilitation of the adult and child with traumatic brain injury* (2nd ed., pp. 383–409). Philadelphia: Davis.

Ben-Yishay, Y., Rattok, J., Ross, B., Lakin, P., Cohen, J., & Diller, L. (1980). A remedial module for the systematic amelioration of basic attentional disturbances in head trauma patients. In Y. Ben-Yishay (Ed.), *Working approaches to remediation of cognitive deficits in brain damaged persons* (Rehabilitation Monograph No. 61). New York: New York University Medical Center.

Ben-Yishay, Y., Silver, S., Piasetsky, E., & Rattok, J. (1987). Relationship between employability and vocational outcome after intensive holistic cognitive rehabilitation. *Journal of Head Trauma Rehabilitation, 2,* 35–48.

Binder, L. M. (1986). Persisting symptoms after mild head injury: A review of post concussive syndrome. *Journal of Clinical and Experimental Neuropsychology, 8,* 323–346.

Brooks, N. (1983). Disorders of memory. In M. Rosenthal, E. R. Griffith, M. Bond, & J. D. Miller (Eds.), *Rehabilitation of the head injured adult* (pp. 185–196). Philadelphia: Davis.

Brown, J. W. (1988). *The life of the mind.* Hillsdale, NJ: Erlbaum.

Carter, L. T., Howard, B. E., & O'Neil, W. A. (1983). Effectiveness of cognitive skill remediation in acute stroke patients (visual scanning, visual-spatial, time judgment retraining). *American Journal of Occupational Therapy, 37,* 320–326.

Cermak, L. S. (1980). Imagery and mnemonic training. In L. W. Poon, J. L. Fozard, & L. S. Cermak (Eds.), *New directions in memory and aging.* Hillsdale, NJ: Erlbaum.

Christensen, A.-L., Pinner, E. M., Moller Pedersen, P., Teasdale, T. W., & Trexler, L. E. (1992). Psychosocial outcome following individualized neuropsychological rehabilitation of brain damage. *Acta Neurologica Scandinavia, 85,* 32–38.

Cicerone, K. D., & Giacino, J. T. (1992). Remediation of executive function deficits after traumatic brain injury. *Neurorehabilitation, 2,* 12–22.

Cicerone, K. D., & Wood, J. C. (1987). Planning disorder after closed head injury: A case study. *Archives of Physical Medicine and Rehabilitation, 68,* 111–115.

Cope, D. N. (1987). Psychopharmacologic considerations in the treatment of traumatic brain injury. *Journal of Head Trauma Rehabilitation, 2,* 1–5.

Damasio, A. R. (1985). The frontal lobes. In K. Heilman & E. Valenstein (Eds.), *Clinical neuropsychology* (pp. 339–375). New York: Oxford University Press.

Davis, G. A., & Wilcox, M. J. (1981). Incorporating parameters of natural conversation in aphasia treatment. In R. Chapery (Ed.), *Language intervention strategies in adult aphasia* (pp. 169–193). Baltimore, MD: Williams & Wilkins.

Davis, G. A., & Wilcox, M. J. (1985). *Adult aphasia rehabilitation: Applied pragmatics.* San Diego: College-Hill Press.

Denes, G., Semenza, C., Stoppa, E., & Lis, A. (1982). Unilateral spatial neglect and recovery from hemiplegia: A follow up study. *Brain, 105,* 543–552.

Diller, L., & Gordon, W. (1981). Rehabilitation and clinical neuropsychology. In S. Filskov & T. Boll (Eds.), *Handbook of clinical neuropsychology* (pp. 702–733). New York: Wiley.

Diller, L., & Weinberg, J. (1977). Hemi-inattention in rehabilitation: The evolution of a rational remediation program. *Advances in Neurology, 18,* 63–83.

Diller, L., Weinberg, J., Piasetsky, E., Ruckideschel-Hibbard, M., Egelko, S., Scotzin, M., Couniotakis, J., & Gordon, W. (1980). *Methods for the evaluation and treatment of the visual perceptual difficulties of right brain damaged individuals.* New York: New York University Medical Center.

Dobkin, B. H., & Hanlon, R. E. (1993). Dopamine agonist treatment of antegrade amnesia from a mediobasal forebrain injury. *Annals of Neurology, 33,* 313–316.

Evans, R. W., & Gualtieri, C. T. (1987). Psychostimulant pharmacology in traumatic brain injury. *Journal of Head Trauma Rehabilitation, 2,* 29–33.

Evans, R. W., Gualtieri, C. T., & Patterson, D. R. (1987). Treatment of chronic closed head injury with psychostimulant drugs: A controlled case study and appropriate evaluation procedure. *Journal of Nervous and Mental Disease, 175,* 106–110.

Fleet, W. S., Valenstein, E., Watson, R. T., & Heilman, K. M. (1987). Dopamine agonist therapy for neglect in humans. *Neurology, 37,* 1765–1770.

Gardner, H., Zurif, E. B., Berry, T., & Baker, E. (1976). Visual communication in aphasic patients. *Neuropsychologia, 11,* 213–220.

Gasparrini, B., & Satz, P. (1979). A treatment for memory problems in left hemisphere CVA patients. *Journal of Clinical Neuropsychology, 1,* 137–150.

Gianutsos, R., & Gianutsos, J. (1979). Rehabilitating the verbal recall of brain injured patients by mnemonic training: An experimental demonstration using single-case methodology. *Journal of Clinical Neuropsychology, 1,* 117–135.

Gianutsos, R., & Matheson, P. (1987). The rehabilitation of visual perceptual disorders attributable to brain injury. In M. Meier, A. Benton, & L. Diller (Eds.), *Neuropsychological rehabilitation* (pp. 202–241). New York: Guilford Press.

Glasgow, R. E., Zeiss, R. A., Barrera, M., Lewinsohn, P. M. (1977). Case studies on remediating memory deficits in brain-damaged individuals. *Journal of Clinical Psychology, 33,* 1049–1054.

Glass, A. V., Gazzaniga, M. S., & Premack, D. (1973). Artificial language training in global aphasics. *Neuropsychologia, 11,* 95–103.

Glisky, E., & Schacter, D. L. (1986). Remediation of organic memory disorders: Current status and future prospects. *Journal of Head Trauma Rehabilitation, 1,* 54–63.

Glisky, E., & Schacter, D. L. (1989). Extending the limits of complex learning in organic amnesia: Computer training in the vocational domain. *Neuropsychologia, 27,* 107–120.

Glisky, E., Schacter, D. L., & Tulving, E. (1986). Learning and retention of computer-related vocabulary in amnesic patients: Method of vanishing cues. *Journal of Clinical and Experimental Neuropsychology, 8,* 292–312.

Goldberg, E., Gerstman, L. J., Mattis, S., Hughes, J. E. O., Bilder, R. M., & Sirio, C. A. (1982). Effects of cholinergic treatment of posttraumatic anterograde amnesia. *Archives of Neurology (Chicago), 39,* 581.

Goldstein, M. (1990). Traumatic brain injury: A silent epidemic. Editorial. *Annals of Neurology, 27,* 327.

Goodglass, H. (1987). Neurolinguistic principles and aphasia therapy. In M. Meier, A. Benton, & L. Diller (Eds.), *Neuropsychological rehabilitation* (pp. 315–326). New York: Guilford Press.

Gordon, W. A., Ruckdeschel-Hibbard, M., Egelko, S., Diller, L., Shaver, M. S., Lieberman, A., & Ragnarsson, K. (1985). Perceptual remediation in patients with right brain damage: A comprehensive program. *Archives of Physical Medicine and Rehabilitation, 66,* 353–359.

Grafman, J. (1984). Memory assessment and remediation in brain-injured patients: From theory to practice. In B. A. Edelstein & E. T. Couture (Eds.), *Behavioral assessment and rehabilitation of the traumatically brain damaged* (pp. 151–189). New York: Plenum.

Gray, J. M., & Robertson, I. (1989). Remediation of attentional difficulties following brain injury: Three experimental single case studies. *Brain Injury, 3,* 163–170.

Gronwall, D. (1977). Paced Auditory Serial Addition Task: A measure of recovery from concussion. *Perceptual Motor Skills, 44,* 367–373.

Gronwall, D. (1987). Advances in the assessment of attention and information processing after head injury. In H. S. Levin, J. Grafman, & H. M. Eisenberg (Eds.), *Neurobehavioral recovery from head injury* (pp. 355–371). New York: Oxford University Press.

Gross, Y., & Schutz, L. E. (1986). Intervention models in neuropsychology. In B. P. Uzzell & Y. Gross (Eds.), *Clinical neuropsychology of intervention* (pp. 179–204). Boston: Martinus Nijhoff.

Gualtieri, C. T. (1988). Pharmacotherapy and the neurobehavioral sequelae of traumatic brain injury. *Brain Injury, 2,* 101–129.

Gupta, S. R., & Mlcoch, A. G. (1992). Bromocriptine treatment of nonfluent aphasia. *Archives of Physical Medicine and Rehabilitation, 73,* 373–376.

Hanlon, R. E. (Ed.). (1991). *Cognitive microgenesis: A neuropsychological perspective.* New York: Springer-Verlag.

Hanlon, R. E., Brown, J. W., & Gerstman, L. J. (1990). Enhancement of naming in nonfluent aphasia through gesture. *Brain and Language, 38,* 298–314.

Hanlon, R. E., Clontz, B., & Thomas, M. (1993). Management of severe behavioral dyscontrol following subarachnoid hemorrhage. *Neuropsychological Rehabilitation, 3,* 63–76.

Hanlon, R. E., Dobkin, B. H., Hadler, B., Ramirez, S., & Cheska, Y. (1992). Neurorehabilitation following right thalamic infarct: Effects of cognitive retraining on functional performance. *Journal of Clinical and Experimental Neuropsychology, 14,* 433–447.

Harris, J. (1978). External memory aids. In M. Gruneberg, P. Morris, & R. Sykes, (Eds.), *Practical aspects of memory* (pp. 172–179). London: Academic Press.

Harris, J. (1984). Methods of improving memory. In B. A. Wilson & N. Moffat (Eds.), *Clinical management of memory problems* (pp. 46–62). London: Croom Helm.

Heilman, K. M., Watson, R. T., & Valenstein, E. (1985). Neglect and related disorders. In K. M. Heilman & E. Valenstein (Eds.), *Clinical neuropsychology* (pp. 243–293). New York: Oxford University Press.

Helm-Estabrooks, N., Fitzpatrick, P. M., & Barresi, B. (1982). Visual action therapy for global aphasia. *Journal of Speech and Hearing Disorders, 47,* 385–389.

Holland, A. L. (1967). Some applications of behavioral principles to clinical speech problems. *Journal of Speech and Hearing Disorders, 32,* 11–18.

Jennett, B., & Teasdale, G. (1981). *Management of head injuries.* Philadelphia: Davis.

Johannsen-Horbach, H., Cegla, B., Mager, U., Schempp, G., & Wallesch, C. W. (1985). Treatment of chronic global aphasia with a nonverbal communication system. *Brain and Language, 24,* 74–82.

Kovner, R., Mattis, S., & Goldmeier, E. (1983). A technique for promoting robust free recall in chronic organic amnesia. *Journal of Clinical Neuropsychology, 5,* 65–71.

Levin, H. S. (1990). Cognitive rehabilitation: Unproved but promising. *Archives of Neurology (Chicago), 47,* 223–224.

Levin, H. S., Goldstein, F. C., Williams, D. H., & Eisenberg, H. M. (1991). The contribution of frontal lobe lesions to the neurobehavioral outcome of closed head injury. In H. S. Levin, H. M. Eisenberg, & A. L. Benton (Eds.), *Frontal lobe function and dysfunction* (pp. 318–338). New York: Oxford University Press.

Lewinsohn, P. M., Danaher, B. G., & Kikel, S. (1977). Visual imagery as a mnemonic aid for brain-injured persons. *Journal of Consulting and Clinical Psychology, 45,* 717–723.

Luria, A. R. (1963). *Restoration of function after brain injury.* New York: Macmillan.

Luria, A. R. (1966). *Higher cortical functions in man.* New York: Basic Books.

Luria, A. R., Naydin, V. L., Tsvetkova, L. S., & Vinarskaya, E. N. (1969). Restoration of higher cortical function following local brain damage. In P. Vinken & G. Bruyn (Eds.), *Handbook of clinical neurology* (Vol. 3, pp. 368–433). Amsterdam: North-Holland Publ.

McLean, A., Cardenas, D., Haselkorn, J., & Peters, M. (1993). Cognitive psychopharmacology. *Neurorehabilitation, 3,* 1–14.

McLean, A., Stanton, K. M., Cardenas, D. D., & Bergerud, D. B. (1987). Memory training combined with the use of oral physostigmine. *Brain Injury, 1,* 145–159.

McNeny, R., & Zasler, N. D. (1991). Neuropharmacologic management of hemi-inattention after brain injury. *Neurorehabilitation, 1,* 72–78.

Meichenbaum, D. (1977). *Cognitive behavior modification: An integrative approach.* New York: Plenum.

Miller, E. (1984). *Recovery and management of neuropsychological impairments.* Chichester, UK: Wiley.

Mills, V. M., Nesbeda, T., Katz, D. I., & Alexander, M. P. (1992). Outcomes for traumatically brain-injured patients following post-acute rehabilitation programmes. *Brain Injury,* *6,* 219–228.

Mysiw, W. J., Corrigan, J. D., & Gribble, M. W. (1986). Application of reaction-time monitoring during pharmacologic intervention in traumatic brain injury. *Archives of Physical Medicine and Rehabilitation, 67,* 677.

O'Shanick, G. J., & Parmelee, D. (1989). Psychopharmacologic agents in the treatment of brain injury. In A. L. Christensen & D. W. Ellis (Eds.), *Neuropsychological treatment of head injury.* Boston: Martinus Nijhoff.

Patten, B. M. (1972). The ancient art of memory. *Archives of Neurology (Chicago), 26,* 25–31.

Peters, B. H., & Levin, H. S. (1977). Memory enhancement after physostigmine treatment in the amnesic syndrome. *Archives of Neurology (Chicago), 34,* 215–219.

Pizzamiglio, L., Antonucci, G., Judica, A., Montenero, P., Razzano, C., & Zoccolotti, P. (1992). Cognitive rehabilitation of the hemineglect disorder in chronic patients with unilateral right-brain damage. *Journal of Clinical and Experimental Neuropsychology, 14,* 901–923.

Prigatano, G. P. (1986). *Neuropsychological rehabilitation after brain injury.* Baltimore, MD: Johns Hopkins University Press.

Prigatano, G. P., Fordyce, D. J., Zeiner, H. K., Roueche, J. R., Pepping, M., & Wood, B. C. (1984). Neuropsychological rehabilitation after closed head injury in young adults. *Journal of Neurology, Neurosurgery and Psychiatry, 47,* 505–513.

Rattok, J., Ben-Yishay, Y., Ross, B., Lakin, P., Silver, S., Thomas, L., & Diller, L. A. (1982). Diagnostic-remedial system for basic attentional disorders in head trauma patients undergoing rehabilitation: A preliminary report. *Working approaches to remediation of cognitive deficits in brain damaged persons* (Rehabilitation Monograph No. 64). New York: New York University Medical Center.

Richardson, J. T. E. (1992). Imagery mnemonics and memory remediation. *Neurology, 42,* 283–286.

Rimel, R. W., Giordani, B., Barth, J. T., & Jane, J. A. (1982). Moderate head injury: Completing the clinical spectrum of brain trauma. *Neurosurgery, 11,* 344–351.

Ruff, R. M., Baser, C. A., Johnston, J. W., Marshall, L. F., Klauber, S. K., Klauber, M. R., & Minteer, M. (1989). Neuropsychological rehabilitation: An experimental study with head-injured patients. *Journal of Head Trauma Rehabilitation, 4,* 20–36.

Schacter, D. L., & Glisky, E. L. (1986). Memory remediation: Restoration, alleviation, and the acquisition of domain-specific knowledge. In B. P. Uzzell & Y. Gross (Eds.), *Clinical neuropsychology of intervention* (pp. 257–282). Boston: Martinus Nijhoff.

Schacter, D. L., & Graf, P. (1986). Preserved learning in amnesic patients: Perspectives from research on direct priming. *Journal of Clinical and Experimental Neuropsychology, 8,* 727–743.

Schacter, D. L., Rich, S. A., & Stampp, M. S. (1985). Remediation of memory disorders: Experimental evaluation of the spaced-retrieval technique. *Journal of Clinical and Experimental Neuropsychology, 7,* 79–96.

Scherzer, B. P. (1986). Rehabilitation following severe head trauma: Results of a three year program. *Archives of Physical Medicine and Rehabilitation, 67,* 366–374.

Schlanger, P., & Freimann, R. (1979). Pantomime therapy with aphasics. *Aphasia-Apraxia-Agnosia, 1,* 34–39.

Skelly, M., Schinsky, L., Smith, R., Donaldson, R., & Griffin, J. (1975). American Indian Sign: A gestural communication system for the speechless. *Archives of Physical Medicine and Rehabilitation, 56,* 156–160.

Sohlberg, M. M., & Mateer, C. A. (1987). Effectiveness of an attention-training program. *Journal of Clinical and Experimental Neuropsychology, 9,* 117–130.

Sohlberg, M. M., & Mateer, C. A. (1989a). *Introduction to cognitive rehabilitation: Theory and practice*. New York: Guilford Press.

Sohlberg, M. M., & Mateer, C. A. (1989b). Training use of compensatory memory books: A three stage behavioral approach. *Journal of Clinical and Experimental Neuropsychology, 6*, 871–891.

Sohlberg, M. M., White, W., Evans, E., & Mateer, C. (1992). An investigation of the effects of prospective memory training. *Brain Injury, 6*, 139–154.

Sparks, R., Helm, N., & Albert, M. (1974). Aphasia rehabilitation resulting from melodic intonation therapy. *Cortex, 10*, 303–316.

Stern, J. M., & Stern, B. (1989). Visual imagery as a cognitive means of compensation for brain injury. *Brain Injury, 3*, 413–419.

von Cramon, D. Y., & Matthes-von Cramon, G. (1990). Frontal lobe dysfunction in patients—therapeutical approaches. In R. L. Wood & I. Fussey (Eds.), *Cognitive rehabilitation in perspective* (pp. 164–179). London: Taylor & Francis.

Weigl, E. (1981). *Neuropsychology and neurolinguistics: Selected papers*. The Hague: Mouton.

Weinberg, J., Diller, L., Gordon, W. A., Gerstman, L. J., Lieberman, A., Lakin, P., Hodges, G., & Ezrachi, O. (1977). Visual scanning training effect on reading-related tasks in acquired right brain damage. *Archives of Physical Medicine and Rehabilitation, 58*, 479–486.

Weinberg, J., Diller, L., Gordon, W. A., Gerstman, L. J., Lieberman, A., Lakin, P., Hodges, G., & Ezrachi, O. (1979). Training sensory awareness and spatial organization in people with right brain damage. *Archives of Physical Medicine and Rehabilitation, 60*, 491–496.

Weintraub, S., & Mesulam, M.-M. (1987). Right cerebral dominance in spatial attention. *Archives of Neurology (Chicago), 44*, 621–625.

Wilson, B. (1981). Teaching a patient to remember people's names after removal of a left temporal lobe tumour. *Behavioral Psychotherapy, 9*, 338–344.

Wilson, B. (1989). Models of cognitive rehabilitation. In R. L. Wood & P. Eames (Eds.), *Models of brain injury rehabilitation* (pp. 117–141). Baltimore, MD: Johns Hopkins University Press.

Wood, R. L. (1986). Rehabilitation of patients with disorders of attention. *Journal of Head Trauma Rehabilitation, 1*, 43–53.

Wood, R. L. (1987). *Brain injury rehabilitation: A neurobehavioural approach*. Rockville, MD: Aspen.

Wood, R. L. (1990). Towards a model of cognitive rehabilitation. In R. L. Wood & I. Fussey (Eds.), *Cognitive rehabilitation in perspective* (pp. 3–25). London: Taylor & Francis.

Ylvisaker, M., Szekeres, S. F., Henry, K., Sullivan, D. M., & Wheeler, P. (1987). Topics in cognitive rehabilitation therapy. In M. Ylvisaker & E. M. Gobble (Eds.), *Community re-entry for head injured adults* (pp. 137–219). Boston: College Hill Press.

Zangwill, O. L. (1947). Psychological aspects of rehabilitation in cases of brain injury. *British Journal of Psychology, 37*, 60–69.

Zihl, J., & von Cramon, D. (1979). Restitution of visual function in patients with cerebral blindness. *Journal of Neurology, Neurosurgery and Psychiatry, 42*, 312–322.

Index

339